Christianity and Paganism in the Fourth to Eighth Centuries

Christianity and Paganism
in the Fourth to Eighth Centuries

◆ ◆ ◆

Ramsay MacMullen

Yale University Press

New Haven and London

Designed by Rebecca Gibb and set in Centaur type by The Marathon Group, Inc., Durham,
North Carolina.
Printed in the United States of America.

MacMullen, Ramsay, 1928–
    Christianity and paganism in the fourth to eighth centuries / Ramsay MacMullen.
        p.   cm.
    Includes bibliographical references and index.
    ISBN 0-300-07148-5 (cloth : alk paper)
    1. Church history—Primitive and early church, ca. 30–600.   2. Rome—
Religion—Relations—Christianity.   3. Paganism—Relations—Christianity.
4. Christianity and culture—History—Early church, ca. 30–600.   5. Evangelistic
work—History—Early church, ca. 30–600.   6. Christianity and other religions—
Roman—History.   I. Title.
BR170.M33   1997
270.2—dc21   97-7786
                                                                              CIP

A catalogue record for this book is available from the British Library.

The paper in this book meets the guidelines for permanence and durability of the
Committee on Production Guidelines for Book Longevity of the Council on Library
Resources.

10   9   8   7   6   5   4   3   2   1

Contents

◆ ◆ ◆

Persecution

Looked at from a sufficient distance, if indeed any distance is sufficient for a clear view, what seems to confront the observer of the religious scene in the period of my chosen title is a transition from one Establishment to another. That is the grand event. Thanks to our omniscience, however, we know the ancient Establishment will not survive. In that knowledge we focus our attention on the winner (and it is an old saying that history doesn't like losers). We write off the losing Establishment, we pay it no mind; we look closely only at the rising Church, in which all significance seems to lie. We offer our findings then in terms of the Council of Nicaea, Arianism, monasticism, barbarian kings and their conversion, iconoclasm, perhaps contacts with Islam. The flow of relatively little events sweeps us along, all, Christian. It *is* the religious history of the Mediterranean world from the fourth to the eighth century.

But we could also follow out the engagement of the two religious systems as an event in its own right, taking it to the end. We could try to define when and what "end" might mean and what it looked like, while, on the way, trying also to see what the two did to each other as their quite different strengths were applied and tested against each other. This would be quite a new way of assessing what, after all, no one would deny is the most notable fact within religious history of the fourth to eighth century: that you have one system in place at the start, and another when you finish. What alone could prevent this assessment being made would be the view that really no testing took place, no challenge was protracted, beyond the fourth century; therefore there was and can be no story to tell of the ancient world's religious life much past Constantine.

Whatever might have been said back in the eighteenth or nineteenth century, by the twentieth it had become clear and agreed on all hands that nothing counted after Constantine save the newly triumphant faith. From that point on the "Roman" had become "the Christian Empire." Such was the title chosen for the first volume of the *Cambridge Medieval History* (1911), taking up its account exactly with this emperor and matched by the same title with the same point of commencement in French by André Piganiol (1972). With the new foundation of Constantinople as a Christian capital, the ancient world was over and done with, the Middle Ages had begun; likewise the Byzantine era had begun.

This, the consensus, was rarely called in question before the 1980s. Then hesitant doubts and contrary hints found their way into print, discussion grew animated, new details were added or the old presented in a way to reveal the past more clearly. It is now possible to see that there might well be a story to tell of a good deal of significance, involving the two systems as both alive and interacting to a much later point in time than anyone would have said until recently. A part of the interest in their interaction lies in their quite different structures. I return to the fact in my last chapter. For the moment, I need speak only of their external appearance: how they looked as antagonists.

On the one hand was paganism, no more than a spongy mass of tolerance and tradition, so it might seem, confronting a growing number of people determined to do away with that mass utterly, so as to replace it with what was enjoined upon them by the tremendous will of the one God—such were the opposites making up the religious world of Late Antiquity.

Constantine's conversion in 312 had had almost immediate consequences: legitimacy was bestowed on the church along with other great favors and privileges, while at the same time, under this ruler as under his sons, an increasingly explicit disapproval was directed at the old religious organizations and institutions. In the succeeding generation, Theodosius promulgated harsh anti-pagan laws and ordered the destruction of the huge, the world-famous, Sarapis temple in Alexandria. These are the events that stand out in the Greek-speaking half of the empire. In the Latin half over the same period, after Symmachus' ill-success in debate with Ambrose, Eugenius tested his cause; his failure, involving his pagan supporters, gave great publicity to the ascendancy of the Christian faith in Italy. In Africa five years later on a single day Counts Gaudentius and Jovius "overthrew the temples of the false gods and broke up the images."[1] A synod at Carthage pressed successfully for still more imperial intervention. Everywhere, "the irresistible power of the Roman emperors was displayed in the important and dangerous change of the national religion." So, Gibbon in his notorious twentieth chapter.[2]

Well and good. The triumph of the new religion appeared now manifest and irreversible. The moment had come to accept the verdict of history as it was realized, beyond all denial, in "the Christian empire."

But there remained quite contradictory practices and events to be noticed from time to time post-312, post-400, indeed for many centuries to come, showing the church's enemies not yet swept from the field, the national religion still stubbornly alive. They are to be noticed, yet not easily; for the truth left little mark. We may fairly accuse the historical record of having failed us not only in the familiar way, being simply insufficient, but through being also distorted. How and why this may be so deserves a little attention before proceeding to the substance of the truth.

On the simple matter of the numbers of the two antagonists, we have no estimates made by pagans of Christians, while estimates by apologists like Tertullian or historians like Eusebius are manifestly absurd. We are used to their exaggerations as an expression of the authors' zeal and their sense of the distance traveled by their church since the first century. Similar misrepresentations continued to appear later, for instance in the demurral "if there be any," when emperors of the fifth or sixth century urged final suppression of religious dissent.[3] Yet the emperors certainly knew better.

Beyond numbers, the record of events, personalities, and motives should most naturally be corrected by reports from pagans matching what is provided to us by Sulpicius Severus, Gregory of Tours, or Justinian; yet anyone familiar with the sources post-400, anyone standing before the hundred imposing volumes of the fifth to seventh centuries that are Christian while holding in his hand only the one unimposing volume of Zosimus, can measure their disproportion. Very little of whatever there once was from non-Christian authors has survived. The Christians, not only in their triumphant exaggerations but in their sheer bulk, today, seriously misrepresent the true proportions of religious history.

They misrepresent, first, because what was written in the past had to be transmitted from generation to generation across succeeding centuries, and those centuries, as everyone knows, constituted a differentially permeable membrane: it allowed the writings of Christianity to pass through but not of Christianity's enemies. As a tangential illustration: our sole copy of the sole work about political good sense by the person arguably best able to deliver it to us from classical antiquity, Cicero, was sponged out from the vellum to make room for our hundredth copy of Augustine's meditations on the Psalms. True, much of Cicero did survive, most obviously what could be pressed into the service of homiletics. Similar differences in the various fates of his various works reflect the interested choices made over the generations to replicate or not; to let die, or to multiply and so preserve. No one would expect those choices to have been evenhanded, between pagan and Christian, across the Middle Ages.

Quite to the contrary: at the very point of origin, back then in late antiquity, both secular and ecclesiastical authorities repeatedly destroyed unedifying texts, in well advertised ceremonies, most obviously in sectarian disputes where rival claims for orthodoxy were pitted against each other; whereupon one of them along with its creeds and treatises would be declared heterodox by the other, and measures would be taken to insure that no trace of its existence remained except, perhaps, what might be embedded in victorious disproofs and rejoinders.[4] Non-Christian writings came in for this same treatment, that is, destruction in great bonfires at the center of the town square. Copyists were discouraged from replacing them by the threat of having their hands cut off.[5]

Together with the destruction of unwanted books, unwanted fact itself might disappear even in those books that were not destroyed, because of their partisan reporting. The father of ecclesiastical history, Eusebius, in a particularly serious aside, disclaimed the telling of the whole truth. Rather, he proposed to limit his account to "what may be of profit." His example found favor among successors, by whom all sorts of details were bent out of shape or passed over, events were entirely suppressed, church councils deliberately forgotten, until in recent times even the wrong saint and pope might vanish from the record, or almost.[6]

There is, in the second place, a less familiar reason (though an equally simple one) for the loss of balance in the religious record: sheer numbers of pages to start with. By pagan writers post-400 there was relatively little written; by Christians, much. The physical means of reproducing a text were a part of the explanation. From an earlier period we have the example of Origen, extraordinarily prolific, supplied while still in his teens with seven shorthand writers, seven research assistants, and a number of calligraphers, all very expensive on the slave market but paid for by a rich admirer. In his old age even Origen's sermons were taken down as he spoke them. Then his works were judged unedifying, even anathematized; no good Christian wanted them on his shelves; so most of them have not come down to us in their original form. By contrast, the unexceptionable Gregory of Nazianzus had slave help and his works were saved; Augustine likewise had help with his letters, sermons, tracts and an accumulating catalogue of miracles; Paulinus of Nola could readily provide extra copies of his favorite authors to his friends in high places; while in sixth-century Syria in a not very large town the bishop could boast of seventy amanuenses for the publication of his hundreds of sermons.[7] As the rich and influential became increasingly Christian, or we may say, as the upper ranks of the church themselves became more rich and influential, so the chances improved of their version of things being written down and circulated. At the same time the chances for the pagan version diminished. Whatever bulk of production was achieved, Christian or pagan, much or little, choice then came into operation to preserve it according to its value.

I remind myself of these elementary facts about the shape of our present knowledge of late antiquity only to understand how, on first reading, the record seems to suggest that pagans were not only defeated by the end of the fourth century but had in fact all been converted. Really, however, such was far from true. Historians' consensus, such as it was until at least the 1980s, rested on a corrupt foundation.

Finally, on the subject of the record, there is a surprising reminder: "Saint Augustine did not live in a Christian world. We have studied hundreds of inscriptions illuminating urban life in Africa of the Late Empire. We must conclude that Christianity claims only the very most modest place in these documents." How different from the impression one might gather out of literary sources, on which alone historians most often depend! How striking, too, is the confirmation to be drawn from the curve of dated African Christian epitaphs.[8] Of course, Africa's epigraphic corpus is much larger than can be found in any other comparable region in the fourth and even into the fifth, sixth, and seventh century. Moreover, it is of a different quality from, say, Syria's. Syria's has some size to it but it speaks for a far more deeply Christianized population. But if the Latin inscriptional material is measured across time, the balance of forces, Christian and non-Christian, in the west as a whole in late antiquity seems to resemble the African model more than the Syrian and allows some correction to be made for distortions pervading the literary record.

In Augustine's world not only was the non-Christian to be found alive and well, but in daily relations with the Christians. "He does not openly say, Come to the idol, he does not say openly, come to my altars for the feasting there; and if he said this and you [who are Augustine's congregation] refused, this would be the complaint, this would be offered in disagreement and complaint: that you didn't want to come to my altars, didn't want to come to the temple I revere. He will say this."[9] Confoundedly delightful, those cult banquets! Invitation to them amounted to "another bout of the persecutions"; and superadded was the impudence of pagans even, in return, attending the Christians' saints' day feasts at martyr shrines and cemeteries. Such a problem had to be referred to the emperors for solution; it was just too much for local leaders—this, in the fifth century, with similar evidence from other provinces. Yet the problem arose naturally, for everybody used the same cemeteries to bury their dead. Cemeteries, odd as it may sound, constituted the chief social center for towns and villages in many, even in most, parts of the empire.[10] The fact will be emphasized in a later chapter. Near them, for the faithful of both faiths without distinction, gravestone masons and makers of votive lamps and grave-gifts displayed their wares. A great deal of material on cross-faith contacts, from parades to private consultations with experts, may also be deferred to later pages.

"Everybody" in cemeteries should not be taken to mean the elite, aloof at their grand mausolea; but then the elite went to university all together, regardless of religion: that is, together they attended law classes in Beirut and elsewhere, or the lectures of Hypatia on philosophy in Alexandria or of Libanius on rhetoric in Antioch. Pagans occasionally sought out the masters of eloquence in the very churches, for the brilliance of the performances to be heard there.[11] And high or low, rich or poor, together the two populations somehow met, married, and raised their children in whatever beliefs seemed most natural and profitable.[12] They were bound to do so, so long as the pagan population had any bulk to it, and the church could not successfully screen off its faithful from contaminating contacts. This long remained the case.

After Constantine, of course, the process of conversion went on. The long familiar reasons continued still to operate. But they are not always well understood. Among the most general, it is commonly supposed, was Christianity's attractive openness to two large categories of persons for whom paganism, in all its varieties, nowhere had much room: women and slaves along with the vulgar masses.[13] Yet there are difficulties here. Christian leaders once they emerged anywhere at or near the top of the social pyramid looked down on those beneath them with just the same hauteur as their non-Christian equivalents.[14] As to slaves, the disadvantages which they had suffered under for centuries, even those most favored in the great houses, are well known; but nothing indicates that they were made easier by Christian masters or their congregations. Caesarius could be applauded by his biographer for limiting punishments to no more than thirty-nine lashes on a given day, and Leo from the papal throne corrected church doctrine in the matter of slave-priests: they were to be forbidden not out of fear of complications with a runaway, but because of such candidates' sheer vileness, by which ecclesiastical office would be "polluted." In contrast, slaves in paganism had free access to almost all cults and temples, they mixed promiscuously among most cult groups, and commonly formed their own cult groups with their own priests and officials.[15]

As to women, the churches made special provision for widows, presided over not by male officers but, to avoid scandal, by deaconesses; and there is a very occasional priestess attested, too.[16] Otherwise, women were valued for the renunciation of their sex or of their wealth, while barred from worshipping in groups at a saint's martyrium or entering to offer their prayers (they must use male intermediaries); likewise, they were forbidden to approach the altar or to teach or preach. In the huge homiletic corpus they and their concerns hardly appear: the preacher addresses himself to the "brethren."[17] In paganism, by contrast, if we judge by their presence in inscriptions (the best test) but also in works of fiction, female deities like the ubiquitous Tyche/Fortuna, Isis, Diana, the Matres, Cybele, Caelestis-Tanit, and so forth were quite as often appealed to as the male. Priestesses as wives or as themselves alone presided over their entire provinces in the imperial cult; they led hardly lesser city cults or larger or smaller cult groups, some wholly of women;

presented votive performances in oratory, singing, dance or athletic contests; lectured in public on religion; underwent the full range of initiations if they wished to; and enjoyed sole entrance to one or two cults as men did to one or two others, likewise. In sum, while very much less often found in positions of prominence than men, during the period of relevance post-200, let us say, and while differing in the choices available to them from one city to another, women enjoyed access to a great range of activities, experiences and authority among traditional cults.[18] These were lacking within the church.

And a word more on the question: Within which religious tradition might women feel more secure of a welcome? In the 380s in a town of the Thebaid in Egypt, a man was brought before the governor, a pagan, on a charge of killing a prostitute. The governor delivered himself of his verdict in these words: "You have basely killed a woman who reproached her fate among men because she had lived her life in dishonor, and to the end bartered away . . . [and here as later, a lacuna]. And I have taken pity on the unfortunate woman, because while alive she was offered to all those who wished her, like a dead body. For the poverty of her fate pressed down on her excessively, selling her body to a dishonoring rank and encountering the reputation of a prostitute. . . . I direct that you be struck with the sword as a murderer. Theodora, the poor and elderly mother of the dead woman, who because of her poverty deprived her own daughter of modesty and through which also she killed her, will inherit a tenth part of the property of [the murderer], the laws suggesting this to me and magnanimity, *philanthropia*." Contrast this ethical tradition with that which Jerome presents to us in just the same period and which, with other church officers, he quite accepts: by the lights of which, women were beheaded for extramarital fornication.[19] Exaggerated as the comparison is, and a thing only of isolated incidents (though, notice, all in the open and explicitly acted out to a wide public), it casts further doubt on the question of concern here, whether the women of the empire were likely to see Christians as a more receptive community than that to which they had been used.

However, there is no need to look to a special appeal offered by the church on these two fronts, women and slaves, in order to explain the increase in its membership; for as is well known it boasted a special means of conversion through miraculous demonstration of its claims.

Miracles: as before, the sources post-Constantine explain the winning of pagans to the church in mostly anecdotal form; and, as before, success is sometimes presented as due to the convert's overwhelming conviction that the Christians *are right*, witness this or that wonderful event—for even the stupidest plowboy would know better than to discard all the divine aid of his tradition in exchange for what someone tried to prove in no more than the breath of words. In support of the common sense of this we have the reasoning of a famous example, Clovis, who, "since he was a most astute man, was unwilling to agree to it until he knew it was true. When he saw that the" miracles wrought at the tomb of Saint Martin were as advertised, then he believed. On matters of religion, as his bishop tells the king, it was impossible to "becloud the keenness of Your Subtlety."[20]

Of such undeniable demonstrations of divine power, being also the most familiar and seriously offered explanations for conversion, by far the greater number are those of healing. Against a general background of routine exorcism in the churches,[21] we will be told of someone suffering from a physical or mental disability who seeks out a holy place, a martyrium, or a holy man, a monk, and there asks for relief; and in consequence of being granted this, sometimes as part of a bargain, he accepts the new faith.[22] As Origen had said, on the occasion of a man in his audience breaking out in a fit of raving, "We see the foul spirits being flogged, for by such means many are brought round to God, many are freed from error, many come to the faith"; and Theodoret two centuries later repeats, "Those initiated into the mysteries of the Holy Spirit know its great works and what wonders it performs in men through men, in order by the grandeur of its wonderful acts to draw the unbeliever to a knowledge of God."[23] The driving out of spirits that afflicted the mind, the wonderful drafts to drink, poultices and touchings for afflictions of the body, even infertility amended through a dream—such are the causes underlying conversion that are pressed on readers by our sources. And, though much less prominently, our sources also record conversions through other kinds of wonders besides cures: a holy man may be able to say where some precious possession has been lost; raises the very dead, at the news of which everyone hastens to him for instant baptism; disperses the demons that cause crop-failure, again in return for conversions; overthrows temples by his words of prayer alone and so brings an end to the surrounding villagers' attachment to it; overthrows an idol in a procession by mere prayer and, in its inability to right itself, provides the proof of its nothingness to its worshippers; or binds or freezes the idolaters in their steps, granting them release, then, only upon their acknowledging the wonder-worker's as the one true faith.[24]

We know of these moments and their important consequences because they were much noticed at the time. Accounts of them would spread about informally, as we are told, by word of mouth, or formally in annual memorial orations whose texts are referred to or have come down to us in writing. They constitute that category of conversion which is the most express and which most clearly arises out of religious experiences, experiences in which can be seen the primacy of healing miracles, and next in efficacy, miracles of other sorts. Surely the historical weight of this evidence is to be multiplied enormously, taking into account not only the individuals or groups directly involved but a secondary audience as well who listened and, in anxious moments when traditional resources seemed to fail, surrendered themselves to a new conviction. This multiplication is what we need to reconcile the certainty of increase to the church, by the scores of thousands, with the small corpus of conversion miracles.[25]

Of preaching, very little is said at any time after Saint Paul. Not that there aren't sermons by the thousands from the third and fourth centuries, by the hundreds thereafter up to, let us say, the seventh. But they don't set out to explain their act and setting, which then must be teased out from the contents. Very much as one would expect, they shed no light on the matter at hand: conversions. They are delivered rather to the already converted or, rather, to a tiny segment of that possible audience—namely, rich males.[26] Only in a country town will any more generous socioeconomic sampling turn up for mention—there, and on great feast days, when, however, the bishop might very well not be understood by his audience: their language was not his, literally or figuratively. He spoke Greek, they, Syriac; he, Latin, they, Celtic; and most often, he spoke in prolix complexity according to the rules of his art, so far as he was able.[27] Post-400 as already earlier though less completely, preachers represented the elite to the degree it existed at all in the city or region; they were of the rich and highly educated class, they married within it, they took their membership for granted and expressed themselves accordingly. Theirs was a society of pronounced stratification, the realities of which they are not often seen denying, in any effort of outreach. Even at the end of their lives, their graves might be set apart from those of common folk.[28]

Whatever was done by preaching for conversion was done in rural settings—where, of course, eight- or nine-tenths of the empire's population lived.[29] Just what did the church say? The best answer is sought, and almost only to be sought, in the model sermon to those baptized but lamentably ignorant inhabitants of northern Spain, the diocese of Martin of Braga, whom he had in mind in a sermon presented for imitation to other bishops under him in the 470s.[30] He offers an easily recognizable, very basic outline of beliefs, intended as a reminder to the audience, not as a novelty or any inducement to become Christian. Only at one point (§14) does he speak of eternal life in heaven for the virtuous and (at greater length) the sufferings of the damned, all of whom "in their flesh and for all time to come are dispatched to Hell, where dwells that inextinguishable fire forever, and where that flesh, regained through the resurrection, groaning, is eternally tormented—wishing to die once more so as not to feel its punishments but not allowed to die, thus that it may endure unceasing tortures." It was conventional wisdom among the leadership of the church that fear constituted a most essential element in the mix of motives that could bring an audience round.[31]

Some element of fear, some sense of the Christian God's awful strength, surrounded also the bearers of the church's message. Bishops and ascetics were not persons to fool with, even if, or particularly when, they said or did outrageous things: as for instance, when they brought the disrespectful to a sudden end.[32] There is an account by a bishop, later a saint, in fifth-century Italy who had wished for a wider open space in front of the martyrium he had built, so as to amplify the vista; but the home and workplace of uncooperative neighbors stood in the way of his architectural project. They actually talked back to the saint and resisted, until the martyr Felix himself from his tomb miraculously removed them by burning down their obnoxious buildings. "The gracious favor of Felix had us in mind," declares the bishop, "with this gift."[33]

Christianity in its substance as in its agents post-Constantine thus retained its aggressive quality. No one could ignore it. It made news. Daily exorcisms in the churches, daily healings of the mind and body at the shrines of its heroes, could not fail to be talked about beyond the ranks of its faithful. The impression of power it conveyed through its beneficence was enhanced by the report of what happened to its enemies; and their error was not hidden from them. While in the non-Christian thought-world there was virtually no testing of the merits of my god against yours,[34] in Christianity such testing went on continually, continually defining approved worship as against its opposite. The wrong was to be swept away by every means.

But why? A non-Christian, true to his traditions, might have asked why he might not be left alone—particularly if, by one of his own miracles, he could have pointed to the opening pages, above, conceding how inevitable was the spreading presence of Christianity over the ancient world, how defining and irresistible it had already become by the turn of the fifth century. Why was it necessary to hasten the process of complete Christianization by anything beyond gentle suasion?

Indeed, there had once been talk of toleration. From both sides across the second and later centuries are heard expressions of acceptance the one toward the other. They have been often noted and discussed. It is their quite natural pattern that they should be addressed with the greatest sincerity from weakness toward strength; so they are heard first from Christian spokesmen, then from both Christians and non-Christians (of the latter, Galerius first and then Licinius in concert with Constantine), still from Christians for another generation or two, but in the end from non-Christians with the greatest publicity.[35] Symmachus directed a famous appeal in vain to Saint Ambrose. By then, in 384, it was really too late to speak of toleration.

It was too late because by then Christians were in a position of power allowing the free expression of a deeply felt imperative; and that imperative allowed no rest. None, ever. So long as unbelievers clung to their old ways, and indeed in far more challenging numbers than the Christian record would acknowledge, good believers must fulfill the divine command, "Ye shall destroy their altars, break their images, and cut down their groves; . . . for the Lord, whose name is Jealous, is a jealous God" (Exod. 34.13f.). So spoke their Lord himself. And again, through his angels: "Praise God in heaven! Peace on earth to everyone who pleases God" (Lk. 2.14)—but the displeasing were another matter, with different deserts. "God who speaks truth has both predicted that the images of the many, the false gods, are to be overthrown, and commands that it be done."[36]

It used to be thought that, at the end, the eradication of paganism really required no effort. The empire in its waning generations had suffered a decline not only material but spiritual. Of itself, "paganism had by late antiquity become little more than a hollow husk."[37] To replace it, only a preferable alternative was needed which, when supplied and explained, over the course

of time inevitably found acceptance. But historians seem now to have abandoned this interpretation (even if, outside their ranks, it persists for a time).[38]
The real vitality of paganism is instead recognized; and to explain its eventual
fate what must also be recognized is an opposing force, an urgent one, determined on its extinction. Such a force is easily felt in Christian obedience to
the divine commands of both Testaments, calling for the annihilation of all
error. It was this that controlled the flow of religious history from the fourth
century on.

Long before it could be expressed in actions, urgency was clear in the way
Christian writers described paganism. From the start, it is not easy to find in
the whole of their literature a matter-of-fact, uncolored reference to its beliefs or rituals or (of course, especially) the actual images of gods. Some
touch of denigration is almost always added. We might suppose Christians
therefore lived in a fog of dark disapproval which they were supposed to
breathe in and make a part of themselves, if they listened to their leaders or
read their works, while of course living also in a mist of love—for each
other. Needless to say they could not all, in every moment, respond as they
were bid. Instead they responded only in fits and bits, as one might expect,
not always with outrage toward their unbelieving neighbors nor ever-charita-
bly to their own fellows. Periodic outbursts, however, of hate-filled mob or
gang violence after the mid-fourth century are indeed recorded—reference
will be made to them in what follows—and the role of the church leadership
in exciting them is clear. The leaders' appeals could be heard over a general
background of terms such as "mad," "laughable," "loathsome," "disgusting,"
"contaminating," "wicked," "ignorant," and so forth, characteristic of ancient
invective and freely applied by Christians to everything religious that was not
also Christian.[39] More to the fore were specific demands for aggressive action
by fulminating synods or individual zealots, of whom I may pick out Firmicus Maternus in 346, adjuring the emperors, "Little remains, before the Devil
shall lie utterly prostrate, overthrown by Your laws, and the lethal infection of
a vanquished idolatry shall be no more. . . . The favoring *numen* of Christ has
reserved for Your hands the annihilation of idolatry and the destruction of
profane temples." Adjuration rises to a shout: "Abolish! abolish in confidence,
most holy emperors, the ornaments of temples. . . . Upon You, most holy emperors, necessity enjoins the avenging and punishing of this evil, . . . so that
Your Severities persecute root and branch, *omnifariam,* the crime of idol wor-

ship. Harken and impress upon Your sacred minds what God commands regarding this crime" (and he goes on to work up Deut. 13.6–9, "If thy brother,
son, daughter, or wife entice thee secretly, saying, 'Let us go and serve other
gods,' . . . thou shall surely kill" them).[40] A little more focused than Firmicus'
exhortation will be the legislation of the time with its own version of inflam-
matory name-calling, for example, aimed at "pagans and their heathen enor-
mities, since with their natural insanity and stubborn insolence they depart
from the path of the true religion . . . [in] nefarious rites of their sacrifices
and the false doctrines of their deadly superstition."[41] At the end, most
sharply of all, specific injunctions on specific occasions by leaders to particular audiences, John Chrysostom by letter to the monks or Augustine to his
congregation, demanded action.[42]

Firmicus was writing toward the turn of that point where appeals for toleration also change, from the Christian to the non-Christian. Ecclesiastical
leaders now began to exercise their superior powers proportionately against
their various enemies; what had been words, earlier, became reality and event.
Among those enemies, not to be forgotten, were Jews and Manichees against
whom laws and arms were turned in about the same period and manner,[43]
while sectarian rivalries within the church continued unabated and with freer
use of force, now that it was safe (so, in the century opened by the Peace of
the Church, more Christians died for their faith at the hands of fellow Christians than had died before in all the persecutions).[44] These areas of religious
strife I recall only to make plain in other ways the great urgency lying behind
those Old and New Testament commands cited above, which would allow no
truce with error. Christians might point with envy to the *concordia* that prevailed among non-Christians, just as non-Christians pointed with amazement
at the murderous intolerance within the now dominant religion;[45] but there
could be no compromise with the Devil.

Christian readiness for action carried to no matter what extremes has not
always received the acknowledgment it deserves in modern accounts of the
period. Among them, prior to the 1980s, readers will be hard put to find Firmicus' word "persecution" describing the conduct of the Christian empire
toward its non-Christian subjects. Instead they will find a reference to that
happy moment in 312 "when the era of persecutions ended [!] and Christianity became publicly established in the Later Roman Empire." Still again in the
1990s, congratulation is made on the process of converting the ancient empire

"without society tearing itself apart . . . the fourth century said goodbye to bloody religious strife."[46]

The lynching of Hypatia took place toward the beginning of the fifth century (A.D. 415). Her fate is illuminating. It may be recalled that, snatched from the street by a mob of zealots in Alexandria, she was hacked to death in the gloom of the so-called Caesar-church and her body burned. She was a non-Christian and a prominent voice for her views; she had become the focus of the patriarch Cyril's resentment; the lector had caught his master's wishes and led the crowd that killed her. All this seems certain.[47] In the background, explaining Cyril's heat, were the indirectly connected Greek-Jewish tensions in the city and the patriarch's and the provincial governor's conflict over their respective followings and strength. In the contest between these two, the patriarch called on his *parabalani*, church workers with some muscle, as well as hundreds of monks from the Nitrian wilds with still more muscle. The monks shouted against the governor and stoned him, though he escaped alive. They constituted, with the civil and episcopal authorities and nameless zealots, the available agents of that reforming urgency which governed religious change in the centuries post-400, all conveniently seen in action in the drama that ends with the death of Hypatia.

Their different roles may be best explained one by one, beginning with church members under nobody's orders, carried away by their sense of outrage at religious error, as they saw it. Perhaps that was what got Christians onto the north African police lists as early as Tertullian's time, and it was certainly a problem by the end of the third century in Spain, when idol smashers sought the reward of martyrdom and the church felt compelled to deny it to them.[48] Then we have Augustine at a certain moment trying to lower the temperature of anti-paganism among his congregation with the advice that they should do no more than is allowed by law, lest some landowner lodge a complaint.[49] Emperors chime in occasionally, worried about "disturbance or tumult" in general and particularly about the Alexandrian *parabalani*: would the patriarch please to limit their number to five hundred, since a deputation from the city had petitioned against them in terror? Because appointment to their ranks was sought by purchase (a practice common for government jobs), evidently they attracted predators; and their numbers should not surprise, since even bishops in small towns would have a respectable staff of house-slaves while those ruling over proper cities would have correspondingly more persons under their orders.[50] Such a staff was assumed in Honorius' directive to bishops in the west: he allowed them freely to employ whatever corps of servants they had in the suppression of pagan cult meals, acting in concert with designated Imperial Inspectors.[51] Later in the same century, "Both in this imperial city [of Constantinople] and in the provinces, We direct our officials to see to it with all care that through both themselves and the most holy bishops they inform everyone to seek out according to the law all impiety of pagan superstition, either that there be none or that it is punished"; and in the next century bishops were often called on as informants and spies to report on the enforcement by the emperors' officials of laws defining right religion.[52] Yet another century still, and the bishops assembled in council (at Toledo in 681), like Firmicus quoting vengeful verses from Deuteronomy, called on the civil authorities to seize and behead all those guilty of non-Christian practices of whatsoever sort.[53]

On occasion, bishops might bring monks to bear as a physical force in support of their objectives. At least, this may be seen in Constantinople, Alexandria, and points of the eastern provinces in between; in the west monks were not numerous enough for this purpose and had a different character. They were forbidden to settle in cities in 390, though the law had to be withdrawn two years later. Then long afterwards it was reinstated (even in the east). Ambrose and the first Theodosius could agree, "the monks commit lots of crimes"; in 398, the eastern emperor was of the same mind, and gave orders that they must be confronted boldly by local authority, whatever it was, if they attempted to snatch accused persons from custody, even when their "audacity seems so great that it is thought that the outcome will be a war."[54] The church itself had doubts about them, expressed in 451 at Chalcedon (can. 4) in the reminder that they should respect the authority of their bishops. The admonition begins in measured words, with what experiences behind them, there is no saying: "Since certain persons under the guise of monks disturb church and civil matters, traveling about various towns and presuming to establish monasteries for themselves," let them be aware that they should "embrace peace and occupy themselves only with their fasting and prayer, and remain in the place assigned them, and involve themselves in none of the business of the church nor of the secular world."

Such various mentions in the record assemble themselves into the form of the zealous rustic from some isolated village or tiny landholding, an illiterate man and more used to asserting his religious convictions with a big stick than with willowy argumentation, drawn into a loose community of his fellows by what he had heard about them in the district, and instinctively hostile to any authority but theirs whom he had joined. Nevertheless, men of this sort could be useful to the church's purposes. The patriarch of the eastern capital, John Chrysostom, early in the fifth century would naturally write to their leaders for help in carrying the word to rural areas—one might have expected this in Egypt or Syria, where they were strongest, but in fact he was concerned about Phoenicia (see note 42). From that region had come report of pagan-Christian rough stuff in the backlands, through which "he learnt that Phoenicia remained still within the cult of the demons [*daimones*, customary Christian term for non-Christian deities]; [so] he assembled ascetics afire with holy zeal, and, arming them with imperial laws on idolatrous shrines, sent them forth. The money provided to the workmen and those who served them for the destruction" of temples he had secured not from imperial resources but from the piety of wealthy women.[55] To the rear of his efforts, then, were civil and pacific forces; to the fore, the monks as "shock troops" (so they are often termed in modern accounts).[56] It was they to whom Cyril's predecessor had appealed for help in the destruction of the Alexandrian Serapeum and other shrines in the city back in the 390s, likewise they whom the ecclesiastical historian recalls as having, in the early decades of the fifth century, done the most to convert Syria and Palestine.[57] Trombley rightly describes them as men "who, in youth, had a stake in the village economy, knew the rudiments of agriculture, spoke the local *koine*, had friends and understood the yearnings which lay behind the local cults"—therefore especially effective in work in rural parishes.[58]

More will be said in the next chapter about the presence of ascetics as individuals or small groups in the countryside and their part in the bringing over of the population to their own beliefs. From near Emesa in Syria I may just instance the holy Abraham visiting a village under the guise of a merchant. There he lodged for a few days, raising the volume of his morning prayers from sotto voce to something more audible, until at length he infuriated his neighbors; but he won relief from their wrath by offering to square them all with the cruel tax collector, which worked, and when they, who (most unusually) owned their own little plots of land and so had no big man as their patron, asked Abraham to stay on in that role, he agreed. He set one condition only, that they would build him a church and in due course pay for a priest to conduct services there. So the village was won over.[59]

Acts of patronage and problem solving by monks and ascetics in the eastern countryside of late antiquity are a quite minor part of the hagiographic literature, although, since that literature is itself so abundant, they can be combed out and made to look substantial.[60] I know of only the one case just described where such acts resulted in conversion and therefore need to be considered for my ends. On the other hand, that case shows how, by merely making himself acceptable in an alien setting, an ascetic might induce others to join him in his worship. Abraham the intruder survived and succeeded. It seems reasonable to attribute success also to others like him less fully attested; yet in another region the same attempt was made and the intruders lost their lives.[61] So the need for a nonepiscopal type, a man used to rough stuff, was made plain.

In fact the pagan population did sometimes attempt to defend themselves. When their own beliefs were ridiculed, they answered indirectly through comic pieces on the stage, in both western and eastern cities. It was an age-old tradition to present the Olympian family as a target for laughter but something new to add the local saint or bishop; and perhaps against the church another tradition was invoked as well, of free speech against despotic or dictatorial force such as the little people in the audience as individuals would never dare to voice out loud—for that matter, like the theater in Communist-occupied Czechoslovakia.[62] Then, too, in Italy in Symmachus' lifetime there was some pamphlet warfare of which only the Christians in prose or verse can still be heard, excepting Symmachus' famous protest itself. That piece made the other half of a diptych with Ambrose's answer. In the same way, a letter from the unbelieving Faustus to Augustine is preserved only through Augustine's reply.

Once, like the passionate speeches invented by Tacitus for oppressed barbarian chieftains, pagan villagers are given a voice in reply to the preaching of a bishop. The scene lay some fifty miles north of Paris, toward the mid-seventh century. Gathered for a festival in the square before the church, the population of a village are addressed by him from its steps, in ingratiating phrases: Away with your "disgusting, your criminal, your ludicrous superstitions!" (etc.). One of their number replies, "No matter how often you rebuke us, Romans, you will never succeed in tearing out our customs. We will rather perform our rites as heretofore, and always and forever gather for them; nor will there be a man ever to prohibit our ancient and dearest festivals."[63] The story ends predictably. The bishop presents a fearless front: he continues talking, while the intransigent among his audience are evidently seized by a demonic spirit: for they continue their festal dancing! At such a miracle, all the rest in panic beg for a Christian cleansing, which being administered, five hundred join the church.

Less dramatic because acted out entirely on paper and by a scholar, the prodigiously productive Abu al-Hasân Tabith of Carrhae-Harran near the empire's eastern edge offers another protest of unregenerate heathendom. Tabith (d. 901) writes:

> Although many have been subjugated to error [i.e., made Christians] by means of torture, our fathers, by the hand of god [Aziz], have endured and spoken valiantly, and this blessed city hath never been defiled with the error of Nazareth. And we are the heirs, and transmitters to our heirs, of heathenism, which is honored gloriously in this world. Lucky is he who beareth the burden with a sure hope for the sake of heathenism. Who hath made the world to be inhabited and flooded it with cities except the good men and kings of heathenism? Who hath constructed harbors and conserved the rivers? Who hath made manifest the hidden sciences? On whom hath dawned the divinity which giveth divinations and teacheth the knowledge of future events except the wise men of the heathen? It is they who have pointed out all these things, and have made to arise the healing of souls, and have made to shine forth their redemption, and it is they also who have made to arise the medicine for bodies. And they have filled the world with the correctness of modes of life and with the wisdom which is the head of excellence. Without these products of heathenism the world would be an empty and a needy place, and it would have been enveloped in sheer want and misery.[64]

Perhaps all the peculiarities of the passage, as it comes from an area so long since lost to the empire, need not concern us. It is enough to acknowledge the loyalty Tabith offers to the rich, complicated faith of the persecuted—beyond that, declaring the greatness of "Hellenism" in the sense so insistently preferred by fourth- and fifth-century champions of the entire culture in which paganism was the matrix, or vice versa.

Words of pagan protest sometimes were addressed in court to a judge. To turn back from the ninth century to the 380s: strictly within the terms of the law of his time, Libanius directed an open oration against the destruction of temples around Antioch, accepting the legal limits to the exercise of his faith but insisting that they had been complied with; Augustine has been heard at a later date cautioning his own congregation to do nothing contrary to the law; and the heroic Shenute in Egypt actually was sued by the victims of his heroism.[65] In shifting and narrowing areas legislation thus gave warning to vigilante zeal. But enforcement was uncertain because of the peculiar nature of government.

The subject arises in the course of my attempting to describe the four agencies at work for the church in the eradication of nonconformity: individual zealots, monks, bishops, and civil officialdom, as they can all be seen in the nexus of events around Hypatia and in various other illustrative texts, incidents, and persons. Now to go further in the description of the process, to compulsion beyond words, beyond sticks and stones, to arms, it needs to be explained how that ultimate force might be applied, or threatened, in support of the law; for only the emperor's agents might wear a sword, and those ultimate adjudicators play an increasing role in the fourth century and thereafter.

The law, let us say, is the Theodosian Code. That great compilation was presented to the empire as a Christmas present in 438. In it, decrees from Constantine forward were gathered in rational categories, including a Book given to religion, and a section therein of twenty-five titles all concerning "Pagans, sacrifices, and temples." One might suppose, especially considering the veneration due to the monument called Roman law, that we need to read only this one section to know the course of church-pagan relations at least through the first third of the fifth century; instead of which, we find windows in the Code opening upon much unmistakable backtracking and inefficacy, upon apparent disregard of what had been earlier decreed, consequent repetition, and threats of action against the emperors' own agents for not doing as they were bid. Whatever the importance of legislation—and it was great—the workings of it depended on a complicated fabric of forces beneath the emperor's omnipotence.

At their very birth, imperial decrees arose not through an ordered system, let alone any grand policies, but from personalities and pressures of the moment. In deciding to bring arms to bear against unbelievers, certainly individual emperors had their own ideas and might issue whatever decree they wished when and as they pleased; but they spent their lives in their palaces, dependent on others to tell them what was going on outside and what needed to be done. In regard to their religious policies they had to rely most on bishops. Bishops, as is plain from their correspondence, in turn received information from priests or subordinate colleagues and shared their information at provincial meetings, occasionally at ecumenical meetings. The request that they serve as his eyes and ears has been heard from the emperor, above, matching their appeal to the throne from the Council of Carthage for help in suppressing religious error. In addition, individual churchmen might have access to the throne and could ask for help or offer advice. They stand behind much of a Roman emperor's legislation[66] or, for that matter, a Germanic king's,[67] in circumstances which we can, for the most part, only guess at. No doubt those circumstances resemble the plausible fictions of Mark's *Life of Porphyry*, and more reliable details may be added from what is known in general, really a great deal, about the power structure of the later Roman empire and its rules and customs.[68]

Then, next, when a decree was issued in response to whatever influence or need had been brought to bear, various officials would have their part to play. From top to bottom, however, the government of the later empire was seen as the property of its servants, virtually all of whom had had to pay good money for initial appointment and subsequent promotions and who (as was to a much lesser extent true also in the church) saw their positions as a source of income, through the selling of their action or inaction on a given matter, regardless of what the law directed.[69] Accordingly, it could be taken for granted that law enforcement would fall far short of the literal.

Furthermore, since there were not and never had been any state prosecutors, detectives, or police force in the empire, so that all criminal charges arose, in modern terms, as civil suits brought by private citizens, a person who was thought likely to retaliate was likely to be immune, or a person well protected by highly placed friends, likewise. Everyone high or low knew this and accordingly tried to keep in constant repair around him a protective web of influence and favors owing to him. The extent to which government power lay in the hands of one's friends would thus count for a great deal, quite as much as the letter of the law; so it is an important fact in the history of paganism that the offices of praetorian prefect or provincial governor, military commands, and posts in the palace itself before the turn of the fifth century rested mostly in the hands of Christians—important, too, that as their grip tightened on the upper ranks of government, laws could be passed explicitly reserving all imperial service for their coreligionists (in 415 and 425) and legal practice itself in 468.[70]

This domination within secular authority developed quite rapidly following the conversion of Constantine. The senatorial ranks in Italy included a significant number of Christians in Constantine's reign attaining a parity with non-Christians in the highest civil positions in Constantius', this, despite the fact that the senators were as a group very conservative in their religion. Indeed, they were once seen as the empire's paganism *tout court*, the whole cause and, in Symmachus' day, the last holdouts.[71] However, before the change in their allegiance is seen as developing more quickly than it really did, it should be noticed that pagans regained a temporary domination in office under Julian and, before as after Constantius, for a generation or two, were more likely to hold more than one very high office in the course of their careers. Given that they constituted only a few score out of sixty million in the empire, it is their ability to attain and wield power that is worth counting, not their absolute numbers. The wielding of power on behalf of coreligionists lies at the center of my discussion.

By 400, as I just said, government in the east had become overwhelmingly Christian, and non-Christian officials even in the western provinces increasingly rare, to the vanishing point. But the connections between government and citizens might suggest otherwise. *Exceptiones probent legem;* let some odd cases suggest a more complicated reality: and first, Rome's pagan prefect Pompeianus in 408. He listened to envoys from neighboring Narnia, who had saved their own city from invaders by a miracle obtained through the old gods; and he performed the best old rites himself up on the Capitol in hopes of similar success against Alaric. In vain. He was killed by the mob before long, for apparently unconnected reasons.[72] Toward the same date the municipal senates of several north African centers remained in the hands of pagans.[73] The same was perhaps true not just of a few but of many centers for many decades; but sources to confirm the possibility taper off to nothing. It is at least apparent that Christianity had made no clean sweep of the summits of power and publicity.

Then in the east we have the Quaestor of the Imperial Palace, Isocasius, removed from the capitol to Bithynia in 467 to be interrogated about his religious loyalties, considered suspect and the target of riots; but through his friend and coreligionist, the emperor's personal physician, he got off with no more than compulsory baptism. The physician's services had been recognized by the rank of Count and statues of him placed by the senate in positions of honor. He was clearly a person with the most important connections; and they sufficed for himself and others as well.[74]

Looking at a lower level among the leading persons of important centers, we find Aphrodisias (fifty-odd miles inland from Ephesus, well excavated, and its remains, especially its inscriptions, well published) a Christian city. It could fairly be called that. A certain Pytheas, however, in the late fifth century had his statue set up in a place of honor, unrolling his imperial titles magnificentissimus and illustris; a second time was honored for a handsome gift to the city; and a third time was saluted as if by Aphrodisias in her own voice, "city of the Paphian goddess," bestowing on him her "blessings appropriate to a goddess." His contemporary, fellow citizen and coreligionist Asclepiodotus, appears in other flattering inscriptions and literary texts: "at that time he took pride in the honors and dignities with which the emperor was loading him and was a leader in the municipal council."[75] We have then two prominent, rich, influential, untouchable non-Christians in the town, and certain other indications in public texts of tensions between them and the Christians.

From the west subsequent to the occupation of Africa by the Vandals and of Spain and France by other tribes, since the sources are so few and the cities likewise few and shrunken, we cannot expect many matching figures to defend the old beliefs; but they do appear occasionally.[76] Kings and chiefs play more of a role, but are more often remembered in ecclesiastical sources for their conversion and cooperation—likewise, the odd leader of peoples beyond the eastern borders.[77] I should explain at this point, however, that my treatment of my subject takes in only the areas lying within the borders of the "classical" empire of, let us say, Severan times. Non-Christians encountered in more remote regions post-400 therefore lie beyond my reach.

Below those personages important enough in our sources to be named, whom non-Christians might look to for help, a comfortable layer of unidentified sympathizers in various official posts offered protection from the emperor's decrees. He addressed them angrily through those same decrees: his will must be enforced. Woe betide anyone who was slack about it, whether imperial official or urban magistrate! "If any of the governors, through the sin of connivance and the trickery of dissimulation, should fail to execute the present law, he shall know that he will forfeit his official rank and . . . his office staff also . . . shall be subject to a fine of twenty pounds of gold, in addition to the punishment of its three primates. Moreover, if the members of the municipal senate, out of favoritism to the persons subject to punishment, should keep silent . . . , [then, for them] deportation and forfeiture of property."[78] In a string of such enactments from the mid-fourth century past the mid-fifth, frustrated emperors, echoing the imperatives of frustrated bishops, reached further and further down into the layers of authority beneath them, to the lowliest of their bureaucrats and the most obscure city fathers, looking for responsive zeal. Eventually their rage subsided; rather, it was directed elsewhere. Italy had fallen to Vandals and Huns, everything west was lost to the empire, and Byzantium was occupied with attacks on its northern flanks and, internally, with a score of heresies, most especially the Monophysite. The problem of pagan sympathizers in government, or at least of corruptible law enforcement, could not at this point in the 450s engage the embattled emperors' attention. Sympathizers, however, had not disappeared: Pope Gregory discovered the governors of Sardinia accepting bribes to permit heathen sacrifices.[79]

Augustine felt confidence in legislation: whatever might be said against the laws that attacked idolatry, "yet," said he, "many people are corrected by them and have been turned toward the living God, indeed daily are converted."[80] True; and much more needs to be said in the next chapter about them. Despite the autocracy from which laws flowed, however, at the local level they were (to repeat) tempered with considerable accommodation, venality, pretense, compromise, deceit, and plain kindness, where neighbor must confront neighbor and where persecution to some degree reflected the balance of beliefs in the community. Progress toward the extirpation of religious error could only be slow. Two centuries after Constantine's conversion, still the old cults lingered, still they declared themselves insolently. "A thousand terrors of the laws that have been promulgated, the penalty of exile that has been threatened, do not restrain them. . . . But straightway they sin with such audacious madness . . . !" In these terms Theodosius II reacted to we know not what reports of quite open cultic acts.[81]

Pagans danced in the very streets, as Augustine described them; in the the-

atres they laughed aloud at takeoffs on communion and martyrdom, as I
mentioned a few pages earlier; they wrote open letters and speeches in their
own defense, they even went to court to assert their rights—all this, far into
the fifth century. On rare occasions when the rites or homes of their gods
were physically attacked, pagans even resorted to sticks to beat off the attack-
ers, and killed some, in incidents both before and after 400.[82] Thus the imperative to which Augustine and others of the ecclesiastical leadership responded, utterly to extirpate every form of worship but their own, must resort
to arms. At the end of the fourth century the bishops called in troops to various points east and west; an imperial Procurator and Tribune of Soldiers
used his men to destroy a gigantic Caelestis temple at Carthage in 421; but
barbarian invasions in the west thereafter prevented cooperation of this sort
until the end of the sixth century.[83] It was otherwise in the eastern provinces.

Under the emperor Zeno (474–491) we hear of a pagan prominent in
Aphrodisias, the physician Asclepiodotus, who rallied his coreligionists in the
town to the revolt of the Master of the Soldiers, the Isaurian Illous in the
early 480s.[84] A Neoplatonic intellectual and lecturer, Pamprepius, well known
in Athens and Antioch and, thanks to Illous, holder of a chair in the capital
and Imperial Quaestor, went off to Alexandria to gather more support.
When Illous suffered defeat in a decisive battle near Antioch in 484, he took
refuge in Isauria; but he was besieged, taken, executed, and his head nailed up
for display in Constantinople (488). His cause, presumably including his
troops, had been very largely Christian, himself a Chalcedonian while Zeno
was a moderate Monophysite; or it was political, hardly sectarian at all. No
clear picture emerges of the help contributed by pagans like Asclepiodotus,
Pamprepius, and others whom they recruited. Still, they may have been numerous, certainly fervent; and it could be recalled that in the preceding three
or four generations no fewer than four separate attempts at a coup had been
made, unsuccessfully, by pagan diehards.[85] Men of their faith evidently could
be dangerous. Therefore the pagans supporting Illous were pursued into their
various cities and severely punished (484/5). In Alexandria, those arrested
and tortured to extract the names of confederates included professor Horapollon. He endured interrogation in silence. Yet his school of rhetoric was
closed through rioting instigated by the patriarch, and, with other suspects,
he retreated to a safer city, to Athens. Eventually he like others of the time
apostatized.[86]

The rioting just mentioned arose by coincidence out of another train of events described by Zacharias in his biography of a man later bishop of Antioch (Severus, 512 to 518). In their youth Zacharias and Severus were students together in Alexandria and then Beirut. In those two cities and in a number of others in the east, Christian "Zealots" as they called themselves (or in code, by other names) formed societies and, under their chosen chiefs, served to channel the ardor of still others like them. When a friend of Zacharias made taunting remarks about the pagan gods and community leaders, his audience of pagan students beat him up. Zacharias took the matter to the local Zealots and the patriarch. The latter aroused the whole Christian community. Students of a Christian professor entered the fray, too. The next step was to lodge charges with the prefect and his secretary (respectively a pagan sympathizer and an open worshiper). The Zealots challenged the right of these men to hold office at all and railed against them at the hearing. In the face of such angry opposition, the accused lost heart and fled the city. Among them was that same Horapollon, sympathizer of Illous. Behind him he left the anti-pagan outburst to be resolved in ceremonious idol burning.[87]

From Alexandria, Severus and Zacharias removed to Beirut to study law. There they learned of the discreet paganism of certain leading citizens, whose servants and friends could be persuaded to expose and inform against them. The first victim of the Christians' efforts fell at their feet in terror, asserting his true Christian faith and lamenting what had only been a recent lapse from it. He convinced them of his sincerity and they let him off, but kept an eye on him. Their success encouraged them to form a small society, to elect a president, receive further denunciations, and bring charges against various fellow students before the bishop. Public hearings held by the latter and the city Recorders culminated in a second bonfire, this time of suspect books, and in the flight of the accused. One who fled was able to buy a safe return; a second was allowed back once he had submitted to baptism.[88]

With these events the fifth century concludes. Times had become distinctly more difficult for even the wealthy and well placed if they persisted in the religion of their fathers; the pagan population as a whole had become more clearly a weak minority. Savage penalties were more loudly advertised by the impatient autocracy of the emperors, to offset the irremediable venality and favoritism of their servants. The means of persecution available to the church thus had more of an edge.

Especially so under Justinian (527–565). A brutally energetic, or energetically brutal, ruler enjoying a very long reign, he pursued the goal of religious uniformity as no one before him. "He did not see it as murder if the victims did not share his own beliefs." Those he disagreed with he was likely to mutilate if he didn't behead or crucify them; and among a number of highly placed pagans who escaped baptism by suicide, at least one he pursued to the grave, and buried him like an animal; apostates, he declared, should be executed.[89] Persecution came in waves, or at least it is so reported, toward the start of his reign, again in 545/6 and 562, and at the very end: "There was a great persecution of pagans, and many lost all their property. . . . A great terror was aroused . . . [with] a deadline of three months to be converted."[90] Troops were used to destroy the remotest temples still active as centers of worship, in Egypt;[91] in the center of the realm, in Anatolia, "many straightway went everywhere from place to place and tried to compel such persons as they met to change from their ancestral faith. And since such action seemed unholy to the farmer class, they all resolved to make a stand against those who brought this message. So, then, while many were being destroyed by the soldiers and many even made away with themselves, thinking in their folly that they were doing a most righteous thing, and while the majority of them, leaving their homelands, went into exile. . . ." The account (which for a half-page is directed to a particular group, heretics, against whom also, along with Jews in Palestine, the emperor's wrath was even more implacable than against pagans) returns at the end to the point at which it began: "He [Justinian] then carried the persecution to the 'Greeks,' as they are called, . . . and any of them who had decided to take on merely the name of Christian, evading their present circumstances, were, most of them, soon arrested at their libations, sacrifices, and other unholy acts."[92]

After Justinian's death there was a short lull in the course of persecution. Tiberius (578–582), however, was determined to take up the cause with vigor. Toward the beginning of his reign he ordered the local army commander at Baalbek-Heliopolis in Phoenicia, where the Christians were a miserable poor little community, to move in and teach the non-Christians some manners toward their scruffy neighbors. This charge the commander Theophilus, notorious for his savagery against the Jews in earlier years, most readily addressed, "and seized many of them and punished them as their impudence merited, humbling their pride and crucifying and killing them." When their like were denounced "in every region and city of the east, especially Antioch," he proceeded against these populations, too, summoning the high priest of Antioch to him at Edessa. The old man killed himself, but his elderly associates were terrified into denouncing as his fellow-worshiper no less than Anatolius, the vice-prefect, provincial governor, and apparently a senator as well. Anatolius was therefore remanded to a Constantinopolitan court (ca. 579), tried and found guilty, tortured, torn up by wild beasts, and then crucified, while his aide died of his tortures. "On information received," other criminals were identified in Antioch; "the populace in the grip of divine zeal" renewed their rioting, seized their bishop who had been implicated in the case, and burned him alive; whereupon the emperor had to call off the hunt and send more troops to enforce calm. He was not, however, ready to confess excessive zeal on his own part. Lest anyone within reach of his voice should doubt whether his severity had been intended, Tiberius summoned to the palace the entirety of his highest officialdom and the senate, too, so as to have read aloud to them, from morning till night, the accounts he had received of the actions taken at his orders against nonbelievers.[93]

Tiberius' reign ended as it had begun in a vigorous campaign against paganism that lasted well into the next reign, that of Mauricius (582–602).[94] Mauricius saw to it that pagans were brought before the courts "in every region and city," and in particular, in Carrhae-Harran. Here, the bishop toward the turn of the seventh century received the emperor's orders to institute a persecution. "Some he managed to convert to Christianity, while many who resisted he carved up, suspending their limbs in the main street of the town." The local troop commander himself was denounced as a secret pagan. He had passed as a Christian, his name was "Danger-free"; yet he was crucified.[95] It was his ambitious assistant who betrayed him, and one might therefore suspect a false charge, were it not for the particular probabilities in this particular city.

Harran still had many more non-Christians than Christians at this time, and in 639 when the Arabs threatened and a deputation had to be sent to deal with their commander, it was all pagan.[96] In due course the city was chosen as an Umayyad caliph's capital (ca. 745). It was an important junction for caravan routes to Asia Minor, Mesopotamia, and Syria. The residents were still permitted "to carry on with their rites quite openly, venturing even to the point of decorating the sacrificial ox with precious hangings, crowning him with flowers, hanging bells from his horns, and parading him about all the public squares," before he was sacrificed—this in an account of a continuing practice in the second decade of the ninth century. Not long afterwards for a second time the pagans negotiated with an Arab commander (a. 830), on this occasion facing the loss of their freedom of religion; yet once more they were successful—just how, makes a vivid and amusing story, but too long to tell. The pagan community continued to repeat its annual New Year's prayer "for the revival of the religion of 'Uzûz [Aziz] which used to be in the place of those things we have described," that is, temples replaced by a mosque, a Melkite church, and a women's market.[97]

Harran's very close neighbor, and one may say its twin city, Edessa, continued in the open celebration of its old religious spring festival at the end of the fifth century; but under Mauricius all such practices were severely restricted and the reluctant done to death.[98] Christianity had long been established there, earning fame for hymns in the local tongue, and the head of the community had under him seven subordinates in the region around him, including even an embattled bishop of Harran. But the Edessene church chose the weaker side in its theology and suffered greatly from the emperors' cruel measures. Its literary tradition ended. Harranians on the other hand, though likewise in Syriac, gloried in their fostering and transmission of Greek learning: Hermetic, astrological, philosophic (especially Platonic), medical, exact-scientific—as "descendants of the ancient Greeks and keepers of the ancient faith (however they understood it)." Their voice has been heard, above, through Tabith. They played a crucial role in the transmission of this heritage to later times, through Arabic, themselves maintaining their open faith and temples into the eleventh century, and their descendants, so it may be, in the form of the Subba in southern Mesopotamia at the present day.[99]

◆　◆　◆

Paganism's history in late antiquity could only be ecclesiastical history. It lay with the church to supply the shaping force. Therein, the logic of this chapter, or the excuse for it. Further, under most emperors from Constantine through Justinian and Zeno and others even later, it is not easy to separate ecclesiastical history from imperial, since to one degree or another emperors regarded themselves and were accepted as having a most important voice, indeed very often a decisive voice, in church affairs. The two forces, ecclesiastical and imperial, have been seen working together, sometimes the one at the behest of the other, sometimes contrariwise, but always in agreement about the one essential, to rid God's world of nonbelievers.

On review, that determination can be seen slowly changing character in response to the weight and confidence of church membership. At first, from 313 on, legislation was a chief means to the end; but it was of uncertain tenor for many decades, with afterthoughts, concessions, posturing beyond real intent, and contradictions. These, especially in the earlier laws, have caused scholars all sorts of difficulties; something (but not very much) must be said about them in the sequel. Then also, so long as pagans still had any friends in court, the law could be used by pagans in self-defense. A time would come, however, at different points in different localities, when government would have passed into the hands of Christians alone, or in such preponderance that the legal system became wholly an instrument of persecution—by 450, let us say. In turn, that point was prepared and preceded by the rising proportion of imperial officials who were Christian, a majority by the 360s or 370s.

Apart from legislation, only one significant missionary effort is attested, by John under Justinian. That, and individual efforts by monks like Saint Martin in rural areas, will be recalled in the next chapter. In other respects the conversion of people from their traditional faith continued post-400 in just the same ways, perhaps at just the same rate, as over the preceding couple of centuries. That is, by miracles the claims of the church were validated; and to the extent or in the moment that a person doubted the efficacy of Zeus or Caelestis, recourse was instead had to such powers of succor as the church promised, in return for exclusive fidelity.

Positive inducements in the form of cash handouts, employment, and advancement in the fourth century and later, too, played their part. Negative inducements, however, were the chief instrument of legislation, returning us to that most important means by which the church pursued its ends.

Certainly the decision to practice the faith of one's fathers had become, for non-Christians, a somewhat risky business by the mid-fourth century in some cities and by the mid-fifth, in most. Just how risky, evidence doesn't say. It was illegal (the various layers of activity attacked by legislation will be reviewed in the next chapter); but there are no anecdotes to tell us if fines for inaction were in fact imposed on the aides to some governor, or a flogging for participation in some festival, on some humbler citizen. While there is in the fifth century a good supply of incidents in Italy, Africa, Thrace, Egypt, Syria, and the eastern capital where physical violence is used against pagans, the agents are not lawful—rather, mobs and monks. Not till the sixth century are the emperors' threats actually realized and so reported. They are, of course, bloodcurdling. The higher level of judicial savagery in the late Empire, however, lies along a curve that rises steadily through the whole period preceding, and it was not directed at religious dissent any more than at any other target. It does not seem to represent any special urgency to finish with paganism for good and all.

Its effectiveness cannot be measured. In the ancient world outside of Judaism and Christianity, no belief is attested in some divine reward for worshipers who died in the acts of their worship. Rather, in the view of the pagan Lucian in the second century as of the Christian Procopius in the sixth, dying for such a cause was mere idiocy. Baptism at the point of a sword is therefore more often mentioned than endurance to the end.

Reviewing the impressions to be formed from this flow of evidence across time, a flow always pointing toward the extinction of paganism, it is natural to look beyond the obvious to some greater depth or precision. Just what were the crucial phases in the process? In view of the varying fates of different regions, reflected in the different abundance and character of the written sources, is it possible to quantify the evidence? If so, and if pagans and Christians approached a parity in numbers at the turn of the fifth century, when was the three-quarters point reached? When was the process "over"? And was there then no paganism?

These, it seems to me, are in fact not the right questions to ask, however natural the sequence of them may appear. But before approaching the truth more nearly, some preliminary matters need to be explained.

♦ 2 ♦

The Cost to the Persecuted

Apart from Judaism and, in due course, Christianity and Manichaeism, the essential characteristics of religion in the empire were, I would say, these four: the acknowledgment of innumerable superhuman beings, the expectation that they were benevolent and would respond kindly to prayer (all but those who might be bent to wicked uses by magical invocation), the belief that some one or few of these beings presided especially over each place and people, and a substratum of rites addressing life's hopes and fears without appeal to any one being in particular.

This religion had no single center, spokesman, director, or definition of itself; therefore no one point of vulnerability. Everyone was free to choose his own credo; anyone who wished could consult a priest, or ignore a priest, about how best to appeal to the divine. Appeal found expression in a great variety of words, acts, and arts, which, in each great city like Athens or Rome, or in each village, had been woven into the deepest levels of daily life and culture, the secular included. Witness the favorite form of mass entertainment, by narrative dance: it drew on Greek mythology for its most popular themes, whether in Carthage or Edessa. Or witness the reliefs on the stone boxes that rich folk were buried in: no motifs for their panels were more popular than those drawn from the same source; and this was true whether a sarcophagus was manufactured in Aphrodisias for Spain or in Rome for southern Gaul.

Not only motifs but people circulated everywhere—meaning worshipers with their religious ideas. Over the course of many hundreds of years of peaceful stirring about, the mix became constantly more complex and intimate, at least in urban settings. Variety itself became a characteristic binding together the whole fabric of religion into one whole, across space, as, on the other hand, the long peace of the pax Romana had bound communities also to their past.

A very resistant thing, then, this paganism—to anyone who wanted to do away with it.

Quite true, apostates from it were constantly won to the church in response to miracle, argument, and worldly advantage. Something about these positive inducements has been said, though more remains for the pages that follow. Perhaps apostasy could have been accelerated had church leaders undertaken some organized missionary effort. They chose not to. Was that because they were simply more comfortable speaking to their own kind in their own churches? Or because they disliked the idea of delegating authority to an inevitably independent advertising force? In any case, they relied almost exclusively on negative inducements. These must have seemed all the more necessary because, without them, progress was so slow, complete victory apparently impossible; and, unlike positive inducements, they had their own drama, their own triumphs which can be traced through dates and headlines. A sampling has been offered of particular attacks by individuals, groups, and mobs which grew more and more frequent as the third century turned into the fourth, fifth, and sixth.

Such acts, however, had their limitations. They were illegal. They might occasionally be punished as crimes, for physical force was supposed to remain the monopoly of the emperor. On this, too, the limitations have been described. So long as those outside the church remained numerous, influential, or at all likely to resist, the emperor had to consider the costs of going to war with his own subjects. There was a lesson to be learned from the massacre at Thessalonica in 390. When, therefore, an answer was sought to the "problem" of paganism—which is obviously how it was considered, in many high council meetings—only piecemeal measures could be seen as possible. Only those in actual fact were attempted.

Where should the attempt begin? Initiative rested ordinarily in the hands of bishops, joined after a time by monks. Even when laymen acted, monks' or

bishops' speeches to arouse them are often attested, perhaps always a preliminary to action. In turn, the settled purpose of ecclesiastical leaders was stimulated to action by whatever they saw as intolerably open, defiant, disrespectful, an insult to their face. Their sense of the degree of respect due to them
and to their faith encroached steadily on the areas of life left free for paganism, as, over time, the church gained power and paganism lost it.

If in the mind's eye one conjures up scenes of challenge to the church that
might be judged intolerable, they are most easily envisioned in the streets and
open places of cities. There, persecution should have had its start. But two
anomalies immediately present themselves: the imperial cult and the festal
calendar. These should have been but they were not the first targets of attack.
Let these two be explained away before going any further.

As to the imperial cult, the difficulties in seeing it clearly must always require a special effort of understanding on the part of any observer raised in
the Judeo-Christian tradition. It is familiar that superhuman beings were in
antiquity (as in numberless other points of human history, ancient and modern) seen as differing in degree of superhumanness. Some like Zeus were very
great, some like Penates, little. Any of them might be called "god" in Greek
or Latin. Rulers in particular were so honored. They were divine. In Constantine's day this fact could be sensed in a thousand temples, priests, and ceremonies of the very first prominence in their communities. "God," however,
for Jews and, on the basis of Old Testament texts, for Christians also was a
term reserved to the one superhuman being whom they worshiped. The numberless others they called angels, prophets, saints, and "demons."[1] There was
no place in their universe for human beings who were superhuman.

When Constantine, therefore, at the very center of his capital, the New
Rome, placed his image portraying him as the Sun God, with rayed head and
thunderbolt in hand, atop a huge red stone column, there receiving sacrifices
and prayers exactly as Caesar's statue on *its* column in old Rome had once
been the object of prayers and offerings, or again, when his smaller image was
paraded about the hippodrome in the so-called Sun Chariot, among torches,
and saluted ceremoniously from the royal box—by his successors, on their
knees—no doubt ecclesiastical protest should have been instant. Likewise at
the sight of the many statues of himself and others of the imperial family in
Rome rendered in precious metal, which, as all the world knew, was reserved
for and advertised only superhuman beings.[2]

But who would bell the cat?—who, correct the autocrat? The bishops had learned the strength of their tremendous friend at Nicaea (to mention only that one moment in their education). Accordingly they kept quiet. Kneeling to emperors, which Constantine expected, his successors likewise expected, without ecclesiastical objection into the fifth century and beyond. In council at Elvira a few years before Constantine's conversion, the bishops had indeed banished priests of the imperial cult from their churches—the emperors were, after all, their persecutors—but a few years *after* 312 they only required such priests not to perform the usual sacrifices in person. The election of them was approved of and regulated by Constantine himself. African senates, as we happen to know from the epigraphic evidence, continued to elect them until the Vandals came; in the same province's ecclesiastical councils, the delicate subject of emperor worship and its increasingly Christian presidents was never raised at all.[3] By orators, careful to say only what was safe and more than safe, Christian emperors from Constantine on continued to be addressed to their face as "god-like," *divinus,* or even as "god," *deus;* still at the accession of Justin the Second in 565 the poet laureate rejoiced that kings offered him their bowed heads, "tremble before his name, and adore his divinity." Flattery played on the words "numen" and "nomen." But there was of course more than play intended.[4]

During his lifetime Constantine referred to his father as divinized and made elaborate arrangements for his own worship after his own decease. He was duly memorialized in inscriptions and coins as "deified," still *divus* in the mid-fifth century; even Julian was piously recalled by Christians as "deified" ("god" to his supporters); and Theodosius' father toward the close of the fourth century, by a Christian governor, could be portrayed in stone as deified—not only portrayed but given as company, on either side of the relief, the city's guardian goddess Artemis and Athena. This, on display at Ephesus.[5]

For many observers of the fourth and fifth centuries, the rituals surrounding the emperors no doubt seemed quite obviously pagan. Otherwise there could be no explanation for the cult acts offered at the porphyry column in Constantinople, nor for a description of the like in Antioch in Theodosius' day: "for those among the [pagans] entrusted with the care of the rites worship the emperors more than as masters, more than even idols, and by reason of this fear they faithfully attend their images."[6] Accordingly, Christians sometimes deplored emperor worship and tried to limit participation in it by their coreligionists, as was noted in connection with the councils of the earlier fourth century, above.[7] But it was manifestly welcomed by Constantine (and his successors), whom the church venerated as a saint and hailed in its councils as the defining agent of their faith: "May the emperor's faith prevail!" they shouted in unison at the Council of Constantinople in 536.[8] He continued to be addressed and thought of as existing at a level somewhere above the merely human.

If no one much wanted to challenge his position on religious grounds, for the most obvious prudential reasons, the acceptance of it might be called instead a civic duty without religious content. The interpretation minimized the offense. Cult offered to the emperors had never had quite the same seriousness as the worship of Caelestis or Cybele. Its terminology, its attested acts and symbolism have been minutely examined to identify the differences. Of course no one can say just when it came to be seen and felt as purely secular by every single soul in the Mediterranean world; but a gradual secularizing, which was from the Christian point of view its purification, went on by itself and at its own pace with a certain inevitability, even if the rate cannot be measured.[9]

There was a further reason not to attempt the conscious destruction of this part of paganism: people of all sorts and beliefs greatly enjoyed it. It was folded into elaborate celebrations of the January kalends. In Rome and later also in Constantinople these were led by the new consuls in sacrifices for the good luck of the state and brought them at the high point of the day to the palace, there to salute the monarch with what a poet and bishop in the mid-fifth century called "the opening salutations and auspicious exchanges" of the New Year.[10] The senate offered oaths and prayers of luck and loyalty, so did the army, so did everyone in public places in cities. No one particular deity was addressed, though the consuls naturally repaired to the Capitol with their sacrificial bullocks or, by the sixth century, to the churches. They also signalized the day by handouts to the populace: small coins, sweet things to eat, and so forth. Everyone was to have a good time and feel happy because, so it was believed, the kalends had a prognostic quality: as on that day, so for the whole year. It was important, therefore, to live it up.

The same wonderful quality invested the day, and indeed the following two, for the whole population in both the open streets and their dwellings. On the night that began the kalends one never went to bed, instead joining in dancing, singing, joking, drinking, and feasting with one's neighbors at tables set up in the streets and plazas and, when morning came, decorating the doors with laurel branches, offering prayers to the Penates, and going about with presents and good prayers to all one's friends' houses, even from town to country or country to town. At the end of the first day, dancing and feasts resumed till dawn of the second; then rest at home, a family time, the relaxing of all constraints between master and slave, parent and child; on the third day, civic ceremonies and public prayers; in the circus, horse races, wild beasts to be fought, and pairs of gladiators; the public baths crowded, and masked parades and mummery including cross-dressing in the streets. The emperors before the end of the fourth century had declared all these kalends customs a public holiday, one of only four authorized for the Roman world at large (along with the emperors' own birthdays, and those of the two capital cities).[11] To keep the urban populations happy, to leave their traditional pleasures as little disturbed as possible, was an imperial duty regularly acknowledged in legislation.[12]

Libanius, faithful heathen, and John Chrysostom describe the kalends celebrations as presided over by the gods, among whom, as late as the second half of the sixth century, Malalas speaks of Janus and Saturn paraded through the streets of a Lydian city. In the capital, the merrymaking involved monks, clergy, even bishops along with the highest secular and military officials; cross-dressing, too, and dancing and masks, some of which survive from the thirteenth-century palace; yet elsewhere the kalends celebrations were seen only as a rustic custom. In the west in this and later periods the participants dressed up in masks representing Saturn also, along with Jupiter, Hercules, Diana, and, evidently, Cernunnos, favorite deer-headed deity among Celtic populations of northern Italy, Spain, Gaul, or Britain (Cernunnos whose image in stone till modern times sat cross-legged among the foundations of Notre Dame at Paris); and Boniface in 742 reports and decries the annual parading, singing, shouts, and loaded banquet tables in the open squares of Rome around Saint Peter's itself, on the traditional date and "according to pagan custom," "by heathen ritual." Masks had been long familiar in religious parades in Rome and elsewhere; in some or most of these later western processions there were heifer masks worn as well as deer masks and much riotous cross-dressing.[13] As a parallel for the costumes, officials called alytarchs and amphithaleis presided over the Olympic games in various east-

ern cities—in Antioch, in white, bejewelled, and silvered cloaks and so forth
to look like Zeus and Hermes, respectively; and in the festival games celebrated in Rome in Macrobius' day around 430, the images of the gods were
paraded about and greeted with applause.[14]

Perhaps there is a hint of how the practices of the New Year festival could
spread from Italy, outwards, in the charter drafted by Caesar for the incorporation of Urso in Spain. Its bronze tablets direct that the city senators shall
agree with contractors "to supply all things requisite for sacrifices and religious acts" (§69), the two-man executive shall appoint supervisors in charge
of "chapels, temples, and shrines in such manner as the senators shall re-
solve," and the latter "shall determine the manner in which" games and sacrifices are celebrated (§128). It would be tedious to follow out from this early
point, through a forest of question marks, just how the several recognized
types of communities in the western provinces and, by quite different rules,
how urban centers of the eastern provinces were brought into some degree of
conformity to the Romans' religious calendar. Over the centuries somehow
it happened. History supplies one significant coincidence, in the date of
the Urso charter: it was drafted within a few months of the birth of Roman
ruler worship. That cult, offered first to Divus Iulius right on the Roman
Forum, was to become the most easily identifiable force behind the spread of
the Roman New Year rites. To what extent the connection was encouraged
from the center, to what extent by local initiative, there is no saying. Attested
in the barest mentions during the better known period of the empire, the
kalends festival only emerges more fully into the light in the fourth century.
By then it had become a panimperial phenomenon recognizable if not in-
dentical in every community. It could not be ignored. Loud, long, totally dis-
ruptive of normal life, and sheltering under the name of patriotism, it constituted one of those offenses in their very face that the bishops found the
most provoking.

But against it they found no easy point of attack. Though they were no anthropologists, they were clear that the rites were not just a big party; rather, an
act of worship. A pagan friend, more likely some author of earlier times like
Varro, might have instructed them. "Pagan" is what they called those rites,
which were "sacrilegious" and "of the Devil." Of course!—with all those
demons paraded about. The bishops could not fail to recognize (though
some of their congregation did not see) that there was a religious element, a

precatory recognition of superhuman forces, even or especially in drinking, in jokes and comic turns and whirls and dances.[15] Without legislation to help them, however, they could do little more than preach. Preach they did, then, and often, but in terms not easily accepted. How, for instance, could Asterios, Maximus of Turin, Augustine, or Caesarius of Arles persuade their congregations that giving friends presents was *wicked*?[16] In their councils together on a dozen occasions almost up to the eighth century in the east, and much later in the west, the bishops joined in anathematizing all such diabolical rites. Disciplinary and regulatory tracts and collections gave still wider circulation to their decisions.[17] Again and again, far into medieval times, pressure was renewed. It cannot have been very effective.

The second anomaly to explain away, in addition to the imperial cult, is the festal calendar. Here again, the offense was to both eye and ear, most obtrusively. So far as regulation had rested with the central authorities through lists of days to be observed by the army or by any city sufficiently duteous to notice them, the world changed with Constantine's conversion, for Christian emperors, outside of the imperial cult, could not prescribe pagan days and rites as an obligation. The change did not immediately affect the local calendars of cities for their own use. In the eastern ones, oddly, the Roman Brumalia of November 24th to December 17th were expensively celebrated in the sixth century at Gaza, as we happen to learn by chance, and remained widely popular at the end of the seventh century, while in the capital they persisted in vigor, with celebratory bows to the emperor, even into the reign of Constantine Porphyrogenitus (913–959).[18] So, too, the birthday of Helios at the winter solstice persisted, on December 25th, as did the vernal equinox of March 21st;[19] also a first-of-March festival of which little is known.[20] Joshua the Stylite describes a festival with mimes on the usual Olympian subjects in sixth-century Edessa, and the so-called Maiouma, a month-long bathing festival enjoying (where the bathing was nude) great notoriety, survived in the very capital of the east into the sixth century; to the same period, there, too, the Brytae remained highly popular until forbidden by the emperor.[21] Otherwise, traditions of local independence were too long established to be much affected by incorporation into the Roman empire; shared festivals were few, and each city observed its own holy days. Almost nothing is known of these past the third century, for lack of sources; but we know they continued in some places for hundreds of years.[22]

Quite remarkably alive to a quite remarkable date was the Nile festival celebrated on the night of January 5th to 6th at Giza, within sight of the Great
Sphinx on the banks of the river, when those banks and an island in mid-
stream were illuminated by thousands of torches. The population of the city
there (Old Cairo or Babylon) stayed up to enjoy the most lavishly laid tables
and most joyful music and dance, breaking off from the feast to bathe in the
river and insure by the act that no illness could touch them. It was the Night
of Immersion. The best description, in which both Muslims and Christians
appeared together very happily, survives from the tenth century.[23]

In the west the picture of survival is very similar, so far as the evidence survives—which is not past Augustine's day in the north African provinces, for
obvious reasons, and irregularly and almost wholly through ecclesiastical
sources elsewhere. Days of the week kept their names, of Hermes/Mercury,
of Aphrodite/Venus, and so forth, in Greek or Latin across the population
regardless of their faith. The bishops alone (it may be guessed) saw meaning
in that, and objected, quite in vain. A rest from work assigned to the fifth day
"of Jove" was also maintained at least in many communities.[24] Of festivals,
the Maiouma appears in the sixth century at Ostia; in the capital, the Saturnalia of December 16th–19th in Macrobius' day, the Lupercalia of February
2nd, object of the pope's outrage in 494/5, Cybele rites on March 27th, and
the Megalensia on April 4th; in Gaul on the 22nd of February the Caristia,
deplored by the council of Tours in 567, with the Vulcanalia in August and
the Neptunalia on July 23rd still in the eighth century; to return to Augustine's north African world, there were the winter solstice and the Attis-day in
late March; and so on to the occasional mention of unidentified holy days
in this or that western locality during the course of the fifth to eighth centuries.[25] These are no more than chance mentions in a rather meager body of
evidence, sufficient, however, to show how very difficult it proved to weaken
the grip of the old religion upon the flow of time itself.

Where even such grudging evidence survives we can thus expect to learn of
open, in-the-streets paganism into the sixth century in some scattering of
towns in the east and to a considerably later date in the towns of Italy and
Gaul in the west. By dipping back into the half-century before 400 with its far
more abundant documentation, and from there, if we will, to the second century, descriptions of the old ways on view in urban and occasionally rural settings can be easily collected and compared with the later ones so as to give a

sense of the continuity that governed religious practices throughout the empire. We can see across this long stretch of generations an unchanged liking for the processing of crowds, often carrying holy images on litters under baldachins, and certainly with floral decorations, wearing choice costumes taken from storage or borrowed from rich friends, with wreathes on every head, and musical accompaniment.[26] The crowds in holiday mood and very much caught up in what they are doing, as our longer texts make clear, also make clear why they are still to be seen to the advanced dates that are attested: they are or were strong in numbers. No denunciation to the authorities by some personal enemy or zealot could have much disturbed them. Nothing less than a cavalry charge could have cleared them away. So long as a critical mass of coreligionists could still be gathered at the traditional time of the year, mindful of their ancestral ways, there was not much anyone could do about it. Only the bishops preached, which is why any report survives; they preached because the crowds seem usually to have included some of their congregations, for the moment gone astray. More must not be lost. Addressing at least this supreme provocation, law eventually decreed the death penalty for Christians joining in pagan festivals. There is no sign it was enforced; the irritation it was intended to remove had yet to be endured awhile.[27]

A glimpse of the irritation appears toward the year 409: at Calama in Africa Proconsularis, "at the June 1st festival, the impious ceremony of the pagans was celebrated without hindrance from anyone, with such impudent audacity as was not ventured in Julian's day: an aggressive crowd of dancers in this precinct passed directly in front of the church doors. And when the clergy attempted to prevent such an outrageous thing, the church was stoned." So the priests had come out to the street and shouted at the crowd, which no doubt knew its passing would be taken as a provocation; and they weren't stoned but the building was, and the same again a second time, and a complaint was lodged with the town senate, and tensions escalated from then on to a major outbreak of violence against the Christians. A century after the Peace of the Church, Calama was one of those towns that had not yet joined "the Christian empire."[28]

From earlier times, yet another glimpse: of a festival parade going along the main avenue of the city, an eastern one (Ilium, Delos, Andros, Epidauros, it made no difference where), with an ox for sacrifice in the midst, the ox being the main idea of the procession; and painted on its broad flanks the name of the donor, with the man himself leading it so as to gain all possible honor.[29]

Here was both a provocation to the bishops and a point of possible attack, indeed a salient one. One single, well-known individual had come forward in the name of piety to address a supernatural being of choice, so it may be expressed: meaning the city's guardian, Artemis of Ephesus, Caelestis in Carthage, Jupiter in Rome; for only a guardian would receive the compliment of an ox, costing in comparable terms roughly what a car would cost today. Without such acts how could good fortune be assured, for Rome so late as the fifth or Antioch in the sixth century?[30] There would follow in the natural course of things the communal feast, the distribution of the cookout to the whole assemblage of citizens, and at some point other distributions, other entertainments: music especially hymns, dances, races, recitations of Homer, displays of oratory, perhaps some high-minded sermonizing against rough bloody spectacles, after which everyone could turn with a sharper appetite to the day's fare at the arena.[31] Such would be the religious feast deluxe, at least throughout the Greek-speaking regions of the empire. Full descriptions of it belong to times happier for paganism, those of the local patriot Epaminondas of Akraiphia in Boeotia, of Dio Chrysostom or Menander the Rhetor. From the first, second, and third centuries with their relatively large variety of sources, I offer these three names rather at random. Even in more briefly described versions, however, as I have indicated, such deluxe displays went on well into the period which properly concerns me.

That was against the law. For Constantine had spoken and legislated against the slaughter of animals in offering to the gods; so had his son, followed by Theodosius most sternly in the 390s. Close to Theodosius' laws, Libanius speaks with all respect and accurate understanding of what was by then allowed and what wasn't. Yet still, within a morning's walk, blood sacrifices continued to be offered in the little town of Touron at least to 396 —continued to be quite openly referred to in speaking with the bishop of a north African town, or of Chalcedon itself, in the fifth century, and to recur in scattered mentions elsewhere during this period and up into the reign of Justinian and beyond.[32] It is safe to say that the law was not enforced in any quite Prussian manner; yet the emperors certainly meant what they decreed. Any of their subjects who offered sacrifices should be executed, this in 352, in 356, and again in 451; should be exiled, perhaps more realistically, since before Justinian we hear of no one in fact put to death for this particular crime; should be dismissed from rank and office; or should lose all property and rights to bequeath it, thus bringing his relatives to bear upon him. In the fullness of time and in the fashion described in the previous chapter, the persecution of this particular rite in the traditional ways eventually prevailed.

Just what it all meant may need some clarification. The slaughter and roasting of an ox or a ram on a great altar was indeed a prominent act of piety. In the scenes described, it rewarded the ordinary participants in several different and important ways, most obviously through uniting them in their worship and affirming it communally. Naturally, too, it made the community as such feel safer against life's dangers. For those whose prerogative it was to preside—the elite of a city or province, consuls, governors, and so up to the emperors—there were other but no less important rewards. To be deprived of these was a serious loss. Like religious processions, however, a day of sacrifices was public and publicized, therefore obtrusively offensive to at least some Christians; and besides, if divine aid were to be sought for all together, whatever person addressed the divinity in their name could only be seen as their leader, and the occasion as quasi-political. Any emperor would most naturally pay some attention to this aspect, which no doubt accounts for Constantine's severe law of 324, and the successive tightening of it in 341 and subsequently. Of course from a different point of view the bishops welcomed this flow of legislation.

But, one may say almost coincidentally, animal sacrifices involved ordinary folk in their ordinary lives, as family groups or at least not in any grand corporate fashion. Reverting to the passage in Libanius' Thirtieth Oration, which was was just referred to: he says of the rural population (§17f.) that, innocently, they do sacrifice,

> but for a banquet, a dinner, a feast, and the bullocks were slaughtered
> elsewhere [than in temple grounds]; no altar received the blood offer-
> ing, no single part of the victim was burned, no offering of meal
> began the ceremony nor did libations follow it. If people assemble in
> some beauty spot, slaughter a calf or a sheep or both, and boil or roast
> it, and then lie down on the ground and eat it, I do not see that they
> have broken the laws. . . . Even if they were in the habit of drinking

together amid the scent of every kind of incense, they broke no law, nor yet if in their toasts they sang hymns and invoked the gods.

For a time, then, the faithful could enjoy their freedom to continue their group meals. At these, a god might be invoked and honored. He would be "the fulfilling participant in all cult associations, who ranks as their leader of toasts, the symposiarch among them whenever they assemble" (so, Aelius Aristides had seen it in the second century). Friends invited to a religious feast would be asked to join whoever issued the invitation "at the couch of the Lord Serapis," if that were the deity favored, or Hagna Thea would herself be named as the host who assembled the party; by the same pretense, priests might issue the call "to partake in blessedness," "the ancestral god [Zeus] summoning all mankind to the feast daily to share in his universal love"; or again, a layman who was also a priest might remark, "It is not the abundance of wine or the roasting of meat that makes the joy of festivals, but the good hope and the belief that the god is present in his kindness and graciously accepts what is offered" (so Plutarch). As to the consumption of wine, the participants "drink there into the evening—they think they will otherwise not be heard" (so, Ambrose, with the same thought in Caesarius of Arles).[33] And there was a tangible reminder of the worshipers' view of the nature of the occasion in the form of prayers and holy signs impressed upon the participants' sacrificial cakes or inscribed on sacrifical wine dippers and strainers. The consecrated cakes you could take away to eat, to insure your good-keeping at home; the silverware added a prayer to your glass, "Long life!" or "To [the god] Faunus."[34]

Just as at the kalends festival, so at meals taken in shrines, the moralists spoke out. They condemned the heavy eating and drinking. In due course bishops joined them, first teaching Constantine to reprobate his un-Christian subjects: "Away with you, impious ones! Away with you to your slaughter of victims, your banquets and festivals and drinking, pretending worship but bent on pleasures and debauchery, enslaved to pleasures!"[35] Worship was certainly joined with the delights of the table and of one's friends and kinsfolk. To be called a sacrifice lover, *philothytes*, came to mean "fond of guests," a sure enough recognition of the conjuncture of rewards in sacred meals.[36] But the evidence offered from such pagans as Plutarch and the rest, in the paragraph just above, shows plainly enough that dining in the divine presence and precincts was much more than a social act, however much hostile observers then and now might seek to demean and secularize it. It was religion, and understood as such by the participants.[37]

Perhaps, therefore, it was inevitable that legislation aimed at first at sacrifices conducted by high personages in the name of whole communities should be broadened intentionally to include those more ordinary folk and more ordinary acts that Libanius declared innocent. "It shall in no wise be permitted to hold convivial banquets in honor of sacrilegious rites in such funereal places [as temples, honoring not the living but only "dead" gods], or to celebrate any solemn ceremony. We grant to bishops of such places the right to use ecclesiastical power to prohibit such practices," and provincial governors shall second them without excuse or delay. So decreed Arcadius, Honorius, and Theodosius II in 407, repeating the law the next year.[38]

Inevitable, too, was noncompliance. The realities of law enforcement were described in the first chapter and, above, many chance instances of continuing blood sacrifices post-407 were offered. It would be easy to add still further, similar scenes of religious life going on as usual in response to the balance of forces in any given setting. They are reported to us most emphatically through ecclesiastical legislation in Gaul.[39] There, practices persisted into Carolingian times in overtly pagan form, that is, as religious feasts in sacred precincts. Some idea of their scale can be sensed through excavation that uncovers, here, a grand banquet hall built some time post-Constantine and still in use in the days of this very law; there, the remnants of the animals slaughtered on the spot by the thousands and tens of thousands, in times leading up to the law. But evidence accumulates for the impact of the law, too, in the form of detailed destruction and desecration of certain such sites toward the turn of the fourth century.[40] Persecution indeed had its successes.

Once more, it is important to define just what was lost to religion through this law, on top of recent prohibitions even to set foot inside temple precincts. And first, of secular considerations: as Libanius pointed out about the recent laws, poor-relief suffered, because of the "expulsion of people who by their personal care provided relief for poverty among old men and women and fatherless children, the majority of them suffering from severe physical handicaps"; then, the population of priests and caretakers, rarely mentioned in the sources because they were of a humble class, but explained by the site-plans of holy places with a few or a lot of little cells and rooms adjoining the god's home proper—they too would be swept out. And money changers and small traders accustomed to use the area, especially on holy days, as their fairground, would have to forgather elsewhere.[41]

As appears both in site-plans and literary sources, temple precincts provided the favored or the sole place for the display of several arts in the service of religion. In the courtyards and in temples proper, those very houses of the gods, were statues; on the walls, reliefs and paintings that served to illustrate divine narratives and to glorify their chief figures. Paintings needed care not to deteriorate, and few have survived outside of Egypt or Syria; but they are often mentioned in written sources.[42] Theaters or seating arrangements around courts were a common feature in those provinces but also throughout Gaul, north Africa, Italy, and so forth, in great numbers. On the secular stage the Olympians were as much laughed at as revered (and for comparison, recall the reverence for Shakespeare on the American stage some generations ago, conjointly with an almost equal taste for burlesqued versions of his plays); but in temple theaters the treatment of divine themes and stories was reverent, and ordinarily in the form of danced narratives.[43] Dance was inseparable from worship, and recognized to be so.[44]

A word on this subject, if only to introduce it; for, even more than ornamental prose (prime art of classical antiquity), ornamental motion is undervalued in our view of the past—undervalued for the very good reason that, while ancient eloquence survives in huge amounts along with its rules and commentaries, the report of dance was barely attempted by contemporaries. Depictions do exist in fourth-century mosaics; better known, those in the service of religion on the walls of the Pompeian Villa of the Mysteries. The two illustrations may explain the sparse report: the former, in mosaic form, being secular and indecent, the latter sacred. Perhaps it was felt that what was sacred should not be too casually revealed. As to the secular, Romans of the class that wrote, thereby controlling our picture of the past, looked on it as beneath them. They left it to moments of little or no *gravitas*, or to entertainers of loose morals, no better than prostitutes (male or female). In the Greek-speaking world similar prejudices are heard from the pulpit, sophists preaching, like Dio Chrysostom, or ascetic-minded folk like Apollonius. Lucian notes that, in some regions he knew of in Ionia and Pontus, festival times found the Bacchic dance "performed by men of the best birth and first rank in every one of their cities, not only without shame but with greater pride." He was surprised.[45]

A heavy three-step in the liturgy of the most anciently respectable gods was performed in Rome by the most select of select society, the Arval brethren, until close to 400, when the inscriptions happen to run out, while something perhaps not much more graceful enlivened the feast of Anna Perenna, by the very least select, on the banks of the Tiber; and from the earliest empire into the late fourth century the importation of eastern cults brought dance to the capital's sacred precincts in honor of Isis, Cybele, and the rest.[46] In the east, often to the accompaniment of hand-clapping and with pipes, citharas, timbrels, castanets, or other instruments, dance was a regular feature of mystery presentations or a form of prayer or exposition of belief through miming. It invited everybody's participation, especially through teenage choruses, for the worship of ordinary civic deities in Elis, Sardis, Pergamon, or the Nile valley.[47] Both men and, more often, women took part. The ubiquity of the practice embraced the north African provinces and the northwest, where the rebukes aimed by bishops at the kalends festival speak of dancing in the crowds; likewise, in a setting of other festivals, in northern Spain, in the south of Gaul in Caesarius' day (d. 542), near Tours in the sixth century, a little south of Amiens toward the mid-seventh century, or in reference to Gaul generally.[48] So, exactly like the dancing kalends of January, the practice was a demonstrably universal feature of paganism at every season in the period of my study. Its role in exposition of beliefs and as a form of prayer was occasionally recognized in so many words. And it was this that the law aimed to bring to an end.

Descriptions of sacred dancing ordinarily associate it with singing. Sometimes singing only is mentioned by itself, as in the fourth century Panathenaia that Himerius describes, at Petra for the local goddess and in Alexandria in the Kore temple toward the same date, for the Castores in Rome of the 490s, near Trier in the mid-sixth century, and so on. A number of other passages have been noted just above.[49] Menander the Rhetor in his handbook on speech-making reminds his fellow worshipers of Apollo that "he continues to give us abundant harvests and to rescue us from dangers, and we propitiate him with hymns." He makes express what people thought they were doing in their song, just as John Chrysostom refers to the pagan songs at sacred feasts as invitations to the gods to join the party. Likewise (with Augustine and Jerome) John refers to the practice of keening at funerals, while preferring more cheerful tunes at the subsequent all-night graveside feasts. These latter were a custom well attested at the start of my chosen period in both eastern and western settings. I describe them, below. I may add the invocation of the appropriate male or female deity in work songs, weaving, or wine-pressing.[50] But these take me too far from temples, where the chief business of sacred song lay and where it is most richly attested. There is, for example, more to be learned about actual tunes in the ancient world from musical notation inscribed on temple walls for the guidance of worshipers than can be known from any other source.

In second-century Antioch, competitions among women were held in the recitation of hymns, the winners to be named as priestesses.[51] Let these represent the high level in the art generally aimed at. Hymn masters, male or female *hymnodoi*, were familiar institutions, training the young and reminding adults how to envision and address the gods. Prose hymns, or call them eulogies or encomia, were also familiar in temple settings, an ordinary accompaniment to the larger festivals, at least in the Greek-speaking areas. They, too, offered visions of the divine shaped by tradition. Libanius offered one such (his Fifth Oration) to Artemis in thanks for healing, with a richly ornamented description of her bounties and miraculous powers; still better known are Aelius Aristides' rhetorical thank offerings to Asclepius; but the best is Dio Chrysostom's, centered in the statue of Zeus before which it was delivered and bringing into play the ideas also of the best known poets and philosophers. It has been called "perhaps the finest oration surviving from the time of the Roman empire and worthy of comparison with the work of the Attic orators. It is beautifully organized, and it deals with cosmic subjects and noble art. Man and god, Homer and Phidias are brought together on the field of Olympia for the edification of Dio's contemporaries."[52] From such a performance, or again, from the versified encomia inscribed on temple walls, worshipers might receive instruction in their beliefs, so far as they wished to receive any; from priests and religious tourists like Plutarch chatting in the shady porticos, more might be learned; from temple libraries, too; and from theological lectures like those of the wonderful Sosipatra's son Antoninus at the Isis shrine in Menuthis.[53]

An important service performed by the likes of Dio, Plutarch, or Antoninus was the reconciliation of the better read, more analytically minded worshiper with traditions that had their birth in much older times. To men like these three and their listeners, Olympian fables seemed ridiculous, half of

Homer was not sacred text but an embarrassing joke, and the rituals addressed to stone, even to ivory and golden idols, offended all reason. Yet Homer still deserved the reverence of those able to see (as Dio Chrysostom put it) that he "spoke in parables and images."[54] In a long tradition from before Plato's day down the centuries through the Stoic school especially, not only were the stories about Kronos or Zeus or Aphrodite defended as inspired revelation (if properly understood), but so were the baboon and crocodile deities of ancient Egypt and any number of apparently nonsensical rituals; and discussions of this explanatory sort continued into the late empire, no less important even then as a shield against attack from Christians.

According to the enlightened fashion, at the level of thought just illustrated by Dio, pagans may be heard in Augustine ridiculing idolatry. One such replies, "I myself do not worship the stone, but I rather adore the divine power of some certain sort, invisible, that presides over the image"—a defense that the bishop dismisses *ad hominem*.[55] On the other hand, actual life in images, which Augustine heard some people deny, he also heard defended. Accounts of images that sweated, smiled, wept, moved, or rose a little distance from their bases were all known to the traditions of paganism and well vouched for. At the more accepting end was the theurgy in which Neoplatonists and initiates like the emperor Julian were interested; or, from earlier times, an account by the apologist Athenagoras may be recalled, that "Ilium has images of Neryllinus (a man of our own time), Parium the images of Alexander and Proteus [Peregrinus, described by Lucian]. . . . One of the [Neryllinus] statues is believed to give predictions and to heal the sick, and for this reason the Ilians sacrifice to it, gild it and wreathe it. Then there is the statue of Alexander and that of Proteus, . . . also said to offer predictions. To the statues of Alexander . . . public sacrifices are celebrated and festivals, and it is treated as a god who hears men's prayers."[56]

In fact quite a number of superhuman humans could be accommodated within true paganism. Most of them came into their own in pre-Roman times, but a dozen or more are known to us from the first three centuries A.D. With some imprecision, they may be sorted out into several different types. First, it is natural to mention the more worthy Roman emperors, Augustus as much as any of them, to whom veneration and, by some of their subjects, prayers for favors were directed. Their temples stood, very grand, in every large city. Just what their nature was conceived to be, and how different from

that of ordinary mortals, has been often discussed; but no one has argued
that they inserted themselves very deeply into their people's daily lives and
problems. Yet Vespasian, the very last person of whom one would have predicted it, received credit for miraculous healing. Incidents were reported from
his touring around in the east before he won the throne. Septimius Severus
and his son Caracalla effected miraculous cures and were thanked by votive
inscriptions of the sort commonly set up in sacred precincts.[57] Their powers,
however, gave rise to no special, continuous cult; so these all are different
from Neryllinus, Antinous, and so forth. In this latter category of superhuman beings we should include, perhaps, a certain priestess Ammias of Thy-
atira in the province Asia, at whose tomb petitioners could put their questions and be told the truth "always, any time of day or night." Such figures as
Antinous or Ammias are to be distinguished, though not very sharply, from
those especially who died young as "heroes" and "heroines" and were conceived of as living on among the blessed—in that respect and no other,
"heroic." Call these the third type. Beliefs that surrounded them were of a
grieving, memorializing sort; they had no temples built to them. Fourth, and
likewise without shrines, ascetic people who devoted their lives to thinking
and talking about the divine also might be seen as superhuman but in an active and beneficent fashion: Proteus Peregrinus counting as one of these in
the second century because of his great wisdom and leadership in defining
right worship, Apollonius for these qualities but for advising communities as
well, and improving the morals of their youth by his sermons. There are, fifth
and finally, Homeric figures like Protesilaus and Achilles. Theirs was a more
ancient cult, but they proved themselves still active in their more individual
benefactions into the third century. Philostratus devotes a rich account to
their shrines, festivals, and miracles, especially of healing, in Thessaly and
elsewhere in northern Greece; and he ties them in with a statue in Ilium of
Hector "which performs many good deeds," just like the ones Athenagoras
reports.[58] There is, as Apollonius is reported to say, something more ap-
proachable about the heroes than about the higher divinities. Their worshipers seem also to be drawn more spontaneously from among the general
populace, without intervention by the elite. Yet even they had their temples,
hymns, and sermons.

Pausing here for a word of summary: the activities, facilities, and physical
fabric of sacred precincts can be seen defining religion even without exerting

any particular normative pressure. They affirmed its truth through the concurrence of all the arts, all the classics, philosophy, tradition, and the participation of fellow citizens and civic leaders. Whatever measures struck at such points of union could not fail to have an effect on much that was invisible but essential to belief.

Phidias' art is movingly recalled by Libanius when he addresses Theodosius in defense of the temples. Perhaps because protected by such piety, the chryselephantine Zeus lasted well into the fifth century.[59] Then it fell victim to accident by fire. It was the last great survivor. Flames had consumed the Alexandrian Sarapis of equal fame in the 390s. Still earlier, even while being themselves persecuted, Christians had directed their zeal against holy images and, once clear into the Peace of the Church, had been led in idol-smashing by Constantine, and thereafter through isolated incidents into the reign of Theodosius.[60] Then was the fated moment for the assault on Sarapis. At the head of a great mob of Christians, "one of the soldiers, fortified more by faith than by arms," with an axe smashed at the jaw of the god, and others joined in to hammer off the head and burn the whole.[61] The scene exactly recalls another of only a few years later in Augustine's province, where, starting the fifth century with a bang, a Christian mob smashed off the beard of the cult image in the Hercules shrine. It had just been regilded, affording a provocation; and they had heard of the recent destruction of a Hercules in Rome.[62] Here in Africa, "Hercules wanted his beard gilded. But," Augustine tells the congregation at Carthage, "obviously I misspoke, saying he wanted it to be, because he couldn't; for what can mindless stone wish for? In truth he wanted nothing, he could do nothing. But the people who wanted him gilded blushed at his being shaved. . . . Brethren, I deem it more shameful for Hercules to have his beard shaved than to have his head taken off" (and so forth, making great fun of the incident, and having to raise his voice over the eager shouts of his listeners). In a public letter that he circulated, again he promises sarcastically, "we will certainly make good that Hercules—metals are to hand, no lack of stone, different kinds of marble, lots of workmen. We add the ochre to depict his blushes," etc. Mockery had had a prominent part in the treatment of the Sarapis statue, too, and of the inner sanctum at Alexandria. The bishops' aim was of course to demonstrate as insultingly as possible the ridiculous nothingness of sacred images.

What made things easier for Augustine and the like-minded was an imperially funded and decreed campaign some eighteen months earlier conducted by two high officials to destroy all sacred images in the province, and the further request by the bishops in council in the very year of the Hercules incident that the emperors should please command such action more generally through their laws.[63] In 408 the bishops got just what they asked for, a call and license for the tearing down of images that were the focus of worship. I suppose images generally survived thereafter in the many urban shrines where continuing worship is attested (above), and in rural shrines in a story to be told a little later; but they otherwise receive specific mention only rarely from this date forward. The law seems therefore to have been well timed to suit the balance of beliefs, of influence, force, and zeal; and that it worked appears not only in the written record but in the mutilation of statuary post-400, which excavation uncovers from time to time. From fifth-century Ephesus comes one particular witness to the latter process: on the reused base of a statue of the city's guardian Artemis, the text in verse, "Destroying the deceitful figure of the demon Artemis, Demeas raised this monument of truth, the cross of God that drives away idols. . . ."[64] Happy Demeas!

Happiness depends on one's point of view—as may be imagined through another inscription in verse much earlier written on the base of a statue of the "Great god, mighty Silvanus, most holy shepherd: . . . attend here favoring to me, holy one, and bring to bear your divine power, for I have offered you as you have deserved a likeness and an altar, which I had made for the sake of my masters' and my own safekeeping, and that of my family too, praying for them and bringing them a favored life and a boon. Stay close at hand as my supporter . . . and 'joyfully refresh yourself after your good service'."[65] Similar early texts often add that the image was set up in obedience to a vision of the deity (ordinarily meaning a dream); and the dreams or visions no doubt would have been shaped by such likenesses as the Zeus statue that Dio Chrysostom describes—invested by Phidias or any great sculptor with life, tangible reality, and benignity.

All those qualities must be lost to belief through iconoclasm post-408. It is to suggest the meaning of the loss that I offer the Silvanus text. One might sense it equally from scripture (Ps. 74.4–11).

The law of 408 called for idol destruction specifically where cult was offered. This limitation responded to a concern lest zealots proceed to the breaking up of all religious statuary in all the cities, to their great loss in sec-

ular terms. In fact, from Constantine on much of the sculptural treasure of
the old beliefs had been preserved, even in honored locations in the New
Rome as in the old, in Verona as in Athens. Laws from the turn of the fifth
century on directed the careful removal of divine images from places of worship to secular sites.[66] Removal or destruction, however, served equally to
change temples from living, functional structures into mere monuments and
then, by neglect, to mere shells. Worse still, the same law that invited the destruction of idols decreed also that their homes henceforward should belong
to the imperial fisc. Some were reduced to ruins—as was expressly ordered
by another law of 435.[67] They had once been, some of them, grand big things,
made of huge monoliths. It wasn't easy, absent Samson, to tear down their
columns and walls, a job for which in fact miracles might be needed, or at
least regiments of strong arms. The Asclepius shrine in Athens required such
an effort, some time around 475. Narses' men in the 530s evidently spent
weeks methodically smashing the feet and faces off the relief figures of the
Isis temple at Philae. They gave equal attention to the pharaohs, whom they
couldn't tell from the gods.[68]

Elsewhere in Egypt the work begun with the Sarapeion in Alexandria had
been promptly carried forward, we are told, "throughout every Egyptian city,
fort, village, rural district, riverbank, even the desert, whatever shrine could be
found or rather, tomb [of the "dead" gods], at the urging of every bishop."
So exclaims the enthusiastic Rufinus.[69] In Asia Minor, Constantine had
shown the way against famous shrines at Aegae and Aphaca, but other sites
suffered only in the last quarter of the century; in Africa, the counts' campaign against images in 399 extended also to temples but hit only a few select
targets. The mile-long Caelestis shrine in Carthage remained to be leveled by
the local imperial land manager only in 421. Not long afterwards its site was
described as being, "through disuse over some period of time, overgrown
with the prickly bushes that surrounded it, and the Christian populace
wanted to claim it for the use of the true religion." Pagans tried in vain to defend the sanctity of the place with their shouts, only further inflaming the
Christians, of whom a big crowd gathered from all points under the leadership of a number of their priests. They helped the bishop to "set up his
throne and seat himself in it," this highly symbolic act being divinely affirmed
through the discovery of a nearby stone bearing his very name, Aurelius.[70]

I leave the bishop enthroned where once Caelestis sat, amid his exultant congregation, and turn to the role played by temples in worship not by groups or communities but by individuals. To what extent might persecution touch these latter? They too as such sought out their favored shrine. The church of the third century indeed looked with envy on their faithful daily attendance. Religious tourism and pilgrimage were familiar in every province, instances of lifelong loyalty to some one cult are reasonably often attested, and the voices of individuals in moments of particularly strong religious feeling are occasionally heard in tones easily recognizable and most naturally expressed in a formal setting: that is, in a shrine of some sort. Routines of priest-led worship at fixed hours of the day gave definition to the religious impulse.[71] To destroy a temple meant also to disturb habits of awe, loving gratitude, devotion, or humility to which the ancient cults could give expression. In the nature of the thing, religion must have feeling.[72] So much was recognized as essential—one might even say, as operational. For insincere prayer, prayer touched with any spirit of doubt, wouldn't work. Everyone knew that. "Those who call upon you [Isis] in faith behold you"—just as a holy man after his death could be seen only by that follower whose faith was whole.[73] Invocation would be better heard, a vision better received, where the elect gathered or the god's image resided. Destruction touching stone therefore touched much else besides.

It naturally included testimonies on shrine walls. It is these that have the most to tell us about religious tourism. Where the hammers of zeal later missed them, to this day they record how devout travelers paid their visits and their respects at the home of whatever deity it might be. The latest such testimonial dates to the second half of the fifth century. Also displayed on the walls of shrines would be inscriptions recording answers to prayer, many of these being quite substantial narratives, still more being in the abbreviated forms that one generation of the faithful learned from another. "Great is the god!" they might end their declaration, in a shout of belief and gratitude. Telltale grooves in some temple walls show where dust was scraped from the gods' own home to be treasured for its miraculous properties, perhaps drunk in a dilution.[74] Still more common were testimonies without words: reliefs on plaques of precious metal, bronze, terracotta, or stone depicting the affliction healed, or figurines or large carvings in wood (preserved for excavation only in the northwestern quadrant of the empire) of whole figures or limbs or heads offered in requital to the gods—even very rough portraits of the grateful.[75]

Figure 1 The faces of worshipers at the Seine-Source shrine. Courtesy Musée archéologique of Dijon (= Deyts [1994] pl. 15,4; 14,5; 14,2)

To see their faces around one when one applied for divine aid or to see almost with one's own eyes the cures testified to by anatomical thank offerings, did wonders for one's faith. A visible display of proofs like these could preach even to the deaf; it could be read by the illiterate; and for the lettered, there might be an equally full written record of miracles of healing provided to worshipers by those in charge of the shrine.[76] At least the unwritten testimonials continued to be offered into the sixth century. But what was required for such affirmations of belief, and by then hardly to be found, was a temple undamaged.

Ordinary individuals turned to their favored shrine, whether at this late a date or any point in the past, seeking answers to their ordinary problems. "Foolish men," says an unbeliever, "they never tire of asking the gods about getting married or taking a trip, about blindness or illness," the gods serving thus, "in most people's lives, as useful oracular sources for the discovery, it may be, of a slave's flight, the loss of some object, a land purchase, a business deal, a marriage, or anything else of the sort for which people in awe and wonder pay homage to the gods with the blood of a cock or the slaughter of a steer or a bull, or cakes . . ."—all, about little everyday concerns. And if it were not an oracle, or lot casting, then it might be a god-sent dream that gave an answer;[77] and accounts would circulate by word of mouth or in written life stories or in inscriptions of thanks, testifying to the effectiveness of divine assistance.[78] In more rural shrines, the worshiper applied for the cure of his ox or his horse[79] or, urban or rural, for the repair of some affliction of his or her own mind or body.

By far the most often attested business of prayer was health; by far the greatest number of shrines and deities answered such prayers almost exclusively or as the principal part of their usual benefactions. So there were hundreds of Asklepieia in the eastern half of the empire and various adopted versions of the god, through syncretism: the petitioner thus applied for help to Asclepius Zimidrenus or Asclepius Culculsenus.[80] Some of the old Olympian logic persisted in paganism after all; the Greco-Roman gods sometimes did realize their mythological roles. But then, sometimes they didn't, and Silvanus cured as well as Asclepius, unmindful of his proper raison d'être; so did Mercury, Hercules, in fact any deity one could think of. One scholarly discussion after another particularly given to some pagan deity will conclude that he or she was essentially a healer; and any number of essentially healing deities are known: in eastern Gaul for example, those eighty and more different ones presiding over cures by water at springs and lakes.[81]

It was said long ago, it was "a cure-seeking world," in which the chief attraction for special journeys to temples was "the longing for cures."[82] Well, we must remember the realities. Most things that could happen to you in those distant times were at least intelligible, if not manageable. The rich had their power of the purse, the poor had their patrons, for most predicaments of living. But what was to be done about the growing goiter which you nervously measured with your touch each day, or the loss of speech after only a brief faint, or pain in one eye and the darkening of it followed by the ominous onset of pain in the other?—a thousand afflictions beyond household herbs and medicine, with no doctors' offices to go to, no hospitals, no miraculous intervention of Science. Only temples supplied all these deficiencies, or one might hope so. Only they and their benignant Power, under whatever name, offered some promise of help made credible by all the testimonials spread about the walls, presenting real cases of real people really cured. For individuals as opposed to groups and communities, temples were thus very close to the central concerns of life, as by the same token experiences in temples lay close to the center of religious faith.

Facilities were often to be found for sleeping through the night near the god's house, so-called incubation, in the course of which the god would appear in a vision or a dream and reveal an answer or a command. The proce-

dure was known to the shrines of every province.[83] Ordinarily, however, petitioners' address took the form of an offering of some sort, most commonly
a small coin tossed into a well or basin or coin box, often a pinch of incense
on an altar, perfume in a perfume bottle, a little oil lamp lit and later thrown
away, or wax candles likewise to be lit in special numbers on the god's own
day; by the rich, of course, gold or silver lamps, huge candelabra; at some
shrines, figurines or statuettes; in rural shrines, fruits, game, anything small
from one's fields. The evidence particularly for festal lighting in active pagan
worship is very abundant for all regions and goes on up through the fourth,
fifth, sixth, even the seventh century, though the later mentions carry the
story into almost entirely rural settings. Whatever of an offering was not used
in the act went to the priest to support the upkeep of the shrine. The finds at
shrines run into the hundreds or thousands of such objects, often bought on
the spot from a handy vendor: "Buy lamps, sieves [for wine offerings], statuettes," reads an advertisement inscribed on an African lamp.[84]

Laws of the fifth and sixth centuries reached beyond blood sacrifices to
forbid offerings of incense or wine.[85] Nevertheless such cult acts went on in
some cities quite openly if quietly. In Corinth near the edge of the built-up
section of the city was a cave containing a natural spring which, fitted out
first as a bathing place, later was given to the worship of the spirits resident
in it. They were termed, in one graffito, "The Angels Below." To these, perhaps also to other beings here, were offered thousands of lamps; hence the
name given to the site by the excavators, Fountain of the Lamps. Among the
motifs decorating these objects, Eros was most favored. The shrine was active
well into Justinian's reign.[86] The date to which active cult was maintained
here, evidently focusing the loyalty of large numbers of people, is best explained by the site not being a temple; so, while apparently at odds with the
times, its history only brings out the quite different nature of more formal
shrines and proper temples. *They* couldn't be ignored, they were vulnerable,
therefore they didn't last even though old habits of worship still obviously
surrounded them.

Another point of vulnerability in paganism was perceived and attacked:
the economic. Confiscation of all income-producing property from temples
was decreed apparently in 382 by legislation not directly surviving and perhaps little observed at the time; but its intent was reasserted in the 390s under
Theodosius and again in the same year that temple destruction was decreed

(407/8). What was then seized by the state was to be transferred to churches.[87] There is considerable known about both the regular income and the expenses incurred by temples of any size in Rome and in various eastern cities, especially in Egypt and in Arsinoe above all others. Without going into such material for its own sake, it is enough to say that paganism in its "upper parts," its "deluxe," community-wide cult acts and buildings, required extremely large portions of the regular municipal funds each year and was to that extent at the mercy of such laws as the Christian emperors passed, and passed again.[88]

Those same upper parts depended also on individual acts of noblesse oblige, for which we now borrow the Greek word evergetism. Without evergetism—hugely generous or hugely obligated by social position, but in any case the gift of the municipal elite to their fellow citizens—Greco-Roman cities could never have paid for their religion in anything like the form familiar to themselves in, say, Constantine's day and familiar to us as well in all our learned publications. Hence such laws as that of the later fifth century declaring invalid all gifts and bequests to shrines.[89] Sheer lack of money was intended to reduce paganism to such humble places and practices as have been revealed by excavation at the Fountain of the Lamps.

In addition, the elite, taking their money with them, could be induced to apostatize. A large subject, that.[90] Here, too, I need not go into it at all, except to point out what is obvious: that a millionaire senator who joined the church would no longer express or secure his place in his world by repairing the roof on the Jupiter temple or buying the feast that delighted the populace on Jupiter's day. Apostates there were—the knowable among the great names of the empire, all known to indefatigable research. From whatever mix of impulses, in a steady stream they joined the emperors' own great congregation. The emperors could accelerate the process by favoring their coreligionists for appointments and promotions, while eventually commanding all citizens to turn up in church with their wives and children, on pain of having their property seized and themselves sent into exile. This was in the 420s.[91] In the same decade and repeatedly thereafter, pagans were banned from all imperial service; and they were forbidden also to serve as lawyers, in 468, and in due course as teachers in the schools.[92] Two years after this latter legislation (of 527) came the reign of terror in Constantinople in which large numbers of the most prominent pagan personages were arrested, jailed, interrogated, and tortured: lawyers, career bureaucrats, noblemen, but also grammarians, sophists, professors. No doubt they had half thought they were safe, after so many generations of avoiding so much persecution and so many laws.

After or at the same time as its campaigns against idols and their homes and after forbidding community worship, the persecution thus turned its edge against individuals, choosing the elite for obvious reasons. They had always supported those idols, homes of idols, and community worship with their wealth and position—of which being deprived, they were no longer able to support the upper parts of the religious structure called paganism.

A particular problem though a narrowly based one, from the point of view of the persecutors, were the high exemplars and justifiers of paganism. They were persons focused on their religion to a degree beyond the reach or taste of all but a few, pointedly abstinent in diet, hard on themselves in other ways like the famous Apollonius of Tyana or, later, Plotinus and his disciples. Some Plotinus drew out to his Campanian community from the Roman senate itself. In Egypt certain priests could be found who regulated their lives in an ascetic fashion, one that admirers of "philosophy" could recognize; and, quite outside of the temples, specially devout individuals formed themselves into a group which we happen to know about from their correspondence. A single letter survives between two of them, recalling how "our friend Callinicus was testifying to the utmost about the way of life you follow even under such conditions—especially in your not abandoning your austerities. Yes, we may deservedly congratulate ourselves, not because we do these things, but because we are not diverted from them by ourselves. Courage! Carry through what remains like a man! Let not wealth distract, nor beauty. . . ."[93]

Their very differentness gave such persons a certain importance. They were talked about, attracted curiosity, and gave rise to stories about their superhuman powers. It was believed they could control the very winds. Some could call out evil spirits from the possessed. Apollonius could do this, others also whom Plotinus knew and accepted in contradistinction to the false exorcists that worked through incantations and so claimed to heal. How could these latter believe in what they did? Their tricks were for the masses, not for sensible folk. Other unchallengeable heroes spent long periods atop stone pillars, "whom *hoi polloi* believe to be up there in the company of the gods, requesting benefits for the whole of Syria"—so, one sceptical account.[94]

Piety of a sort so disembodied offered no real target for persecution. Exemplars could only be few in any period; they required no elaborate funding, no elaborate space or facilities. In the sources they have left few traces of themselves in the best of times and none at all post-Constantine. But piety of a different sort, more organized and academic, did present itself in a vulnerable form, centered in the philosophic lecture halls of Antioch into the 460s and in Alexandria even after Hypatia's death into the 480s, among such figures as Asclepiodotus, as was described in the first chapter.[95] The school in Athens lasted even longer, defining itself anew and with increasing fervor and distinctness in the course of the four or five generations up to its dissolution in 529.[96] Its membership, certainly its leadership, pursued their careers to some extent as conscious rebels in the face of a hostile establishment, some very incomplete glimpses of which are afforded through a school president, Damascius, of the early sixth century. He describes the arrest and flogging of one member of the school group and the interrogation and renewed ordeal of others at the direction of a certain orthodox bishop, Athanasius, evidently hand in hand with the secular authorities, at what date is unclear; also, what the victims thought of their persecutors: "A race dissolved in every passion, destroyed by uncontrolled self-indulgence, cringing and womanish in its thinking, close to cowardice, wallowing in all swinishness, debased, content with servitude in security, such is the life of those who belong to the present generation." The passages survive, as we would expect, only as excerpts and by accident, very much as the school members themselves survived, *disjecta membra*, moving about in flight or exile among their friends in Alexandria, Aphrodisias, Epidaurus, Beirut, and so forth, in the 480s and 490s, and to Carrhae-Harran when, in 529, Justinian ordered the closing of the school. There we may leave Damascius and his companions, barely within the empire, barely alive. The persecution of the intellectuals had done its job, finally.

That the high pagans of this one little university town should have been able to hang on so long without hiding their religious loyalties—should have been able even to weave their beliefs into their open teaching of philosophy better called theology—can perhaps be explained by the reverence of the eastern bishops for their own learned culture. A number of them had sought out such stars of the academy in their youth in one center of learning or another; their professors had recalled their own studies in Athens. Then came Justinian, not one to tolerate the intolerable. The story of the town remains, however, a little puzzling. Of course, it may not have mattered much. The world around it wanted none of its learning, to which in fact the empire's eastern neighbors, Persia and before very long the Arabs, gave a better welcome. Gutas and other scholars can explain that, which does matter.[97]

The Fountain of the Lamps in Corinth may serve as a reminder of the unconverted in eastern cities who, unlike the holdouts at Athens, had no prominent visible community; who had no access to great images or altars, gathered in no crowds for their various festivals, persisted without the means of openly expressing their religion, so it would seem. They appear in the surviving evidence only by accident, through graffiti, or as the market for mosaics and objets d'art bearing religious messages too clearly wrong for any Christian buyer. Denunciation by private enemies discloses their loyalties, as may an oppressive sickness that sends them on a hunt for health even to a Christian source (where they are converted, a miracle! and so we hear of it). Scattered among the various notes to this chapter, they present a puzzle, so far up in time even as the seventh century, though by then pretty rare. A puzzle, because how were they able to persist, being so stripped and starved?

The answer lies in what may be called private worship. Let me present some gleanings on a subject almost never talked about, yet permeating everybody's life in one way or another, in those Greco-Roman times, and so inevitably turning up in the record now and again by inadvertence. Very much like a city, domestic religion had its calendar, its festivals, its shrines, but in the homes of the living or the dead. Of the living, at least in a Latin setting, the hearth was and is well known as family worship's focus, in every sense. In Spain and Gaul the custom of making an offering on the flames happens still to be mentioned in the late sixth century.[98] Latin worship of the Lares and Penates in their wall niches and similar tiny chapels is familiar, too: often practiced daily, the images or painted portraits often flanked by the owner's particular choices among other traditional deities, or the untraditional, or favored emperors. Literary mentions are obliging enough to extend beyond Rome into other parts of Italy and Spain. In Pompeii, matching less abundant archeological evidence from Mauretania or Pannonia, literally hundreds of portable altars have been found in interior rooms, exterior ones, and gardens. Such worship—the very Lares in private homes!—was declared illegal in 392, by a law never heard from again. Jerome accepts such cult as still routine, subsequently, and the rooms of a mansion built in Ostia in the early fifth century provided the usual niches for the gods of the inhabitants. Greek households, too, had their little stone altars for an equal variety of specially

chosen cults, with reliefs of a god like Sarapis on the wall, or images for favored cults in the peristyle or gardens of rich dwellings. In Egyptian excavations, household gods as little images are found by the thousands in contexts
as late as the mid-fifth century or mentioned in literary sources up to the
sixth century: in one home of no great size, no less than forty-two to satisfy
every prayer. Reliefs and figurines next to doorways in Arles or Rome as in
Alexandria kept away mischance.[99] All of which adds up to the ubiquitous
and most meaningful conduct of religious life right in one's home, from its
doorway to its most private recesses. Persecution could not effectively reach
this, though the picture of paganism somehow retaining its vitality and its
satisfactions, with such private worship and nothing more, needs further explanation (see chapter 4).

The religious calendar which could be found in a family as in a city recognized principally the birthdays of its members; and for the family as a whole,
the annual Dear Kin Day came around in February. This was an old Roman,
that is, an Italian holy day but in due course was taken up generally in the
western provinces and remained a public festival past the mid-fifth century.[100]

And in homes or at businesses, the old gods presided over contracts, too.
They were invoked in oaths and sometimes, in the west up to the end of the
sixth century, in pagan forms and rituals.[101] But this can only be called a
recognition of the traditional faith, not an act of worship.

A page or two earlier, private cults were said to be discoverable in the
homes not only of the living but of the dead as well. That meant tombs. In
some, the family displayed their favored deities: best known, Minerva and
Harpocrates in a second- or third-century mausoleum in the necropolis beneath Saint Peter's in Rome.[102] To other tombs, as we know from much and
widely scattered material, the surviving family gathered for memorial dinners,
inviting their friends as well, the deceased, too, and making a night of it. The
rite was immensely popular, quite as much as the feasts alfresco that enlivened
the precincts of the gods.

Artemidorus in the second century, that most learned professional dream
interpreter, recounts how one of his clients "dreamed that cronies and brothers in an association to which he belonged suddenly appeared and said to
him, 'Receive us and give us dinner,'" which, with more of the dream, the interpreter easily understood in terms of "the custom for companions to go to
the dwelling," that is, the tombs, "of the deceased members and to dine there,

and the reception is said to have been given by the deceased because of the honors paid to him by his fellows."[103] The obvious analogy is the hosting of meals by grander immortals like Sarapis, Zeus himself, also Hagna Thea and the range of deities mentioned above (see note 33). Graveside banquets of the sort are in fact indicated by inscriptions, funerary reliefs and mosaics, banquet tables and the remains of all the drinking and cooking vessels needed for the meal; by late poems, too, and still later (thirteenth century) reminders from the church that the faithful should not indulge in such pagan customs. They are indicated by a law for all the empire, in a part of the general proscription of pagan practices of 408.[104] In earlier times, Lucian described how families brought costly picnics to the dead and insured the full sharing by a pipe let down into the tomb through which wine pure or mixed with honey could be poured; and just such arrangements have been found in sarcophagi from a Greek area.[105]

All this material is eastern, only to be teased out of a most reluctant, quite exiguous body of material on the private or family aspects of religion. In western areas there is only a little more to be learned, but it is exactly similar in quality: that is, telling of graveside evening meals for which wine-mixing and cooking facilities were sometimes built, adjacent, or for which the tomb top itself slanted to form a *triclinium* surrounding a dinner table, a *mensa*. The tomb or the sarcophagus might have a lead or terracotta pipe led into it with a wine-strainer at the top for toasts to be shared with the deceased, who, himself, is depicted in a large and well-known variety of frescoes, recumbent on the dinner-couch with his glass raised on high. Old Roman custom required a special chair or seat to be reserved for the deceased to join the party. In the western capital, in the well-known cemetery of Peter and Marcellinus, the frescoes of pagan burials show the usual dining scenes with details regarding the various foods to be eaten, and a mid-second-century burial beneath Saint Peter's provides an example of the lead pipe arrangement, perhaps for something less refrigerating than wine, since it is a child's burial[106]—"refrigerating," because the mood for family visits to the tomb was celebratory, easy, happy, and the Latin term for them was *refrigeratio*, "refreshment," or *laetitia*, "joy."[107] Their religious character, however, was recognized in the word "sacrilegious" thrown at them by Christians.[108] They seem to have taken for granted, of course, life after death, living and almost tangible in the very grave. About this, people in fact had their doubts, very serious doubts, more often than not. The subject is debated still. Debate, however, was no obstacle to the ubiquity of the graveside evening and nighttime feasts.[109]

Review of private paganism, as it may be called, commences in the home; but it cannot end there. It must move on to the cemeteries that ringed the ancient city. Once arrived there, the scene opens out still further, to the countryside, with the realization that everything said so far in this chapter has regarded only city life. However important city life may have been, quite disproportionately so, and however much better known, yet in a demographic sense it could only be a minority thing. If we should say arbitrarily that "urban" designates the population in centers of at least five thousand, we have accounted for only a fifth or less of the empire's total—leaving four-fifths still to be included in the story of paganism and its persecution post-400. Those four-fifths certainly can't be forgotten, for no one would expect the church to ignore the challenge from this great majority—that is, when the bishops gave any thought to it. It was of course a matter as little or as seldom on their minds as it was on the minds of their peers in secular society, whose preoccupations were always city-bent. Consequently, rural persecution comes relatively late to the story.

The target was not easy to get at. Away from the cities, the expression of religious beliefs was as diffuse as the population itself. For illustration: the Cloud-driver or Weather-man, able to control storms, either to bring them with their rain or to avert them and their hail, and to do so as himself a wonder-worker, being possessed of the right powers, never mind in what god's name; for in fact such persons seem not to have any home, temple, or any one single deity to explain them.[110] They resemble rather the men and women capable of cures, predictions, and far-sight who are also reported because of their supernatural gifts in the isolated districts of the Peloponnese, the Anatolian highlands, Bithynia, Syria, and elsewhere, though (I assume by the mere chance of the record) almost only in the east.[111] They had no built amenities around them, no sacred home. Everyone nevertheless knew who they were and applied to them as needs arose.

The rustic population obviously had needs different from those of city folk—weather, for one, which ruled their lives. Care of animals was another. It is not in urban shrines that one finds votive horse- or ox-sculptures or inscriptions giving thanks for their cure (see note 77). It was common also in rural parts to send up a prayer in the form of a ribbon tied to a tree or to offer cult to specific great monarchs of the forest or to divinities dwelling in groves. Fillet-prayers and tree worship are both attested in all regions of the Mediterranean world, a reminder of the remarkable degree of uniformity that had been attained in cult by A.D. 400. Both had been forbidden by fourth-century laws as they were again by Pope Gregory in the 590s; both were continually preached against by bishops up through the sixth century in the west; both came under repeated physical attack by ardent priests and monks of eastern and western provinces alike into the latter half of the seventh century; both were identified by western church councils as the practices of pagans still in the tenth.[112] Yet they proved close to ineradicable.

Unlike trees, hilltops did not disappear from the tangible record, so archeology sometimes supports the written mention of their little shrines or altars.[113] Similarly we know of shrines principally for healing at lakes, ponds, and ordinary springs as well as at the occasional thermal one. They were indestructible. It was the usual practice to apply the water to the ailing part of the body or to drink it and, in return, to cast an offering of some sort into the water. Coins were favored and sometimes help to date the life span of sites.[114] Pre-400, a heavy stream of pilgrims brought fame and some wealth to places like the nameless shrines near Lake Bracciano or at the Sources de la Seine; but the examples should not suggest that there were not similar ones in eastern provinces. The ubiquity of water shrines brings out once more the degree of homogenization, or perhaps only of parallel development, across the whole of the empire and its religious landscape, while their known numbers, by the hundreds upon hundreds, are proof of their importance.

To put an end to them, one Christian ascetic could simply curse them and dry them up; to level a temple or blast a cult image, others need apply no more than a prayer.[115] But such help was not always available; resort must be had to unassisted human powers. Sacred cypresses, center of a living cult in Lycia, fell to the axe of a zealous monk; a hilltop shrine was overthrown by another, with the help of the rustics themselves, whom his miracles of crop and domestic animal protection had converted.[116] In the first chapter I had something to say about the important and vigorous part that monks played in breaking down the country dwellers' faith. There is a fair amount of hagiographical literature on the subject, or at least on episodes in the story.

A still more important part was played by landowners. The church had an ever-increasing network of rural priests, *chorepiscopi* as they were called, and little churches and chapels to go with them. These served as so many eyes open upon the backward, least populous areas, but they were only observation posts. They had no muscle, no force or authority other than the fear of hell that could be brought to bear on unbelievers.[117] John Chrysostom pointed the way to more effective pressure, urging individual landowners to set up priests and chapels on their holdings.[118] No doubt other bishops preached to the same effect. Being, some of them, great landholders, titular owners of whole villages, they could certainly insure a pretty good compliance with their wishes among their own peasantry.[119] As the grandest landowner of all, the emperor too could discipline his own estates and keep them clear of obvious, built shrines; and he could demand the tearing down of "temples in the country districts" in general, "for when they are torn down and removed, the material basis for all superstition will be destroyed." But no penalties or responsible offices at this time are specified. It is only in 472 that a further, more effectual step was taken: owners of pagan places of worship (which can only mean temples on private land) were to be identified and stripped of rank and property or, if mere lowly individuals, tortured and sent to the mines.[120] By this decree, what Chrysostom had asked for was at last given some force — just how much, it must be said once more, no one knows because no information survives to indicate the success of enforcement. Was there in fact any at all? Yes, of course; but to what degree or at what rate? By definition, obscure localities will remain obscure. To the surprise of Constantine Porphyrogenitus in the tenth century, a little corner of southern Greece still sheltered a wholly idolatrous, good-old-fashioned Greek population.[121]

Advice offered by the emperor to his agent in Damascus, just quoted, regarding "the basis for superstition," had been offered with a different emphasis not many years earlier by Libanius to Theodosius: "temples are the soul of the countryside; and the property that suffers thus [through their destruction] is destroyed along with the zeal of its peasantry, for they believe that their labors will be in vain, being deprived of the gods that direct those labors toward their needs."[122] The orator goes on to picture the religious feasts of the peasantry, their toasts to draw the gods to their celebration, the big happy crowds of them gathered at the landowner's on days of worship. All such means of survival, with the human enjoyments attending them, they stood to lose.

Justinian in 542 secured the services of a certain John as titular bishop of

Ephesus to convert the backlands of the four provinces of Asia, Caria, Lydia, and Phrygia; and the bishop with the help of four energetic deacons in Asia, others elsewhere, and ample funding from the emperor, over the course of decades proved very successful: eighty thousand souls reclaimed at three triens each, and ninety-two churches built with another ten monasteries.[123] A poor man could live most of the year on a triens, employment on the churches would have been welcome, and, all in all, John's visits in any locality must have made a most favorable impression. Speculation is idle, whether in these very long-"Christianized" regions, indeed some of them lying almost within Saint Paul's general orbit, the number of converts represented the very last pagans in existence, and, let us imagine, a tenth of the population (perhaps a tenth of the adult males, and therefore several times the figure of eighty thousand), or whether an equal number were left in other odd pockets here and there, still to be converted after the bishop and his men had come and gone.

The same story in the western provinces must be told in somewhat different terms. Here, the intent of the authorities was equally serious, the ecclesiastical and secular similarly worked together well, and the instruments of persecution were the same: laws, monks, and landowners. However, the archeological sources are much more abundant and throw light on corners that in the east are rarely illuminated. Moreover, the degree of urbanization is very much less and diminishes significantly post-400, so that the history of the countryside comes close to being the history of everybody and everything.

Excavation uncovers great amounts of minutely smashed building elements and statuary in or near holy places, most but not all in Gaul, just as can be seen in the east but far more frequently.[124] The associated coin evidence commonly runs out toward the turn of the fifth century. The fact by itself can't be used to date what happened; but, for much of the destruction, fitting with the coins, Martin (d. ca. 397) may be fairly blamed or credited. His area of activity can be plotted on the map and aligned to some extent with archeological evidence. He was by no means the last monk so active.[125] The foundation of monasteries in the more remote areas served also to supplement the establishing of rural churches and chapels, thus bringing Christianity among the population; and preaching based there went on with occasional moments of success, along with the physical destruction of cult facilities.[126]

In the towns and from a steadily growing number of rural pulpits, preaching addressed the wealthy, meaning the landowners of the neighborhood, and called on them to take an active part in the rooting out of religion as their tenants, dependents, and slaves knew it. They should see to it that any temples were broken up and sacred trees felled, and anyone who resisted should be beaten and flogged. So urged Caesarius of Arles, as, earlier and in Italy, Maximus of Turin had urged toward the turn of the fifth century along with Gaudentius of Brescia, Peter Chrysologus in Ravenna, or Augustine in just the same terms in north Africa. Again, toward the turn of the seventh century, Pope Gregory directed his campaigns at the still totally rural population of Sardinia through their masters, recommending far harsher measures. It was the masters' fault if any sacrifice continued to be offered, if any idol or temple still stood on their land; they were as good (or as bad) as accomplices to the breaking of divine and man-made law.[127]

It is not surprising to find, in step with bishops as individuals, that assembled councils issued instructions to the same effect. The first to do so was in Spain, where successive canons grew more and more furious, ending in 681 with a recommendation of capital punishment for recalcitrant peasants unless their masters took action first, to lock them up and flog them.[128] By then, most of the peninsula had long reverted to paganism.[129] To do the actual beheading, it was of course not the masters but the secular authorities who were called on. Imperial legislation for the east had involved landowners since 392, but nothing further seems to have been determined for the west along these lines—naturally enough, given the barbarian invasions post-400. Instead, of course, it was the barbarian kings and queens who must be taught to enforce the law. In due course they obliged: they forbade their rural nobility to tolerate traditional piety. Clovis was flattered and converted and smiled on those of his subjects who joined him; Charlemagne laid down fines against the cult of trees and springs, and was sanctified; Egica toward the turn of the eighth century found and deplored "idolatry everywhere or other various errors of the Devil's superstitions"; Brunigild of the Franks was favored with a personal note from the great pope Gregory inviting her attention to her crypto-pagan subjects; while Childebert specified a hundred lashes for any cult act ventured by a person of the lower orders.[130]

From the late date of much of this evidence for paganism still surviving, one might conclude that the Christian powers had never been in earnest about converting the masses on the countryside. The machinery of enforcement, ecclesiastical and secular, certainly didn't work very well. But the conclusion really seems ridiculous. Rather, very serious efforts were made within the kings' and bishops' capacities, defiance invited severe punishment, and yet, nevertheless, the story went on in the familiar way: familiar, that is, from the centuries pre-400, with slow but very incomplete response to Christian argument, pacific presence, and miracle. Hence, another conclusion, apparently more reasonable: the old religion suited most people very well. They loved it, trusted it, found fulfillment in it, and so resisted change however eloquently, or ferociously, pressed upon them. Left to themselves by the receding tide of imperial and ecclesiastical authority, they drifted away from the church in Britain; likewise in Spain. The depth of Christian belief had perhaps always been limited and the evidence of conversion, in counting bishoprics and churches, easy to exaggerate. Even from the longest-evangelized, most completely church-ed area down in Provence, in the 580s, when a man took passage on a vessel bound for Italy, he might find "a great crowd of pagans getting aboard along with myself, among all of whom, that crowd of country people, I was the only Christian."[131] The incident is very revealing, not least in the matter-of-fact tone of the narrative. It fits easily with all the other evidence accumulated in the notes above, showing in still more advanced periods the persistence of this or that pagan custom, the survival of one or another ancient rite.

In the definition of paganism offered at the opening to this chapter, one element suggested was "a substratum of rites addressing life's hopes and fears without appeal to any one being in particular." At this level, persistence was particularly marked because particularly hard to get at and counter. Though calling it all "superstition" raises problems that must be addressed in the next chapter, to do so seems the quickest way of introducing the subject; and there are at the moment enough problems of quite another sort, arising from the obscurity of the material. "Superstition" was in fact something not much talked about by the kind of people likely to leave a written record, and, without their explanations, the archeological evidence, such as survives, is hard or impossible to understand.

I attempt only a superficial sampling of the evidence, beginning with the belief that there were bad things—disease, or hexing, or misfortune—that one could keep out of one's house by marking its entrance with some certain sign. The practice has been noticed, above. An ankh would do, the ancient Egyptian cross with a loop which meant "life"; and the custom touched the west and aroused the hostility of the bishops in Spain. They speak against it in puzzling periphrases, to forbid "making empty depictions of deceit in front of one's house."[132] In the countryside, equivalent protection could be secured to one's property by walking its periphery or erecting boundary posts with proper rites. They would keep away hail, blight, storms, everything.[133]

Protection of one's person lay through amulets tied around one's neck or worn in any other way, some inscribed "Sarapis [or Isis or whatever deity] triumphs!" The elder Pliny instances a piece of paper worn in this way by a most distinguished contemporary, inscribed with two letters of the alphabet, to prevent eye illness; and he goes on, in a rare passage, to collect out of his own society and personal experience all sorts of familiar little habits rather than acts of cult (though he calls one of them "worship"): for example, the attributing of prognostic meaning to sneezes.[134] Prognostic or prophetic rituals of the do-it-yourself kind took many forms: one well-known, the so-called Virgilian lots, whereby the *Aeneid* (a copy in many a home) was opened at random and one's finger set down at random, too, and whatever the line pointed to, that was to be interpreted like an oracle. There was another usage that Aelius Aristides notes in his diary: "I heard propitious remarks from both children and from others—right while I was approaching, and in their play, they cried out, 'Hail to the Master!'"[135] It was the freedom of the message from any rational human intervention that was thought to insure its divine origin, very much like bird flight observations but on an individual, domestic scale. Plainly, persecution could never reach such moments.

A burial custom is worth mentioning, too, if only because mention might be expected: the placing of a small coin in the mouth of the deceased to pay Charon, which everyone knows about. Juvenal says a penny will do, a very small tip indeed for the ferryman. Cemeteries in the region of Tournai offer some fifth-century illustrations of the practice.[136]

And finally, fears that the moon would disappear for good: to an eclipse or the end of the month, the response that we hear about from the western provinces was to make a great racket with horns and bells. The bishops from the fifth century on called the practice sacrilege, the Devil's work, and tried to end it by their conciliar legislation on solemn occasions and by their preaching far more often; but it persisted till the ninth century.[137]

◆ ◆ ◆

Looking back over the chapter, perhaps nothing stands out more clearly than the degree to which ordinary human needs were answered by traditional religion. This is the first thing to notice. A different world is certainly conceivable: needs could have received purely secular answers; but that was not what happened. For example: man is a social animal. The need to share oneself with others after work was satisfied by most people in antiquity through groups divinely hosted or addressed to the divine. There were meals in shrines and at the graveside (which became a shrine, and the meal was shared by the deceased). Most people simply did not meet their friends or kinfolk in any other setting—most people, of course, not meaning the great and rich, bishops and senators and so forth.

At such meetings the need for art, which may likewise be called biological or of the species, received satisfaction in ways characteristic of the culture of the Mediterranean world at the time: that is, through song and dance above all. While both could be seen on the stage with or without religious meaning, and while songs pervaded secular life as well as religious, dance as a thing to participate in is not attested except in moments of worship. And make-believe, sheer inventive effervescence, may be called of the species, too. Where could it be better found than in the religious processions that the pagan world delighted in? They are richly, one may say lovingly, described in a variety of genres and texts. Or they are hatefully described, of course, by bishops. Alternatives to them are conceivable. In the younger Pliny's day a grand lady might have her own private troupe of entertainers for her postprandial diversion. Most people, however, only got close to such displays through participating in worship. Similarly the other arts: the art of elaborate prose and poetry, of sculpture and painting. These in urban settings and more crudely, too, in the rural could only or chiefly be enjoyed in connection with worship, unless one lived among the privileged.

In addition, humanitarian impulses may be said to be of the species. So far as they needed expression beyond a patron's role, beyond evergetism, they were expressed through religion: temples provided poor-relief and refuge from enemies.

All these answers to common needs, and never a word about religious needs! Whatever those might be, and however restless was the search for satisfaction within paganism—however constant was the invention of slightly new answers, new acts and styles of engagement with superhuman powers, new adaptations and combinations of belief, new rules for Bacchants in Italy of the second century B.C., new liturgical practices at Panamara in the second century A.D., new deities like Sarapis, Antinous, Glycon, and a radically re-modeled Mithra—no single desperate point of emptiness appears. Taken as a whole system, paganism worked.

Among the novelties to challenge its old ways, pre-Constantine, the most marked and successful had of course been Christianity. In three hundred years it succeeded in winning over perhaps a tenth of the population; then, many times that number in the next three generations. The contrast points to the role played by secular support in bringing up the total to a half, or close to a half, of the population at the beginning of the fifth century.

But if the church now embraced so many, that wasn't enough. The second thing to notice, I would say, is the difficulty experienced by ecclesiastical and secular forces conjoined in completing the process of conversion. What the difficulty indicates can only be an emptiness, call it, or some mix of deficiencies, in Christianity itself. Therefore anyone whose particular needs were better answered by an alternative and who would not respond to the social and economic inducements held out by the "Christian empire," nor to the arguments and demonstrations proving the rightness of Christianity, must be persuaded by other means. It is a striking indication of the urgency felt within the church, that the ideal held up for imitation in accounts of evangelical efforts were heroes that would lock an old man for life in their private dungeon of some sort, or burn a heathen priest to death.[138] Government, too, at the urging of the bishops weighed in with threats, and more than threats, of fines, confiscation, exile, imprisonment, flogging, torture, beheading, and crucifixion. What more could be imagined? Nothing. The extremes of conceivable pressure were brought to bear. Thus, over the course of many centuries, compliance was eventually secured and the empire made Christian in truth.

A third and last thing to notice: in the process of eradicating paganism, the most provoking, accessible, vulnerable aspects were attacked in sequence. A space of some two hundred years is seen to lie between the first serious moves against blood sacrifices, by Constantine, and the earliest opposition to moon-racket (as I have called it). Persecution that first focused on acts sponsored by community leaders only later turned to those involving no-account people, the poor and the rural. Public religious ceremonies came under attack some generations before the private and individual—the family ones and those conducted in the home. In rough terms, we may say paganism was dismantled from the top down. As a consequence, the aspects that survived longest were those closest to the rural masses, closest to home, closest to "superstition." The fact has given rise to various interpretations which the next chapter will explore.

◆ 3 ◆

Superstition

The mix of acts and beliefs to be called religious, especially in the West, included some of a particularly long history post-312 that were certainly not Christian. In a loose sense, instead, they were, or are today, called pagan. Some discussion of them obviously belongs in these pages, and leads into wider areas of inquiry.

To begin with, their identity. I mean the word in its literal sense. Across a great length of centuries, is it one cult that reappears from time to time, or are the several appearances of successive different cults?

Diana worship may serve as illustration. Classical temples flanking the city square, idols with golden beards, parades of sacrificial animals, donors, and priests might all fade from the scene, but Diana lived on, at least in Spain, Celtic Italy, and Gaul.[1] Her name, like the name Mercury for this or that favored male deity in the same region, was by a familiar practice attached to female deities whom Latin writers judged unpronounceable and unintelligible to the ordinary reader—deities who somehow recalled Diana in her classically Greco-Roman form. Perhaps the similarities amounted to nothing more than female gender and woodland habitat. In the 380s, Diana cult provoked the bishops of north Italian churches; again in the opening years of the tenth century the abbot Regino of Prüm found somewhere in ecclesiastical records of the ninth what were there termed "great crowds" of women who, reporting on their experiences during deathlike trances, had careered about the skies with a mistress at their head named Diana. In the eleventh, the fourteenth, the sixteenth century her worshipers had nonsense phrases on their lips, strange new names for the objects of their worship, strange couplings with Satan. Bishops became more than ever disgusted; their persecution became ever more angry and particular. It was a witch-hunt.[2]

Is Diana to be interpreted as a survival, then? A bit of the goddess of vegetation hanging on? Fertility rites? Is her cult *folkloric*? In odd forms from odd lands, it emerges from time to time out of silence, like the arched back of a dolphin in a distant school, seen only when it unexpectedly surfaces. Is that, the observer wonders, the same dolphin's back each time, or some other? Diana of the 880s, let's say, in Germany: is she the goddess that Maximus of Turin points to, or Peter of Ravenna in the 380s? Or is she a Frankish import a little naturalized? The intervals of time and space separating the attestations of this particular cult are too great to permit an answer. Whether Diana was post-Roman meaning post-pagan in my sense of the latter word, or whether she was Roman meaning Italian, or perhaps pre-Roman, or even entirely alien in origin, who can say? At least in the northwestern empire, after New Year's day of A.D. 407 and the flooding in of Vandals and the rest, questions of the origins of beliefs and practices need special caution.

And exactly what would *folkloric* mean? Belonging to a pre-Roman, even prehistoric, Durkheimian world? To be found among all peoples of the earth, therefore capable of being reconstructed out of similarities noticed across many cultures, in an anthropological way, and in that form capable of being applied to a fuller understanding of medieval phenomena?[3] But of course reconstruction must proceed on the level of theory. Whatever might then be formed in the mind can have no more than heuristic value for historians. They will go on to look for theory realized in some actual time and place; but they will not find the materials they need in the area and period examined in these pages. Whether Diana and her midnight rides preexisted the Roman empire as a part of general human culture and thereafter passed into that empire and beyond, to later ages, cannot be known. It may certainly be doubted.

"Folkloric" might instead be declared to characterize what was "popular," regardless of origin. This definition would be less difficult to understand and substantiate. Underlying it would be a distinction between the beliefs and practices of the majority, the masses, the *populus, vulgus,* lower classes, uneducated, the simple or unlettered or however they might be labeled, as opposed to some dominant minority, however that might be labeled. As the progress of persecution showed, whatever was least structured and elaborate in religious behavior and most remote from the eye of authority proved the most likely to survive. The requirements precisely fitted the *populus* and its religious usages: what was "popular" turned out to be safe. Therefore it survived into much later times. Rather attractive, this line of reasoning. It will be tested in the next chapter and the support for it pointed out.

To return, however, to Diana worship as illustrative of the problems presented by medieval and later paganism, so-called: from the abbot Regino's day forward, the trances that women succumbed to in some private home went undetected, and so almost uncorrected. At least they escaped the full attention of the ecclesiastical authorities. But the illustrative material here is suspect because of its uncertain origins. My purposes require something more clearly originating within the classical Roman empire, where paganism took shape, subsequently attested in a close-set series of mentions long afterwards. The exchange of gifts on the Kalends will do; similarly, the hanging up of ribbons as prayers on trees or, at springs, the tossing in of a coin; the lighting of a lamp or marking of a good-luck sign near the door. These and other "popular" rituals differ from Diana cult in being clearly traceable from at least the beginning of the empire to an advanced period. They differ from Diana cult also in addressing no one particular superhuman being. Thus they make a much better fit with the definition of the substratum offered at the beginning of the previous chapter—that is, the less articulately defined area or level of belief.

Pre-Constantine, practices of the sort are discussed at length in an unusual passage from the elder Pliny, he who died in Vesuvius' explosion. Speaking of the beneficial properties of various plants, minerals, and other substances, he digresses. "Pig's fat," he says, "was quite sacred for people in olden times; and more, new brides on entering their homes even nowadays ritually touch the doorposts with it." In contrast, people of his own day: they have risen above beliefs so senseless, though the acts nevertheless remain customary. Further, he says, "To point out how remedies return once again after a thousand years is to mock at life. The ancient Romans even held that wool had religious power and had their newlyweds touch it to the doorposts." In the same line of thought he offers the comment, "Those people established these things in the belief that the gods take a part in all matters and at all times." And, last: "Our Vestals of today we believe can, by their prayers, fix [or immobilize] runaway slaves in their place, so long as they have not left the city; but if this reasoning is once accepted and the gods harken to certain prayers, or are influenced by certain words, the thought must be applied across the board. Indeed our ancestors were forever reporting such things," meaning, the operation of spells or incantations or magical formulae.

He continues: " . . . reporting such things, even (the height of impossibility) that lightning can be induced." The nonsense-strange quality requisite in the necessary sets of words he finds quite "ludicrous." "As a body, the public at all times believes in them unconsciously, though the really wise in their wisdom and as individuals sharply reject them." Such subjects, for politeness' sake, he mustn't pursue any further. Let different people have their different ideas. They are defensive and rather touchy about them.

And yet, only a few pages later, he does go on! He cannot resist quoting at length certain magical prescriptions from an ancient author too silly to believe, a great nuisance to the ears, he says, by whose folly he is thoroughly disgusted. He is plainly aware of the appetite for the wonderful and the readiness indeed to credit it among some part of his readers; only he will not withhold, rather, he draws attention to his own less accepting view.[4] He himself is no universal doubter, no atheist; rather, a respectful believer in the gods and their beneficent powers, though his degree of Stoicism renders his faith a little abstract, or, one may say, renders his gods a little abstract. Yet he thinks he lives in a day much different from that earlier one at least some generations past, one in which beliefs beyond belief existed among people of his own class. They once thought of the divine as forever present and active in the daily minutiae of life. No point existed in which its immanence was not assumed and, too, its susceptibility to certain rites, perhaps even to be controlled, though just how control worked, perhaps nobody pretended to understand.[5]

In the next century the discussion is carried a little further along the same path, Plutarch recalling a dinner-table conversation which turned to spell casting and the evil eye and which opened out to consider reports of the supernatural in general. How should one address these? The answer that persuaded the company was drawn from knowledge of empirical data observed in nature. To think, thus, along lines of reason, along lines of the likely, is the distinctive sign of "philosophy"—using the word as we ourselves once did in our term "natural philosophy." Today we would say "science."[6] For Plutarch and his friends, unthinking report of extraordinary phenomena need not be summarily rejected; rather, it should be tested against what is known of commonly observed cause and effect. "In general," he says, "the person who looks for what's reasonable does away with what's wonderful." The guests' discussion is thus set off into commonsense parallels, simpler models, the mechanics of sensations, and so forth. They grow quite learned, though their learning, needless to say, falls short of our own science.

And then, in the third century, the last great voice of ancient philosophy, Plotinus. Speaking as an old man in the 260s to his disciples, on the subject of certain sectaries (Gnostics, it is surmised, though which particular ones, among all the various Christian groups so-called, scholars are not agreed), he rebukes their care over the special wording of prayers and goes on to expose the folly or rather the impiety of supposing they can control such ills as physical disease by casting out the demons to blame. It isn't a question of demons, he insists; and anyway the real gods wouldn't respond to spells. Cure must rather be sought through disciplined diet and temperance such as philosophy teaches. There are medicines, too, hot applications, and so forth. When you consider the logic of exorcism, tested against common experience of fevers or the like, all arising from natural causes like fatigue, overindulgence, or dietary deficiencies, the whole demon idea is "ludicrous."[7] So, Plotinus.

To sum up the aspects of these discussions that are useful at the moment: they offer us a view onto a thought-world seen across a great length of time, in which, as we would expect, a spectrum of religious ideas is readily sensed. At one extreme are the highly educated, among whom ancestral belief as such is thought to deserve no special reverence. Their tradition or cast of mind in the Roman world can be picked up in Cicero's day, emerging, with the help of a Greek education, from the credulity of a more primitive Rome. The most listened-to among them are persons with some, or much, training in analytical thought—"philosophy" in their terms as in ours—and so habituated to the applying of their minds to everything observable in nature, by which as much of their experience as possible is to be explained. Many other explanations favored by the quite uneducated they dismiss as laughable; for their part, "the masses [at least as they are observed in Alexandria around A.D. 200] are in terror of Hellenic philosophy, as children of goblins, fearing it may delude them."[8]

The educated elite themselves believe in the supernatural, like all good pagans; they cherish their gods, acknowledge and revere them. They attribute to them the great goings-on in the world, of the size of earthquakes or better; they will even hope to influence such things by prayer.[9] They do pray, themselves. They have recourse to the gods for the cure of bodily ills, like, for example (the most obvious and predictable example) Galen. He is at ease with others' reports of successful prescriptions imparted by Asclepius, and himself was a beneficiary, so he tells us.[10] So says Marcus Aurelius, too, of his own experience. Galen's friend Lucian counts as another like these two: caustic on the subject of cures by spells, exorcisms, and phylacteries tied to the affected part, while indignant at the charge of impiety. "I revere the gods and I see their cures and the benefits they bestow by restoring the sick to health with drugs and medical treatment."[11] Men of such faith were only reluctant to see the operation of superhuman beings where it was enough to invoke natural causes. They would be guided (so far as it could take them) by the accumulation of sensory experience, the examination of which must always be the first step toward understanding. Because of their reading, travels, and conversation with others like themselves, in fact they were thus able to explain relatively large areas of life.

The three writers and their like constituted a circle or stratum of some size and very considerable repute, acceptance, even influence. Otherwise they would hardly deserve quotation. More names could be added to theirs, with roughly similar views: Seneca, Aulus Gellius at least in certain passages; Celsus. But, as anyone would expect, the spectrum of attested beliefs is very wide even among the educated classes. Interest in manifestations of the divine shades off from the analytical individual to the personally devoted, or to the idly intrigued: to Aelius Aristides, Apuleius, or readers of fictional temple scenes or ghost stories. Some are credulous, also defensive, in part because they haven't stopped to think. They like what they want to believe; yet sometimes they doubt. In illustration, we have Aelian, retailer of wonders, enemy of sceptics, ready with "a certain Euphronius" as a warning to anyone who listens to them too much. For Euphronius was almost won over to atheism. Then he fell gravely ill. Pneumonia. No physician could help. His friends took him to Asclepius, by whose advice he burned his atheistical books and applied the ashes to his chest, was suitably rewarded, and "his friends were instantly filled with great joy because he had not ended up made a fool of and dishonored by the god."[12]

With Aelian we are still well within the upper class, far removed from "the simple-minded," as their betters describe them, "the thoughtless," "rustics," "yokels," "superstitious masses," "contemptible women," "scum of the marketplace."[13] For such compliments, a pamphlet by Celsus directed at Christianity in the second century is a rich source; but they were generally dealt out by non-Christians and Christians in equal amounts in the course of religious debate. They make clear the reality of the differences marking off the further end of the spectrum. We cannot more directly penetrate the mind of the contemptible masses so as to understand what "popular" religion really was. We must rely instead on what outsiders who were contemporaries care to tell us; and of course we readily accept their view of the world, as being so much closer to our own. They see nothing but superstition preyed upon in the villages or in the darker corners of the towns by persons claiming special powers, special secrets. Juvenal and others describe these in urban scenes, Lucian in both urban and rural, through Proteus Peregrinus and Alexander of Abonoteichus. Unthinking belief is good for social order, observers like Plutarch will say; or it is bad, others (and many laws) will say because it breeds magic and millenial unrest.[14] In any case, it is different—different from "ours" and "us." More direct or less distorted glimpses of the "popular" pre-300 are not worth collecting for a general understanding: they are too few and exceptional.

Most of the authors and evidence serving my discussion so far have come from the second century. To carry it into the third and so almost up to Plotinus, there is Philostratus' famous biography of Apollonius. Here, at a decent remove from the Roman empire, in the far east among the Brahmans (3.15) and in the far south among the Ethiopians (6.27), the miraculous happens right before one's eyes; but Philostratus is cautious about attributing immortality to his hero (8.29) and reluctant to credit him with bringing the dead to life (4.55). A balance, then. These and other passages and their nuances have been often studied. They place the author comfortably within the company so far surveyed, at least among the less rigorous-minded. To learn more about the next generation, however, we really have no one to listen to but Plotinus. And he may be said to bring the series to an end.

His disciple Porphyry and the latter's disciple Iamblichus chose to travel quite a different path. Porphyry wrote an account of Plotinus emphasizing Plotinus' wondrous powers and deeds; Iamblichus, a biography of Pythagoras and that sage's ability to predict the future and deflect plagues, storms, and earthquakes (§92, 135), to be in two places at the same time, to see things beyond ordinary mortal sight (§136, 142). Both men were as seriously given to thinking about the divine as Plotinus had been. As an even more stupendous guide and inspiration, however, Porphyry had in his hands and preferred the questions to, and responses directly from, the divine in person, as those responses had been solicited from an oracle in the earlier half of the century and compiled into a theology.[15] It was warranted by the ultimate authority, Apollo himself. No need to figure things out for one's self, no need for philosophy as Plutarch had used the word. With the works and teaching of Porphyry and Iamblichus, the century closes in resort to magic and mediumistic trances for illumination, the invocation of spirits, and knowledge through direct, divine revelation.

Of the same habits of mind, hear Diocletian describing Manichaeism as "certain most delusive and wicked teachings of superstition" which depart from "everything the immortal gods of their grace have deigned to impart," abandoning "what was determined and laid down by the Ancients once and for all." It is "a new-fangled, unheard-of sect at odds with the more ancient faiths divinely granted to us."[16] There could be no disagreeing or, one may say, there could be no reasoning with beliefs thus declared divine in their very origin. Contrast is clear between the three and the one: between Pliny, Plutarch, and Plotinus on the one hand and Diocletian on the other—even while he is claiming his superiority to superstition!

The significance of this comparison needs to be brought out, first, by asserting the typicality of Diocletian (A.D. 284–305). As with the three writers, if there were not others of the same mind, there could be no profit in considering him. But of course very many of the emperor's subjects must of necessity be of the same mind because he was what he was, ruler over all, possessed of the loudest voice. In trying to form an accurate impression of whole populations, where evidence is of the sort and quantity in fact surviving from antiquity, one may indeed, and quite fairly, instance single individuals provided they are such as had to be listened to, like an emperor, or undeniably enjoyed great influence in setting styles of thought or behavior through their conversation, orations, or writings, or were, perhaps, not them-

Figure 2 Diocletian and Maximian (above), Maximiam and Maximin (below). Vatican collection, photo from H. P. L'Orange, *Studien zur Geschichte des spätantiken Porträts*, Oslo H. Aschenhoug, 1933; the coins, from the Louise Wodden Collection, Yale University and the American Numismatic Society, New York (ANS-HSA 22143)

selves of a high position but were addressing a large audience whom they must please, or at least not offend; so whatever they said must chime with views held generally. Such witnesses would include public speakers from whatever sort of platform.

Commonsense rules of evidence hardly need to be spelled out in pausing on this one Diocletian. He emerges from his career as a man dangerously decisive, himself disciplined and demanding discipline of others, an activist and doer in novel, ruthless ways and, in his solutions to problems, fond of square corners and fixed drill. In short, an army man. It was from that career that he rose, bringing with him his closest associates, all self-made army men from backward provinces. The camp was of course no place for wide reading and independence of mind. Contemporary historians in somewhat muffled passages in fact declare the regime of Diocletian low-brow.[17] The origin of its upper ranks and presumably its lower lay among the unprivileged, fitting its intellectual character. They came from remote and little urbanized regions; one of the leaders (Galerius) was born of a peasant mother from the backlands.

Under Diocletian's rule the rate of increase in government was hugely accelerated. Increase continued more slowly over the next century or so. Impossible though any exact census of the administration must remain, still, it is safe to say that the roughly three hundred career civil servants in the reign of Caracalla (a. 211–217) had become thirty to thirty-five thousand at any given moment in the later empire, a change attributable in the greater part to Diocletian.[18] Over the same period, the clergy, too, grew enormously. Some indications of this growth have appeared in the first chapter. Enough to say that at the episcopal level the total in 400 was many times what it had been in Plotinus' day, toward 260. Given their numbers, no one would suppose they were all of the class, beliefs, education, and habits of mind that distinguished the three, Pliny, Plutarch, and Plotinus. Certainly not. The cultural resources of the empire would not stretch so far, nor even approach such a level of demand. In proof, when the older elite is heard from, commenting on the new, the report is just what we would expect: while the elegantly lettered have been in lucky moments sought out and rewarded and can accordingly make their careers, the majority of the new aristocracy are small-town curia members or of that general stratum, equipped with some clerk's skills and generally to be looked down on.[19]

The radical expansion of the upper ranks of society produced an equally radical development in the history of thought. So says the argument of this chapter. The flood of new office holders, ecclesiastical and secular, joining the elite, reshaped it in their own image. Diocletian's regime at the very top illustrates this more general process affecting positions of influence. Habits of mind discoverable in the empire's elite of Pliny's day, even of Plotinus', were thus overwhelmed and lost among others quite different, more "popular." The spectrum of belief lost its sceptical and empirical-thinking extreme. What was left were the middle and the more accepting end. These latter together have been described as no longer a two-tier but a one-tier system of beliefs, all the same. It operated in turn to reinforce the tendency of the anti-pagan persecution in "popularizing" the religion of later times.

I should say in passing, however, that "tiers" as a metaphor, though it makes the change in religious thought easy to grasp, also invites misunderstanding: first, because it suggests a clean distinction between two thought-groups, and second, because it too easily becomes entangled in other, less fundamental qualities of thought. My first warning draws attention to the confusion of beliefs actually to be found among the elite, if that group is defined in political or socioeconomical terminology; for some of the elite certainly shared the views of the nonelite; and, if the latter were known in the slightest detail, no doubt we would find the reverse was true, too. I prefer the metaphor of a spectrum because it makes room for such very numerous exceptions.[20] My second warning is needed where there is any danger of forgetting what the spectrum measures: not, for instance, complexity or even bookishness of religious views such as distinguished the church leadership from its congregation or the urban from the rural population, but rather, to repeat, the degree of acceptance of superhuman intervention in life as lived and observed—"moving things around, for instance."[21] Much very good history of thought or "mentalités" can be written in terms of city versus country, rich versus poor, elite versus masses, and, within an ecclesiastical narrative, clergy versus laity. Obviously these categories will impose themselves on discussions of superstition at one point or another. But my own concern is rather with a distinction which transcends these others and does even more to signal diachronic differences, changes across whole eras, B.C. to medieval and even to the Enlightenment—from which we moderns emerge with our sense of the difference between science and religion, reason and superstition. A transcendent distinction, indeed: the question dominant over all others in the history of European thought for a thousand years and more was not "which religion?" but "how much?"

But to return to my much tighter focus on the change that brought an end to the series, Pliny, Plutarch, and Plotinus: proof of any underlying demographic cause, or anything like direct demonstration, can't be hoped for. Those mostly small-city, small-town, and to some extent rural upper and middle classes from whom the augmented aristocracy of the later empire rose in the period after, say, A.D. 250, left almost no record of their thoughts about the divine and the supernatural. There are only disconnected little hints to be noticed almost at random: for example, an apparently growing readiness, certainly not among the educated aristocracy, to respond to millenial prophecies—this, from around the turn of the third century forward; but whether this is relevant or means much is unclear.[22] A generation later, there is the miraculous appearance of a rescuing deity seen by the faithful of a certain city in the air above, so says the historian Herodian; a generation before the turn, we have Apuleius' picture of the well-to-do landowning sort in a small north African town, confronting philosophy which may be magic, or vice versa, and showing themselves utterly benighted, naive, and sunk in superstition—a quite vivid and believable piece of evidence, this. Would that there were a dozen, a hundred similar from a dozen locales spread across at least the later second and the third centuries! But wider views and more trustworthy indices to show how these classes thought, these new recruits to prominence and influence, simply don't exist.

In the absence of what we might hope for, we can at least determine what the new recruits thought of two key ingredients in the making of the minds of Pliny, Plutarch, and Plotinus. The three and their like had been taught by *philosophy* and *books* to restrain their resort to the divine in explaining experience. Can it be shown that these instruments of understanding were less valued by the privileged and prominent in society, less used, as time went on? Was the explanation of experience through the immanence and direct action of superhuman powers therefore left free to prevail?

The attempt at a demonstration can begin with a programmatic statement bearing on both instruments alike, philosophy and books. It is proposed by an anonymous third-century writer: he would have every serious student pursue "that uncomplicated love for philosophy which lies solely in knowing God through continual contemplation and holy piety. For many confuse philosophy by the complexity of their reasoning . . . by combining it with various incomprehensible intellectual disciplines through their over-subtle reasoning." He goes on to insist that there can be only one reason for "our knowing the size of the earth, depth of the sea, force of fire, and the operation and nature of all these things: so as to marvel at, adore, and praise the mind divine."[23]

It needs no emphasizing how utterly opposed the views here are to those of Pliny, Plutarch, and Plotinus. In common usage, the word "philosophy" (with "philosophize" and "philosopher") had in fact been shifting slowly from what would match our modern sense toward a meaning more like "ascetic piety," and the latter was increasingly emphasized so as to displace the former by the turn of the fourth century.[24] It was then, in Diocletian's reign, that Lactantius had before him and admired the passage just quoted, its author a pagan in a tradition of Greek mixed with Egyptian religious thought, while Lactantius was of course Christian. Lactantius' career took him from Africa to Diocletian's capital at the emperor's request, then to the western capital, and eventually (ca. 316/7) to Trier as tutor to the crown prince, son of Constantine. He was thus at various junctures in a position of great influence. Widely read in both languages, "Lactantius is in fact, despite his learning, the most forceful representative of that Latin Christian development that rejects learning.... [He] rages against science." He demands to know "what purpose knowledge serves?—for as to knowledge of natural causes, what blessing will there be for me if I should know where the Nile rises, or whatever else under the heavens the 'scientists' rave about?"[25] The passage from so very influential a teacher of the west was still unanswerable in the mind of that fictional Jesuit of 1925, Mann's Leo Naphta.

To pause here a moment: the evidence for a shift along the spectrum, among the cultural and intellectual elite, away from the views of Pliny and his like and further toward the "popular" end, has thus far been drawn entirely from non-Christian society. Henceforth, Christian sources take over. But there is no difference in their position on the spectrum. None is to be expected. Little pagans and little Christians of more or less the same social stratum went to school together, went to the baths together, and together watched and learned from grown-ups of every religious persuasion dealing with an illness in the family, a bad harvest, or other similar challenges to understanding (on this social mixing, there will be more said in the next chapter). I suppose childhood and early adolescence are the age at which fundamental habits of mind develop. They will determine how much of life is to be thought out afresh by each individual, how much accepted from authority; how much of experience is to be explained by nature and science, how much by divine intervention. Ideas of this order lie too deep in the individual's maturing or are too widely diffused in the society around him to be dictated by sect or theology. Or so I suppose.

In any case, the shift that the evidence indicates can hardly be attributed to conscious teaching, for which no empire-wide machinery existed. To assign it to empire-wide political or economic change(s) is equally impossible. None can be suggested that will fit. The breakdown of high political order in the mid-third century does not correspond to the shift as this is to be measured across time, nor is there any attested connection between the shift and the life-experience of particular individuals who seem to reflect a new age. Stability and prosperity in the fourth century such as north Africa enjoyed, and most of the eastern provinces still more plainly, cannot be shown to have reversed the shift, later, sending everyone back to their books and philosophy and "science."[26]

I am therefore inclined to look, not to new ideas somehow getting into people's heads, but rather to new people with their old ideas getting into positions from which they could be more heard—in short, a demographic explanation of cultural change. I suggested this long ago, in Italian (and I recall Rostovtzeff's comment on his less-quoted papers, "Rossica sunt, non leguntur"). By chance, an Italian-speaker, Arnaldo Momigliano, offered the same suggestion at exactly the same time, but in English. He too reached back to the beginning of the era among writers of Livy's generation to define the norm up to the end of the third century: he too detected the collapsing of the spectrum into a single "popular" religion or superstition—the two, identical—and he too explained the change by the movement of outsiders, as they had been, into novel situations of power, rather than by any external historical factor.[27] Such are the arguments, however incomplete they certainly must be, in explanation of what can be observed.

To pick up the story now using the evidence of Christian writers, we have that Latin Christian tradition referred to a page earlier, which begins with the often-quoted challenge by Tertullian, "What has Jerusalem to do with Athens?" He poses the question in the midst of his thorough excoriation of all philosophy, with its endless aimless clever perplexities and sectarian controversies, taught to man by "that wretched Aristotle." "For ourselves there is no need of any wish to learn, except of Jesus Christ." What God wanted us to know is just there and in scripture, nowhere else; the itch to know more is of the Devil and the fallen angels; and even to search elsewhere is to violate God's wish and plan.[28]

From Tertullian, the tradition in the west is taken up by Arnobius, dismissing all non-Christian religious thought as so much argy-bargy and quarrelsome obfuscation;[29] then by Lactantius, as we have seen; and next by Constantine, a new recruit but well taught by Lactantius or Ossius, dismissing Pythagoras, Socrates, and Plato as sorry quibblers and impostors.[30] The series rises through Ambrose and minor writers like Chromatius of Aquileia, Victricius of Rouen, and Philastrius of Brescia, the last-named declaring:

There is a certain heresy regarding earthquakes, that they come not from God's command and indignation but, it is thought, from the very nature of the elements, since it knows not what scripture says [at Ps 103.32]. . . . Paying no attention to God's power, they presume to attribute the motions of force to the elements of nature, . . . like certain foolish philosophers who, ascribing this to nature, know not the power of God.[31]

These views have Augustine as their most authoritative proponent. For him, inquiry of any sort that we would call science is a target for ridicule. The Greeks, silly men, lavished their time and effort on the identifying of the elements in nature, etc., etc.; but "to the infinite number of points regarding such matters as they have discovered, or think they have discovered, a Christian will pay no mind." No need to know how nature works, for such pretended knowledge is irrelevant to blessedness. Rather, in Augustine's mind and day, "the Christian, the educated pagan, and the illiterate peasant all shared basic assumptions about the world they lived in . . . the workings of the whole cosmos were commonly seen as effected by animate beings," immanent and continually at work, and "not determined by impersonal laws or mechanistic forces. Thus whereas Cicero had been able to maintain that events came about either because they were willed, or because of fate, or chance, or through natural causes, Augustine will go back a stage further and argue that all events (ultimately) depend upon the will of God."[32] Why bother with books and philosophy?

In the more sophisticated Greek-speaking world, a generation after Tertullian's outbreak on Athens and Jerusalem, a man like Origen still stands apart from the uneducated masses, still notices from a distance how ready they are to condemn subtlety of argument as wordiness.[33] They mixed scorn with fear, too, in the presence of book-learning, confounding it with magic. So a certain Eusebius was to discover in the 340s: a student of philosophy at Alexandria under Constantine, made bishop of Edessa, and run out of town by his enemies under the accusation of dark knowledge, astrology or whatever; and similarly others too-learned after him in other cities and situations.[34] To a different Eusebius of the same period, this one the familiar church historian, "Investigation of natural phenomena is superfluous and beyond the human mind, and the learning and study of these matters are impious and false." A successor in ecclesiastical history, Philostorgius, agrees.[35] In the interval between them a variety of high churchmen declare truths of the same sort already heard from Latin writers. I instance only Basil and John Chrysostom, beginning with Basil. He is consistently contemptuous of pagan thinkers of the past because of their disagreements with each other, in contrast to the single infallible authority of scripture. He advises his listeners to "put a limit to your thought, so that your inordinate curiosity in investigating the incomprehensible may not incur reproach. . . . Let us Christians prefer the simplicity of our faith, which is the stronger, to the demonstrations of human reason. . . . [For] to spend much time on research about the essence of things would not serve the edification of the church." Chrysostom, just like earlier bishops, vaunts the wisdom of the believing unlearned over the unbelieving learned; ridicules and rejects Plato and the other great names of the philosophic pantheon, just as Constantine had done; dismisses their teachings as mere cobwebs; and in the end approves only "rustics and ordinary folk."[36] His is the cast of mind prevailing in the Byzantine world to come.

Where he lodges his trust is in the population that gave rise to the great exemplars of religious life in the fourth century and afterwards, made heroic in the person and biography of Saint Anthony. Of this type, the character was sketched earlier (p. 16f.). It has been pronounced by Father Festugière, no doubt our century's best authority on early eastern monasticism, as "anti-intellectual in tradition," suspicious of any refinement of argument or any elegance of expression, not only not seeking human knowledge but glorying in its rejection, and for the most part illiterate, even lacking spoken Greek.[37] A favorite moment in the life of such paragons, treasured by their biographers, provides an opportunity to confront the enemy, the learned believer (or occasionally pagan) who propounds subtle questions and is rebuked, discomfited, made to look utterly foolish by the extreme simplicity of the ascetic's answers.[38] The apparent loss of reason, and certain individuals among the monks called holy fools, are held up for admiration in that tradition.[39]

With this, we are fairly into the intended period of these pages, post-Constantine. There does now exist an empire-wide instrument of education: the church. What bishops, even emperors, made plain in the honor they rendered to Saint Anthony or Saint Symeon, what could be heard in broader terms from every pulpit, was an agreed upon teaching. Every witness, every listener should know the great danger to his soul in Plato's books, in Aristotle's, in any of the philosophical corpus handed down from the past. The same danger threatened anyone using his mind according to their manner, with analytical intent, ranging widely for the materials of understanding, and independent of divinely imparted teachings. In particular, the physical universe and its operations were to be seen only as a lesson in themselves, making manifest the greater glory of the creator, all parts of which must respond to divine direction. In any corner or instant of the universe, that direction might show itself. The over-all message in every respect accorded with, or we may more truly say, the message *was*, the "popular" or "of the people" at large. In contrast, the other end of the spectrum of beliefs once represented by Pliny, Plutarch, Plotinus, and their like, determining just where to draw the line between the natural and the divine, had simply disappeared.

Perhaps the disappearance should not after all be called simple. In fact the phenomenon was a complicated one. Beyond the effect of general education from the pulpit, just outlined, a second factor must be recalled from previous chapters: institutions of higher education had been largely destroyed. The emperors' attacks had centered on the chief of them, Athens and Alexandria, in the late fourth century and were turned against them again toward the end of the fifth and in 529. By the later fourth century, a lover of learning could say of Alexandria that "the various disciplines are not silent in that city *even now*," anticipating the lament of another admirer of Alexandrian wisdom in the 480s: being asked, How fares philosophy? he answered, In past times conditions were good, "but philosophy and culture are now at a point of a most horrible desolation." His interlocutor planned then to seek for something better in Athens.[40] As to the initiators of the persecution, the emperors themselves, a steady decline in their level of cultivation has been noticed.[41] Thus books and philosophy were bound to fade from sight.

A third factor—this, too, dealt with above, but I repeat it as a part of my summary—was the rise of some tens of thousands of persons in each generation, for a half century and more, to ranks of greatly enhanced influence. So a certain cast of mind, certain reflexes of understanding characteristic of a class, were ennobled; explanations of things that would once have been smiled down were now taken seriously; and this can be occasionally seen in non-Christian circles even post-Constantine exemplified in figures of the highest culture. There was, as Momigliano saw, no distinction in the later empire between "popular" and elite in viewpoint, no marking off of the incredibly supernatural from the naturally credible.[42]

Finally, a fourth factor which arose specifically out of the ongoing conversion of the empire, namely, the doctrine of demonic causation. Far beneath Zeus or Sarapis or any other universal deity, at a correspondingly great remove from their great powers, had always lain those everyday concerns which ordinary people must every day ponder and in some way explain, in order to address them. In such a situation, the likes of Pliny would have turned to books and reasoning. Well, countryfolk had other explanations. That much we learn from chance mentions in poetry or fiction. A diseased flock, infertile wife, deranged daughter, unresponsive lover, or a long run of bad luck might, any or all, be due to superhuman agencies; but explanation of such ills might turn, not to Zeus or Sarapis or Mercury, bringers only of blessings, but to the level of "magic" and "superstition." Here were hexing, haunting, and inexplicable mischief in general. All such was recognized, yes, but most often recognized in the ancient sources (who, after all, are not countryfolk) only to be dismissed. To be made respectable, the operation of maleficent forces on any large scale must await Christianity; and it was of course Christianity which was to form the medieval and Byzantine world.

The church not only through its sermons and writings but at the very doorway, through the words of baptismal rites, taught the infinite number, ubiquity, and immanence of certain superhuman beings under a great monarch, Satan. The radical dualism of its doctrines, as they were insisted on and came gradually to be accepted, allowed or rather invited a supernatural explanation for all suffering not inflicted by God himself: Satanic agents were to be seen as the cause not only of wars and rebellions, persecution and heresy, storms at sea and earthquakes on land, but of a host of minor or major personal afflictions. So, in consequence, Christians were forever crossing themselves, whatever new action they set about, and painted crosses on their foreheads, too, from Tertullian's day forward, responding to their leaders' urging them to do so. It would protect them against all evil, so said Lactantius.[43]

These teachings proposed in the second and third centuries were fully established throughout the empire by the fourth and carried on thereafter. Explanatory reflexes always natural to the great rural majority of the population, so far as it can be known, were thus blessed by the bishops, most evidently in just those areas of individual concern that had been most often brought to the gods of old: that is, health, whether mental or physical. Nothing had been more advertised and talked about in and around the edges of early Christianity than the exorcism of demons from the possessed; the same advertisement now continued unopposed. The rituals of initiation themselves dramatized possession and the exorcistic cleansing of anyone who joined the church; and (as was sometimes denied, more often taught from the pulpit) demons could be invoked, too, through spells, and people could use them for wicked purposes. In late antiquity, aggressive hexing is better attested in the eastern provinces; in the western, wizardry and demonic invocation. Whatever the regional differences, the proponents of these various but fundamentally integrated views sometimes made express their hostility toward alternative, empirical explanations, thus reinforcing what the church had to say against books and philosophy in other contexts.[44]

If, next, we want to illustrate the changes in religious views that I have been describing, texts are easy to find among a great abundance of biographies, encomia, and other genres of relevant literature. Most familiar is the contrast in treatment accorded by Lucian to Proteus Peregrinus, seen as holy (though not by Lucian), and that accorded to someone like Antony by Athanasius (along with all the world of that day). Athanasius credits the saint with control over savage beasts through his sheer sanctity, something Eusebius had personally witnessed in other saintly beings of more or less the same period; and he recounts exhibitions by Antony of far-sight, predictions about the future, exorcism, and the like. Other writers describe how Antony passed on his gifts to a long line of similar ascetic miracle workers.[45]

A particularly rich genre of literature developed among these latter and their disciples throughout the east, celebrating the sanctity of monks and, in the course of so doing, celebrating also the demonstrations of their supernatural powers. In illustration, exorcism scenes, in one of which a woman possessed by demons is led into a church to seek a cleansing through a certain Saint Theodore; and they so terribly control her that she is seen to rise above the ground and whirl about in the air. While the community in which this and similar accounts originated is one of simple folk, nevertheless hagiography was addressed to and read by an audience of every level of society and culture, and had an acceptance made manifest in writings of ecclesiastical historians and others of the cultural elite.[46]

The church historian Socrates (high among the educated—like Augustine and Sozomenus trained as a lawyer) offers as real events awe-inspiring apparitions over battlefields to settle the outcome, as Paulinus of Nola and Eusebius had done, earlier, and John of Ephesus was to do, later.[47] Still another church historian, Theodoret (bishop of Cyrrhus 427–449), writes of the saving of Nisibis from Persian armies by the prayers of its bishop from the battlements, bringing down a plague of gnats upon the enemy; and he mentions with less detail the dragon reduced to dust by the signing of the cross in its face by a holy man.[48] Dragon-encounters by church officials and holy men are often recorded in the eastern regions as well as in the west.

The salvation of Nisibis brings out the importance of these same ranks as patrons, often under that name, over cities and smaller centers served by their supernatural powers. They could, for example, prevent the onset of epidemic—so says the church historian and bishop, Evagrius (536–ca. 600); they could fly through the air, so say Socrates and others. Theodoret, again, honors them with the patron-titles traditional for many centuries.[49] Bishops for their individual fellow citizens could produce cures beyond explanation in terms of natural science: thus, by Uranius bishop of the Iberi, Eutychius of Amaseia, and so forth.[50] They presided, too, from the fourth century on, over those high points of the ecclesiastical year with its saints' festivals, when the beneficent wonders of martyrs, ascetics, and bishops were recalled in encomia. Many survive.[51] Their authors elevate, elaborate, they personally vouch for what they extol; no one could withstand their eloquence. And, in addressing the illiterate gathered out of the countryside, they use healing shrines as so many classrooms for populations ordinarily beyond the reach of the educated.

One eulogy by a deacon gives the details of a cure effected on a blind man by the holy waters and oil from an Archangel Michael shrine, at Germia in Phrygia, in gratitude for which, near his own home, the grateful petitioner erected a memorial church with other buildings and an endowment drawn from various of his estates.[52] It served as an advertisement for his grateful convictions. It was not only such high folk in their provinces but, notoriously, the very emperors of the whole world who paid homage to the miraculous favors bestowed by the holy—so, Theodosius II and the women of his family, with maximum publicity—or who applied to them humbly for a share of their benefactions, as Valens did, asking Saint Basil to heal his son. Theodoret describes the moment. There was Justinian himself to hear of the incredible

survival of a boy convert even in the glass-furnace of his wicked Jewish father—to hear, to believe the account, and to seal his belief with the crucifixion of the father. A lady in purple in the very midst of the flames had
brought the boy water and cooled and preserved him.[53]

In all this material it is not, of course, the miracles themselves which hold
so much interest for the modern observer, remarkable as they certainly are.
Rather, it is the high distinction of many of the narrators and witnesses that
helps to define the mentality of the times. They are of the type or class that
should have produced a Pliny, a Plutarch, a Plotinus; yet what they took for
granted was utterly different, utterly of their times. The change is by no
means difficult to document—quite the reverse. In their day, by far the most
abundant forms of literary production expressed and celebrated a new acceptance of the wonderful, and did so broadcast across the regions John of Ephesus traveled so widely or, again, in Mesopotamia, too, and Syria and Egypt.

From this end of the Mediterranean, passing around its southern corner,
my survey of thought comes next to north Africa. Here, post-400, the catalog
of Saint Stephen's relics was drawn up on an Augustinian model, retailing
how the *patronus* of Uzala, as he is called, wrought remarkable wonders for
those who came to him, drawn at first by his portrait; and that, which hung
in chapel, had been given by some pious person or an angel ("for this is nothing unheard of or beyond experience") to the subdeacon for display. The account is a useful one in the history of thought. But Augustine himself is the
obvious figure to focus on, to determine the place of the wonderful in his
most mature thinking. The last book within his major opus is the best place
to look. Here he recalls the excitement at Milan, when he was last there, over
a miraculous restoration of sight brought about by Saints Protasius and Gervasius. The prior miracle by which Ambrose had recently discovered their remains was on everyone's lips; this other, of healing, was witnessed by huge
crowds. From the recollection, Augustine turns to the cure of a man's anal fistula at Carthage in circumstances which physicians in terms of their science
could not account for; but the bishop Aurelius' prayers, with Augustine's
added, provided explanation enough. Then, some further cures (one, prescribed through a dream) by the application of baptismal water, or by the
touch of earth from Jerusalem, which a local landowner had brought back
with him to keep in his bedroom for protection against illness; but then with
Augustine's advice he placed it in a special shrine for general use.[54]

Fuller description is given to the entry of a water demon into a local youth who is rendered insensible by the invasion and is carried to a shrine which contains certain relics of Protasius and Gervasius. There the demon, driven out of his victim by the hymns of the lady who owns the land, seizes the altar "with a terrifying roar, unable to move, as if chained or nailed there, and confesses with a great howl" (like the demon that Ambrose on another occasion exorcized before the eyes of his whole congregation) "just where, when, and how he had entered the youth." As he leaves, he pulls out one eye of the youth, but, replaced, it is as good as ever. To all this, the witnesses were the lady, her slave women, various nuns, and the sister and brother-in-law of the youth. Thus there could be no doubt about it all.[55] Augustine's catalog then moves on to a number of cases of dead persons raised to life by appeal to Saint Stephen in his shrines of Hippo and nearby Calama, over the course of only a couple of years, and concludes with a most particular and dramatic long report of cures wrought by Saint Stephen's altar in his own basilica, seen by Augustine's own flock and instantly reported to him. He had written it up and read it aloud to the church the next day with the healed person present as proof before the congregation—whereupon, on the instant, yet another healing was accomplished. The scene is important to imagine, as illustrative of the educational role and the effectiveness of the ecclesiastical elite. Many other illustrations might easily be recalled.

In medieval France, as we must call it post-400, what the elite thought about the operations of the divine can be read first in Sulpicius Severus, whose hero Martin could raise the dead to life, among his other supernatural acts and powers; Bishop Germanus (d. 448) doing the same; and there is the priest of Caesarius of Arles telling how that bishop's staff, planted on a hilltop overlooking a farmer's fields, protected them from bad weather and guaranteed their rich crops; also Nicetus of Trier impressing a Lombard monarch with scenes from around the shrines of various saints in France, dramatic with healings, where "the afflicted (those having demons) are suspended and whirled around in the air and confess the [power of the] Lords [i.e., the saints] that I have named to you."[56] Just as in other regions, the ecclesiastical leadership inculcated its habits of mind through reports of wonders wrought by the heroes of the church: Victricius of Rouen in his sermons, or renowned orators at bishops' invitation attending saints festivals, such as Faustus of Riez.[57]

No encomiast of wonders is more familiar than Gregory of Tours (ca. 538–593). His Saint Stephen from the tomb flies to the rescue of distressed mariners and, returning dripping wet, wets the floor of the shrine.[58] Everyone could see the fact, in support of the subsequent testimony of one of the men he saved. Gregory's Saint Caluppa, ascetic in a cave, is visited by dragons which, when he makes the sign of the cross at them, decamp; and the account is confirmed by the detail that as they left they farted monstrously. So Gregory had heard from the old man himself.[59] The bishop is a personal guarantor of wonderful cures granted to himself or to members of his family; he personally with holy relics could dispel storms.[60] In addition to his hagiographical writings he advertises the rewards of saints' festivals and makes the most of them.[61] He sees portents in small matters where Pliny and those like him would have seen nothing at all: as for instance in the fact that the wicked Arius died in a public latrine, at stool. Divine judgment could abase the wretch no lower; and in his fate, any quantity of eastern bishops likewise had read meaning.[62] The thought-world that Livy once recalled as long past had reappeared.

In Italy, the land of Livy's birth, various literary figures in the later empire write about and evidently credit such wonders as the apotropaic powers of the sign of the cross, protecting flocks and herds; dramatic exits of demons from the possessed; and the riveting of a sinner in his place, unable to move, paralyzed, until carried to the tomb of the saint he had dishonored where he confesses and is freed.[63] The writer is Paulinus of Nola. Another Paulinus, biographer of Ambrose, describes the bishop's relics able to drive out spirits from those who were brought to him in his church; and "there the throngs of demons shouted aloud how they were tormented by him, so that you couldn't stand their howls."[64] Like other writers, Ambrose himself bestowed the term "patron" on the saints of Milan Protasius and Gervasius, as Paulinus of Nola did on Felix, seeing in them a force to shape the history of their homes.[65]

And another Gregory, the Great, credits the bishop of Todi with exorcisms, restoration of sight to the blind, even restoration of life to the dead; credits Benedict with many wonders, too, and the bishop of Placentia likewise, able to control the flooding of the Po by dropping a letter of command into its waters.[66] A voluminous writer, Gregory was nevertheless an enemy to much education, of which he often expressed his distrust: "The wise should be advised to cease from their knowledge," to be "wise in ignorance, wisely untaught." He concludes, on the subject of a natural phenomenon like eclipses, "So it has pleased the idle endeavors of philosophers to assign these to true but merely proximate causes, since they were quite unable to see the cause above all others, God's will."[67]

Last in the circuit of the empire is Eugippius, priest and later abbot (ca. 465–535). He describes Severinus' mission to Noricum some generations earlier in which a chief instrument were the bishop's demonstrations of divine power, to resuscitate the dead and banish blight from the wheat fields; even, by marking boundary posts with the cross, to ward off floods.[68]

With Severinus we reach the edge of a darkness in which a part of the empire is swallowed up for good. No further word is heard of it; and how its population, high or low, took in and made sense of life around them cannot be surmised. The same darkness closes in on north Africa, Spain, Italy south of Rome, and so forth. My purposes require, however, not political but only religious or intellectual history. There is no need for more than the survey just supplied (tediously, it may seem, and too well known), so long as it is clear that no further great shift in habits of mind took place after A.D. 400. What was already apparent before, in the comparison of Pliny and his like with Pophyry or Lactantius remains detectible thereafter wherever the sources allow any appraisal at all, for many hundreds of years. The Middle Ages supervene, so-called because they lie between what people of the Enlightenment felt to be their own illuminated times, and the illuminated times of antiquity.

❖ ❖ ❖

The grand change from classical antiquity to the Middle Ages, so far as it registered in people's fundamental ideas about causation, is entirely familiar. Everyone knows that the world after the Decline differed from antiquity, everyone has some sense of what "medieval" means when "science" is mentioned and how the explanations offered by the one differ from those offered by the other. The sense, too, that the eastern as well as the western Mediterranean lands underwent the same change is pretty general, though much less clear. In due course thereafter, that is, in modern times, medieval wonders ceased, or at least the expectation of them, to be replaced by "a more rational idea of existence." In short, Enlightenment. But that would carry the story up to the seventeenth century.[69]

This long-drawn-out succession of states of mind began in a period on which historians are agreed. In the earlier years of the present century Gustave Bardy had only to refer to it in an aside. "Is it not," he asked, "one of the most characteristic traits of the third century—that blind faith and irrational engagement, by the best minds, in diviners of every sort and origin, in wonder-workers and prophets? Historians have yet to explain this invasion of the Mediterranean world by the worst superstition."[70] The reminder amounted to a challenge, and a fair one; but no answer was attempted, so far as I know (though my reading has been perhaps too narrow), until the two little essays of the early seventies, my own and Momigliano's; and then, nothing since. Given the proportions and significance of the phenomenon, such lack of scholarly interest seems odd. I think I understand it but, being no specialist in nineteenth- and twentieth-century intellectual history, I don't attempt a serious explanation.

There is, however, a single point to notice: the detection of a loss of "rationalism" as the central event in the story. Many observers have drawn attention to this both before and after Bardy.[71] In their minds as in the minds of those like Lucian or Lactantius who illustrate the event, the word "rationalism" or its opposite can only arise out of a personal belief in some superhuman being(s) or force(s), malignant or benign, weak or strong, immanent in every tiniest event and object of experience, to be addressed by prayer or spell or any other means; or, rather, in some superhuman being(s) or forces only exerting remote control mediated through the familiar laws of the physical world; or, as a third possibility, existing (if at all) beyond any human address whatsoever. From one or another of these alternatives the use of the terms "rational" or "irrational" may follow, in describing another person's religious beliefs and acts. That it follows is logical; it can be discussed and explained. But only if it is made explicit. Otherwise at least one of the terms must seem dismissive or contemptuous, a cause of trouble.

I illustrate the usage in the notes above, one of these focused on Lucian.[72] He was that irritating publicist who went out of his way to expose religious idiocy, as he perceived it. Galen described the lovable tendency in his friend; the man himself boasted of it. At one point it nearly provoked a beating from those whose faith he challenged. He would have deserved what he got. People do not like to be told their faith is utter nonsense. Witness in a very different age the reactions to Gibbon's famous twenty-eighth chapter, shot through as it was with contempt for "ignorant rustics," the "vulgar," "the prostrate crowd," and the transfer to the church of "the superstition of paganism."[73] How must believers feel, reading this?

Per contra, it was also provoking to the highly educated to have *their* faith confronted with unanswerable revelations vouchsafed to persons they considered their social or cultural inferiors, mere "silly women," "peasants," and so forth. Such misguided folk knew nothing of the proofs of the impassivity of the divine, nothing of the benignity of Plato's God, nothing of his infinity. They feared the consequences of inadequate worship: *feared* God, sheer superstition! as any educated Greek-speaker would tell you, using the Greek word for superstition: *deisidaemonia* (fear of the gods). As to divine impassivity, once the conviction was settled, then throwing pennies in a stream, burning incense, or lighting candles in the daytime must seem an absurdity; and no one could suppose the infinity of Athena or Zeus could be contained within a stone idol. What then of ceremonies of adoration, tales of Hecate smiling? Superstition again! The dictum of De Maistre, that "it is certainly not believers who ever get annoyed about the manifestations of an over-simple faith," is just as certainly not true.[74]

The contempt shown by Lucian and his like for their inferiors was not, it should be emphasized, a thing unheard of in later times—times when the views they had once scorned now generally prevailed. It is in fact easy to find the masses looked down on or at least seen as very different from the educated among the upper crust of the church in Basil's day, or Augustine's, or at any point thereafter. Illustrative passages have been cited at various points already, and discussion in modern sources appears just below (note 80). Certainly there was a gulf separating many a bishop from many or most of his congregation, and they held correspondingly different views about any number of questions. Even in hagiography some range may be sensed along a line of straightforward, literal acceptance, or more theologically complex acceptance, of miracles and such.[75] But bishops and congregation nevertheless did not disagree about the central question of concern in this chapter: how much of what one saw in the world was to be explained as the action and immanence of the divine.

Take the learned Agobard of Lyons, bishop until his death in 840: he writes a treatise titled, though perhaps not by the author, "Against the stupid opinions of the masses," in which he begins, "In these parts nearly everyone, noble or lowly, citified or rustic, old or young, thinks that hailstorms and thunder are within the control of man"; and from here he goes on to describe a universal belief in practitioners called *tempestarii* or weather-men who can be called in to control the source of these phenomena, which most folk say come from a sky-land called Magonia and are borne along on celestial ships. Now this, says Agobard, is madness, a great stupidity; and the most profound stupidity of all which he recently witnessed was the exhibiting of four people tied up and held in the public prison who, it was advertised, had accidentally tumbled out of the ships! Some similar silly explanation of a pest among the cattle was recently passed around and "credited by everybody, who were not thinking rationally." Instead, he says, over a good many pages of argument and with very extensive quotations, we have scripture to tell us the truth: that weather and things like hail and wind and rain are God's to direct, and by his power alone are they controlled; so that it is not only error but a heresy and a sin to credit *tempestarii* with any special efficacy. The contrast, however, between the learned Agobard with his citations of authority, and the ignorant around him, is one thing; between himself and Pliny or Plutarch, quite another. Pliny and Plutarch sought to explain natural phenomena in natural terms, arising out of the movement of air and so forth. It is this latter contrast on which I focus.[76]

In modern times, tension in debate over what one person may have called faith and another "'irrationality' (and attracted condemnation from non-believers and empiricist historians alike)," can still be felt (and I here quote a scholar of the 1990s who champions "irrationality").[77] Moreover, the passage quoted above from De Maistre enters modern debate thanks to a second historian who, even while exercising his craft on a period of late antiquity, would prefer more faith than history in the account. Eusebius had set the style. His preference arose out of assumptions about the universe: in a word, religion. Yet today it may be troublesome to explain. To do so would require openly positioning one's self along the spectrum of belief, risking "condemnation" at the hands of the "empiricists."

They can exert much more pressure nowadays than ever lay within the command of Pliny, Plutarch, or Plotinus. Yet it is not hard to imagine what these latter three would have had to say about medieval beliefs: about Gregory the Great, bears made into sheepdogs, lions into smiling beasts of burden, dragons at the door, people flying through the air or walking on water, salt water made fresh by a mere wish; or the spectacle of the chief citizen of the ancient capital, Leo III, leading an Assumption Day procession of all his clergy and the faithful of the city, up to the entrance of certain ruins near the Santa Lucia church; and there challenging the occupant of the ruins, a great serpent, a basiliscus as the Greeks call it, which had killed everyone who approached with its foul breath and with its mere glance, Leo put the beast to flight by his prayers. He concluded with an oration to the crowd. They cannot be imagined in anything but awe of the scene; yet it strikes a modern observer as very remote from the Rome that Pliny knew. Habits of mind formed in his day from books and philosophy would have dictated the use of scornful terms for the performance, back then; still more, today. In consequence, historians' trouble with terminology: "superstition" or "folklore" or "the masses" as opposed to "the educated," where quotation marks are added as if to disarm the words.[78]

Terminology would be a lot less troublesome if the religious phenomena being discussed were clearly pagan or clearly Christian in origin. But (to revert to the opening of this chapter) lineage is often indeterminable. Part of the problem lies, naturally, in the darkness of the Dark Ages and the paucity of evidence through which to trace a thing to its origins along a known trail of occurrences, all the way back from Carolingian times, let us say, to Pliny—which would make it demonstrably pagan, and "superstition." It somehow persisted through "survival."[79] More often it appears first among "the masses," and who can say where their ideas came from? Hence a great deal of debate expended on the nature and definition of "popular religion" and its relation to the church. The phrase in quotation marks recurs continually in discussions of religion post-400, to be distinguished from what may be found among "the educated" or "elite."[80] I have indicated at various junctures, above, my own hopes of staying within those areas where the texture of the evidence is fairly close, where origins and nature can be shown through an adequate pedigree, and one need not rappel across great gulfs of ignorance on gossamer threads of conjecture.

Finally, a difficulty growing out of the question, whether non-Christian beliefs and practices, whether they be called folkloric or pagan, should be counted as religious at all. The denial is perhaps inadvertent. Let us hope so.

So far as concerns ritual acts rather than beliefs, which observers thinking only of Christianity will not recognize in their own modern churches, the problem is easily solved by a little anthropologizing. "Let us," suggests J.-C. Schmitt, "take the example of dancing, which was no empty waving about of one's hands but a social practice, that is, the conduct of religion: for who could believe that people for so long danced in cemeteries and churches because towns and villages could provide no other places big enough for free dancing? 'Popular religion' was therefore dancing."[81]

With this last point so well made, my chapter returns to its commencement in the primitive and popular; but Schmitt's words lead naturally into the next chapter, too, in which answers to all these questions must be given, or at least implied, in the course of describing the "non-Christian" within "Christianity."

◆ 4 ◆

Assimilation

Ritual dance as a custom of north African Christians was familar to Augustine post-400 as before; and how could it not be, since in the opening year of the fifth century it was to be seen both at martyr tombs and "throughout city precincts and squares." It spared neither the close vicinity of the churches nor the saints' days themselves, as the bishops in their council described the sight. Most of them objected to it, especially for the sake of women coming to worship, who might be the target of sexy remarks.[1] It was a case of the bishops against the vulgar, the latter offering the equivalent of a prayer in the language of gestures, just as their prayers in their native Libyphoenician were unintelligible to their betters; but dancing was also a practice the bishops recognized for what it was, or what it had been in unreformed days for their congregation: a rite performed in the sanctuary before the temple in traditional pagan fashion.

A generation earlier, an eastern bishop addressing his flock on the feast day of a martyr asked them, "What offering shall we bring to the martyr in repayment, what gift in thanks? . . . Let us, please, dance to him in our usual way." And Chrysostom, listening to the celebrations in Antioch from his sickbed, described the rural population drawn in to the martyr days reserved for them, "a people remote from us in their tongue [Syriac, like Libyphoenician in Africa] but not in their faith," "who have danced throughout the whole city."[2]

That was all right for them; it drew no rebuke; but when Chrysostom turned to his ordinary urban audience, he would have none of such behavior: his sermons harshly reproached moving and stamping of feet and waving of hands in the nave, exactly (he says) as in the shows at the theater. Perhaps so, but he might more truly have said, exactly like the worship offered in the temples. Indeed on other occasions he did draw a distinction between what would be customary among the heathen as such, and what should be, among Christians.[3]

In Cappadocia, Gregory describes those who attended church festivals as dancers as well as feasters, and in the 370s he appealed to Basil for help in dealing with a deacon in his bishopric, Glycerius, who was adding holy dances to the services and festivals. Glycerius headed a group of young men and women who looked to him rather than to the *chorepiscopus* for direction, and was not easily corrected, since, it has been suggested, all he and they were doing was native to their oldest local traditions. Basil himself complained about Easter dancing in the congregation he spoke to directly; the Council of Laodicea complained about dancing at weddings; Ephraem, about wreathed dance groups in Edessa; there was general disapprobation of hand clapping with the rhythm; but in Isauria, there was approved dancing at the Saint Thecla festivals; a similar report from Evagrius with apparent approval as he watched the crowds of pilgrims gathered around the shrine of Saint Symeon near Antioch in the later fifth century; the same again from Choricius of Gaza toward the mid-sixth century, in connection with the festivals of Saints Sergius and Stephen.[4] Still later mentions of dance within the practice of religion can be deferred for a page or two.

For the so-called Messalians in Syria and Meletians in Egypt, dance was a daily practice in the church, though the two groups were at odds with the majority of their fellow Christians on other grounds.[5]

From all of which, it seems evident that over some generations before 400, as over some centuries afterwards as well—and especially among the people we hear least about but who, off in the country, constituted the vast majority of the population—dancing and eastern Christianity went hand in hand quite commonly; and this was so, whether or not bishops from their urban pulpits openly confronted what they generally didn't approve of. The church, while its leadership maintained the effort to exterminate paganism, had in fact adopted this form of offering cult, with local variations: hand clapping, instruments, and so forth.

In the western provinces toward the turn of the fifth century, the bishop of a French city is heard preaching over relics on the occasion of a nighttime "Joyful," a *laetitia* as such festivals were often called, in which groups of monks were present whom he singles out for mention, along with a boys' chorus and a young women's chorus, too, to carry the cross—the latter urged to "Sing out, holy untouched virgins! Sing out! and in your chorus strike with your feet the path which leads to heaven!"[6] To give a salvation-directed character to a practice which was a reflex of traditional worship was the object of these flowery words, in an oration of the very best style; so also Ambrose's object as he tried to reform the impulses of his congregation: let the limit be set at "spiritual dance," where evidently he saw too much of the other kind.[7] His not perfectly obvious idea needed to be explained to the young; or perhaps he had been challenged to say what was wrong from a scriptural standpoint in the dancing practices of David or of Jesus himself; so he resorted to allegory.[8]

When the bishops saw women's unrestrained movements, unrestrained smiles and hair and even ankles, they saw also the near approach of fornication; and the train of their thought directed the characterization of dance as of other social customs they disapproved of.[9] They themselves had better company-manners than plowboys, too, and saw men's dancing, no doubt rightly, at times, as mere "jumping." In New Year's celebrations, this would be on display; in martyr shrines likewise during vigils, about which, more on a later page. But in addition, of course the bishops knew what they saw was religious, and of an alien and therefore hostile character: satanic, "un-Christian," and to be corrected by Caesarius' sermons or ecclesiastical council decrees of the fifth, sixth, and seventh centuries.[10]

They had indifferent success; witness the reports of dancing by the laity or clergy at festivals in the churches of various corners of Europe up to the present century.[11] On Saint Michael's day the celebration at Barjols in southern France brought or, for all I know, still brings crowds of families to the churches where, at the customary point in the service, the dance began with mothers holding up their infants in the air and bouncing them rhythmically, the older children joining in on their own feet, and next, their parents and every adult, with their song as accompaniment. Derivation of the custom here or at any one locale from classical antiquity is beyond demonstration: the texture of documentation is, to my knowledge, too thin. Why should the impulse that may have introduced it in this or that other place, in prehistoric or ancient times, be lacking among the citizens of Barjols in 1800, then and never before, just as the midnight rides of the Diana enthusiasts perhaps derived from post-Roman times?—in which case, the custom might appear ancient and primitive, but really be relatively recent. Care is needed in causal explanations not to stretch the train of attestations, nor stretch credulity, too much. Nevertheless, taking the population as a whole, and the train that is reasonably secure within that large group and area, clearly in the western as in the eastern provinces the pagan custom of address to the divine through dance was absorbed into the churches and maintained among them to some significant degree far into the medieval period and, it may be, much closer to modern times.

The fact may be denied easily enough through the defining of "religion" as distinct from "culture . . . 'the way of doing things,'" whereas "Christianity" is described as "belief" and the Christian as someone who has "seized upon a doctrine" in terms of which his life is wholly directed and shaped. To the extent that Christianity today remains centered in a book, while it is also the lens through which "religion" may be and most often is defined, the understanding of this term will screen out much that an anthropologist or historian would rather include: it will screen out, it will simply not allow as "religion," dancing and other communal or individual cult acts. Witness, for example, a description of scenes drawn from France, north Africa and Spain of the fourth to seventh centuries: "The crucial question, however, is whether the pagan practices described in these sources" (from Augustine on up to Eligius' biography) "were consciously pagan at all. . . . The inhabitants of the village near Noyon where Eligius risked martyrdom thought their festivities were justified because of the ancientness of the custom; there is no indication that they worshipped pagan gods, and it seems probable that they were Christians who still continued rituals closely bound up with the rural processes."[12]

The author of these words, like others who could be quoted, puts into separate boxes, on the one hand, "practices," "festivities," "custom," or "rituals," and on the other hand "worshiped." The possibility that they all belong in one and the same box doesn't occur. Of course, you may say, it is only a matter of terminology. It can have no effect on the reality of what was said, done, felt or thought in the past, so far as that can be determined. Granted. But it must be granted, too, that the church authorities most carefully insisted on terminology, and their insistence was real, and was expressed in what they said, did, felt, and thought. "God" was theirs alone, no name for Zeus or Jupiter. Their definition of the word "worship," *adorare*, to reserve it to their deity, like their definition of the term "deity" itself—*theos* not *daemonion*—constituted a fact of history, indeed a most potent one; their definitions of "Christian" were equally real and effectual. Struggles over them made events, which must then be seen for what they were and so described, as best we are able.

Yet the definitions insisted on by those engaged in the struggles of the past need not infect the present. We do not ordinarily accept them as our own— for example, by their dictates, avoiding the terms "god" and "worship" to describe the pious Athenians on their Acropolis, or expunging from American or English history, or from the annals of Communism, those actors who once suffered on the losing side, in one or another Revolution. If we did so, or reduced them to the status of "demon deluded," "deviants" and "heretics," or put them in quotation marks as "so-called" This-or-That, we could only distort historical proportion, weight of significance, reality.

Presentist loyalties distort the shape and proportions of the past nowhere more often than in the treatment of religion, and most obviously, our own. The reason surely lies in the overwhelming nearness of the object to be understood; only when seen from a distance does comparison with other religions make clear the peculiarity of Christianity's structure.[13] It was a religion of the book, as it has so often been called, developed around certain sacred texts very gingerly chosen. For centuries it had had no temple; it filled the streets of no city with its crowds and celebrations. Celebration instead was kept simple, not to distract from focus on the Word; and the too-enthusiastic acting out of response to that Word, except in a moral life, was discouraged.

This simplicity of structure was generally well protected. Change was suspect. An apparent exception may serve to test the rule. In the period of my study, one remarkable novelty was admitted: the ascetic life.[14] Though it was lived for the most part by those who could not read the Bible, nevertheless it had at its core their prayers and verses known by heart, indeed the whole Bible known thus by some heroes of the desert. Everything else of their former lives they had stripped away; nothing of the pagan, nothing of the peasant remained to them except, perhaps, the accent of their voice heard from within a cell, chanting psalms. Doctrine had been reduced to the very bone. The novelty they offered therefore could provoke only admiration among the directorate.

In paganism, on the other hand, sacred texts, doctrine, and directorate had no place. Civic leaders of the type of Pliny, Plutarch, or Plotinus who might best have claimed to say what was or what ought to be good religion well understood their public role. It was not to censor or exclude. It was to pay, and to smile on the traditional. Within tradition, what lacked any supporting scripture or even any conscious reason they might think foolish; but they accepted it as harmless. It had been handed down from so long ago. In their own worship—as in their secular moments, for that matter—they themselves did not dance as they did not sing at their work; they did not readily approve drinking to excess on a good night out, or in their temples; they did not communicate in dress-up or gesture. In these and other points of behavior they were of their class, just as popes were, and patriarchs, and bishops. But the structure of their religion (as I persist in calling it) was a very great deal larger and looser than the Christian.

Singing as the accompaniment of address to the gods, whether by individuals or communities, was close to universal within the empire's religious traditions.[15] It included (I can't say how commonly across the whole empire, but widely attested) wild, sad wailing notes at funerals and gayer songs at weddings;[16] sober choruses in temple precincts; also, apparently everywhere, convivial tunes at sacred feasts. Among Christians, singing was at first limited to psalms, as had always been the custom among Jews. After the mid-fourth century, however, more is heard of a different sort of music not only at private parties, where the words that went with the tunes might contain the names of pagan deities, evidently in telling their stories, or where, in a love song, they might offend morals; not only in the obstreperous New Year's and New Month's rituals which Christians freely joined, though forbidden to do so by their bishops; not only in rallies and processions led by their bishops; but in the very churches as well, with flute or cithara accompaniment.[17] The intrusion of music into a sacred setting must obviously be credited to the old cults. Converts brought with them their traditional forms of address to the divine, leaving behind only the words of old hymns, Sophocles' and the rest.

They still favored a beat, a use of the voice, or some other characteristic that bishops thought unacceptably different from Jewish psalmody. Ambrose's initiative, a few years into his episcopacy, to engage his congregation's needs in a new, unmistakably Christian form of music, was promptly noticed and imitated by Augustine and others, with results important for the history of music. But the competition was evidently not driven off the field even within the churches and martyria.

Where it maintained itself longest and loudest was at the all-night celebrations of saints' festivals. Reaction by ecclesiastical authorities was inconsistent. In Cappadocia, Basil complimented his sister's singing at such vigils, and Paulinus in Italy approved, but at Carthage and Hippo, Augustine disapproved. Still toward the end of the sixth and into the seventh century the united bishops of Spain and France anathematized it, evidently because it persisted; and so, in describing it, did Shenute in Egypt.[18] While church and emperor occasionally got their hands on books and burned them when they sensed their evil tendencies, they could not so easily reach the minds of worshipers, among whom the rightness of conduct before the divine was long prescribed by actions observed and handed down, not by scriptures read. Rightness meant joy. Joy was worship. At the Kalends or Attis Day as at Easter, it was an offering of faith to show one's happiness. The point, so far as it was ever made express by those of the older faiths, has been brought out in a previous chapter. The same mood was to prevail in the same way, as a ritual offering, at the tombs of the deceased.

That odd fact draws my discussion into the whole set of customs focused on the tomb, the dead, and the afterlife (so far as anyone believed there was one). Here as throughout this chapter my aim is to describe the flow of practice and belief from the old faith into the new. With that end in view, I sketched various practices in paganism, above, for comparison at this point;[19] and they are indeed evident in Christianity. Christian burials were protected with the usual old invocations of divine punishment upon any person disturbing them; the stone was occasionally inscribed with the usual old formula at the top, "To the gods and the ghosts of the departed," *d(is) m(anibus);* and the disposal of the body by cremation only slowly gave way to inhumation, by a change of custom which took place anyway in the non-Christian population as well, so that its origin is hard to establish and the religious loyalty of the deceased is likewise hard to establish, at least from archeological data. No objection was raised to the tradition of equipping the deceased with favorite or precious objects for the amelioration of eternity; even the coin for Charon sometimes turns up in Christian burials of the west and east alike, bringing the custom up to the last rites of Pius IX in 1878.[20]

It seems safe to surmise that the people in charge of the pope's burial were Christians according to anyone's definition; yet in some corner of their picture of the afterlife could be found beliefs at odds with the picture that would be agreed to by the bishops assembled. Surely such corners exist in everyone's mind. According to the times and the individual, they may be large or small, few or many. They may be consciously valued or not. At what point in time the mixture of pagan-derived burial customs lost any connection in people's minds with piety of the traditional sort, involving a rebelliously different vision of the hereafter from any taught by a bishop, is of course unclear; but at least as late as Charlemagne, in his legislation on the subject, these customs were seen as religious, and therefore from a bishop's point of view wrong. That is, they were still at that date to some degree pagan within Christianity. One may fairly say the same of the bag of coins put into the pope's sarcophagus.

Evidently people loyal to these customs took over from the non-Christian thought-world the certainty that the deceased continued in some form of life and activity within the tomb. Of sanctified martyrs, this is seen to be true in accounts of the early medieval west, noted above; but there are various express statements of the same view descriptive of the humble dead as well. The bishops at Elvira in the early fourth century, for instance, advised the faithful not to light candles at tombs lest they disturb those sleeping beneath; Augustine agreed with everyone else around him, that the dead took pleasure in attentions paid to them.[21] That belief was, at any rate, ubiquitous and obvious in the practice of memorializing after burial.

Early testimonies to the practice are archeological: stone chairs for the deceased in the Roman catacombs and elsewhere in the west, of the third century and later, or sometimes an inscription on a nearby wall making the invitation to the dead explicit: "Join in the refreshment, the *refrigerium*, in a holy spirit."[22] For the living in attendance there were stone tables to eat on, fashioned separately near the grave or out of the top of the burial itself, which projected a little above ground, or in the lid of the sarcophagus in a mausoleum; there were inclined stone couches which, with cushions, served the usually recumbent diners; perhaps an exedra, too. Such arrangements may be seen in third-century Spanish, German, Italian, and north African Christian cemeteries; and in eastern church directives they receive, not condemnation, but a reminder that priests should feel free to join in such cheerful banquets. Foods usual at banquets are indicated in relief, inscriptions, frescoes, or surviving remains; the wine drunk is clear from inscriptions, surviving shards of broken cups, receptacles on the spot for wine or water, and wall paintings in which the diners call out to the slaves who wait on them, "Irene, hand the hot water," and "Agape, mix it for me." Occasional tombs have a tube or pipe running down into the sarcophagus, ending, it may be, at the mouth of the deceased, whereby wine could be shared with the dead.[23]

The identical nature of the Christian and non-Christian cult of the dead appears not only in its physical details themselves, all of those just reviewed being of the third century and so at the earliest end of the chain of information we possess; but they are clear as well in the impossibility, sometimes, of determining which religion is represented by a given piece of evidence: for example, in the line of a third-century epitaph from Mauretania, where the dedicants recall how "We decided we would add on this stone table," *mensa*, to their mother's grave. For various reasons, none of them decisive, this epitaph and burial may be judged Christian or not; but it hardly matters. Sarcophagi with symbols and reliefs made for pagan customers were used by Christians.[24] Since, as has been shown in earlier pages, the faithful of both religions sought out the same cemeteries, there to mourn, though cheerfully and even boisterously to mourn, the recently deceased, and then periodically to return to recall them in the company of their friends of any faith at all, in a social gathering—since these were the facts of their ordinary life, there can be nothing surprising in the ambiguity, call it, of our evidence. Or it may equally be said: for hundreds of years, the pagan cult of the dead was a common part of Christianity.[25]

For, in the fourth and later centuries, the evidence continues in the same character. Finds in cemeteries and other excavations repeat in detail all of that picture of graveside banqueting which is more sparsely available for earlier times: the bones and shells of animals and seafood eaten on the spot, the wine vessels and cups, the lamps needed because banqueting extended past sundown, the facilities for cooling water, the built structures for dining, the term *refrigerium* in inscriptions, all are the same, indicating the same mood and purpose in groups around the graves. The calendar for particular celebration is unchanged: in Africa and Spain at various sites into the fifth century; in Rome in the very Vatican and on the Tiber island into the sixth century; in Naples, Nola, Milan, and Syracuse; in Sardinia in particular abundance up to the seventh century and with a particularly fine scholarly treatment; in Salona in the former Yugoslavia; in France so far as it was governed by the third Council of Arles (452), and there and in Germany much later still; in Syria (sarcophagi pierced for the introduction of liquids, with lamp shards nearby) in the fifth century; in Egypt into the eighth; and, floating loose in eastern contexts, miniature sarcophagi like doll furniture to serve as reliquaries, with little holes in their tops, just like real ones of the fifth to seventh centuries.[26] That the archeological record extends no more widely around the east is surely the consequence only of the patterns of modern on-site investigation. So much appears when literary sources are used to supplement the material data. They take us beyond Augustine's Africa, beyond Zeno's north Italian home, to Gregory's Cappadocia.[27] There, at the memorial feast of a certain beloved priest, his brother priest was able miraculously to supply the favorite dish for just such occasions. Franz Dölger, who noticed this little moment, was able to carry the story up to the nineteenth century in Turkey, where celebrants of memorial rites at the graveside, with the priest joining them, poured wine down into the tomb; Einar Dyggve published a photo of the 1930s in which, in Yugoslavia, a family came together around a tomb spread with a tablecloth, on which women of the family set plates of food, and Martin Nilsson pointed to the rites of Psychosabbaton in the Greek Church today—the custom of holding meals in churchyards.[28] These scenes have been offered as convincing indications of a changeless religious usage. It seems safe to assert not only this much but, further, the virtual universality of the Christian grave cult in the Mediterranean world at the commencement of my period of study and for a period thereafter—in some regions, only over the length of a few generations but, in others, for a very much longer time, even to our own age.

This matrix nourished the cult of the martyrs, to which I turn next. As might be expected, the eastern provinces provide the earliest evidence, through the description of Christians meeting at Polycarp's tomb in a *laetitia*. The date is not far into the second half of the second century. By Constantine's day, joyful illumination, singing, eulogies, feasting and drinking were well established as features of martyrs' day vigils and appear so in mentions by Julian, the Cappadocian Fathers, and various other fourth-century bishops.[29] By then—indeed, from around the mid-third century—similar mentions appear in Rome and north Africa. In the latter area, Cyprian was the focus at Carthage, where Augustine used to preach at the memorial shrine titled the "*Mensa*, the Banquet Table of Cyprian." Then from Dougga a somewhat amateurish inscription of Augustine's day declares, "Holy and most blessed martyrs, we beg you to bear in mind that /// a simposium are offered to you, [signed by several donors] who made these four dining places, *cubicula*, with their own outlay and labor"; and at a second inland city, Timgad in Numidia, excavation presents us with a fifth-century martyr's burial half-sunk at mid-nave of its chapel, the raised part of the tomb being equipped with a hollowed-out cup, a strainer, and a funnel leading down into the tomb to the mouth of the skull beneath.[30] In Rome, the focus of cult was naturally on Paul and Peter, at various times and points in and about the city. The apostles were the object of pilgrimage recorded in hundreds of graffiti, the largest number under the present-day San Sebastiano. Here as elsewhere, the faithful acquitted themselves of vows to provide the martyrs with the refreshment of a banquet in return for their favor. One memorial was pierced to receive the pouring in of wine, while the pair together under San Sebastiano were equipped with a handy dining area and benches.[31] There is nothing to distinguish the physical arrangements for martyr cult from all those that so commonly surrounded the unsanctified dead. The latter setting indeed proves useful to explain the former.

It is convenient to begin a more detailed account around the turn of the fifth century, with the verses of Paulinus, bishop of Nola. It was he who there put Saint Felix on the map, so to speak, by advertising and richly patronizing the martyr's tomb; and since his acquaintance numbered the very most cultivated, the very richest of the western empire, to whom his accounts were well known, as he wished, clearly he is describing nothing that he thought odd or shameful. He is therefore a good witness for the practices of his day. His building program at the shrine included a cleared space (already mentioned, above, at p. 11) enfolding a porticoed court decorated with frescoes showing appropriate religious scenes. For the walls of the chapel in which lay the tomb, he commissioned inscriptions to describe and glorify the martyr; on other walls he dedicated the shavings of his youthful beard, and he notes the testimonials on display, hung up by grateful ex-sufferers.[32] The slab over the tomb itself was pierced, the burial filled with aromatic unguents by the faithful; also with wine, "for they," the worshipers though not Paulinus, "believe, wrongly, that the saints delight in having their tombs bathed in the fragrant wine." They came with candles and torches, bringing votive incense, silver, and rich textiles. On festival days, the banquets of slaughtered animals as offerings which the local rich contributed, like those in temple precincts of yore, drew the poor to share in them; there was singing, of course, and for the *laetitia* everyone stayed up all night.[33] It is a picture of worship even to its slightest points of action and belief recognizable by Pliny or his like, were he only supplied with one necessary clue: that graveside cult and some admixture of temple cult could flow together.

Contemporary with Paulinus and, incidentally, well knowing the scene at Nola, Augustine describes the practices he for his part saw at martyrs' tombs in north African cities and towns—practices traditional in a modest form within his own family.[34] Their centerpiece were feasts celebrated, as has been seen, in all-night gatherings with dance and song.[35] He objects to the fancy rich foods and excessive wine, as non-Christian moralists and other bishops had been prone to do likewise. Sometimes it is hard, too, to separate his condemnation of martyr-festival moments from entirely similar feasting in or around the churches on other days of the Christian calendar; for of these he disapproved just as strongly. Their place in life is suggested by the title of the whole church in Carthage, the Basilica of the Banquet Rooms.[36]

Western sources provide a glimpse of unsettled views on the subject: Paulinus, for example, giving a color of tolerant condescension to his descriptions of the pious and their customs around Saint Felix, whereas Ambrose would have none of them. From scenes near Lyon, Sidonius Apollinaris recalls mornings after the vigil for St. Sergius, gladdened by jokes and funny stories, playing ball and rolling dice; whereas Augustine wanted everything serious. His strictures one day provoked much grumbling from his congregation: hadn't the people, before, who raised no objections, been Christians? The challenge he confronted on the morrow with carefully chosen words.

> That it might not seem as if we wished to put down our forebears,
> who had either tolerated or did not dare to forbid such excesses of an

unthinking people, I explained by what necessity this bad custom seemed to have arisen in the church. For, when peace came after so many and such violent persecutions [i.e. post-313], crowds of pagans wishing to become Christians were prevented from doing this because of their habit of celebrating the feast days of their idols with banquets and carousing; and, since it was not easy for them to abstain from these dangerous but ancient pleasures, our ancestors thought it would be good to make a concession for the time being to their weakness and permit them, instead of the feasts they had renounced, to celebrate other feasts in honor of the holy martyrs, not with the same sacrilege but with the same elaborateness, *luxus*.[37]

The explanation he offered was of course not quite straightforward; for the "ancient pleasures" that converts wouldn't surrender were not so much, or at all, the feasting that attended worship in the temples, however convenient he found it at this particular moment to depict them as such; rather, what had flowed into martyr cult was graveside cult, and this he chose not to correct.

To another criticism directed at the church by the Manichaean Faustus, he had to reply more severely: Christians, Augustine was told, in honoring martyrs, had turned them into idols, "whom you worship with those same offerings, *vota*, and conciliate the shades of the dead with wine and feasting."[38] Well, such was indeed the pagan view of the rewards in *refrigeratio*, as was acknowledged by bishops quoted above, indeed by Augustine himself in comparing the offerings to "a sort of *parentalia*, very much the same as those of pagan superstition"; and various texts have been quoted also to show that the same hopes of conciliation prevailed among most Christians in the act of martyr cult. More evidence will appear a little later.[39] Truly, if not conciliation, what could possibly have been the purpose of pouring a little wine into a tomb, inhabited, so everyone said, by a superhuman being (though not to be called a god!)? By what claim might you ask such a being to bear you in mind? What point to all the toasts, what point to the invitation that he should "Enjoy the party"? What could be the point of all the other offerings? Augustine, however, avoids these challenges by saying only what may well have been the case: nobody within the clergy had ever stood at an altar proclaiming it to be a saint's and there made any offering.

About the same time that Augustine was obliged to defend the boundaries around martyr cult, so was Jerome.[40] "Why," he was asked by a certain Vigilantius, speaking perhaps from experiences in the west but most recently from a visit to the Holy Land as well, "why must you honor with such great honor, or rather, adore" the martyr in his tomb? And he goes on to say, "We see something close to a pagan rite brought into the church in the guise of religion: in full daylight, a mountain of candles lit," and so forth. To which Jerome replies, specifically, that "we do not light candles, as you vainly and untruly allege, in the daytime but only to lessen the darkness of the night," in vigils (which he must have known was by no means the case). "And bear in mind," he goes on, "that we are not born Christians, but re-born; and because we once worshiped idols, are we now not to worship God?—lest we appear to venerate him with the same honors accorded to idols?" So Vigilantius' accusation must be borne, after all. Yet "what used to be done for idols, and is therefore detestable, is done for martyrs, and on that account is acceptable." His defense at the center of it sounds just like Augustine's: pagan usages had inevitably entered the church in the past, inevitably they still did so and could not be excluded, because converts could not be expected to leave all of their paganism behind them.

As Jerome was writing from the east and in fact moves on in this passage to speak of eastern rites, this may be a natural point at which to outline what martyr cult was like in that region. Of the music, song, and dancing, various mentions have been cited, above; it remains to mention the generous banquets leading into all-night festivities, the torches, flowers, incense, processions. Crowds that attended attracted commercial people, too, naturally not at night; for, in one place or another, the festival might last a week, even a month.[41] There were eulogies of martyrs pronounced often by invited orators, Saint Theodore at Euchaita in Pontus, for example, by Gregory of Nyssa, just as invited orators praised the western martyrs, though more often it was the local bishop. Of their powers we have many exhibitions: Chrysostom's or Gregory's of Nazianzus, expressing the hope (says Eusebius of Alexandria in the sixth century) "that, hearing the hymns and listening to their praises, they [the martyrs] will persuade the loving Jesus to receive the prayers of the moment. So, then, whoever celebrates their memory should do so with all piety, and welcome to the luncheon whoever attends, and make them realize that the martyrs are the table company; and let there be no doubt about this, for in very truth, they themselves are present at the meal with those who celebrate the memory of the saints." The derivation of all this from beliefs prevailing at sacred feasts of pagan days is plain, down to the very words chosen to express the thought, though in this coincidence of course only by chance. There is the additional detail of an *agon*, of all things the most Hellenic: the custom of a competition to see, or hear, who among the practised orators present could best exalt the saint—in this case, Saint Thecla in Cilicia in the mid-fifth century.[42] At her annual festival, after a week of high and holy times, a special banquet would bring the event to a climax, at which, once, a pilgrim's eye was caught by the beauty of a girl also present. With shame he confessed it. The reader is transported to the description of another high holy time described by Xenophon of Ephesus, where likewise the young of both sexes could more or less decently see and be seen. No society can function without such opportunities.

The identity of most of the beliefs and practices surrounding the cult of the Christian martyrs, and the cult of the ordinary dead, was pointed out in an earlier page, as, of course, it has often been pointed out by scholars in the past—even to the identity of architectural accommodations; but identity appears also between the pagan and the Christian cult of the dead, the latter flowing from the former. That derivation too is recognized.[43] Dom Fernand Cabrol in 1906 was an early observer of this truth; but then there had been Faustus and Vigilantius around the year 400: they too had seen it. It was inevitable that they should do so, as natural and inevitable as it had been from the start for Christians to continue in their cemeteries the practices familiar all around them.

Around them among their friends and neighbors, yes; and in their own families as well—even in their own personal religious practices of earlier years. As Augustine and Jerome agreed in pointing out, so as to excuse their paganism, Christians were not from birth. To a very significant degree, this was still true of the two apologists' own generation. It made inevitable some bringing in of inherited rites and beliefs to the church. But influences and alternatives which their bishops might disapprove of pressed heavily on Christians from their surrounding society, too, even if they had been church members from birth.

Enough has been said already about the fact that they and pagans shared cemeteries and that these places served them as social as well as religious centers. Add, further, that members of one group, assembling for their recollections and celebrations of an evening and under the genial influence of a full stomach and a glass or more of wine, might look over to their neighbors of another faith, involved in *their* recollections, and invite them to share the loving time. To which, the eastern bishops either said, "At least don't overindulge," or, "Better to decline the invitation entirely" (it being the bishops' turn now, also, to pin on the enemy the name they had themselves borne in previous centuries, "atheists"). Western bishops a little later, that is, just at the turn of the fifth century, offered their congregations the same counsel, complaining further that the atheists for their part sometimes tried to intrude on Christians' martyr-day festivities.[44]

The fact shouldn't surprise. Augustine was quite matter-of-fact about having an occasional nonbeliever in the audience for his sermons, while certainly in his youth, like many other clever lads, he heard lectures in the company of students of an alien faith, listening most likely to pagan professors.[45] Christians had recourse to pagan physicians; pagans, to Christian martyr tombs and holy men, for healing. Aside from the many hagiographical anecdotes in proof of both Christian and non-Christian attendance in eastern settings, aside from the mix of votive offerings from petitioners of both faiths at, for instance, the Corinthian Fountain of the Lamps, there is in the shrine of Sulis at Bath a curse-tablet directed at some thief, "whether pagan or Christian, whosoever has stolen from me." Evidently both faiths were known to attend there.[46] There were government offices with mixed staffs, mixed municipal senates, mixed civic committees, and the greatest mixture of all, about which bishops gave warning continually: pagan holy days, or days with holy connotations and connections. On the dreadful Kalends, who could keep the two faiths apart? Other dates with their parties and processions were hardly less notoriously snares for sin. From all of which intermingling, amply documented in the first chapter, we must suppose that ideas about religious practices were sometimes exchanged in civil discourse, since, as the bearers of those ideas, human beings as well as saints were brought together. Some greater degree of tolerance was thus extended to differences among laymen than the ecclesiastical authorities would approve.

In these general terms the derivation of beliefs and practices attending the cult of martyrs may be easily understood. It cannot be understood, certainly, in scriptural terms, which did not exist. But the very center of the cult remains to be explained; for the sanctified dead were not seen as others.

By the second half of the second century in the east and by the mid-third in Africa and Rome, the annual celebration of martyrs' days had entered the ecclesiastical calendar;[47] and by the latter date the favor of martyrs and confessors—these, the faithful who had testified under persecution and were being held against the day of their death—was widely acknowledged as especially powerful in bringing divine help. Belief in the miraculous powers of their relics was established.[48] Beyond these odd bits of information, however, which can hardly be called evidence, the ancient record reveals nothing about the earliest moments in the vision of martyrs as superhuman beings to be called on for aid in one's difficulties or sufferings.

The initiative, had it arisen from among ecclesiastical leaders, would no doubt have left some mark in the written record. Instead, the vision arose from among the nameless. How? Long ago, the answer most seriously proposed looked for an inspiration in the cult of "heroes," in the Hellenic sense of that word, and instances of the new creation, or the reverent perception, of such beings have emerged into the light in more recent times. They could indeed be found as a living force in the religion of a certain large area of the Greek-speaking world. The evidence was outlined in the second chapter; a little more will appear, below.[49] If it played a part in the forming of martyr cult within that area, from the north Balkans into the province of Asia, so much would be natural; but evidence for even that, let alone any wider claim, is lacking. Really the question, how did Christians come to believe that they could get good things from martyrs at their tombs is not an especially important or interesting one (though of course the detective in all of us would dearly like to know just who it was that hit upon such a belief, at what moment, and expressed it in prayer, and was rewarded, and spread the word to others around him). Given the overwhelmingly attested variety of beliefs within the Christian population, producing a constant pullulation of "heresies" (as they all called each other) and, among the non-Christian population as well, given the same vitality of religious experiment in Aelius Aristides' diaries or in the closing pages of Apuleius' *Metamorphoses*—against this background, why would it not occur to someone to direct his cult to the sleeping Stephen, Peter, or Cyprian? The question rather to be answered is, why such an experiment in individual piety should become more general, and at such a rate as it did.

In the most richly documented, comprehensive, and sensible treatment of martyrs' or saints' cult published in this century (and largely written so long

ago as the nineteenth!), Ernst Lucius took note of the remarkable speed with
which this form of worship spread, from a certain point in time. Since his
day, of course, many other scholars have commented on the fact.[50] The country people especially were forever finding another martyr and setting up an
altar on or by the burial.[51] Everyone, meaning rustic and urban nobodies
alike, unbelievable because unauthorized enthusiasts, stole and then advertised other people's martyrs, i.e. relics, in Egypt of the 360s; there, again, some
decades later, showed themselves no better than "drunk with false knowledge,
who say, The martyrs have appeared to us and told us where their bones lay";
provoked an imperial decree from the eastern capital in the 380s to control
the marketing of relics; from about the same date on, accounted for a strange
novelty in France that amounted to fraud in the invention of martyrs, so it
was charged; induced in Africa a resolution from the assembled bishops in
401 "that altars set up here and there in the countryside and along roads as if
in memory of martyrs, in which it is shown that no body or relics of martyrs
have been deposited, shall be overthrown, though, if this is impossible because of demonstrations by the people, at least the population should be ad-
monished"—everyone was eager to advance the cult. The sequence of incidents and testimonies to such spontaneous and unregulated enthusiasm may,
more or less arbitrarily, end with a certain rascal (so seen by the Roman council of 745), Aldebert, who claimed to have been visited by nothing less than
an angel in a dream and vouchsafed relics by which he could obtain all sorts
of wonders from God.[52]

Beyond all or any of this surge of religious energy, Lucius it was who saw
the meaning that lay in a match of dates: the abrupt rise in martyr cult began
in the generation preceding Julian, that is, starting in the latter years of Constantine, just when the numbers of converts began immensely to increase as
well.[53] Here was more than coincidence. The two facts must be bound together as cause and effect. Converts evidently needed what they had put away,
or something very like it.

For, by their own act, they found themselves without gods. A strange way
to put it. Surely they understood that the one Omnipotence was enough. But
no, the answer was overwhelmingly, no. That was because the concerns of little people were little, and they were therefore not accustomed to apply to
Jupiter or Zeus for succor; nor to Jahweh, after conversion. Like the great
Lex, they thought, great gods cared nothing *de minimis;* great gods were lords

and masters, not the fathers they hoped to appeal to (so Apollonius had once put it). Conversion and the repudiation of their old patrons and rescuers among the divine ranks had left an emptiness, a loneliness in times of trouble, not comfortably to be filled by the Power preached from urban pulpits. We find Augustine again and again contesting his congregation's doubts whether God should be bothered about affairs of everyday life.[54] "There are those who say God is good, great, the top, beyond our perception, incorruptible, who will give us eternal life and that incorruptibility which he has promised in the resurrection, while temporal matters and matters of this world belong to *daemones*," to superhuman beings of a lower order, those that scripture calls demons and the heathen, gods. Yet, Augustine insists, God heals both man and beast, yes, even your flocks and herds. "Let us reduce it to the very least things: he sees to the salvation of your hen." "Don't be ashamed to learn this about your Lord God. Take care not to think anything else." He rebukes "those misguided men who count God as necessary for eternal life, for that life of the soul, but think these Powers must be worshiped by us on account of temporal matters." In a very similar strain, a generation earlier, Basil had confronted his people with their inclination, when some minor problem or anxiety beset them, to turn to *daemones*.[55] But there was a Christian answer: sanctified martyrs were the answer. If we happen to know of no miracle wrought by any of them for, with, on, or among hens, yet in Italy at Nola, it was Saint Felix who cured one's larger animals, Felix who found the runaways; in Bithynia, Saint Hypatius, in Cilicia, Saint Thecla; in France, Martin who exorcised a demon from a mad cow or Fides (Foy) who would resurrect one's mule. Perhaps we may add Saint Germanus, though in his living self, not from the tomb, who almost met Augustine's challenge: ministering not to a hen but to a rooster which had somehow lost its cock-a-doodle-doo.[56]

It has often been noticed that people turned to superhuman beings most of all in case of sickness or physical or mental disability. Absent the doctors of today, hospitals, clinics, drugstores, or any accepted pharmacopoeia, what else would one expect them to do? In this realm of difficulty, Christians were well served in Basil's and Augustine's day by the powers from the tomb.[57] The principal business of the martyrs, by far, then as for a thousand years to come, was to restore fertility, straighten limbs, clear the sight, or untwist the mind. Like Asclepieia, like sacred springs presided over by their healing deities, the martyria served as hospitals to urban and rural masses alike—

even as the resort of the wealthiest, once they learned the limits of their medicos. To their memorials, their chapels and churches, their stations of visit of any sort, believers applied with pleas for help—for example (in Egypt) through a piece of mail submitted to "the god of our patron Saint Philoxenus," calling him by the old term of grateful submission and asking advice on how to restore the health of the petitioner's loved one.[58] The need for divine help, as the traditional was banished by mission and persecution together, was no doubt enormous; to supply it, the Christian God might seem very distant; but the beneficence of the sanctified dead was close and comfortable. The religious world of antiquity thus retained or resumed its traditional character "under new management."

The success that marked this area of belief may be measured of course through positive means, in the form of sheer publicity: stories of benefits sought and granted. These can be traced from the later third century on, with a sudden steep rise in frequency and fame from the mid-fourth century. Thereafter, sources within the limits of my chosen period of study describe some thousands of instances. However, the negative means of demonstration should be considered as well: the fact that benefits sought not from saints but directly from God are very rare (I recall seeing only one or two). He assured the greatest benefit of all, salvation from eternal torture; favors merely in this life and on this earth were more naturally in the gift of the saints, thanks to whose great numbers and comforting nearness, the loss of the old gods could be borne.

"To these we flock," Theodoret reminded his fellow Christians, in speaking of the martyrs, "not once or twice or five times a year, but frequently in the celebration of festivals, often in a single day bringing our hymns to their Lord. And healthy people request security in their health, while others at grips with some illness request relief from their sufferings; the infertile request children, the sterile, to be made mothers; and whoever attains the enjoyment of such gifts wants them to be safeguarded." Thus introducing martyr cult, rightly, with the sick and the disabled, Theodoret touches next on the prayers of travelers, only to revert to the principle category of miracles effected at the tombs, where carven representations of eyes, now enjoying their sight, were displayed by grateful petitioners, or of feet or hands with their use restored, sculpted of precious metals or mere clay; "and these proclaim the power of the dead."[59]

He goes on to remind his listeners of the source of that power, God not the saints; and Augustine and other bishops and church writers do the same very insistently.[60] In vain, so we must suspect, much or most of the time. Why otherwise must the reminders be so continually renewed, and why expressed with such exasperated raising of the voice? "Brethren, I warn, I exhort, I beseech you. . . . " Even the educated of the church often expressed themselves in a way that left out God entirely, in the working of miracles, or came to terms with the divinity in saints: John of Damascus, for one, insisting that they were "truly gods."[61] Where, as was the ordinary practice, it was the saints that were said to have performed some miracle, unless it was then qualified as really the act of God through the intermediary, it seems reasonable to assume that the words were sometimes meant as used, and the saint was seen as acting of himself or herself. Of an infinite number of illustrations, a bronze stamp may be instanced, to be used in the manufacture of clay lamps, inscribed with the words, "Receive, O Saint, the incense, and heal all," where the holy Symeon is addressed, and a picture drawn of the suppliant with censer in hand; or the sixth- and seventh-century lots may serve, surviving on papyri from Antinoe and Oxyrhynchus and inquiring about people's individual concerns from "the all-conquering God of Saint Philoxenus" or "of Saint Kollouthos"; but sometimes, instead, the inquiry addresses the saint unassisted.[62] Before as after Vigilantius and Faustus, there were even openly expressed perceptions that conflicted with the sole divinity of God: for, says Augustine, "I know many people are worshipers of tombs and painted representations." He uses a word, *adoratores*, which in his lexicon carries a meaning that reserves it for address to God alone. Yet it was applied quite loosely to various points and elements of the cult of the saints.[63]

In the sudden growth of martyr cult, along with more spontaneous expressions (above), initiatives by bishops played a great part. I instance two cases, one from the eastern provinces, one from the western, showing their purpose most plainly. First, Cyril, patriarch of Alexandria, presiding in 429 over the resurrection of two martyrs' remains to prominence and veneration at a site, Menuthis, only a morning's walk from his own great city. Thus Saints John and Cyrus displaced a long-famous healing shrine dedicated to Isis. Cyril delivered three celebratory orations on the event, explaining that "these districts were in need of medical services from God," and, in that need, "those who had no martyr shrine went off to other [i.e., Isis'] places, and, being Christians, thus went astray; so, out of necessity, for this reason we sought out the remains of holy martyrs." At last, with the situation remedied, "those persons who once went astray have now come here, and let them come, to the true healing given without cost; for no one invents dreams for *us*, no one says to those who come, 'The Mistress has said, do thus and so.'"[64] What he makes plain as his strategy finds an echo in Pope Gregory's directive for the conversion of the Angles, "that the shrines should not be destroyed but only the idols themselves. Let it be done with holy water sprinkled in those same shrines and let altars be built and relics be placed there so that the Angles have to change from the worship of the *daemones* to that of the true God"; and thus, with the shrine intact, "the people will flock in their wonted way to the places they are used to."[65] He goes on to note the tradition of sacral feasting for which also a direct alternative must be supplied, in the form of a festival to celebrate the birth or death of holy martyrs, to be celebrated with religious banquets.

The two passages serve to show the recognition of functions performed by the traditional religion, at Menuthis, to relieve mental and physical illness, and among the Angles, to bring them together in a sort of sacred sociability. Nothing could be more familiar than these aspects of paganism. They were of the essence. The threat they posed had to be acknowledged: at the side of pagans, Christians, too, had been directing their prayers to Isis. Pope and bishop therefore determined on the immediate superposition of saints' cult upon both the physical and social structures of the enemy.

The adoption of the social structures—eulogizing, feasting, dancing, singing, drinking, and staying up all night in the company of the saints—has already been described in enough detail. There is no saying if the feelings of reverence and love toward the divine beings at the center of the traditional ritual inspired the celebrants of the Christian imitation, too, since we lack the same sort of revealing texts from individual worshipers of Christian times that have survived from the pagan; but there is no reason to suppose that much was lost, so to speak, in translation. In other respects the Christian vigils seem to have been nearly identical with the pagan. Too nearly: they were sometimes condemned as immoral by church authorities, as has been seen; yet the authorities also tolerated them, having little choice, or, like the pope, actually instituted them.

As to the choice of a site, to challenge directly and so far as possible to displace the past, there is a great deal of evidence for that strategy. Enough to mention examples in the heart of the Holy Land; there are many elsewhere just as clear but less familiar.[66] Their success appears in the seamless join of the old to the new. Occasional accounts of miracles at the tombs show us pagans making their appeals to the saints in uncertainty as to just what wonderful being was to be found there, and by what name. Sometimes conversions resulted.[67] The converts had cared little for sect or theology, only for relief from what ailed them. Cosmas and Damian, so legend told, had to explain to their worshipers in Constantinople that they were not, contrary to a wide misunderstanding, Polydeukes and Castor.[68] They resided in a big, famous resort for healing in the capital, and, like John and Cyrus, charged nothing. At one of Asclepius' best known centers, in Aigai in Cilicia, not very long after Constantine had destroyed the building, the cult of Cosmas and Damian became established as "his real successors."[69] Similarly, Apollo's healing spring in Bithynia was turned into a center of healing by Justinian, presided over by the archangel Michael, the latter being "quite obviously" the successor.[70]

To leave the subject of "ordinary" saints, for a moment, and pursue the angelic: Michael, like Cosmas and Damian, maintained an important residence in the suburbs of Constantinople, built for him by Constantine and extravagantly amplified by Justinian. Justinian also built or improved a Michaelion near Perge in Pamphylia and another, elsewhere; later, likewise, the emperors Leo and Zeno. The church historian Sozomen recalls how he himself was made whole by the archangel in the Constantinopolitan center, like many other suppliants whose wonderful stories were to be heard there, pagans included; and pagans applied to Michael at his Colossus home, too, where he had brought a spring forth from the earth and healed through its waters.[71]

Michael's services to the church and the high honor in which he was manifestly held throughout the empire from Italy to Syria were at odds with the condemnation of angel worship in the 360s, by the Council of Laodicea.[72] The reason behind the canon must have been a fear of offense against the first commandment. Of this, Christians in Africa were in fact charged by outsiders, and, in the sixth century in Syria, by the bishop of Antioch, apropos the archangel's portrait which he saw on church walls. However, the cult of Michael in particular was suspect, yet especially hard to eradicate, because it was long entwined in both paganism and Judaism. He was thus at home in all three religious systems; but the home was itself too magical. In a good number of apotropaic texts on stone or papyri in combination with hocus-pocus or dubious superhuman associates, he is asked by Christians to protect their fields against hail, to bring relief from illnesses, or as psychopomp to bear the souls of the dead safely to their final haven. Accordingly, once again toward the end of the fifth century, a church council warned against calling on angels for protection against illnesses or evil spirits. The angels are themselves demons.[73] The emperors by their magnificent offerings to Michael taught their subjects a different lesson.

Accounts of the archangel's miracles of healing, for which he was especially noted, add details to the broad outline of his cult: that suppliants to his power, like those in scripture but in all paganism around them, too, need only believe to receive his healing; that he worked his wonders through the application of water from his sacred springs, as did Cosmas and Damian or Cyrus and John, or Thecla; and somehow the fish in those springs were also sacred to Michael.[74] Fish in ponds sacred to a resident deity were to be found in various localities in the pagan world, especially Syria; sacred birds, there as well, recalling the birds sacred to Saint Thecla; a sacred spring, at Ephesus the property of Artemis, sacred water from a shrine in Egypt carried off to heal, and pagan sacred ponds and springs at western healing sites literally by the hundreds. In the approved tradition, Gregory of Tours applied the waters of a spring, sacred to Saint Ferreolus, to the relief of his fever.[75] Through the cult rendered to Saint Michael, he thus serves very well to represent in miniature, as it were, various points of identity between saints' cults in general and the paganism all around them.

A last point to notice in the usages of his shrines is incubation. By this term was meant the age-old practice of receiving visions of deities during a night's sleep at the shrine, "advised in a dream" as so many Greek and Latin votive inscriptions say. They are matched by as many literary mentions.[76] Episodes centered in Michaelia of Egypt and other eastern provinces describe the rewards to petitioners through dreams; likewise, to the petitioners at Thecla's shrines, at Cosmas' and Damian's, and at Menuthis, and at Ephesus (to gain advice from Saint John the Evangelist), and at many lesser martyria. The descriptions of epiphanies—how the saints appeared, spoke, and were thanked with hymns and offerings—make use of the vocabulary and phrases familiar in, for example, the worship of Asclepius.[77] One locus of that cult opens up a most illuminating picture: Athens' famous and beautiful

Asklepieion on the south slope of the Acropolis. Its destruction must be dated through the archeological evidence "possibly as late as 485, while the earliest church on the site appears to have been constructed before the end of the fifth century. . . . The church included not only the site of the temple of Asklepios itself, but also the earlier stoa of incubation, the sacred spring, and what was probably the *katagogeion* [hostel] of the sanctuary"—so, T. E. Gregory.[78] As Gregory points out, the possibilities here must be interpreted within a context of much else that is probable or certain, much that has been presented in enough detail, above.

The traditions that surrounded divine healing seem thus to have flowed forward from eastern pagan to eastern Christian without check or change. There was in addition a flow to the west, though not so well attested. Incubation was known to Augustine at the Saint Stephen shrines in the district.[79] In Italy, too, attested sites include Ferentinum and, in many of its churches, Naples, too, where it was customary for priests to inquire about the suppliants' dreams and to explain them, and where sometimes the suppliants had to reside for weeks or months before obtaining relief (as happened, too, at eastern *martyria*). These practices exactly recall those of the second century that Aelius Aristides reports from Pergamum. As to Christian Gaul (or France), there, sleepers received their cures at the tombs of Saint Illidius, Saint Abraham, or Saint Martin. Around the relics of Saint Fides (Foy), of a night, a visitor might find the church too crowded with sleeping forms to move around in. The custom carried on into the later Middle Ages.[80]

Much of what could be seen at *martyria* of one sort or another may be recovered from hagiographic literature and celebratory sermons. In particular, many texts of the latter sort survive; for bishops stood a good chance of sanctification, themselves, and, like college presidents awarding honorary degrees to other college presidents, rejoiced in such festal oratory.[81] In the course of it, they tell of the crowds, the arrangements for lodging, the priests on hand to answer questions, the joyful vigils, feasts and fairs, the animals and other offerings. All these have been touched on in earlier pages and their roots in older traditions have been noted. Mention has been made, too, of the representations of holy scenes and personages on the walls of Italian and African shrines in the generation around A.D. 400, just as in temples, to which should be added at Uzala a painting of Saint Stephen donated by an angel— whether "angel" in the literal or colloquial sense, our reporter is unsure.[82] An early instance of such art is praised by Gregory of Nyssa. It decorated the walls of Saint Theodore's church at Euchaita in what is now northern Turkey. At the moving sight of the martyr's sufferings and deeds, Gregory says, the faithful will want to offer some gift and perhaps take away a pinch of dust as a gift in return.[83] Many fourth-century bishops speak of such depictions, some even in private houses (Chrysostom, on Saint Meletius), and the series carries on, then, to the archangel Michael on church walls in Antioch around the turn of the sixth century; in the first half of that century, the depiction of Saint Eutychius' miracles, in a painting or in the round; and toward the end, Saint Martin, at Tours, on the walls of his cathedral.[84] As the saints' cult originated in the east, so did the art of it; and it is thus suitable that we should have, even if more than half effaced, a portrait of Saint Stephen from perhaps the 530s. A local bishop set it up in a great Isis temple at Philae in Upper Egypt after a unit of Justinian's army had driven away the worshipers and their priests.[85] Pagan origins of this art have been noted, too, in earlier pages.[86]

Those origins were of course troubling to Augustine, in speaking of misguided *adoratores* of the representations of martyrs; troubling notoriously in the provinces of the iconoclastic controversy, much later; and troubling still at the turn of the millennium to the monk Bernardus of Angers, hagiographer of Saint Fides (Foy). He described her miracles and cult in the village church of Conques, some twenty-five miles from Rodez in the south. There she sat enthroned, a little less than life-sized, covered with jewels and herself (at least her face) of pure gold. The devout had somewhere found the image of an emperor of Julian's time or thereabouts and used it to make a reliquary.[87] Thus as the focus of imperial cult in the fourth century, from the ninth on it gained in fame as a worker of wonders, generally of healing but of many other acts, too. Bernardus was challenged to defend what appeared, to "the learned," to be "very much like the rites of the ancient worship of the gods, or rather, of demons." He concedes that "statues of the saints can by no reasoning be tolerated unless because of an ancient, incorrigible abuse and inborn habit of the ignorant," but it may then serve quite properly to stimulate the awe of the peasantry. The true character of this extraordinary image, the oldest surviving from the medieval west, has been rightly described as "marking the continuity of the Christian religion with the pagan" in sculptured terms.[88] It may be imagined borne about on a litter, for such was the frequent practice of the monks in charge of it, and on its peregrinations in the neighborhood it

Figure 3 The Majesté of Saint Foy (Conques). Photo A. Allemand, Atelier du Regard (Orsay)

wrought some of its miracles. Processions of images had always been at home both in this part of the world and elsewhere throughout the pagan empire, still inviting condemnation by the bishops in the eighth century.[89] The ritual accounted for Saint Martin's mistake in thinking that a funeral procession which he met on a country road was rather a religious parade. Celebration and advertisement of the saints through the parade of their relics or perhaps their images (they are termed "the martyrs") Gregory Nazianzenus described as early as the 380s, with, of course, a familiar history subsequently. The flow from non-Christian into Christian usage was thus unbroken.

This may be the place to mention early images of Jesus, with Paul and Peter on display in places of worship—a practice, it need hardly be said, originating neither in Judaism nor in primitive Christianity. Nor did it originate among the Christian leadership. The Council of Elvira of ca. 306 forbade it inside churches.[90] It had nevertheless become a popular element in cultic settings by the third century, best known through Roman tomb paintings, in which Jesus is shown as a bearded male figure and sometimes in guises familiar to pagan painting and sculpture (as a shepherd, or as the sun god). In a passage often noticed, and pointing to what was surely the invention of common people of the third century, Eusebius reports the statues he had seen at a little town some twenty-five miles inland from Tyre. The bronzes there were a pair: a standing male being petitioned by a kneeling female, long taken by the inhabitants to be Jesus and the woman with an issue of blood. "There is," Eusebius says, "nothing remarkable in the fact that common pagans long ago, for favors granted them, would have done this [that is, erected the statues] for their benefactors . . . naturally, since people of long ago, unguardedly, in their pagan fashion were accustomed thus to honor those who saved their health."[91] And, he adds, he also saw (apparently in the same town) paintings of Jesus, Paul, and Peter, which can only have been in some church and of some age.

In the same years as this account, another pair of statues was set up, these by none other than Constantine and in the basilica of San Giovanni in Laterano. They were of a precious metal reserved for emperors, silver, 260 pounds of it, and almost life-sized. Both represented Jesus enthroned like a Roman magistrate, facing the congregation down the nave, and facing the bishop in the opposite direction, in the apse; and John the Baptist's statue was placed in the baptistery, with gold lambs.[92] So much for the bishops of Elvira! Constantine's ideas of proper forms and symbolism were very much his own and must have greatly embarrassed his coreligionists, until they could wipe out the traces of them, as they did in due course. What could one do, after all, with a man frank to acknowledge to the chief of his churches, "We have received from Divine Providence the supreme favor of being relieved from all error"?[93] Meanwhile a rule had been broken. A jeweled gold image of Jesus was provided to the Peter shrine by the emperor at Xystus' request. Statues of Jesus, Mary, and the apostles in both church buildings and private homes receive mention in literary sources of the sixth and later centuries and are uncovered by excavation in both the east and the west during the same period. It is assumed they were common. They were destined, however, to arouse controversy.[94] Naturally. Their external origins were too apparent, along with the conduct that attended those origins. In Justinian's reign a challenge was raised against images in the round by the bishop of Ephesus, who nevertheless could tolerate paintings; and, responding to violent objection against even these latter, Pope Gregory made the same distinction.[95] Until grown familiar, however, veneration of images could hardly ecape suspicion as heathen idolatry.

Eusebius goes on to mention the plant found nowhere else but at the foot of the Jesus statue, growing in the dirt that gathered there, which the pious picked and used for healing. Just so, the pious picked simples and herbs in Artemis' temenos at Ephesus. Whatever place plants grew, near a grave or in a cemetery or a sacred precinct, it had much to do with their medicinal properties. Somehow they absorbed something from their environment.[96] Saints' tombs everywhere supplied healing power of this sort, through every kind of growth, even grass and weeds, portable (to be conserved and taken home) and infallible.[97] Similarly, dust. Gregory of Nyssa has been quoted, above, reminding the faithful that they might want to take some from the saint's tomb as his gift to them; more from Saint Demetrios' tomb was requested by emperors, Justinian and Maurice, and presented to them by the archbishop in charge. The faithful of earlier, pagan times had done just that at their temples, sometimes making it, indeed, by scraping the stone walls of a sanctuary. The ancient signs of the practice may be seen near the entrance of that Isis temple at Philae referred to above. The custom continued into Christian times in Egypt; it does so still into this century, there; and in Italy and France, it continues.[98] More to the purpose: accounts of the miracles wrought by the saints from Mesopotamia to Germany through the dust around their burials run through the hagiography of the fourth to the eighth century and beyond, highly approved by ecclesiastical authority and therefore, no doubt, all the more universal and pervasive in Christianity.

Closer to the power of the saints, far closer, to the point of being in fact the very saints themselves, were objects they had touched while living. From Saint Paul people took his handkerchiefs as instruments of miraculous healing; from Saint Cyprian, handkerchiefs and napkins wetted by his blood at the time of his execution (and the power of the blood of someone dead before his time was known in eastern parts to be highly effective in wonder-working).[99] Ernst Lucius points to the quarreling over the bodily remains of martyrs in Palestine: Eusebius spoke of it, but disapproved, and so would supply no details. Saint Anthony's fellow monks quarreled over one of his garments after his death; the fringes of Saint Martin's cloak were found to be full of healing.[100] In life, the saints rubbed their spit on blind eyes to restore sight; the application of their tears would work wonders on the ailing; their very toenails, too.[101] But, until the second half of the fourth century, references in our sources to martyrs' relics and their potency are few and obscure.

It is at that point that we have the first attested incident of the translation of relics: Saint Babylas'. A few years later we have Basil's mention of the gift of dust from a martyr to suppliants (above), and the revelation to Pope Damasus of undiscovered sanctified remains, through his dreams.[102] It was by dreams that the martyrs sometimes provided not only curative prescriptions to their suppliants but news of their own whereabouts as well. Audiences were eager to receive this news, since, over the course of time, a church was thought to be hardly complete without the remains of some hero of the persecutions. Bishops were eager, too, by reason of their pastoral concerns. They wanted a means of confronting and bringing an end to the paganism by which they were still surrounded; so it may be said without too much exaggeration that "it was in fact the bishop who invented the martyr."[103] Babylas promised to be a good ally in the struggle: he worked miracles, or at least miracles were wrought in his cause. He later appeared to Chrysostom in a vision, encouraging the advertisement of his great merits.[104] Similar heroes may be recalled from earlier pages: Saints Cyrus and John, brought in to Menuthis to displace Isiacism. In charge of the effort was the patriarch Cyril. It was he also who opposed the alleged paganism of the city's prefect and thereby lost one of his own most zealous supporters, a monk, Ammonius; for, in the course of rioting, Ammonius so cleverly threw a rock that it opened the prefect's head and covered him with blood. Ammonius was seized and tortured to death. Cyril recovered the body, deposited it in a church under the new name of Saint Wonderful, and delivered the usual panegyric on the martyr.[105]

The battle logic, as it may be called, accounting for the promotion of many a saint appears in hagiography. It appears, occasionally, in physical remains. On the model of the Athenian Asclepius shrine (above), transformed into a church with the least possible change that might affront its servants, we

have the chapel to Saint Hilarius in France, built by the local bishop just by
the shrine where a goddess presided over a lake—the shrine, partially excavated, and the lake named Helarius. Displacement was to be literal as well as
littoral; and there was real need for action. Many of the baptised attended the
centers of water gods and goddesses, altogether too many.[106] Their piety
could only in part be redirected. The locus long dedicated to worship had to
be accepted, the inflow of crowds thereto encouraged as desirable, but the divine object of their visits was to be no longer Rosmerta or whatever heathen
deity, of course, but rather God and his saints. Similarly around the empire,
a number of sites—Athens, Carthage, Menuthis, Philae—have been mentioned where a temple was made into a church; many other examples might
easily be added to the list.[107] To some degree, the pagan past thus determined
the distribution of points of worship for the Christian future.

   In the course of advertising the powers of the martyrs, a bishop, Theodoret,
was quoted some pages earlier exulting in their curative power in those regions
he knew best, the eastern. He instanced as proof the display of body parts in
effigy, to show the points of suppliants' afflictions and to testify to their re-
covery. In the western regions, Paulinus notes with pride the effigies covering
the walls of Saint Felix' shrine.[108] Of the whole picture empire wide, there is
an assessment in Gibbon's notorious twenty-eighth chapter: "The walls were
hung round with symbols of the favours which they [suppliants] had received; eyes, and hands, and feet, of gold and silver, and edifying pictures,
which could not long escape the abuse of indiscreet or idolatrous devotion."

   Quite right; but Gibbon goes on to add what is no better than a half-truth:
"The most respectable bishops had persuaded themselves that the ignorant
rustics would more cheerfully renounce the superstition of Paganism, if they
found some resemblance, some compensation, in the bosom of Christianity."[109] Indeed and truly, Paulinus does smile with tolerant superiority at the
crowds around Saint Felix; but his condescension is directed at their illiteracy
and their uncomplicated perceptions. It is not true that the church's more educated leadership differed in their fundamental view of miracles and con-
spired to impose on their congregations what they themselves did not believe.
So far as concerns the central matter of Saint Felix' miracles, Paulinus was as
truly persuaded as the rustics; likewise, the rest of Gibbon's unnamed bishops. The point was argued in the previous chapter, as it has been by others in
the past, with illustrations drawn from a variety of contexts—some, offering

miraculous cures vouched for by the ancient authors, Augustine and others, as personal witnesses from the church' upper ranks; some, affirming the martyrs' sterner powers to punish, if they should be too closely provoked. Augustine it is who recommends that oaths of disputants be taken in the presence of Saints Gervasius and Protasius, who could (like good pagan gods, of course) be counted on to show in some dramatic way which was the liar.[110] More decisive still, the bishops themselves wrought miracles of healing, by common report, and so were sought out for that blessing; and even in death they continued to provide miraculous cures. The facts are very well known, thanks once again to the large surviving hagiographical library: the sick applying to Basil for his wonderful aid, in Cappadocia, or to Martin in France, while Severinus in Noricum, too, wrought wonders of healing and, from his tomb, long afterwards continued them; at the time of Cyril of Alexandria, another to be mentioned, Nestorios, "a man gifted with prophetic powers; and the holy one once a year was accustomed to visit the city to heal the infirm"; slightly later in the west, Lupus bishop of Troyes, or a century later still in Provence, the holy Leobinus whose garments drove out spirits, who restored sight to the blind, who could check the spread of fire; and so forth.[111]

With these figures, however, a second generation of saints has stepped upon the stage: not martyrs but persons of a life so devoted to worship that they had gained a share in divinity itself. However far their antecedents may be traced back in Egypt or Palestine, however often and widely attested was the readiness among the eastern populations to see and acknowledge divine beings before them in the flesh,[112] Christian heroes really were something new. At the very least, they were new in the attention they attracted, from the latter decades of the wonderful Antony on through the centuries, and through the genius of Athanasius, too. He found for his biography of Antony exactly the length and tone, exactly the proportions of anecdote, ornament, and praise, to make the new saint talked about. The Greek text was promptly translated into Latin.

It might be said that, in the latter years of Constantine when Antony's unwritten life was already serving as an inspiration to others, the type of the second generation had been already and independently established, and would have spread without special advertisement at a slower rate but inevitably. Word of mouth was always a most effective medium. It explains the propagation of ascetic models among communities and regions quite untouched by

Athanasius' work. As paganism receded, news spread of new heroes almost as much to be honored and imitated as the martyrs in their tombs. An ideal denial of the natural man and devotion to the divine had of course long been the aspiration of a few; a tradition of asceticism was familiar in paganism, above all, in Egypt.[113] But only those lucky people who had much had aspired to do with less, meaning the well-to-do and educated. Such was certainly not the class of Antony nor of those like him: individuals of similar temperament who became so prominent a part of the eastern landscape, from the second quarter of the fourth century onward. Their general type was described earlier.[114] By their way of life and their rapidly growing numbers they made a remarkable place for themselves.

Beyond their own needs of individual temperament and piety, however, they filled the needs of a much larger population around them. They lived and had their being outside of cities, often in isolated farming regions. Here, the suppression of traditional worship by their efforts or by other ecclesiastical orders left a gap needing to be filled by the miracles the monks themselves notoriously wrought. Thus, once their repute was established, they were sought out from afar by petitioners able to make a pilgrimage, of the same sort that came to martyrs' shrines — for that matter, of the same sort that would in the past have come to Artemis or Caelestis. Monks were asked to respond to the problems brought to them in this way; they were more often asked to handle local problems for which solutions in the past would have been sought from gods less distant and imposing. Surviving accounts illustrate their activities.

First, as to their closeness to the land, people, and past: in Lycia of the mid-sixth century,

> the clergy of Plenios came in a procession with the congregation of
> the faithful, chanting and with the venerated crosses, and met the ser-
> vant of God [Nikolaos] at the chapel [of St. George]. From there he
> went with them with seven calves. They went into the chapel of the
> holy George and he sacrificed the seven calves, and the crowds gathered
> so that there were two hundred couches. The servant of God supplied
> enough to distribute a hundred measures of wine and forty measures
> of wheat, and everyone ate and was filled and thanked God who gave
> grace to his servant Nikolaos

(and so forth, describing identical visits on Nikolaos' rounds of the territory). A scholar of long ago, Gustav Anrich (friend and editor to Ernst Lucius), rescued the picture from oblivion: "The description," he explains, "shows us the survival of the old sacrificial meal made over into Christian form. The churches or oratories are still the place for slaughter, feasting and drinking, the slaughter is ordinarily described as a sacrifice (θύειν, θυσίας ἐπέδωκεν, εὐχαριστῶν τῶι θεῶι). . . . The Laodicean synod had already in the fourth century forbidden the holding of agapes in churches, but, since the Trullo synod of 692 felt obliged to repeat the ancient canon, it shows that the custom nevertheless persisted."[115] Anrich compares the scenes described by Paulinus, to which still further parallels could be added from other regions and dates within the period of this study.

Then, next, the sort of help that men of God could provide: no doubt most commonly, healing by their touch or by the signing of the cross or prayers of intercession. Evidence comes most abundantly from Antony's life, as it should, and most tangibly from his successors, through written appeals to anchorites on papyrus still surviving (one such from an Athanasius, possibly the great bishop himself).[116] For other kinds of legendary aid there were other heroes of almost equal powers, earlier as later: Gregory the Wonder-worker, to name one such, who planted his wonder-working staff where it could prevent flooding, according to accounts that a local bishop picked up in the century afterwards; and a cross set in the ground by Theodore of Sykeon would do the same; or, in Noricum, Saint Severinus worked miracles of flood control by his staff, too, while, in Italy, Sabinus the wonderful bishop of Placentia had his wishes in a letter dropped into the Po bidding that great river to respect the lands within his see. It worked—a species of phylactery to which I return a little later.[117]

Elsewhere, miracles against other common dangers: fire[118] or blight in the fields[119] or hailstorms. These latter might be averted by prayer alone, by Hypatius, Theodore of Sykeon in Galatia, Julian, or Martin.[120] Or by *horoi*, again through Theodore: "In the village called Reake, a fierce cloud from time to time visited the land and brought hail upon the vines when the grapes were full; and the men of the village were in bad straits, being unable to harvest any of their crop, over a good length of time." Accordingly they fetched the wonder-worker from his monastery, exactly as they might apply to a "cloud-driver." "Forming a procession, he went round the vineyards and village territory and, with a prayer, planted four wooden crosses at the corners around its edges, and so departed for the monastery; and through his holy prayers the fierce cloud no longer visited there. In gratitude for this benefaction, from then to the present day"—so says the biographer in the succeeding generation, at some point a little before the mid-seventh century—"the men of the village bring annually to the monastery a certain measure of wine and grapes."[121] F. R. Trombley notes the presence here of a practice reaching back behind Gregory and Severinus into both Greek and Roman antiquity; and he goes on to indicate a similar spell from sixth-century Lydia: "Exorcism for the turning back of hail. I adjure you, O Demon [of the skies] . . . I adjure you by the power of the God of Hosts and the throne of the Lord, go outside of the *horoi*. . . . I adjure you by the letters of the planets. . . . You archangels Raphael, Ragouel, Israel, Agathoel, make a seal around the village of Ennaton"—so reads a plaque protecting an area which is marked out, still today, by the corner-stones.[122]

I pause a moment here to note the vision of the universe latent or express in the accounts quoted. They understood blight in the fields to be inflicted by superhuman beings; and not only blight but plagues of grasshoppers, too, and destructive great gusts of wind or hail or conflagration, lack of water or too much water and subsequent flooding. Demonic causation ruled their thought. It followed that contrary, benevolent forces must be brought to bear to restore the balance. Such a vision of the universe was discussed in the preceding chapter and contrasted with the ridicule of spells to avert hail. Seneca saw them in the same light as Pliny, who was quoted. Seneca writes,

> Incredible, this: at Cleonae [a few miles south of Corinth] there were official hail guards on the lookout for hailstorms on the way! When they gave the signal that hail was at hand, what do you suppose? That people ran for their winter cloaks or leather raincoats? No, everyone for himself offered up a lamb or a chicken; and, directly, those clouds veered off elsewhere, since they'd had their taste of blood. You laugh at this? But here is something to make you laugh yet more. If someone had neither lamb nor chicken, he turned on himself, without inflicting any hurt to speak of, and (don't think the clouds greedy or cruel) pricked his finger with a good sharp stylus, and so made his blood sacrifice; nor did the hail veer off any the less from his little field than from some other prayed for with larger victims.[123]

Evidently they all believed, these unenlightened folk, that the sky and earth, fire and water, worked in the same way in which Pliny's country neighbors believed, in Italy, or as did the peasants of Mauretania, for that matter, who offered their grateful sacrifices to the Spirit of the Mountain for averting windstorms—or, again, like Augustine's country people who relied on spells; or, last, at the turn of the seventh century, as the people of Madaba believed. On the floor of the Elijah church they wrote in mosaic letters, "Prophet, thou who to our prayers hast providentially stirred the rain-bearing clouds and pitied the populace, remember the donors of this humble city." Elijah in this dry land had succeeded to the local sky god of the pagan past.[124]

In the eastern provinces in the period of this study, where once the holy Pythagoras of pagan legend had averted plague, hail, and storms, the "cloud-drivers" were credited with the right powers to bring or keep away blasting or blessing movements of the air, and church councils of the fourth century and so on up to the end of the seventh, again and again, forbade the pious to resort to such men. Councils in the west over the same period and much later, too, issued the same commands.[125] Everywhere, life demanded, or if not life, then hope demanded wonder-workers. Shamans, dervishes, wizards, medicine men, *nephodioktai, tempestarii,* Pythagoras or Theodore or Elijah must be at hand; and choice only lay among the means that offered, Christian or non-Christian. The bishops were determined on a Christian answer; their congregations, on whatever worked. The proportions of their success are beyond any good guess, so far at least as concerns the rural scene—measuring the entrenchment of tradition against the efforts of chorepiscopi and the reports (generally no more than reports) of saints' miracles; for saints' shrines, whatever their total number empire-wide, were thinly scattered about, beyond most people's easy visiting. Similarly, most people never laid eyes on a holy man.[125]

Whatever worked governed the choice of access to prediction, too. For anyone about to go on a journey, which might very well be dangerous, or to undertake anything else important and risky, certainty about what might happen was beyond price. The pagans' constant attendance at oracular shrines in search of foreknowledge was described, with contempt, by Eusebius in the passage quoted above (p. 77). Emperors perhaps needn't bother much with hail or runaway slaves, but even for them, it would be wonderful to know the future. They made their arrangements accordingly: along with their senate and consuls, they continued to make use of specialists who understood the necessary arts, into the fifth and sixth century, officially, while also spasmodically banning these same specialists; for prophetic powers were suspect both theologically and politically. As Salvian reminded his readers, having in mind such writers as Varro, Cicero, or Pliny as points of comparison, "just about everything is still being done that even those ancient pagans thought to be useless and laughable."[126]

The laughter had died out long ago. Prediction in Salvian's own day was known to be entirely possible. Christian Powers, the saints in their martyria at Antinoe or Oxyrhynchus, replied through sortition to the anxious queries posed to them in precisely the forms that pagans once had used; Christian holy men gave insights into the future on demand. The evidence is largely eastern.[127] They were nowhere near able to satisfy demand, witness the ubiquitous resort to less well accredited and even commercial prophets known in their localities as "wise women," seers, and so forth. Against all these, so commonly sought out by their flock, the bishops spoke very harshly.[128] There was still more frequent resort to divination through little events that signalled the operation of some superhuman agency: lots or dice cast by expert readers of such signs, thunder, sneezing, the shape of the flame on the altar when the incense was burned, or words of children at play.[129] At a most famous moment, Augustine had relied on this latter means of learning divine wishes, in fully pagan fashion. He combined the guidance of what he heard with scriptural lots, modeled on the pagan *sortes* but using a copy of the Bible instead of Vergil. It was best if the Bible was placed on the altar during consultation. The practice, though commonly condemned by the bishops, was also commonly employed by them, by lower clergy, and of course by the laity. Martin was chosen bishop obedient to its dictates;[130] it led to "the use of clarifications exactly comparable to the pagan manuals for drawing lots," that is, preset interpretations for each type of Bible passage that might turn up, written into the margins of manuscripts.[131] This convenience had been long familiar in earlier tradition and simply continued in common use under slightly different forms.

In describing devices to control weather, I mentioned word sets employed on a letter dropped into a river or on a stone set up with *horoi* to protect a field. Thanks to the dry sands of Egypt a great quantity of such texts have survived on papyrus and can be compared with scattered others elsewhere inscribed on various hardier materials and in many regions. A particular category are well known because associated with burials; so archeologists are likely to find them. They are the hexing spells called *defixiones,* often scratched on lead. They turn up all over, in Britain or Syria or at any point one wishes in between. They invoke a mixture of superhuman beings from any universe, the more various, the more outlandish, the better. It is notoriously difficult to tell the character, Christian, Jewish, or non-Christian, of many of these documents, on whatever medium.[132]

Since belief in the operation of malign spirits could be found universally, and preoccupied people of every class and tradition at frightened moments of their lives, one would not expect it to be easily eradicated by the church. Rather the church, as has been seen, greatly fortified it. It did so through its doctrine of demons, particularly dramatized through rites of cleansing. In turn, the word sets to accomplish this are best known through what priests recited at baptisms, that doorway to the church. Every entrant thus received instruction in the doctrine. It explains why one unhappy victim paralyzed by hexing, in hopes of help, applied to Saints John and Cyrus. Sleeping in the martyrion, he was vouchsafed a vision and advice from them: to roast a pig's lung and rub it on his body with wine; but also, to dig near his bedroom, to discover and disarm the *defixio* buried there by his enemy. The desired cure was thus ensured while the doctrine of demonic causation was confirmed.[133]

Procedures that restored the use of this petitioner's limbs are familiar within almost timeless contexts. Compare Pliny. Exactly how the body worked, even he—enlightened polymath who smiled at others' absurd ideas regarding natural phenomena—was at a loss to understand; so some of the treatments he recommended went beyond any possible physical explanation, to the supernatural: that is, for example, his recommendation to make use of a sheep's spleen first placed against a patient's spleen area, if it were afflicted. There might be some idea here of a physical effect to be expected. But Pliny goes on to say that the sheep's spleen must thereafter be plastered into the wall by the bed, with a word set recited over it for good measure.[134] Between this method of treatment and the spells against fevers easily found among surviving magical papyri, there is really no difference, just as there is no difference between the prescriptions of the learned senator, and of Saints John and Cyrus.

With more or less complication, and perhaps strengthened with certain symbols, spells survive on a great number of Christian amulets as on non-Christian—again, without differences between them. Such amulets may indeed be imagined in most households: little stone or metal plates or pendants engraved, for instance, with a line from the Ninety-First Psalm—that special favorite. Many called on the archangels, a thing vainly condemned by the church. Many were supplied by the clergy, though Caesarius reproached them. Or instead, as so-called ligatures, a text might be inscribed in ink on paper and worn in a tiny sack around the neck. The wearing of ligatures, common in the pagan world, was often condemned by church authority, perhaps aiming only at partly or wholly non-Christian texts. Gregory the Great as a special mark of favor sent one to the Lombard queen in Milan. He describes it as a phylactery with a few lines of scripture written on it and a piece of the true cross enclosed or accompanying it; and he himself wore a favorite phylactery.[135]

Among not only ordinary folk but the privileged of sixth-century France as well, protective spells "were by common custom tied about the neck for health's sake, with exorcistic writings," while, around Saint Peter's, they were displayed for sale in Boniface's day. The symbol of a fish was one of the popular ones to ward off evil, and gave a shape to amulets not only for the living but to those buried with the dead throughout the western areas, from pagan times up into twentieth-century Italy and Sicily. In eastern martyria you could buy stamps to impress a spell on paper, showing a saint or his or her name and the words "Blessing of . . . . "; or you could buy medico-amuletic armbands for the pilgrim trade inscribed with the five-pointed star (the pentalpha or Solomon's seal), the lion-headed snake (Chnoubis), the Annunciation or Women at the Tomb, bits of Psalm 90, and so forth—a jumble of mostly Christian but also non-Christian symbols and word sets long in circulation.[136] A sampling of archeological data of this sort spread across Syria, Palestine, and Egypt of the early Byzantine period "reveals a world thoroughly and openly committed to supernatural healing, and one wherein, for the sake of health, Christianity and sorcery had been forced into open partnership."[137]

Evidence for hexing is not very prominent at any point in the first or the fourth or eighth century. Ugly, criminal, and feared, it remained a thing for dark corners. Only, occasionally, it emerges into the light of some lurid trial scene. So much is true at least of the literary sources. Beneath their level, however, the thought-world in which it had its being is revealed as the ordinary daily one of ordinary people. Hexing, which acknowledged and em-

ployed demonic force against one's enemies, was only the dark side of an
equally commonplace belief in the operation of spells which acknowledged
but opposed the demonic causes of disease, as of other ills, and did so through
appeal to better and more powerful agencies. This too, this belief in phylacteries or amulets and all that their operation implied, is not easily discoverable
in sermons, theological treatises, histories or biography. It rather appears in
exorcistic texts, baptismal or other; in clay, metal, or stone talismans with
spells on them; or in sharp but brief rebukes by church councils. Nevertheless, it too belonged to ordinary life and ordinary people. Opposing views
once held by Pliny, Plutarch, Plotinus and their like had long since been
crowded out. Bishops and their slaves, aristocratic landowners like Melania
the Younger and her many thousands of peasants, high and low, all agreed
about the essentials: about relics, saints, angels, demons, God, and Satan. No
sharp division separated the different classes within the whole population
calling themselves Christian.

Nor did sharp differences, so far as these essentials are concerned, divide
the Christian from the non-Christian. Which is certainly not to say that the
extremes of the one were just like the other. Certainly not. They were at war.
But among spells on whatever medium there is a very large representation of
non-Christian ways mixed into the Christian address to superhuman beings;
mixed into ritual, too, and language and conceptualization. What else could
one expect, given the common, almost routine resort by Christians to pagan
or Christian spell-makers, *prae-* or *incantatores* or *harioli* as they are called in the
Latin west? They would be recommended by one's non-Christian friends if
one had a fever or the like. *Herbarii* who cut or picked medicinal plants would
be called in, too, to the same end, or priests to advise, the two sorts of experts
alike using spells to secure the full benefit of the plants, and the spells of
Christian character drawing on, and often mixed in with, those traditional in
the pre-Christian past. They were in use in the west into the sixteenth century
and beyond.[138] Over the same long stretch of time, against spell-makers, conciliar injunctions or pulpit admonitions were repeated again and again, clearly
because the old religious traditions persisted among the baptized; against
herb gatherers, likewise, the western church authorities spoke out again and
again. Yet in wording, tone, and strategy, though not in the deity addressed,
the old traditions persisted also among the bishops and lower clergy themselves. They wished only to redirect appeal for help from a confusion of su-

perhuman beings, to the authorized: from the old Powers or conjurations, Solomon or Abrasax, to the saints, or to Jesus himself through relics (the nails or wood of the cross), or to God, through especially potent lines of scripture or liturgy.

Crosses to keep out illnesses or any other evil marked doorposts just as the sign of life, the ankh, had done, or some other symbol or phrase: "Jesus Christ lives here," equivalent to the common "Here lives Hercules," or "Christ conquers!" equivalent to "Ammon conquers!" On the lintels of the new John and Cyrus church where Isis once reigned, as at Philae where, too, she had her home, Christians in good time inscribed their own sign of triumph and safe-keeping; on doorposts they planted their kisses upon entering, just as pagans did; and at doorways in Rome, statuettes of Saint Symeon were placed where there had been other guardians before—perhaps a little Hercules.[139] Crosses marked on the heads of one's herds and flocks saved them from pests; and of course crosses were often inscribed on amulets for the same purpose—on one western example, with "Abrasax" added for good measure.[140] The later Christian practice was a translation of an older pagan one.

And even on the eucharistic bread, a cross stamped before baking represented the continuation of the old practice of marking the loaves of sacrifice and sacrificial meals.[141] Psalms drove demons away, that was well known, as pagan priests also used music for apotropaic purposes; and an illustration of that turned up in Taragon, in the form of a small bell. Cut into it was the owner's name and purpose: "The tinkler, *cacabulus*, for the imperial cult, by Felix of Tarraco, assistant announcer and slave. Good luck to the Senate and Roman people!"[142] Bell-ringing during cult acts was common in Roman temples and, to keep away demons, in tombs throughout the empire; subsequently, of course, in Christian ritual. At many points and places, as is familiar to the present day, offerings of incense and candle- or lamplight framed the acts of cult. The frame, too, had been assimilated.[143]

In my survey of assimilation, these latter pages on magic may need two words of explanation. The first is today easily offered, where, even a generation ago, it would have required considerable discussion: namely, the relationship between magic and religion and the exact meaning of the two terms. For historians of the west, knowing only their own discipline and only the one Judeo-Christian religious tradition, these matters used to be intellectually as well as theologically indigestible. Now, the lessons of anthropology grown familiar, it is common to accept the impossibility of separating magic from religion and to move on to more interesting subjects.[144]

The second word must be demographic and sociological. Clearly the baptized (as for convenience's sake I continue to call them, meaning no more than "Christians" in some declared sense) held to different views among themselves regarding all sorts of religious questions. Aside from the schismatic and theological, which have little to do with my subject, they differed about ritual acts, on which this chapter has especially concentrated; and they differed about many ideas lying behind their acts. For the most part, we know about the differences because they are pointed out to a contemporary audience, and so to us, by bishops in their didactic moments, declaring this or that practice wrong in terms of their own beliefs: plain bad.

From listening to the dialogue, historians sometimes conclude there were two systems of belief at odds with each other, one to be called of "the people," the other of "the learned." This distinction was looked at in the preceding chapter; but it was denied, there, that it existed in any deep, sharp sense. No two churches existed, no two tiers, rather a "spectrum" of beliefs, to recall that useful term from the preceding chapter: a spectrum at one end of which was the very most authoritative, best thought-out Christianity, formed of long education in ecclesiastical traditions and literature, while at the other end lay the most careless and ill-informed. Even at the authoritative end it is worth noticing a good deal of self-contradiction, in both rejecting as heathen and accepting as Christian the very same novelties. Many instances have been offered in the text and especially in the notes, above.

Inflow of novelties into the church was perpetual. And why should this not be so since the period post-Constantine brought about the baptism of so many persons raised in another religious faith? Though baptized, they were nevertheless not easy to reach for more perfect instruction: they were poor and rural and hard to get at, rarely to be seen in church. Yet they counted in the tens of millions. Small wonder that the church which included them, looked at sociologically and demographically rather than theologically, underwent a significant change of character in the process of taking them in.

At the edge of conversion were those most lightly touched: on the Arabian frontier, a whole tribe brought over as a result of the miraculous curing of the sheik's son by a holy man; an entire rural population in Armenia, without Greek at all, brought over by a similar healing miracle, this by John Chrysostom himself; or at Brioude in France, in a third case, all of a village visited by a savage storm as a threat to their impiety from Saint Julian in his nearby tomb; and in terror, promising to accept Julian as their patron and his God as theirs, they were all baptized.[145] Suppose they believed, then, with perfect certainty that the God they might apply to at the saint's tomb was the true master of everything, and a lord willing as well as able to help them; suppose they acknowledged the full force of a blessing beyond all they had ever known of medicine. Let their sincerity be conceded; likewise, in a host of similar incidents which might be quoted to show instant converts accepted and formally designated as "Christians" by bishops singly or in council from the fourth century forward. Yet the circumstances outlined did not allow them to gain any clear understanding of what baptism meant in their bishop's mind or what they were getting into.[146]

Just what might result can be seen in a fourth scene, also on the edge, near the Euphrates among farmers and shepherds. An anchorite who happened among them found them never meeting for worship and ignorant of the most basic parts of the liturgy. He asked them, "'Tell me, my sons, are you Christians or Jews?' But they were indignant at these words, and they say, 'O! indeed, blessed man, we are Christians.'" They explained that they had not laid eyes on a priest for as long as anyone could remember, and in the interval they had forgotten whatever they or their ancestors had once known of Christianity.[147] Yet they were certainly of the faith.

Likewise those Christians that Isaac of Antioch (d. ca. 460) encountered in Syria; yet they continued in the rites and celebrations of the old gods and goddesses. "In our day," lamented Isaac, "we prepare tables on the housetops for the Gadde [the Tyche or patron deity]. There are torches lit above the springs, and lanterns around the streams."[148] "How many," exclaims another Syrian voice, "how many are only Christians in name but pagans in their acts . . . , attending to pagan myths and genealogies and prophecies and astrology and drug lore and phylacteries, observant of the day and the year, of auspices and dreams and birds' cries, hanging lamps by springs of water where they wash themselves, noticing of chance [prognostic] encounters, dining on the flesh of sacrificial victims . . . ," and so on through a catalog of all their heathen behavior, down to their dancing and hand clapping.[149] Many of the points of reproach recited here were touched on in previous pages, as common, whether or not approved, among congregations elsewhere in the empire.

And still in these Greek-speaking regions, the uncovering in the sixth century of persons in the highest positions who were active in the old faith as well as in the new, so far as it was safe and even beyond safety—these too were indicated in earlier pages. Against such, the decree of the Justinianic Code spoke out: "Since some persons have been discovered given over to the error of the unholy and wicked pagans, performing acts that stir a loving God to just wrath, . . . who offer sacrifices to insensate idols in insane error and celebrate festivals replete with every impiety, even those persons who have already been judged worthy of holy baptism," let them now be killed.[150]

On such practices as have been indicated in these latter passages, there is Augustine explaining patiently to his congregation, "God doesn't wish to be worshiped along with those other [pagan deities], not even if he is worshiped a great deal more and those others a great deal less" (though one would have supposed the idea needed no explanation).[151] He recalls with reproach, "regarding the superstitious pagan celebration on Saint John's day, how Christians were going off to the sea to be baptized there," at a time when he himself was out of town—though the misguided folk of Hippo protested a little indignantly on his return that they wouldn't have done it if anyone had told them it was wrong. The day, in the old faith, had its old meaning which involved a ritual bath, and the Christian displacement of the pagan celebration had not fully taken hold.[152] In Gaul, Caesarius confronted the identical problem; and at other junctures in the year, other similar violations occurred, more or less innocently or at least ignorantly. Bishops of course couldn't see it that way. To them (Basil, Caesarius, east or west, early or late), whoever was under their charge and at the same time took part in ritual banquets of nonbelievers, as was entirely common—even if he made the sign of the cross on the meat he ate!—had committed a serious sin.[153]

The bishops might nevertheless hear the rejoinder, "Indeed I do visit idols, I consult inspired men and soothsayers, but I don't leave the church of God. I am a Catholic."[154] The remark from one of Augustine's congregation only illustrates the broader phenomenon just looked at: of the Christian who saw himself as such and was formally a member of the church while at the same time, or at least in certain moments, acting the part of someone faithful to the older gods.

His type is not easily distinguished from another, more suspect: the probable hypocrites. Augustine naturally knew of these, too. He describes their faith as merely nominal. Even in church, their hearts were still fixed on the old gods. As individuals, he says, they pretended what they did not feel in their search for promotion; they wanted the favor of more powerful persons who were Christian, or at least wanted not to offend them. Collectively, as a cadre or class in their community, they behaved in the same prudent way. So, for example, just in Augustine's day, at Kourion in Cyprus, the town senators eloquently thanked their richest citizen for his wonderful munificence toward the town, he a Christian but they subtly pagan still. The buildings he paid for were decorated with grateful inscriptions, roundly acknowledging Christ but at the same time hailing the benefactor as a new Phoebus, surrounded by quite traditional, that is, not specially Christian, personifications of Reverence, Temperance, and Obedience-to-Law.[155] Similar inscriptions and abstractions might be cited from Ephesus or Aphrodisias of the fifth or a later century.

With the civic leaders of Kourion my survey of assimilation has moved a great way up from the shepherds of the Euphrates valley to emblematic figures like Reverence. I close, now, with a very brief look at higher culture such as those Cypriote leaders thought suitable in compliment to their native son.

To begin with the world of letters: it was ruled by patrons. If patrons were Christians, who would remain a nonbeliever? There were conversions, of Nonnus, Kyros, Synesius;[156] converts became bishops; yet we might look for some retrospection—some hint of Persephone (or Lot's wife) in, for example, the verses of Ausonius. Christian literature in either learned language was permeated by the allusions, thought, symbolism, mythology, and esthetic of the pagan past, inevitably.[157] Inevitably, too, the pagan classics permeated the life and thought of the highly educated. Tags of Vergil or Homer could not be kept out of their very epitaphs, however Christian the deceased had been; they intruded on the dreams of ascetics in the desert, so we know from the famous confession of Jerome in the 370s.[158] In fear of such contamination of the mind, the bishops tried, without much success, to displace the older canon with truly Christian equivalents, to banish nonbelievers from the school- and lecture room, and to forbid at least the clergy to read outside their faith.[159]

Similarly in the fine arts, the canon (as it may be called) intruded from the past into the indefinite future. It could hardly be excluded, serving as it did not only for decoration but as the very language in which the artist's ideas must be conveyed. Such symbols as the wreath, grapevine, or birds were thus granted a second life; on reliquaries, such animal forms as were traditionally apotropaic; such postures as the *orans* with upraised arms or the rider a-horse, for Coptic hero-saints; such figures as Endymion, enormously popular for a time in explanation of Jonah.[160] For depictions of Jesus, as for those of pagan gods, much imperial symbolism was borrowed, explaining the ball (orb, *globus*) held in the hand, the throne (for bishops as well), the little tent (baldachin) above the throne—except that the baldachin may have come to the emperors from the gods, and only thereafter to Christian art and ceremony.[161] There were symbolic gestures borrowed, too: proskynesis, for example.[162]

Finally, an illustration of the flow of art from pagan to Christian settings: a well-known horde of silver objects found on the Esquiline hill in Rome, dating to the later fourth century, with various dishes and various reliefs showing the ancestral deities of the city; also, a bridal casket showing on one of its panels Venus at her toilet surrounded by her Nereids, and in a conspicuous place the dedication to the nuptial pair, "Secundus and Projecta, may you live in Christ!"[163]

◆　◆　◆

Now, the third and last word of explanation: about the meaning and perceptual content of much that has been described—ceremony, gesture, symbol, terminology, myth, or allusion. Original in paganism, naturalized among Christians, perhaps all these things had lost whatever of religion once invested them. Otherwise they could not have persisted among Christians.[164] Their presence or toleration in the Christian community would then have nothing to do with religious history.

Let me extend the interpretation of this point offered near the beginning of this chapter. No one will disagree with the common sense of saying, there are things that are religious and things that aren't. But it is rare to find the least discussion given even by the most careful scholars to the question, how to define "religious."[165] Without that definition agreed upon, nothing can be classified. So, would attendance at divine services count? I might say yes only if it wasn't looked at as mere entertainment.[166] I would thereby imply my definition: "religious" means "invested with thoughts about the divine." It would be intent that counts. But I could never make any useful application of this, given our available information base. We cannot poll the past; and adequately self-revealing moments in our sources are too few to support much generalization about what any given act meant to the participant.

To determine what phenomena still should be counted as religious during the period in which they were taken up within the church, I can suggest only a resort once more to that useful word "spectrum." Some phenomena can be defined as inclining toward the unarguably, the most explicitly conscious, focus of thought on the supernatural; and that focus lies at the center of religion in common parlance; while others, toward the opposite extreme, verge on the "secular." And, when in doubt how history should interpret some instance, "the better practice tolerates contradictions."[167] There will be things both (or partly, or to some people) religious *and* secular; and the impossibility of being more precise must inevitably blur the edges of our picture of the past.

◆ 5 ◆

Summary

In the opening century or two of their existence as a religious community, Christians lacked a distinctive poetry, rhetoric, drama, architecture, painting, sculpture, music, or dance—all, arts serving the older faith richly. They lacked arts of play and celebration that other faiths enjoyed. They had almost no special language of gestures or symbols in which to express their feelings or their wishes to, or regarding, the divine, such as pagans had developed; nor were they sure just how to conceive or address most superhuman powers acknowledged in their world: the souls of their dead, heroes or holy men, angels or prophets, Abrasax or Solomon, to say nothing of the gods commonly so-called. Powers beyond the human that did not appall and stupefy by their greatness, Christians had none to turn to; but pagans did, and resorted to them constantly.

Some pagans responded to deep-felt impulses generated by reflection on the old big questions: how to understand fortune, death, cosmogony, or the spark of self. They took up a life of focused thought and self-denial in a temple or among a group of the like-minded, or solitarily. But Christians of such a temperament had not discovered how to meet their needs in a particularly Christian way. Their brothers and sisters of an opposite temperament, gregarious and joyful in worship, were equally ill served.

Nevertheless the church remained remarkably attractive to certain sorts of person and continued to grow in membership, in acceptance within surrounding communities, and in the breadth of its distribution across the empire. It even gained some measure of wealth. By the turn of the fourth century, it could claim a substantial minority of the population in the eastern provinces though only a small minority in the west. Thereafter, as it registers more clearly in our surviving sources, an estimate of its place becomes less uncertain. It constituted perhaps as much as a half of the population by A.D. 400. The figure is not likely to be far wrong; unlikely, then, that the far lower estimate for the church is wrong, either, at the moment when Constantine was converted; for rapid growth in the intervening period is quite evident. Constantine and his successors held out many new and effective inducements to join. In the course of the response, greater numbers but also a greater diversity of human types and temperaments were swept into the church and, along with them, a far greater diversity of demands and expectations. In consequence, the deficiencies noted just above began to be supplied from paganism, partly unopposed, partly against the leadership's wishes, but necessarily, because of the numbers of newer converts and the impossibility of entirely reeducating them.

The inducements to conversion were described in the first chapter, above, where the negative and the material appear most prominently. Their prominence only reflects what is to be found in the sources. As time went on into the sixth and later centuries, the negative gained in importance, at moments quite dramatically. Conversions were made, because they could only be made, through intimidation and physical force. So the authorities evidently judged. The level of resistance reflected Christianity's deficiencies. It could not successfully appeal to a wide range of religious preferences, however attractive it had been and continued to be to persons looking for other, different rewards in the exercise of their faith. Two hundred and fifty years after Constantine was converted and began the long campaign of official temple destruction and outlawry of non-Christian acts of worship—250 years after great buildings in the capital, great estates in the west and east alike, and great sums of cash and precious metals were first lavished on his coreligionists by the first Christian emperor—Justinian was still engaged in the war upon dissent. To this end he bent his armies and his treasury, his power to mutilate or crucify, exile or bankrupt, build and bribe. His general, Narses, assigned a regiment to the minutely careful smashing of offensive wall carvings in a temple which we happen to know about because it has been excavated and studied, while his agent in charge of the peaceable side of the effort, a certain John, was supplied with the equivalent of many months' wages to offer to each person willing to be to baptized. Eighty thousands were the harvest of John's efforts, as we happen to know because he very naturally boasted about them. Yet, where he had worked, into the eighth century, non-Christian acts continued to be reported, though rarely; beyond the reach of my study, they continued into the ninth and tenth centuries, at Harran in the old province of Osrhoene or at Giza at the point of the Nile Delta.[1] In these regions of course the Christian population had been very largely won over to Islam. In the west of the same later period, though new conquerors had brought in and supported their traditional faiths, yet the old worshipers remained, ever a thorn in the side of kings and bishops.

So much for my first chapter—and at its conclusion I make no attempt to determine when the thorn was finally removed, or when paganism had disappeared for good and the Grand Event which I set out to describe was over. In fact the event in some sense, I would say, never ended, at least not if the disappearance of paganism is what's in question.

The paradox explains itself in the way the persecution developed. In following its course in the least detail, the likely consequences emerge. Chief was the likelihood of needs no longer being satisfied; for the old means of satisfying them were denied or destroyed, and the equivalent in Christianity did not exist. Unlike the forms of expression developed by communities of Christians in the first century or two of their history, those developed by non-Christian communities had had a very long time indeed to incorporate the arts and pleasures of life into worship. In the worshiper's address to any immortal being—to the lord of the skies, or a divinized hero, even one's loved ones and ancestors—place could be found for the deepest thoughts and feelings, or the lightest, in awe-filled solitude, or among one's dearest neighbors, friends, and family. The remarkable diversity of cult-centered arts, activities, and psychological rewards, in the traditional forms, fills up my second chapter. All these, church leadership wished converts to surrender.

Many or most converts simply could not make so great a sacrifice. It could not and did not happen. Instead, in different degrees according to individual cases, they continued to satisfy their needs in worship in their traditional ways. Especially was this true of people who were not of the old elite and who did not live in cities. Together, these categories constituted eight- or nine-tenths of the empire's population.

At this point, some necessary explanations drawn from my third chapter. For reasons having nothing to do with the rise of Christianity, the habits of mind once characterizing the elite—the more intellectual, analytical, comparativist, and empiricist elements in ancient thought—lost favor. What was left were assumptions and views of natural phenomena that had always prevailed among people less widely traveled, less widely read, and less educated—elements of religious thought that Pliny, for example, or Plutarch, or Plotinus would once have rejected. In loose terms, the change in thought-habits among the elite may be assigned to the latter half of the third century. Less science, more superstition, one might call it, also in very loose terms. For an illustration: the sociocultural equivalent of Ambrose, but of the period before 250, would have explained hailstorms to you in natural terms; but after 250, whether Christian or pagan, high or low, such a person would have explained it in terms of supernatural agencies.

As a consequence of the change, the elite of the church (or of secular society, so far as that counted) opposed no barrier to the basic religious ideas of the masses, even from the poorest corners of town or the remotest villages. Elite and masses were in broad agreement about how the universe worked, though they put different names to the superhuman agencies at work in the world and preferred different forms of address to them. Across a broad front, then, the way lay open to the acceptance of novelties in rite and belief, as the church confronted the surge of new recruits and their needs.

It must not be forgotten, since both pagan and Christian spokesmen drew attention to the fact, that conversion under pressure was unlikely to reach very far down into the mind. Prudential considerations, to curry favor or gain a rich wife, or not to lose one's job or one's life, diminished the meaning of conversion. True, post-Constantine, everything encouraged a sense of triumph and conviction among the crowds attending church; but everything also encouraged hypocrisy.[2] In the nature of the case no one today can make any good guess at the depth or prevalence of the converts' inner feelings. Only, no one can doubt that loyalties and preferences, the conscious and the unthinking, expressed or not, still attached them to the old ways. The bishops certainly thought so and say so often enough in both eastern and western sermons.

The results of the surge of recruitment, as they are described in the fourth chapter, were not destructive of the church. Quite the reverse: a wonderfully dynamic phase in church history commenced in which the deficiencies outlined in the opening paragraphs above were largely made good. The initial and lifetime appeal of the new faith was enormously enhanced. Christianity became (as a salesman would say today) a "full-service" religion. Converts could find in it, because they brought in to it, a great variety of psychological rewards that had been important to them before, when they had addressed the divine within the pagan tradition.

Foremost was the cult offered to the immortal in humans, the everliving spark or spirit of the dead. Its beliefs and practices as they were to be found among most pagans in every region of the empire flowed into Christian communities and their cemeteries. The cult of the dead became equally widespread and flowed into and was gradually replaced by the cult of the specially honored heroes of the Christian history: the martyrs. Additionally, in due course, prayers, offerings, and thanks were offered by pagans and in due course by Christians to living or dead men (not women, at least for some centuries) whose habits of life expressed an extraordinary concentration on the divine—themselves "divine men" in the traditional Greek phrase, *theioi andres*, wonder-workers, who appeared to be addressing the divine and acting out its teachings in their every waking moment.

Martyrs, divine men, and certain angels together were "the saints." With certain prophets, their worship constituted the chief point of growth, drama, and interest in the church throughout the period of my study. It was, however, no more vital and significant than problematic; for nothing in it lacked obvious antecedents in pagan grave cult. Ecclesiastical authorities declared, while they deplored, the identity of the routines and their pagan character: the identity of feasting, drinking, singing, dancing, and staying up through the night; the identity of joyful, even abandoned spirit. Among strict Christians, of course, there should be nothing of a party mood in worship. The downturned mouth, the sorrowing, gabled eyebrows of Byzantine or medieval piety should replace the smiles of paganism (fig. 1)—should, if the bishops could persuade their congregations.[3] But they were not able.

The creed that was the true heart of the Christian community in the first century or two of its existence was retained untouched by the inflow of new members after Constantine. Church organization, too, showed no effects.[4] But in the ideas and rites just described a large area of new loyalties opened up. Augustine called the sum total of imported paganism among his congregation their "mother," while what he himself would teach them was "the father."[5] They must choose; or he hoped they would. But he could not make them do so. He conceded that they must be allowed some latitude in their manner of worship. At just about the same time, toward the beginning of the fifth century, Jerome made the same acknowledgment: better, worship of saints in the pagan manner than none at all.[6] He was speaking of saints'-cult festivities; but at other points in the calendar the banquets in the churches drew in even bishops. It was religion as a time of communal rejoicing and social intercourse acted out in the company of the divine that converts were used to and could not do without.

The same need forced the invention of many celebrations during the year, since Christians' attendance at events like the Kalends proved too much for the church leadership to control except by competition (and these indeed survived all too vigorously into the sixteenth century and later, west and east alike).[7] A twelfth-century Syrian bishop explained,

> The reason, then, why the fathers of the church moved the January 6th
> celebration [of Epiphany] to December 25th was this, they say: it was
> the custom of the pagans to celebrate on this same December 25th
> the birthday of the Sun, and they lit lights then to exalt the day, and
> invited and admitted the Christians to these rites. When, therefore, the
> teachers of the church saw that Christians inclined to this custom, figuring
> out a strategy, they set the celebration of the true Sunrise on this
> day, and ordered Epiphany to be celebrated on January 6th; and this
> usage they maintain to the present day along with the lighting of
> lights.[8]

By similar inventions other popular pagan celebrations were directly confronted with a Christian challenge. Saint John's day has been instanced, also the festival of Saint Peter's throne; or the Robigalia of April 25th, in protection of the crops against blight, perpetuated for the same ends on the same date under the title Laetania Maior. There are many other examples of the process. The church calendar was thus to some considerable degree amplified (though the names of the days of the week, to be called by plain numbers, were advertised in vain).[9] In the same way, the choice of where to build shrines for Christian worship was dictated by the location of the antecedent pagan ones. They must be challenged and resanctified, if not rather destroyed. A number of cases of this strategy are demonstrable, others boasted about, many scores probable.[10] It is really no wonder that so many worshipers who flocked to them should continue in their old habits of mind, the time and place so reminding them of traditions. Thus, for example, they brought their offerings because they had always done so. They inscribed the Chi-Rho on silver votive plaques of exactly the pagan sort, with the declaration, "Anicilla fulfilled the vow she had promised" (this, from a hoard found in Britain, saved no doubt from some martyrium). The worshipers' too traditional piety, the bishops hardly opposed—indeed, believed, approved and passed on the saying of Demetrios of Thessaloniki to a suppliant in a vision, "Don't you know that the saints are moved to their good offices the more, according to how long an offering," a grand, big candle as opposed to a small one, "works and is alight?"[11]

What Eusebius had ridiculed in pagan practice continued unchanged, except in the Powers addressed; *do ut des* went with prayers for counsel, prayers for miracles, and testimonial dedications. These latter also in the old fashion, hung up on the walls of a church or chapel, earned the bishops' approval but also condemnation (into the sixteenth century).[12] They have been accepted very long since. In due course holy images, also, first of Jesus and John the Baptist, then of other figures, and, by preference, paintings of saints and angels decorated the walls. Such representations had of course always been familiar in paganism but ecclesiastical authorities were divided about their desirability, as is well known. Gradually they became established. I assume but don't know how one might clearly trace a flow of religious usages from non-Christian to Christian images, their display, address, and parading in processions.

The superhuman beings who were appealed to in their churches or chapels responded through the age-old medium of nocturnal visions, granted in Asclepian or Isiac fashion to the suppliant who slept in their presence. The favor most in demand, by far, was the traditional one of healing, whether mental or physical; but prediction, advice in one's personal crises, or punishment of the wicked was also sought still in the old way. Divinity was still expected to catch and chastise the oath-breaker.[13]

In contrast, the bishops sought to direct the focus of prayer, indeed the focus of worship and belief overall, at the concerns of the immortal soul (always, of course, correctly understood). Foremost was the teaching that God himself and no one else granted salvation from Hell-fire; and this went unchallenged. Baptism taught it, sermons reinforced it. But, as it seemed, everything else was in the gift of saints, angels, and prophets—everything else, including those desirables in everyday life at which Eusebius had mocked or Augustine wagged a reproving finger.[14] Against this popular perception, indeed an occasional bishop might protest, while at the same time authenticating it in saints'-day paeans. A whole new area of address to the divine with attendant rites and rewards thus became established.

The language used toward superhuman Powers, whether precatory or apotropaic, borrowed from paganism: candles, for example, or bells, and the marking of objects used in address with special signs and letters, all but the cross a part of pagan tradition. A propitiating kiss bestowed on the doorpost of a temple was just as well given to a church; likewise the honorific bow in the direction of the rising sun, offered "partly in ignorance," says the pope, "partly in a pagan spirit" by worshipers pausing as they climbed the steps of Saint Peter's. The custom could still be observed in twentieth-century Greece.[15]

In turn, the language used by such Powers toward mortals continued in use unchanged—not simply visions and dreams familiar in every religion, nor the augurs and *haruspices* of ancient Roman style whose arts the civil authorities could not dispense with until the fifth century, but other forms of communication, too. Whom one first met as one stepped out the door, or where thunder was heard, how the flame flickered on the altar when incense was dropped on it, what children were heard to say at play, which page one turned to in revered (and readily accessible) texts, these and other chance events were known in the old traditions as intelligible signs communicated from above. The bishops generally consulted them; most or all of their flock did so as well.

In addition, because they were surrounded by superhuman beings of evil intent, Christians made use of various devices to protect themselves. These devices, all but signing with the cross, derived from non-Christian practices. Holy water and holy dust continued in use both to prevent and to cure afflictions of the body; likewise, the blood of holy persons or of persons cut off by violent or premature decease. Phylacteries were popular, little bags tied around the neck with spells inside them written on papyrus. These and other defensive or curative devices continued as a vital part of daily life.

Tempestarii or similar wonder-workers, male and female, who gave hope of protection against hail or drought, had their place on the ancient countryside, all the more important after resort to temples had been forbidden, because everyone's life—life itself—depended on the season. A church which had for so long had its essence in urban settings and whose spokesmen enjoyed the ease and position of Paulinus or Jerome might, just as it wished, forbid resort to *tempestarii* or wise women or spells; it might forbid precatory fillets tied to trees, or coins or little lamps or other offerings dropped into lakes and springs, in pagan fashion. Nevertheless, these suppliant messages continued to be directed to whatever Powers might be, by Christians as by pagans, regardless of warnings from the pulpit, because the realities of life demanded relief, and the teachings of the ecclesiastical directorate did not suffice to fill the demand. Hence, the abundant borrowings, or rather, the continuation, of ancient usages, made tolerable in large measure by the changes described in my third chapter. After some centuries, a part of these usages were reduced, a part reluctantly allowed, a part heartily embraced within official Christianity.

Official Christianity—the older, the urban, the bishop-directed—might be declared the whole, all that counted or deserved the name: a community with a creed, resembling as closely as possible the community sketched in the opening paragraphs, above, with all its deficiencies—a religious system, then, of a certain strict, narrow structure. The pagan system had a very different structure which events forced upon the church and so in good measure reshaped it. So runs the argument of this book. It requires, however, the defining of religion as something more than a creed; it requires a definition more in the style of pagans, or of anthropologists (though of the ancient bishops, too), rather than in the style of yesterday's historians.[16] One must go beyond the world of those who delivered sermons to those who seldom or never heard one or understood it. One must accept such people as having, nevertheless, full weight and meaning in history. One must acknowledge their religion to be what they thought and called it, Christianity—as much Christianity as anything Paulinus or Jerome preached at them, or even more, perhaps, since after all, the mass of any religious system can only consist of the masses.

On the edge of villages in western Cyprus where I have seen the fillets of prayer tied to the trees, I truly believe the people count, and are Christians, and fillets are therefore a part of Christianity (though banned by the Christian emperors more than seventeen centuries ago).[17] Perhaps in southern Italy

I could still see phylacteries hung about children's necks, certainly popular into the nineteenth century.[18] In the nineteenth century the inhabitants of Eleusis still attributed the fertility of their fields to Saint Demetra, hung garlands on her kanephoros statue, and lit lamps to her on festival days.[19] A female image of pagan times near a spring in Savoie, a mother-goddess-made-Saint-Mary, wrought miracles of healing attested from the seventeenth century, through the water that flowed first from her breasts and, then, when for decency's sake these were hammered off, from a pipe issuing at the image's base, into the second half of the twentieth century. Into the same century, from eastern and western churches, petitioners for health scratched a pinch of dust from the walls and drank it down in water, so as to carry healing to their bodies, just as had been done by the ailing in pagan and earlier Christian times.[20]

"Into the sixteenth century, the *herbarius* Bock declared the clergy to be greater practitioners of magic than the laity," in all the special rites required for the collection of simples—rites not greatly changed since Pliny's day in the western provinces; and into the nineteenth and twentieth century, animal sacrifices have continued on holy days and churchyard feasts and graveside lamps in the tradition of the Caristia in eastern provinces.[21] Also, certain burial customs.[22]

Dancing in churches persisted or still persists in the practices of Egypt, Spain, Germany, Switzerland, and France. It was described above.[23]

Enough of such a random miscellany, which I should, in my ignorance, leave to ethnographers. Yet it serves to support once more my chief point: that the grand event which I have tried to describe did not and could not conclude in any sort of a total eclipse or displacement of the past. The triumph of the church was one not of obliteration but of widening embrace and assimilation.

Notes

◆ ◆ ◆

Nothing said about the mentalities, behavior, norms, or proclivities of millions of people can be taken seriously without proofs proportionate to the size of the sample. One individual from the past, one single thing said or done, no matter how striking or evocative, can support no general truth. So, in the notes that follow, I have tried hard to supply enough material to match my broad themes and interpretations.

The abbreviations I use for primary sources as for secondary are current and conventional, or fuller and clearer; but I list below three of the most commonly recurring (others, convenient in the Liddell-Scott *Greek Lexicon* or the *Oxford Latin Dictionary*):

    PL and *PG:* the *Patrologiae cursus completus, series Latina* and *Graeca,* ed. J. B. Migne (Paris)

    MGH: Monumenta Germaniae Historica in several sections, e.g., *SRM* = *Scriptores Rerum Merovingiacorum* (Berlin, Weimar, etc.)

Chapter 1: Persecution

1 March 19, 399: Aug., *Civ. dei* 18.54, cf. Quodvultdeus, *Liber de promiss.* 3.38.41 (*PL* 51.834A).
2 Synod of Carthage in canon 58 of a. 401; Gibbon in the J. B. Bury edition, New York 1946, 1 p. 578.
3 Triumphant absurdities, e.g. *CT* 16.10.22 (423), "regulations . . . shall suppress any pagans who survive, although We now believe that there are none"; Theodoret., *Graec.*

affect. curat. 8 (*PG* 83.1033), "the shrines of their [the pagans'] gods were so utterly destroyed that neither the outline of their form survives nor do men today know the look of their altars"; Aug., *En. in ps.* 149.13, *mortuus est paganus*, in Thébert (1988) 283.

4 The fate of Origen is the most striking, perhaps: attacks on his views from the mid-fifth century raged fiercely and by the mid-sixth had "led to the loss of the major part of Origen's work in its original language," cf. H. Crouzel in the *Dictionnaire de spiritualité* s.v. "Origène" (1981) 957. For the official burning of heretical works from these later times, cf. Soc., *H. E.* 1.9 (*PG* 67.88C), Arian books, and *CT* 16.5.66.1 (Nestorian books in Constantinople, a. 435) with *CJ* 1.1.3.3 (a. 448); *CJ* 1.5.58 (Apollinarian books, a. 455); Zachariah's *Vita Severi*, Kugener (1903) 62f., 68f. (Beirut of the 490s); Victor Vitensis, *Hist. persecut. Afr. prov.* 3.10 (*CSEL* 7.76), non-Arian literature burnt; *Liber pont.* 51 (*MGH Gest. Pont. Rom.* 1 p. 116), Manichaean works destroyed in the 490s by papal order, in the piazza before S. Maria Maggiore, and again under Pope Symmachus (ibid. 53 p. 122, a. 498–514) and Hormisdas, ibid. 53 (a. 514-23); and Thurman (1968) 37, on burning and mutilation as criminal penalties under Justinian (with *CJ* 1.5.16.3 and *Nov. Just.* 42.1.2 on Manichaean and Nestorian texts).

5 To evidence in MacMullen (1984) 125 n. 15 on Celsus and Hierocles and at p. 164 n. 49 on Sibylline oracles, add Thurman loc. cit. on the campaign against the texts of Porphyry, which were targeted earlier also, cf. Soc., *H. E.* 1.9 of 325 (*PG* 67.85A) and *CJ* 1.1.3.1 (a. 448); also, unspecified pagan writings targeted in 529, Constantelos (1964) 375; again in a. 555 at Antioch, cf. *Vita S. Symeon. Iun.* 161, Ven (1962–70) 1 p. 144; and in 562 in the eastern capital, Malal. 18f. p. 491 Dindorf and Michael Syr., *Chron.* 9.33 = Chabot (1899–1910) 2.271, two episodes, one involving thousands of books in "Asia." Contrast the careful copying of accepted writings on the best materials, e.g. Hier., *De viris ill.* 113 (*PL* 23.707).

6 Euseb., *H. E.* 8.1; cf. Hier., *Chron.*, *PL* 27.497f., on the Arian bishops' doings in Antioch *quorum idcirco tempora non digessi, quod eos hostes potius Christi, quam episcopos iudicem.* I owe the reference to the kindness of Dr. C. Galvao-Sobrinho, who reminds me also of other much fuller examples of partisan distortion like the *Historia acephala*, the Coptic ecclesiastical history of Alexandria edited by T. Orlandi, and the suppressed Council of Antioch of 324/5, as discussed by H. Chadwick (1958) 293 and 298. On the erasing of the record of other church councils, see MacMullen (1984) 124 n. 15. The story continues down to saint and bishop Leo absent from the *New Catholic Encyclopedia* (1967), comparing *A Dictionary of Christian Biography, Literature, Sects and Doctrines*, eds. W. Smith and H. Wace 2 (1880) 480ff.

7 On Origen, see Euseb., *H. E.* 6.23.1f.; Nautin (1977) 49, 57–59; and Teitler (1985) 91, 180f.; on Augustine and others, ibid. 193, 196, 189 (Gaudentius), and passim; regarding Augustine's routinizing of the preservation of miracle stories, see Meer (1961) 544 on *Civ. dei* 22.8.20, and ibid. 132 on his ready duplicating of his own works to be sent to inquirers, *Ep.* 230.4; on his sermons copied, Zellinger (1933) 103 n. 42. The copyists might be nuns, p. 217, or deacons and readers, Teitler (1985) 108, 114, and passim. Further on dictating sermons in the fourth and fifth centuries, Gain (1985) 33; on Paulinus multiplying copies of Sulpicius Severus, Rousselle (1983) 29; and on the Syrian bishop Jacob of Serugh, Moss (1935) 88.

8 Lepelley (1979) 372, "n'a pas vécu dans une chrétienté," going on to say (373), "on ne trouve pas le moindre allusion au christianisme sur les multiples inscriptions qui évoquent la vie des cités"—which is not in conflict with the conclusion from a large cemetery near the edge of town that Christians were "truly woven into the fabric of urban society by the fifth century," Stevens (1995) 269. For the epitaph data, see fig. 3 in Galvao-Sobrinho (1995) 464, in the context of this whole remarkable essay, cf. figs. 4f. (Spain and Viennensis), pp. 463f., and below, chap. 4. n. 53.

9 Aug., *Sermo* 62.15 (*PL* 38.422); cf. canon 60 of the Synod of Carthage, in Joannou (1962a) 297, *illud etiam petendum* (from the emperors), *ut quoniam contra praecepta divina* (i.e. imperial decrees) *convivia multis in locis exercerentur, quae ab errore gentili attracta sunt, ita ut nunc a paganis christiani ad haec celebranda cogantur* [!—but the bishops must mean, by social pressure], *ex qua re temporibus christianorum imperatorum persecutio altera fieri occulte videatur: vetari talia iubeant*—and the appeal goes on to add a request for fines, and the notice that *etiam in natalibus beatissimorum martyrum per nonnullas civitates et in ipsis locis sacris talia committere non reformident* (the pagans). In the east, compare Basil, *Ep. canonica* 81, in Gain (1985) 243, protesting against Christians joining non-Christian feasts in temples, around a. 375.

10 For both non-Christian and Christian burials in the same cemetery, see for example Testini (1958) 306, in Phrygia; Rémondon (1952) 71f., Egyptian cemeteries of fifth to the eighth centuries; Albertini and Leschi (1932) 79, in Mauretania; Stevens (1995) 267ff. at Carthage in the fifth to the seventh centuries; Frantz (1988) 69, in Athens; and in a variety of western cities, Rome most familiarly, cf. Galvao-Sobrinho (1995) 443 n. 57.

11 For sources on Hypatia, see below, n. 47. For the mixing of faiths in the schools of Alexandria and Beirut (law), see Canivet (1989) 131, Roueché (1989) 85, or Whitby (1991) 121, drawing on Zacharia's *Vita Severi* for the 480s, or a little earlier, Livrea (1989) 29 on the pagan law professor there whose brother was a bishop; for pagans in Ambrose's audience and in a brother bishop's of north Italy, see MacMullen (1984) 22 and nn. 11f., and in Augustine's audience in the early fifth century, cf. Dolbeau (1991) 53, speculating whether they were there "out of curiosity of cultivated folk encountering a celebrated orator," or (I would say, quite impossibly) because he had stimulated their own peasants to pressure them into attending.

12 Much has been written about the effect of marriage on the growth of the church; virtually all that is supported by evidence tells us only about the highest aristocracy and pre-400—therefore of a limited significance for my purposes. Among studies of later periods, I notice only Sivan (1993) 84f., showing how certain women, by *not* marrying, might signalize their families among at least the highest aristocracy. For the less prominent, the decision of the Council of Arles (a. 314) had significance, threatening excommunication to younger Christians who married out of the faith, cf. Vogel (1952) 63 on can. 11, and MacMullen (1984) 136f. n. 31 on the mixed evidence of permissibility of cross-faith marriages through the fourth century.

13 I pause over this supposition about the church's increase because of such statements as I find in Brown (1981) 46, "Women had been [a] blank on the map of the classical city[!]. . . . By contrast, the Christian church, from an early time, had encouraged

women to take on a public role, in their own right, in relation to the poor: they gave alms in person"; Chuvin (1990) 47, "pagan cults were so deeply exclusive . . . Christianity claimed to break down barriers . . . [a] kind of universalism"; Cameron (1991) 202, on Christianity's unique ability "to work horizontally in society," overcoming barriers between classes servile and free, or any other; Salzman (1992) 454, with bibliography to show that "it is generally believed that . . . women were particularly attracted to Christianity"; Praet (1992–93) 46f., Christianity in contrast to paganism "open to men and women alike . . . [its] appeal especially to women"; H. Chadwick in McManners (1993) 69, "the egalitarianism by which aristocrats and their slaves shared in one and the same eucharist was extraordinary"; and Kreider (1995) 18, "Christianity made the least expected social groups articulate—women, slaves, people who had been discarded . . . social inclusivity and generosity"; or a nonspecialist, Stark (1996) 95, declaring "that Christianity was unusually appealing [to women] because within the Christian subculture women enjoyed far higher status than did women in the Greco-Roman world at large," a "fact" to which he then devotes a chapter of explanation. To correct these perceptions at any length might try readers' patience, but see below, chap. 2 n. 40.

14 Some of the passages showing snobbery are gathered in MacMullen (1990) 264f. and n. 29.

15 On Caesarius, see the *Vita* 1.25 in Klingshirn (1994) 158; Leo's decisions of *Ep.* 4.1 (*PL* 54.611A) in Klein (1991) 602, with context, 603ff. In rural settings exceptions had to be made for slaves to become church officers, even bishops, cf. Gain (1985) 61 and 65; yet more representative is the *Statuta ecclesiae antiqua* 11, in Munier (1960) 81, *Ut episcopus de loco ignobili . . . non transeat, nec quisquam inferioris ordinis clericus.* On obstinate pagans condemned to slavery and consigned as such to the church, see Charlemagne's law (*MGH Leg.* 2, 1.69 cap. 21) in Harmening (1979) 57; and more broadly on the church and slavery, MacMullen (1988) 145f. For slaves in pagan settings, see such evidence as Vogliano (1933) discusses, with odds and ends in MacMullen (1981). The epigraphic material is of course very rich.

16 Deaconesses in Geo. Alex., *Vita S. Joh. Chrys.* 56, in fifth-century Constantinople, cf. Halkin (1977) 233; N. Thierry (1977), Cappadocia in the sixth century; and Basil, *Ep.* 199.44 (*PG* 32.730B) and Gain (1985) 112 n. 211, Basil's deaconesses and his rules for them, with full bibliography; and a πρεσβυτίς in fourth-century Thera, Feissel (1977) 210, 212. Frend (1984) 429 and 469 very acutely notices that "at Cirta it is interesting that the church stocked far more female than male clothes and shoes" (on the text, see MacMullen and Lane [1992] 249). The disproportion I suppose might show that women of wealth were more likely to give their surplus to the poor than men, or felt more keenly for their sisters, or (less likely) that the stocks were drawn down by more indigent men than women. Lane Fox (1986) 309f., without indicating any source, takes up the items-numbers and turns them into a proof of women being correspondingly more numerous in the church, drawn into it principally by "the church's offered charity"; and Stark (1996) 98 quotes and believes this.

17 On Basil's and others' bans against female groups at martyria, see Février (1978) 1.2; women in the compound around St. Symeon's tomb, see Theodoret., *H. E.* 26.19, in Kötting (1950) 122; Conc. Laodicense can. 44 a. 343/381 in Hefele and Leclercq

(1907–52) 1, 2.995, "that women shall not come to the altar"; women are not to speak during the church service, can. 70 of the Council in Trullo, in Joannou (1962) 208; on the ban against teaching or preaching by women, Nürnberg (1988) 57 and 72; and as a reflection of the more severe Christians' view of women, the story presented for admiration, that the holy Jacob [d. 338] living near Nisibis was offended that the washerwomen working by his path didn't avert their gaze or veil their faces at his approach, and so by his curses he dried up their well and brought premature aging upon them. See Theodoret., *Hist. relig.* 1.4. On the ignoring of women in sermons, see (what any skimming will confirm) note 26 below.

18 A sampling of the evidence only: as priestesses of the imperial cult in their own right, see the possibilities in Kearsley (1986) 184ff. and at least one incontestable, 190; also Fishwick (1987–92) 2, 1.480 n. 35; Paus. 18.11f., priestess in charge of Athens' Artemis cult or (1.20.2f.) of Eileithyia at Elis; of a Dionysiac cult group, Vogliano (1933) and Nilsson (1988) 2.359; as orators at cult festivals or in charge of choruses, Nilsson (1945) 66f.; worshiping freely with men, in Pompeian frescoes or in the mix of votive inscriptions to e.g. Minerva in Piacenza, in Roda (1981) 248f.; an association solely of women for professional and cult purposes at Luna, Angeli Bertinelli (1990) 61 and passim, comparing other groups of priestesses in Rome and Saepinum, and a small number of cults in Rome open only to men or only to women, in Dorcey (1992) 124f.; Sosipatra teaching in Pergamon, in Eunap., *Vit. soph.* 469f. and on Hypatia, *Suidae lexicon* 166, ed. Adler 4.644, among other testimonies; Paus. 1.16.2f., Elis' womens' track meet and dances; 1.38.6, 3.10.7, 5.16.6f., womens' dances at Athens, Sparta, or Elis; or Nilsson (1988) 2.361f. on female choral dancing; on female deities beyond the obvious, note the Nymphae and Matres prominent in Gaul, e.g. in Lavagne (1992) 224 and passim or the goddess Sin at Carrhae, cf. Segal (1963) 202 ; for a woman zealous in many initiations, see e.g. the third-century Favonia Flacilla at Ephesus, in Nilsson (1988) 2.342.

19 BGU 1024 of late fourth century, cf. Poethke (1981) 459; translation based on Bagnall (1993) 197f.; and, indicating that the *hegemon* is not a Christian, notice that he invokes *philanthropia* in another case also, p. 5 of the text at line 15, and that on page 4 lines 13f. he exclaims, "By Zeus," νὴ Δία. For the response by the authorities, which were Christian, to extramarital sex, see Hier., *Ep.* 1.3–15 (*PL* 22.10ff.), noting the presence of church officials at 1.12f., and 147.4 (*PL* 22.197), where he offers no comment on the death penalty for women taken in adultery. Contrast with Jn 8.7 is a reminder that Christianity like other religions was dynamic and changed over the course of centuries.

20 Nicetus, *Letter to Clotsinda* (*CCSL* 117.421f.), in Hillgarth (1969) 79; Avitus Viennensis, *Ep.* 46 (*MGH AA* 6, 2.75), *vestrae subtilitatis acrimoniam schismatum sectatores . . . visi sunt obnumbratione velare.*

21 There is no better reminder of the frequency of this service than the *Statuta ecclesiae antiqua* 62 of the latter half of the fifth century in Gaul, *omni die exorcistae energumenis manus imponant,* cf. Munier (1960) 90. On the central and much advertised powers of Christian belief in exorcism, see MacMullen (1984) 27f., 112, and idem (1990) 135 n. 27.

22 For specific moments of conversion through healing, from Thrace down to Syria— those instances marked with an asterisk involving not only individuals but crowds of converts—see MacMullen (1984) 27f.; Dattrino (1987) 255–61 on Rufinus, *H. E.*

1.10f. and 2.6, noting this author's special fondness for healings as the instrument of conversion; *Athanas., *Vita Anton.* 70 (*PG* 26.941B—44A), Basil's *Vita Theclae* II 2 (*PG* 85.568f.), in Kötting (1950) 152, and Theodoret., *H. E.* 4.14 (*PG* 67.1157C), all these three being pre-400; post-400, *Geo. Alex., *Vita S. Joh. Chrys.* 59, in Halkin (1977) 237f.; Callinicus, *Vita S. Hypatii* 22.8—10 and 21; *Life and miracles of S. Thecla* 14, 17, and 18, in Dagron (1978) 90, 328, 336, and 340; apparently, Soz., *H. E.* 2.3 (*PG* 67. 940Cf.), and the *Narratio de miraculo a Michaelo patrato*, both in Rohland (1977) 87, 95f.; *Archippus, *Miracle of St. Michael at Colossae* 3, in Nau (1908) 549; *SS Cyri et Joannis miracula* 38f. (*PG* 87.3570f.), in Seiber (1977) 90; *Cosmae et Damiani vita* in Deubner (1907) 101—4, 113ff. (similar to Rupprecht [1935] 54f.), and 117f.; the cases of two Saracen sheikhs in *Cyril Scythopolitanus, *Vita Euthymii* 10.18 in Festugière (1961—64) 3, 1.71ff., and in Theodoret., *Hist. relig.* 16.16, in Trombley (1993—94) 2.171; and *Vita S. Symeon. iun.* 141 and 143, in Ven (1962—70) 1.130f. For healing miracles that convert in western areas, see *Paulin. Nol., *Carm.* 27.547—51, the crowds at St. Felix' tomb converted by *sanctorum opera in Christo . . . aperta; *Vita S. Severini* in Thompson (1982) 117; *Meyer (1904) 60, a text of the first half of the sixth century; *Greg. Turonensis, *De virtutibus S. Martini* 1.11, in Barlow (1950) 2f., a heretic cured and converted to orthodoxy with his people, where Isidore, *De viris ill.* 35 (*PL* 83.1100) seems to credit Martin of Braga with the conversion by making Martin's advent and the healing simultaneous; *Vita Amandi* 24 (*MGH SRM* 5.447), a blind woman cured and converted; Sulp. Severus, *Vita S. Martini* 5.2 (13.9) on the very great effect of miracles, though not only of healing, in conversions (of healing, e.g. 6.3 [19.2]); *Greg. Turonensis, *De passione et virtut. S. Iuliani* 5f., in Stancliffe (1979) 57f.; and Bede, *H. E.* *2.2 of ca. 600, and 2.9.

23 Origen, *Homil. in Sam.* 1.10, ed. Nautin (*SC* 328) 134, ca. a. 240 (with my thanks to A. Kreider for the reference). Hällström (1984) 22 sums up nicely, "It is hardly exaggerating to say that they [σημεῖα καὶ τέρατα] are *the* motive for belief among the *simpliciores*, or more exactly, among multitudes past and present." For Theodoret, see his *Hist. relig.* (*PG* 82.1292Bf.), going on to say that whoever doubts the miracles he will relate will doubt also those performed by Moses or Jesus; for he had his stories from none but eyewitnesses.

24 For the (conditional) finding of lost objects that leads to a conversion, see Callinicos, *Vita Hypatii* 40.27ff.; for raising the dead, see the *Vita Amandi* 14f. (*MGH SRM* 5.438f.), and *ubi hoc miraculum longe lateque divulgatum est, statim incolae regionis illius cursu celeri ad eum cucurrerunt, ut eos faceret christianos;* for exorcisms of bad weather conditions, Theodoret., *Hist. relig.* 28.1—5 in fifth-century Gabala in Syria, or Greg. Turonensis, *De passione et virtut. S. Juliani* 5ff. in Stancliffe (1979) 58; burning down of a temple by divine fire and conversion of its worshipers, Amélineau (1888—95) 1 pp. 116ff. (the later-fifth century *Panegyric on Macarius of Tkôou*); overthrow of an Egyptian temple, *Vie de Moïse* 2 (of the 560s?), Amélineau (1888—95) 4, 2.686ff., leading to the cessation of the cults in and around it; overthrow of an idol on a wagon, Greg. Turonensis, *Liber in gloria confess.* 76 (*MGH SRM* 1, 2.343); or, on "binding," see first *On Apollon* 26—29, in Festugière (1961—64) 4, 1 (*Enquête sur les moines d'Egypte*) pp. 54f. and *The Miracle of Saint Michael* 5 in Nau (1908) 552, with other, western examples in Paulinus Nolensis, *Carm.* 20.103ff.; Sulpicius Severus' *Life of S. Martin*, in Manselli (1975) 56; Greg. Turonensis,

Hist. Franc. 6.6; idem, *Liber in gloria confess.* 61 and 76 (*MGH SRM* 1, 2.334 and 343f.);
Excerpta ex collatione episcoporum coram regem Gundebaldo (*PL* 71.1154) on early sixth-century
miracles and their results; of about the same date, Iona, *Vita S. Vedastis* 7 (*MGH SRM*
3.411), at Arras, St. Wast's miracle brings *multi ad salutem*; and *Vita Walarici* 22 p. 169 in
Musset (1976) 141f.

25 The importance of word-of-mouth passing around of miracle stories is suggested in
MacMullen (1984) 40f. Of other, wordly, inducements to conversion, see below, at
nn. 78 and thereafter.

26 On the preacher's audience pre-400, see MacMullen (1989) 510 and passim, adding
Monaci Castagno (1987) 82f. and 87 on Origen; on Basil's audience, sometimes very
mixed socioeconomically in a backwater, cf. Greg. Nyss., *Explicatio apologetica in hexae-
meron* (*PG* 44.64f.) and Bernardi (1968) 49f., 336ff., noting the high degree of slave-
ownership and little concern for the poor or rustics; on Chrysostom, esp. Dekkers
(1980) 122f., the bishop particularly in Constantinople addressing only an elite; similarly, Chrysostom's *In Acta Apost. homil.* 18.4 (*PG* 60.146), *In Mt. homil.* 70/71.4 (*PG*
58.654 and 660), *In Ep. ad Rom. homil.* 17.4 (*PG* 60.569) and 112.6 (491f.), *Homil. in
Coloss.* (*PG* 62.349), *Homil. in Philipp.* 10 (*PG* 62.259), and Pasquato (1976) 230–34 on
the great wealth of Chrysostom's usual audience, but occasional huge mixed crowds
on festival days; on Augustine, Meer (1961) 135 citing *Sermo* 9.4.4, 51.5, 82.8.11, 132.4,
211.5.4, 224.2f., and other texts, leading him to suppose that "there were literally
slaves in every house"(!); post-400, *Vita S. Caesarii a discipulis scripta* (ed. Morin vol. 3),
that the saint "often" addressed his listeners on their duty to their slaves, confirmed
by Caesarius, *Sermo* 6.3 (*CCSL* 103 p. 32), addressing small landowners, *rustici*, but only
when he was on a tour of country churches, cf. Delage (1971) 319 n. 1 (and even so,
they have each their *villa* and vineyards, §§4ff., their *prandia luxuriosa quae nos occupant ad
vesperam*, §1, and can be expected to buy books or hire a reader of the Bible if themselves illiterate, §§2 and 8, pp. 31, 36); by exception, listeners include *pauperes* with
daily labor, 91.8, on which Gurevich (1988) 16 and passim builds a much mistaken
picture of the normal audience; whereas listeners own slaves in *Sermo* 12.60 p. 62,
13.66 p. 68, 34.141 p. 148, 41.174 p. 182, 47.203 p. 213, and 42.180 p. 188 (*concubinae*, with
43.182f. p. 191f. and 44.188 p. 196); and they can be appealed to for charity as *divites*
(25.107 p. 113, 27.113 p. 119, and 30.124 p. 130), they are landowners taking in their own
harvests (30.126 p. 131) while saying, quite against the evidence of their high living,
that they are poor (31.128 p. 134); a single reference to *artifices*, 76.3 p. 317; and they are
almost invariably addressed as males, *fratres* (in contrast to wives not present, 42.178
p. 186); Lemoine (1956) 259f., 279, on the Hierapolis audience of bishop Philoxenus
around the turn of the sixth century; and Severus of Antioch, *Homil.* 100, Guidi
(1929) 247f., and 105, Brière (1943) 652f. and 658, on the gold and jewels, power and
servants of his listeners.

27 The difficulty in following sermons of late antiquity will be painfully evident to
readers today, of course, and has (besides philological study of *clausulae* and the like)
received comment from contemporaries themselves, rarely—Greg. Nyss. loc. cit. in
the preceding note—or from modern scholars like Dekkers (1980) 120 on the eastern style, Klingshirn (1994) 81 on the western. A view like that of Cameron (1991) 8,

36, 39, and passim, is incomprehensible to me: that "It is true of Christianity (and one of its major strengths) that it was inclusive in a way in which pagan culture always remained elitist"; "Christian groups were open"; and its "discourse" was of a style "to address itself to all sections of the public."

28 Février (1983) 34 notes the segregation of rich burials in Rome of the third and fourth centuries.

29 Preaching to the unconverted in the fourth century is rarely attested, as by Vigilius, *Ep.* 1.1 (*PL* 13.550D), or at Edessa (if credible—see below on the city as a pagan stronghold), in Drijvers (1982) 39; post-400 more often, e.g., *Vita Amandi* 20 (*MGH SRM* 5.444), though with no success; south of Amiens in the 640s, Audeonius, *Vita S. Eligii* 19 (*PL* 87.553), with much success, noticed by Musset (1976) 141f. along with the *Vita Wandregiseli* 16 (*MGH SRM* 5.21); or Greg. Turonensis, *Liber in gloria confess.* 2 (*MGH SRM* 1, 2. 299). Other rare references to "preaching" (or "carrying the word," or the like), where there is no mention of success, I may omit.

30 On Martin (bishop from 556) and his *De correctione rusticorum* of ca. 573, see McKenna (1938) 84ff. and Barlow (1950) 2ff., 159ff. Compare Aug., *De cat. rud.* 6 (10), *si forte se divinitus admonitum vel territum esse responderit, ut fieret christianus* (in a work where Augustine suggests no other motives for conversion other than wordly advantage), or again, 25 (47), *fuge, ergo . . . illa tormenta* (while holding in mind the contrasting delights of heaven).

31 For example, Origen seeing fear as instrumental in bringing listeners to God, cf. Monaci Castagno (1987) 224f.; Zeno, *Tract.* 21 *de Ps. 100* 2 (*PL* 11. 460B), of the semi-faithful, neither *fideles* nor *infideles, multos Dei metus in ecclesia continet*, and passages in MacMullen (1984) 147 n. 13 from Max. Taur. and esp. Aug., *rarissime quippe accidit, imo vero numquam, ut quisquam veniat volens fieri Christianus, qui non sit aliquo timore Dei perculsus.*

32 For the sudden death of persons who oppose or challenge holy men, see a number of examples of the fourth and early fifth centuries in MacMullen (1980) 29 n. 25 and (1984) 146 n. 3, with others of later periods in Adnès and Canivet (1967) 61 (*PG* 82.1297Cff.) and 63 (1321–24 and elsewhere), Brown (1971) 88, and Trombley (1994) 158 with n. 20 on the holy Habib and Symeon Stylites; Callinicos, *Vita Hypatii* 43.16; Vesa, *Life of Shenute* 82 = Amélineau (1888–95) 1.44f. = Campagnano and Orlandi (1984) 158; the praise of St. Thecla in the *Vita*, she "who knows how to reward the virtuous and to punish the impious and those who do unholy things," in Dagron (1978) 364ff., with illustrations of her wrath in her *Thaumata* 29ff.; many examples of the punishments inflicted by western saints on the wicked, in Gurevich (1988) 46–49, adding Greg. Turonensis, *De gloria mart* 96 (*MGH SRM* 1, 2.103), on the death or disease awaiting anyone who cheats St. Sergius; and the similar powers of the image of St. Fides (Foy) at Conques, Bouillet (1897) 40f., 24, or Taralon (1978) 10.

33 Paulinus Nolensis, *Carm.* 28.60ff. and 148f., *hoc Felicis gratia nobis munere consuluit,* with the final outcome in 270ff. From the point of view of those who lost their homes, Paulinus' triumphant verses hardly qualify him as "perhaps the most beautiful personality among the great figures of the transition from the ancient world to the Christian world"—thus, N. K. Chadwick (1955) 88.

34 I have come across only one instance of such a competitive loyalty to cult, in Juv. 15.35ff., where he recounts a tale he had heard about two villages of Upper Egypt.

35 On toleration, see Tert., *Apol.* 24.5f. and *Ad Scap.* 2.2 (*nec religionis est cogere religionem*), Lact., *Inst. div.* 5.19.9ff. (*defendenda religio est non occidendo sed monendo, non saevitia sed patientia . . . nihil est tam voluntarium quam religio*, etc.) and 20.7ff., in Garnsey (1984) 14f. and Klein (1993) 137f., Klein adding Arnob. 2.65; declarations by Licinius and Constantine, and by Valentinian in his early reign, Garnsey (1984) 20 n. 44; Hilary, *Ad Constantium* 1.6, and Athanas. I p. 363B, in Lasaulx (1854) 100; Themist., *Orat.* 5.67f. and 70A, in a. 364, ibid. 21, Daly (1971) 73 and passim, and Harl (1990) 12; Liban., *Or.* 30, passim; Symm., *Rel.* 3.10 a. 384, "What does it matter by which wisdom each of us arrives at truth? It is not possible that only one road leads to so sublime a mystery"; and, very much out of step with his times and the church itself, Joh. Chrys., *De S. Babyla* 3 (*PG* 50.537), "it is unlawful, οὐδὲ θέμις, for Christians to compel conversion by force and violence, but rather by persuasion and argument." When Garnsey (1984) 25 rejects the statement that Romans were "completely tolerant, in heaven as on earth" (MacMullen [1981] 2), arguing that the gods they tolerated were those of conquered peoples whom they had made subject, he can only have in mind the early and middle years of the Republic, whereas I speak (ibid. p. xii) explicitly of the period after A.D. 125.

36 Aug., *Ep.* 91.3 (*PL* 33.314 a. 408/410), *verax . . . deus . . . deorum multorum falsorumque simulacra, et praedixit eversum iri, et praecepit everti*. And Augustine acts out his convictions with his declaration to his people, This "is what God wants, God commands, God proclaims!" (*Serm.* 24.6, *CCSL* 41.324f., in MacMullen [1984] 95).

37 P. Karmel, art reviewer in the *New York Times* of December 29, 1995, section C p. 26— no great advance over Dr. Johnson's saying, "The heathens were easily converted because they had nothing to give up" (April 15, 1778), and hardly different from Meer (1961) 44, "the whole of ancient cult was nothing but a vast growth upon what had been for centuries a stagnant pool"; the same again in Dodds (1965) 132, "one reason for the success of Christianity was simply the weakness and weariness of the opposition"; similarly in Piganiol (1972) 259, more diffusely in Burckhardt and Seeck quoted by Lucius (1908) 147f., in Cumont (1929) 38f., and in Nock's assessment in the *CAH* XII (1939) 449. For the denial of a material decline in the period crucial to the church's triumph, the fourth century, a phenomenon often thought to have underlain a religious or spiritual decline, see Thébert (1983) 103, very definite about Africa (the debate is now "closed"), and a more general treatment of prosperity in the entire eastern half of the empire in late antiquity in MacMullen (1988) 31–35.

38 Francis (1995) 144: "It was once fashionable to speak of second" [and, I would add, still more, third] "century paganism as a bankrupt religious system that had ceased to command the attention, much less the conviction, of the citizens of the empire. The explanation of the eventual triumph of Christianity was sought in a decrepit paganism riddled with contradictions and plagued with rising 'superstition' and 'oriental syncretism.'" On the special importance that Cumont and his followers attached to this latter phenomenon, see for example a relatively recent echo in Turcan (1972) 78, "les dieux orientaux ont préparé le terrain ou s'épanouit le christianisme"; still later, Praet (1992–93) 44 supporting the view of Case of 1923, that the oriental cults "still had the greatest survival value for satisfying the desires of the populace," and their best features had to be displaced directly by the church.

39 Harmening (1979) 38 combs out a rich selection of obloquy from the Latin Christian authors aimed at paganism, and at random one might add *foeditas flagitiosa et sacrilega* in Aug., *Ep.* 22, or *hostes dei* . . . , *culpa, peccatum, perfidia, obstinatio* in Greg. Magnus'
letter against the Sardinian pagans, Greg. I *Registrum* 1.23 (*MGH Epp.* 1.257f., 261).
Among Greek authors, at random, one might instance Evagr., *H. E.* 1.11 (*PG*
86.2452Bff.), centered on the (mostly sexual) deeds of Zeus and Aphrodite, the
shame, absurdity, and unnaturalness of them, παρὰ φύσιν, and the drunkenness of
Bacchus.

40 Firm. Mat., *De errore prof. relig.* 20.7, 28.6, 29.1f. (*ut severitas vestra . . . persequatur*). The
text was long a favorite to be quoted against paganism, e.g., at Conc. Tolet. XII can.
11 a. 681.

41 *Nov. Theod.* 3.8 a. 438 (trans. Pharr).

42 Joh. Chrys., *Epp.* 126 (*PG* 52.685f., a. 406) and 221 (733, a. 404), in the earlier letter
saying, "word has reached us that the evils in Phoenicia have revived again and the
pagans' rage has risen, with many monks beaten and some killed," and in in the latter, writing to a priest to express anxiety that the Phoenician church is understaffed;
and Aug., above, n. 36 and below, chap. 2 at n. 62.

43 My purposes don't require me to linger on the campaigns against Jews that heated up
over the course of the fourth century and thereafter. A start on the subject can be
found in Nicholls (1993) chap. 6, but I am surprised not to find something for specialists on the period ca. 350–700, using such pointers as may be found in C. Pharr's
translation of the *Theodosian Code*, the Index s.v. "Jews," Maraval (1985) 78, or Werner
(1976) 56 n. 30. For persecution of the Manichees, see Lieu (1992) 144–50 and 192ff.
(chap. 6).

44 For the mortalities, so far as they can be estimated, see MacMullen (1990) 156 and
267, adding for the fourth century *Liber pont.* 38, Hier., *Chron.* a . 378–79, Epiphan.,
Panarion 7.60.2.3 in Williams (1987–94) 2.630, and Paulin. Nol., *Vita Ambros.* 16.1; in
the fifth century, especially the third book of Victor Vitensis' *Hist. persecut. Afr. prov.*,
on the horrors perpetrated by the secular forces driven largely by the bishops; also,
Amélineau (1888–95) 1 pp. xixf. and 157 and the bloodshed in Alexandria over the
patriarchal throne a. 477 in Stein (1949) 22, to which add the fulminations against
no less than twenty heresies in *CT* 16.5.65 a. 428; in the sixth century, the *Liber pont.* 53
on lethal struggles over the papacy, Evagr., *H. E.* 4.35 (*PG* 86.2768); Stein (1949) 173;
the *Libellus monachorum ad Menam* in Maraval (1985) 176f., Kugener (1903) 341, 351, 353,
356, and 384, Nau (1897) 465, and Festugière (1961–64) vol. 3, 2 (*Les moines de Palestine*)
135, on alleged thousands of deaths in several incidents in Syria and Palestine; Greg.
Magn., *Dial.* 1.43 and 46 *exardescente zelo Christiani populi, igne crematus est* (a certain
monk); and several incidents of the eighth century in Rochow (1994) 61ff. McLynn
(1992) suggests no corrective to the causalty statistics in these encounters but would
minimalize the involvement of good Christians, who (as human beings, I agree) had
no more taste for violence than anyone else; violence was the work of outside agita-
tors, "professionals" (16, 36) and "specialists" (16), or it arose from unfortunate mis-
understandings among the authorities; and so forth.

45 On the *concordia* reigning among pagans—amazement, that *ecce illi multos deos falsos non*

divisi colunt—see Aug., *De utilitate ieiunii* 7.9 (*PL* 40.712), the title and text alike, and
8.10 (713), contrasting Christian divisions, along with his *Serm.* 47.28 (*PL* 38.314—
where he still insists on the designation "heretic"); remarks by Joh. Chrysostom and
Theodoret in MacMullen (1984) 160 with others by Basil and Gregory Nazianzenus
summarized in Gain (1985) 376; and from the other perspective, Celsus in Orig., *C.
Cels.* 3.10 and 12, Amm. 22.5.4, and other pagan observers quoted, ibid.

46 Almost in parentheses, Sulzberger (1925) 433 notes, "In 382 the persecution of the
pagans began (Gratian)," but thereafter, I think that Noethlichs (1986) on "Heidenverfolgung" constitutes my first encounter with any scholarly recognition of a pagan
persecution. For the two quotations, see Wilson (1983) 3 and R. M. Price (1993) 184,
who attributes the "absence of intense and continuous religious strife" to "a general
determination in Late Roman society to minimize the divisiveness of religious differences" (yes, by extermination).

47 On Hypatia, I omit problematical details from Soz., *H. E.* 7.13; Soc., *H. E.* 7.13ff.,
especially 7.15 (*PG* 67.768f.); Suidae *Lexicon* 166, ed. A. Adler (1935) 644ff.; and other
sources and modern titles all gathered by Gajeri (1992) 16–24; Trombley (1993–94)
1.33 mentioning the *parabalani*, where Nicephorus blames Cyril's personal force, cf.
Gajeri p. 17; and discussion of Hypatia at a level of learning above my reach by T. D.
Barnes in a book review, *CP* 90 (1995) 92f. Cyril's uncle and predecessor, Theophilus
(385–412), had been the victim of mob action, too, storming his palace, cf. Theod.
Trimithont., *Vita Joh. Chrysos.* 10 in Halkin (1977) 16; but the mob on this occasion
were monks. Again repeatedly in the sixth century monks are the agents of sectarian
battles in the east, cf. Festugière (1961–64) 3, 2 (*Les Moines de Palestine*) 118 n. 279. But I
am not concerned with internal church history.

48 Tert., *De fuga* 13, showing Christians registered *in matricibus beneficiariorum et curiosorum*,
along with barkeeps and minor criminals; for further violence involving Christians in
Alexandria in the mid-third century (?), cf. MacMullen (1984) 90 and n. 7; and, of
ca. 305, Concilium Illiberit. can. 3, *si quis idola fregerit*. . . .

49 Aug., *Serm.* 62.17 (*PL* 38.422), bidding people to await *potestas* and not to act *sine causa;*
the possibility of pagan court action similarly in *Ep.* 47.3 (*PL* 33.185), a. 398, *Et cum
templa, idola, luci, et si quid huiusmodi, data potestate, evertuntur . . .* , and *Ep.* 97.2 a. 408 (*PL*
33.358); earlier, Zeno Veron., *Tract.* 1.25.6.10 a. 360/380; and at a somewhat later date in
Egypt, where the great abbot Shenute is brought to book, *accusatus a gentilibus oppido-
rum Plevit et Sejmin coram duce Antinoopolos, qui et ipse gentilis erat, quod templa evertisset et idola
combussisset*, cf. Zoega (1810) 377.

50 *CT* 16.10.16 (a. 399), posted at Damascus regarding rural unrest; 16.10.24 (Constantinople, a. 423 = *CJ* 1.11.6), rebuking violence and pillage against pagans or Jews, even
if permitted by governors; and, regarding *parabalani, CT* 16.2.42.1 (Constantinople, a.
416), of which there is some anticipation, though not by name of the category of
clerics, in 9.40.16 (Mnyzus in Galatia, a. 398), and some relaxation in *CT* 16.2.43 a.
418, raising the total to 600.

51 *CT* 16.10.19.3 (Rome, 407/8; posted at Carthage) = *Sirm.* 12, use of the *ecclesiastica
manus* in collaboration with three *agentes in rebus*, which Fowden (1978) 53 and 56 takes
to be the beginning of authorization of bishops to act against paganism.

52 *CJ* 1.11.9 (Constantinople, post-472, probably Justinianic, so Bury and others) and 1.18.12, asking bishops to be on the lookout for any crimes against religion and to inform the provincial governors about them (or to inform against the governors, if they are slack); 1.4.22.1f. (a. 529) and 26, 1.5.12.22, 1.5.18.12, 3.2.4.6, and 9.4.6.9, all of Justinian, in Thurman (1968) 19f.

53 Conc. Tolet. XII, can. 11, with Deut. 17.2ff., in McKenna (1938) 129; earlier, Conc. Tolet. III (a. 589) can. 16, *ut episcopi cum iudicibus idola destruant....*

54 *CT* 16.3.1 (a. 390, to the PPO at Verona) and 2 (392, to the same official, the pagan Tatianus); *CJ* 1.3.26, esp. to keep monks out of Antioch, cf. Joannou (1972) 115; Ambros., *Ep.* 1[41].27 (*PL* 16.1120 = *CSEL* 82, 3.160), *monachi multa scelera faciunt;* and *CT* 9.40.16 (a. 398). Callinicos, *Vita Hypatii* 33, tells how Leontios (prefect of Constantinople a. 434–35) fled the city of Chalcedon in fear of threats from the local monks, who would not obey the bishop's wishes that they desist. For Basil's μοναχοὶ καὶ μονάζοντες mentioned along with other subordinates, some of whom he used as *chorepiscopi*, see Gain (1985) 35f., 65f. Monks had shown their defiance earlier when attempts were made (Hier., *Chron.* a. 378/9) to subject those at Nitria to military conscription, and they were cruelly beaten. But very long afterwards (by the Synod of Constantinople, a. 861, can. 9, Joannou [1962] 73) they had to be reminded themselves not to beat people they thought sinful; so the stick had changed hands (it may be seen literally, the monks μετὰ βάκλων, "with their staffs" ready for a confrontation in a church, John, *Vita Severi*, Kugener [1904] 363).

55 Geo. Alex., *Vita S. Joh. Chrysos.* 23, in Halkin (1977) 135.

56 E.g., Festugière loc. cit.; Amélineau (1888–95) 1 p. xvii, "moines-soldats."

57 *Apophthegmata patrum* (*PG* 65.200A) and Soc., *H. E.* 5.16, in Athanassiadi (1993) 14; and Soz., *H. E.* 6.34 (*PG* 67.1396Bf.), reporting that "excluding the city of Antioch and its environs, Coele Syria and Upper Syria were slowly converted to Christianity," though the monks in the process "were hated by the inhabitants of the countryside and plotted against, and had to endure outrage and blows from the pagans"; yet they succeeded in the end.

58 Trombley (1985) 337, in agreement with Liebeschuetz (1979) 18, citing Libanius but using him to contradict Sozomen: monks and ascetics were in fact successful around Antioch.

59 Theodoret., *Hist. relig.* 17.3 (*PG* 82.1420Cff.), the relief money fetched from Emesa, and the lack of a προστάτης = *patronus* carefully explained (1421A). For parallels to such actions of helpful intervention by ascetics, see for example Vesa, *Life of Shenute* 81, Campagnano and Orlandi (1984) 158; the *Vita S. Theodori* 149, Festugière (1970) 2.47ff., of the last quarter of the sixth century in Galatia; or further examples in MacMullen (1988) 248 n. 99, both eastern and western instances.

60 Brown (1971) argued that ascetics like Symeon Stylites "gained power in society" by the continual "hard business" (80f.; elsewhere often, "hard work") of a local Ombudsman's role (the term, p. 91). This view has received attentive reading, some favorable (e.g. Liebeschuetz [1979] 18, Cracco [1980] 375ff., or K. Mitchell [1987] 77 and 86 n. 1), some unfavorable (e.g., H. Chadwick [1981] 12, C. Pietri [1989] 19), or Treadgold (1994) 154 and passim, with a word of reply to Chadwick by Brown [1983]

12). He draws principally on Theodoret's *Historia religiosa;* a wider search might have led to a different result even by his own methods, perhaps more like the description of monks in Diehl (1901) 527–30.

61 In sub-Alpine country in the later fourth century, cf. MacMullen (1984) 113 and more fully Lizzi (1990) 169ff.

62 For comic presentation of bishops, martyrs, and liturgy on the stage in cities like Antioch from the third to the sixth century, referred to as not uncommon but with little detail, cf. Vogt (1931) 625f., 634ff., and Longosz (1993) passim, drawing on mostly eastern writers like Euseb., Greg. Naz., Joh. Chrys., Soc., and Theodoret., but also Augustine.

63 Audeonius, *Vita Eligii* 2.19 (*PL* 87.553f.), the speaker unnamed, the intransigents led by a certain Herchenoaldus, *eo tempore praepositus palatii.* Only Vacandard (1899) 447 notices the passage.

64 Bar Hebraeus' Syriac *Chronicon* 168f., Budge (1932) 2.153, translated with deliberate literalness, though Budge has in Christian fashion capitalized the word "god." Tabith the scholar could boast of hundreds of titles of his writing, ibid. 152. As a religious man, he centered his veneration (doubtless) on ʿUzûz, cf. Brock (1983) 209 n. 20 and below, at n. 97.

65 Liban., *Or.* 30.7, 9, 15–18, and elsewhere; and above, nn. 40 (Augustine) and 47 (Shenute). For an indication of the personal nature of law enforcement, see Marinus, *Vita Procli* 29 in Frantz (1988) 70, remarking how, in the 470s, Proclus in Athens in his illicit worship was careful "not to afford any pretext to those wishing to plot against him." From the emperors' point of view, notice the explicit encouragement of the normal system in *CT* 16.10.12.1 a. 392, "[every idolater] shall be reported by an accusation which is permitted to all persons and he shall receive the appropriate sentence."

66 I agree with Bradbury (1994) 137, that "civil officials [in the fourth century] almost never initiated the coercion of pagans," preferring to wait for a lead from bishops; but against the one instance he offers in support, there are a few more that constitute exceptions, most notably the praetorian prefect Cynegius in the east (Zos. 4.37.4, with other sources), but also the Master of the Horse Lupicinus in the 360s with other unnamed officials, τινὲς τῶν ἀρχόντων ζηλωταί, in Epiphan., *Haer.* 80.2 (*PG* 42.757Bf. = *GCS* 37.487), with *PLRE* I s.v. "Flavius Lupicinus" and *Dictionnaire de spiritualité* 10 (1980) s.v. "Messaliens." After the fourth century instances occur also: *CT* 16.10.24 (a. 423), cited above, note 48, and *Nov. Maj.* 4.1 (a. 458), rebuking the Roman prefect's staff for licensing the unlawful destruction of temples. The correct, lawful way is outlined in *CT* 16.10.18 (to the procos. Africae, a. 399), routed through the governor's office. For individual bishops applying directly to the throne, see for example John of Ephesus in the eastern half of the later empire, *H. E.* 353f., ed. Brooks, in Constantelos (1964) 378.

67 In the western half it would be a king who passed the law, e.g. Clovis or Egica, cf. *Lex Visigothorum,* Suppl. p. 481, in McKenna (1938) 132, of the late sixth century; Queen Brunigild, appealed to for help in disciplining the paganism of her subjects, Greg. Magn., *Registrum* 8.4 (*MGH Epp.* 2.7, a. 597); the urgings in that direction by

Chararic in Spain, an Arian of the mid-sixth century in Greg. Turonensis, *De vir-tutibus S. Martini* 1.11, with Isid. *De viris ill.* 35 (*PL* 83.1100), in Barlow (1950) 2f.; Childe-bert I, *Praeceptum* (*MGH Leg.* 2, 1.2); or Dagobert, *Vita Amandi* 13 (*MGH SRM* 5.436f.) of the second half of the seventh century. On the most familiar case, Clovis of a. 496 or (I would say) 506, see Greg. Turonensis, *Hist. Franc.* 2.21 (30)f., Hillgarth (1969) 73, Dierkens (1984) 9f. and idem (1985) 143, showing that the king's baptism by no means made his people Christian. But in the long run, conversion generally did come from the top down in the barbarian west, cf. Manselli (1982) 94 and Geary (1988) 168. For an eastern example, see Nau (1897) 475, concerning the conversion and mass baptism of the Herulian king and his nobles and army in 533.

68 I don't use the information offered in Mark the Deacon's *Life of Porphyry*, judging it suspect; contra, Trombley (1993–94) 2.261–63, 267f., characterizing P. Peeters' argu-ments against the authenticity of the biography as "pueril[!] and naive," "absolutely ignorant . . . remiss . . . misleading," "entirely frivolous," "summary fabrication," "blunder crassly," and "if Peeters were honest. . . ." Whatever the force of these words, which don't persuade me, Trombley does not address the arguments proposed in MacMullen (1984) 158 nor the contradictory evidence for a vital paganism in Gaza in the second quarter of the sixth century reflected in Choricius' descriptions, cf. Litsas (1982) 427ff. T. E. Barnes quoted in Saradi-Mendelovici (1990) 54 n. 74, and Dihle (1992) 331 n. 42, most recently accept a date for the Porphyry-*Life* post-534. As to how the power structure worked, see MacMullen (1988) 58–170 passim, with valuable pages by Cracco (1980) 361ff. and Bradbury (1994) 134ff.

69 Routine purchase of civil office and shakedowns for reimbursement are described in MacMullen (1988) 137–64; ibid. 164f. with notes, for similar practices in the church, adding Basil, *Ep.* 53 and 290, in S. Mitchell (1993) 71; can. 23 of the Council in Trullo a. 691 against priests charging for communion, in Joannou (1962) 154; or again, charg-ing for baptism, in can. 48 of the Conc. Iliberr. and Gelasius' *Ep.* 14 a. 494 to Italy and Sardinia, in Dölger (1932) 1 and 6, and can. 7 of the second Council of Braga a. 572, in Barlow (1950) 126, forbidden unless payment is offered *voluntarie* (!).

70 Haehling (1978) passim, where, e.g., the last certain pagan *procos. Asiae* dates to 383 (p. 119); *praef. Aeg.*, to 403/4 (p. 191); *mag. milit. Or.*, to 447/50 (p. 242); and so forth— noting (134f. and 418f., concerning provincial governors in the period 392–423) how pagans disappear from the eastern rolls long before they do from the western. Barnes (1995) makes much of Haehling's presenting *offices* filled by pagans or Christians, not individual *persons* who sometimes filled more than one office; but Haehling's is the right way, for the reason explained in my text. On the religion of officeholders stud-ied more recently, and not in conflict with Haehling, see Salzman (1992) 465f., 475 showing parity of representation, Christian and pagan in high offices, only after mid-century and not for good until the 370s. The mysterious and unimportant posi-tions of *archigerontes* and *dioicetae ergasiotanorum* in Alexandria were reserved to Chris-tians in 396 by *CJ* 1.4.5; but non-Christians were also banned from all imperial service by *CT* 16.10.21 a. 415, again by *Sirm.* 6 a. 425, and in 527 by *CJ* 1.5.12.4f. and 1.18.4, cf. Irmscher (1981) 684 with Theophan., *Chron.* 1.276 Classen = p. 180 de Boor and Malal. 18 p. 449 Dindorf, as pagans were barred also from practicing law, *CJ* 1.4.15 a.

468, and again by the Conc. in Trullo a. 691/2 can. 71—though notice that, in the principal resort of legal studies, Beirut, and at a time when this measure should have been fresh in people's minds, it was apparently unheard of! (the witness being the silence of Zach., *Vita Severi*, Kugener [1903] passim). The decree in *CJ* 1.4.19 a. 505 specified that *defensores civitatum* must be Christian, cf. Noethlichs (1986) 1169.

71 Hadot (1972) 85, "l'aristocratie romaine fut longtemps . . . le dernier bastion de la resistance païenne," with similar statements by many authors though in less authoritative publications.

72 Matthews (1975) 290; compare the reviving of old cult at another desperate time for the city, a. 537, in Procop., *Bell. Goth.* 1.25, in Gandolfo (1989) 889.

73 Aug., *Ep.* 50 (*PL* 33.191), the rabid pagan in *vestram curiam tenuit principatum;* 91 (*PL* 33.316, Calama a. 408/410, by the dating of *PLRE* 2 and Goldbacher in *CSEL* 58 p. 27); and 232.3 (*PL* 33.1026f., Madaura, a. 399/407, by Goldbacher's dating p. 62).

74 *Life and Miracles of S. Thecla*, Miracle no. 39 p. 394, in Dagron (1978) 90f., *PLRE* 2.583 and 633, and Whitby (1991) 120; the further references in Theodoret and Malalas.

75 Rouché (1989) 93f.; cf. discussion of the context, 92; and on Asclepiodotus, 88ff.; and on the second Asclepiodotus of Egypt, and various Aphrodisian pagan friends, including the Scholasticus Demochares, see Zach., *Vita Severi*, Kugener (1903) 39.

76 *Vita S. Amantii* 32ff. (*MGH AA* 4, 2.58, ca. 460s near Rodez); Salvian, *De gub. dei* 8.3 (*PL* 53.155), in Africa in the 440s cults are sustained by *potentissimi quique ac sublimissimi;* and Conc. Tolet. XVI a. 693 can. 2 (*PL* 84.538), threatening *sacerdotes aut iudices* who are sympathetic to pagan worship(ers) or slack against them.

77 On Clovis, see above, n. 67; on conversion of the king and at least "a great number of his nobles" among the Nobades in Upper Egypt toward the mid-sixth century, see Nautin (1967) 8; on conversions from the top down on the eastern frontier, see the references to the two sheiks, in n. 22, above.

78 *CT* 16.10.4. a. 352 according to Piganiol (1972) 88 n. 3, 16.10.10 a. 391 for the west and 16.10.11 to Egypt, threatening pagan governors and calling on their office staff to report them; likewise in 16.10.12.4 a. 392 and 16.10.13 a. 395, invoking also the help of western municipal senates and *defensores civitatum;* again, 16.10.19 a. 407, threatening western governors; *Sirm.* 12 a. 408 in Africa, railing at the lack of obedience among governors, staff, and municipal senates (*mala desidia iudicum . . . conniventia officiorum*), and *Sirm.* 14 a. 409, quoted in Pharr's translation. The series ends with *CJ* 1.11.7.2 a. 451, raising the fine for a governor's nonenforcement of the law against pagan practices to fifty pounds of gold.

79 Greg. Magnus, *Registrum* 5.38 (*MGH Epistulae* 1, 1.324f.), a. 595.

80 Aug., *Ep.* 93.26 (*PL* 33.334); 91.8 (*PL* 33.316, referring to *CT* 16.10.19.3 a. 407/8, so Goldbacher cit.); cf. his saying of pagans in response to the laws of 399, *a timore legum abscondunt,* Dolbeau (1991) 48, and, a little earlier, the consciousness of law in the admonitions of Max. Taur., *Serm.* 107.14f., in Lizzi (1990) 168.

81 *Nov. Theod.* 3.8 a. 438, emphasizing in contorted language the public, blatant character to pagan worship, and matching in its tone of total frustration the same emperor's outburst to his African deputy in *CT* 16.5.63 a. 425.

82 Instances above, in nn. 54 and 56. Perhaps most often noticed is the bishop Marcel-

lus, caught in what he thought was a safe reviewing stand for the temple destruction he had arranged, Theodoret., *H. E.* 5.21, and other sources in MacMullen (1984) 163; other examples at Alexandria at the Serapeum, in Soc., *H. E.* 5.16 and other sources; also at Sufes as reported by Augustine, *Ep.* 50 (*PL* 33.191 a. 399); in vague terminology, ἔβρυχον καὶ ἐμαίνοντο at Colossae in Lydia, *Miracles of Saint Michael* 3 in Nau (1908) 549; vague again, at Philae, perhaps violence only feared, in the Coptic *Lives of Coptic Monks* 6, Campagnano and Orlandi (1984) 82; in western settings, only in north Italy, above, n. 60. Post-400, we have in the west no more than threats of force, in Sulp. Sev., *Vita S. Mart.* 5.4 (15.1f.); in Egypt, the legendary account in the *Panegyric on Macarius of Tkôou*, Amélineau (1888–95) 1.xxvif. and 113; in Phoenicia, above, n. 42; and below, in the course of revolts under Justinian.

83 Troops assisted Marcellus in Syria and the destroyers of the Serapeum in Alexandria; temple destruction in 399 in Africa by two imperial commanders, Aug., *Civ. dei* 18.54 with other sources; at Carthage, Ursus destroys the Caelestis temple a. 421, Possidius, *Vita S. Aug.* 16 (*PL* 32.46) and Quodvultdeus, *Liber de promiss.* 3.38.44 (*PL* 51.835Af.), and *PLRE* 2 p. 1192; and at the pope's request for forced conversions in Italy (appealing a. 598 to the Terracina Count, Greg. Magn., *Registrum* 9.205 = *CCSL* 140.764 and *PLRE* 3.864), in Sicily a. 593 (appealing to the praetor, 3.59 = *CCSL* 140 p. 207), and in Sardinia, where the bishops and the Duke cooperate, Greg. Magn., *Ep.* 4.25 a. 594 in Rochow (1978) 251.

84 On Asclepiodotus (there were two of the name, this one not a native but an Alexandrian) see above, n. 75, and Stein (1949) 24; on Pamprepius, Stein (1949) 13, 23ff.; on Illous, besides these scholars, see also Rémondon (1952) 66, Jones (1963) 32, Haehling (1980) 92f., Noethlichs (1986) 1168, Chuvin (1990) 98f., Harl (1990) 22, Athanassiadi (1993) 19, and Trombley (1993–94) 2.72.

85 There is some indication of the pagans' number and feelings in Zacharias, *Vita Severi*, Kugener (1903) 40f. Haehling (1980) 85 and 88 notices three pagan coup attempts from the 360s up to Theodosius I (or, probably, Theodosius II), and so to ca. 450, with a fourth under Leo I (457–74).

86 *RE* 10A s.v. "Zenon" col. 190 (Lippold 1972); Haehling (1980) 93f., citing Suda s.v. "Horapollon" p. 253 Zintzen, Harl (1990) 22, Athanassiadi (1993) 19f., and *PLRE* 2.569f. s.v. "Horapollon 2." Among apostates of prominent Alexandrians at this time, notice Ammonius and Leontius, *PLRE* 2.670. The date of these events may best be placed in 484/5, after Illous' defeat but prior to the long siege of him in Isauria, as suggested by *PLRE* 2.630 s.v. "Isidorus."

87 Kugener (1903) 22–27, with the idol burning described below (students in Athens in the fourth and fifth centuries, for reasons unconnected with religion, were equally given to riots and beatings); on the Egyptian prefect of the time, see *PLRE* 2.394, s.v. "Entrechius 2."

88 Kugener (1903) 47, 55, 60–69, and 73. The removal of Severus to Beirut (489?) and Zacharias (490?) is examined in *PLRE* 2.1194f.

89 The quotation, from Procop., *Anec.* 13.7 ("beliefs", δόξα), by an author who knew him well. Justinian's reign is recognized as the "acme of persecution," Noethlichs (1986) 1169, cf. Bury (1923) 367. Cutting off of hands of "those sunk in terrible blasphemies," Malal. 18 p. 451; hands cut off or crucifixion (ἐφούρκισεν), ibid. 487 a.

555, cf. Stein (1949) 374 n. 2 for the date; "maltreating the bodies" of pagans, Procop., *Anec.* 11.31; castrating for pederasty, ibid. 11.34, the testicles of the victims paraded about the city, Michael Syr., *Chron.* 9.26 = Chabot (1899–1910) 2.221; suicides of pagan notables like Phocas, and disgraced burial, ibid. 9.24 = 2.207 and Nau (1897) 482; Rochow (1994) 61 extends the list of mutilations to heretics under Constantine V (flogging or torturing to death, cutting off noses, drowning in a sack, blinding, etc.); and, to end with, the undated *CJ* 1.11.10, that idolaters who once were Christian shall suffer capital punishment.

90 Esp. Nau (1897) 481f., on events of 546; Stein (1949) 370ff., Noethlichs (1986) 1170f., and Whitby (1991) 112, 116, 118; the quotation from Malal. 18 p. 449 Dindorf = Theophanes, *Chron.* 1.276 Classen = 1.180 de Boor.

91 Narses in 535/9 against Philae, in Procop., *Bell. Pers.* 1.19.36f. and Stein (1949) 300f.; the Zeus-Ammon temple at Augila, locus for ongoing sacrifices and cult, destroyed, Procop., *Aedif.* 6.2.15.

92 Procop., *Anec.* 11.21, Loeb trans., moving on to the Montani in Phrygia and the Samaritans in Palestine, reverting to the statement about "all the farmers" (11.27), and so on to 11.31 and the final quoted part, 11.32.

93 Joh. Ephes., *H. E.* 3.27–32, Brooks (1936) 114–21, mentioning many clergy among the pagans denounced at Edessa (§34), and bishops at Antioch and Alexandria as confederates in pagan worship (§29); the reading of the officials' acts, §33; Evagr., *H. E.* 5.18; Michael Syr., *Chron.* 10.12 = Chabot (1899–1910) 2.319; and *PLRE* 3.72f. s.v. "Anatolius 8," the city of this man's last service being Edessa, where he was also *vicarius.* Trombley (1994) 170–81 gives a rather full narrative of the Tiberian persecution.

94 Ibid. 3.28 and 34, pp. 115 and 123f.; 5.15; and Rochow (1978) 231f.

95 Victims of persecution (for "sorcery") executed in Constantinople in 583, *PLRE* 3 p. 974 s.v. "Paulinus"; ibid. 10 s.v. "Acindynus" and Brock (1983) 209, for the passage quoted from Michael, *Chron.*; Rochow (1978) 234ff., 243f.

96 Recognition of the strong pagan element in Harran in the mid-fifth century, with a crypto-pagan bishop in 536, in Schultze (1987–92) 1.401; mention of the community of "Greeks", Ἕλληνες, in the 740s, in Theoph., *Chron.* 1.657 = de Boor 426; Rochow (1978) 235ff. and Segal (1963) 18ff. on the surrender of the city to the Arabs in 639 and open sacrificing; ibid. and idem (1963a) 202, 211f., with *The Encyclopedia of Islam,* 2d ed., (1971) 3.228, on the bargain of ca. 830.

97 Brock (1983) 209 n. 20; Segal (1963) 21; on a different date for the grant of toleration, not 830 but 842/3, see Gutas (1988) 43.

98 Segal (1963) 18; idem (1963a) 204.

99 Ibid. 216 and 219; Gutas (1994) 4943 n. 3, and, quoted, idem (1988) 43 and 45; cf. Tabith quoted, above at n. 64.

Chapter 2: The Cost to the Persecuted

1 On "gods" and "demons" see, for example, MacMullen (1990) 132–35; on the pitfalls to interpretation see, for example, Bowersock (1972) 206, "No thinking man ever believed in the divinity of a living emperor," where the meaning of the word "divinity" is never considered. For entrance to the complicated debate about the conceptu-

alizing of the emperor by worshipers, see, for example, Fishwick (1991) 39 and (1992) 349, conceding that some people addressed living rulers as superhuman; to the same effect, less reluctantly, G. M. Rogers in a review, *JRS* 84 (1994) 247.

2 Suet., *Iul.* 85 *apud eam longo tempore sacrificare, vota suscipere* [*plebs Romana*], the very birth of the imperial cult; for the column and chariot scene, Bidez (1972) 28 = Philostorgius, *H. E.* 2.17, recording the accusation "that the Christians propitiate the idol, εἰκών, of Constantine with sacrifices and honor with illuminations and incense as a god and offer prayers for salvation" from all ills; further, Lasaulx (1854) 47 on the "wenig beachteten Nachrichten über die Porphyrsäule" in Theophanes, *Chron.* 1.41f., and the Philostorgius text, p. 49; Kitzinger (1954) 91f. and MacMullen (1986) 4 with notes; on the column alone, Leeb (1992) 14–17; and Aur. Vict., *De Caes.* 40.28, in Rome "there are" (note the tense, ca. a. 360) "many statues of gold or silver, and a priesthood of the family of Constantine established in Africa."

3 On proskynesis, MacMullen (1986) 5 and notes; on cult priests, Lepelley (1979) 1.317, 363, 364 and n. 149, finding thirteen instances of *flamines perpetui* post-383, unspecified ones into the fifth century, and the emperor's assumption in *CT* 16.5.52 a. 412 and later laws to 438, that such priests will be routinely elected; also MacMullen (1986) 14 n. 34 on a sixth-century *flamen perpetuus christianus*. The Councils of Elvira and Arles date respectively to 289/309 (best, 305) and 314; the Elviran the more often cited, and its penalties on holding imperial cult office are, perhaps rightly, minimized by Thébert (1988) 311. On Constantine's views of the cult, the key document is the Hispellum decree, on which much has been written, e.g. by Gascou (1967) 609, 648.

4 MacMullen (1986) 7ff. and Rodgers (1986) 71–96, on address to emperors as *deus* throughout the fourth century; Coripp., *In laudem Iustini* 2.129 (*MGH AA* 3.130), *cui* [*Iustino*] *subdita reges / colla parant, nomenque tremunt et numen adorant.*

5 Bonamente (1988) 134; Mango (1990) 59, "the memory of Constantine was the object of a posthumous cult" (with references); on Julian as *divus, CT* 5.13.3 a. 364 and *DE* s.v. "Iulianus" p. 208, adding the many milestones along the road from Gerasa to Philadelphia, inscribed Εἰς θεὸς εἶς Ἰουλιανός, cf. Sartre (1985) 106; on coins and inscriptions, MacMullen (1986) 12; and on the frieze, Miltner (1958) 104ff.

6 Joh. Chrys., *In S. Babyla, C. Iulianum* 7 (*PG* 50.544) of a. 382, contrasting times under Christian rulers when the facilities for the cult are disused and deteriorate.

7 Lact., *Div. inst.* 1.15.27f., demands, *quis enim tam demens, qui consensu et placito innumerabilium stultorum aperiri caelum mortuis arbitretur,* offering entrance then to *deus Iulius;* and Joh. Chrys. in the passage just cited going on to exult in the changed character of the cult ceremonies when Christians take over, seeing the ceremonies as not worship but purely unreligious celebration.

8 Mansi 8 p. 1083, in Peterson (1926) 157; earlier, *ita omnes credimus, sicut Leo ita credimus,* etc., at Chalcedon a. 451, or later hailing "Constantine the Great, the orthodox emperor, the savior of orthodoxy," a. 680, in *DACL* 1 (1907) 244 s.v. "Acclamation."

9 Scholars' estimates of the religious content of emperor worship will depend in part, naturally, on how familar they are with the corpus of evidence on paganism. For the ceremonies seen as indeed religious, see Rodgers (1986) 72 and 92f., for whom references to the emperors' *numen* are more than flattery and not merely honorific;

Thébert (1988) 340f., impatient of any attempt to exculpate Christian toleration of the cult as without religious meaning; also Fishwick (1994) 135, that for the Roman soldier "the *Divi* were . . . set unthinkingly on the same level as 'real' gods." Whether thinking makes religion more religious is a curious question.

10 Sidon. Apollin., *Carm* 7.102ff., *primae salutationes et fausta colloquia*, with further material on the connection with the emperor and civic loyalty gathered by Meslin (1970) 29, 52, 57, and 58 (where, with *CT* 16.10.17, as at p. 61 with *CT* 16.2.5, laws seem misapplied to his argument). For celebration of the festival in an eastern city in 378, see Eunap., *Vit. soph.* 481.

11 Liban., *Descriptiones* 5 Καλανδῶν Foerster VIII 472ff. and *Or.* 9 Foerster I 393f.; Bolognesi Recchi Franceschini (1995) 132; there indicating also Theod. Balsamon, *Canones*, on the Conc. in Trullo can. 62, which paints the scene (*PG* 137.728), summing it up as "rites according to some old customs," while Theodore (d. ante 1195) adds information on usages of his day, 728B–D; Meslin (1970) passim on the kalends celebrations, including (66) the limiting of the consuls' obligations to the costs for a single *venatio* and a single set of gladiatorial combats, by Justinian's law, *Nov. Just.* 105.1, cf. Gascou (1967) 650 on such combats in the west still in the fifth century; for *venationes* in the east in the fourth century, see Pasquato (1976) 64, and in the fifth likewise, in the days of Severus of Antioch, cf. his *Homil.* 76 in Brière (1919) 135, and other sources in Stein (1949) 79; ibid., for those still later; and masks and cross-dressing in Nilsson (1916–19) 84 on Asterios, *Kalend. homil.* (*PG* 40.221), ca. a. 400, and again in the "Spuria" of Joh. Chrys., *Sermo de pseudoprophetis* 7 (*PG* 59.561). On masks in parades, see Wissowa (1912) 449.

12 *CT* 16.10.3 (342), 8 (382), 17 (399); 12.1.145 (399).

13 Liban., *Or.* εἰς τὰς καλάνδας 1f., the festival "rendering honor to the gods themselves," Zeus included, and (§4) it is universally celebrated across the empire with (§6) drinking and Sybaritic tables and laughter; Joh. Chrys., *Homil. in kalendas* 1 (*PG* 48.954), where "the demons [gods] parade about the forum," and *Homil. de Lazaro* 1.1 (*PG* 48.963) on the dancing, music, and drinking at Antioch; Lydus, *De mens.* 4.2 p. 65 Wuensch, "even today in Philadelphia a vestige of antiquity is conserved," with the likenesses of Janus and Saturn displayed on the January kalends; and can. 62 of Conc. Trullanum, a. 691, in Joannou (1962) 198f., against kalends-dancing "under the names of those beings that pagans falsely call gods" with condemnation also of cross-dressing. For the west see Peter Chrysologus, *Sermo* 155 (*PL* 52.611), in 430/450 around Ravenna worshipers *qui se bestiis comparant, exaequarunt iumentis, aptaverunt pecudibus, daemonibus formaverunt*, and idem, *De pythonibus* (*PL* 65.27 = *Sermo* 155bis in *CCSL* 24.967f., ed. A. Olivar), *ecce tota daemonum pompa procedit, idolorum tota producitur officina . . . figurant Saturnum, faciunt Jovem, formant Herculem . . . Dianam . . . Vulcanum*, the attribution of this one-page sermon to the correct author made by Nilsson (1916–19) 82, Meslin (1970) 75 n. 1, Arbesmann (1979) 113, and Harmening (1979) 141; reference to the procession in Ambros., *De interpellatione Iob* 4[2].1.5 (*PL* 14.813 = *CSEL* 32, 1.271), *more vulgi, cervus adlusit*, condemnation of the behavior at the festival in Max. Taur., *Homil.* 16 (*PL* 57.257) and 103 (*PL* 57.491f.), and concern for the masquerade expressed in Gaul in Caesarius' sermons (13.5, *CCL* 103.67 and 193, *CCL* 104.782ff.) and in the

Conc. Autessiodurense a. 573/601 can. 1; in Italy in can. 7 of the Conc. Romanum a. 743 (*MGH Leg* 3, 2.15f.), cf. Homann (1965) 172 and Harmening (1979) 127; and Boniface's *scandalum*, *Ep*. 50 (*MGH Epp*. 3, 1.301; a. 742, ibid. p. 298). On the stag-headed worshipers, see Ambros., loc. cit. and, for Spain pre-392, Pacianus, *Paraen. ad poen.* (*PL* 13.1081), the bare mention of *cervulum facere*, and his lost *Cervulus* and its significance assessed, e.g. by Nilsson (1916−19) 72, Meslin (1970) 81, and Arbesmann (1979) 91; also Mart. Bracar., *De corr. rust.* 10 and 16 of a. 572; for Gaul, *Vita Eligii* 16 (*MGH SRM* 4.705), on the Kalends, *vetulae, cervuli, mensae super noctem, strenae, bibitiones* (drinks) *superfluae; Vita B. Hilari* 2 (*AA SS* Oct. 11 638), in Arbesmann 192, but not the *Vita S. Brioci* 2, in Plaine (1883) 162, *pace* Meslin (1970) 79, since the work is of the eleventh century, cf. *Bibliotheca sanctorum* 3 (1963) 534. Linking the stag-head with Cernunnus, see, among others, Arbesmann 117f. The relief of [C]ERNUNNOS is inventoried in Espérandieu (1907−28) 4.211, with Castor and Pollux and a third god on other sides; context, in Grenier (1931−60) 4.695, 697 fig. 211. On the use of masks in Roman festivals of earlier times, see Wissowa (1912) 449.

14 Robert (1940) 517; Malal. 12 p. 286 (p. 54 Stauffenberg) and 17 p. 417; Pasquato (1976); Trombley (1993−94) 2.84 n. 50; Macrob., *Sat.* 1.23.13.

15 That the festival rites were indeed seen as religious appears in, e.g., Peter Chrysologus, *De pythonibus* cit., *CCSL* 24.967, Caesarius, *Sermo* 13.5 (*CCL* 103.67), *paganorum profana observatio*, or again in 193.2 (*CCL* 104.784), *sacrilego ritu*, or Joh. Chrys., *Homil. de Lazaro* 1.1 (*PG* 48.963), ἑορτὴν σατανικήν, or *Homil. in kalendas* cit., *PG* 48.954, excoriating αἱ διαβολικαὶ παννυχίδες, and denying that wine drunk and high spirits will bring riches in the year to come. Notice Peter Chrysologus, *Sermo* 155 *De kalendis* 5, quoting the worshipers' excuse, *vota sunt haec iocorum*, and Ambros., *De Helia et ieiunio* 17.62 (*CSEL* 32.448f.), on toasts drunk to the good fortune of the rulers, the Christians' argument being that *haec vota ad deum pervenire iudicant, sicut ille qui calices ad sepulchra martyrum deferunt atque illic in vesperam bibunt; aliter se exaudire posse non credunt. O stultitia hominum, qui ebrietatem sacrificium putant.* So late as the mid-seventh century, in Eligius, *Vita S. Audueni* 2.16 (*MGH SRM* 4.705), the religious significance (= sacrilege) of jokes is recognized in the ban on "making heifer['s masks] or deer or jokes" on the kalends; repeated in the mid-eighth century by Pirmin, *Dicta* 22, against *iocus et lusa diabolica*, in Harmening (1979) 277.

16 Asterios, *Homil.* 4 *Ad kalendarum festum* (*PG* 40.216f.); Max. Taur., *Homil.* 103 (*PL* 57.492); Aug., *Sermo* 196.4, 197, and 198.1, in Meer (1961) 55; Caesarius, *Sermo* 192.3 (*CCSL* 104.781), *diabolicae strenae*, or 193.3 (p. 784); and Conc. Autess. can. 1 a. 578/85 in Pontal (1989) 293.

17 In the east, the latest in the series of councils to deal with the kalends, so far as I know, is that "in Trullo" (a. 691/2); the series in the west includes Orleans 541, Tours 567, Auxerre 578 [561/603] can. 1, Clichy 626/7, and others thereafter in Jonkers (1968) 52f.; various penitentials up to the tenth century, Harmening (1979) 135; and Regino of Prüm's *On Synodal Cases* of ca. 906 and Burchard of Worms' *Decretorum Collectarium* of 1007/1014, in Arbesmann (1979) 99.

18 On the Brumalia, see Crawford (1920), proposing a December date, 367f., tracing it to a. 743 in Rome, and, 370−83, into the tenth century, despite a much earlier ban,

i.e., Conc. Trullanum can. 62, cf. Rochow (1978a) 488, Bolognesi Recchi Franceschini (1995) 129, and Litsas (1982) 429 on the Gaza festival patronized by the local army commander of ca. 532/3.

19 For the solstice, Cumont (1920) 85ff., quoting a source of the second quarter of the sixth century in Syria, the source being Ephraem as cited in Epiphanius, *Panarion* 51.22 (*GCS* 31.284f., improving the *PG*-text), where the bishop speaks in the present tense of how, at this point of the sun's increase of light, "the chiefs of idolatry and deceivers . . . in many places on the very night of Epiphany celebrate a great festival"; on March 21st, Thomas Edess., *Tract. de nativitate* 10.61 of ca. 525, *ethnici adoratores elementorum, festum magnum hodie ubique quotannis celebrant*, in Carr (1898) 7.

20 The Trullo council, loc. cit., and Rochow, loc. cit., rites still attested in the fourteenth century.

21 Josh. Styl., *Chron.* 30f., pp. 20, 22, trans. W. Wright, on an unidentified festival; on the Maiouma, Trombley (1993–94) 1.73 and 2.55, attested in mid-fifth-century Caria, and in Constantinople in 770, Theophan., *Chron.* 452.25f., with tableaux inspired by Bacchus and Venus, though the object of the rites is unknown, cf. Pasquato (1976) 268 and Roueché (1989) 72; on the Brytae, Stein (1949) 81.

22 As exceptions, notice below at nn. 28 (Calama), 30 (Antioch), 83 (Aphaca), or Callinicos, *Vita Hypatii* 45.2, reporting how, around 430, throughout the region around Chalcedon "people kept the so-called 'Kalathos' to the horrible Artemis each year, over five days," or Joshua the Stylite, *Chron.* 27, 33, and 46 of a. 497/8 in Edessa, "that festival at which the heathen myths were recited," and a week of preparation at home and in the theater; in Egypt, notice the village and private festivals still celebrated in Shenoute's day, in Wipszycka (1988) 148.

23 The description of a. 942 in the *Muruj* of al-Mas'udi, Fr. trans. Barbier de Meynard and Courteille 2.364f., in Shboul (1979) 14, with Hermann (1959) 49 counting the crowds at one hundred thousand and showing how "ein zeitloser Brauch vorchristlicher Jahrhunderte weiterlebte" (as the birthday of Aion?).

24 E.g. Aug., *In ps.* 93.3, rebuking such terminology as "Mercury's day," instead of *quarta feria*, cf. more generally *DACL* 7.2738f. s.v. "Jours de la semaine," with evidence of Christian use nevertheless, e.g. on an epitaph ἡμέρα Ἀφροδίτης or Latin equivalents of the fourth to sixth century; *Liber pont.* 33 (*MGH Gesta Pont. Rom.* 1.46), pope Miltiades speaking against *quinta feria ieiunium . . . , quia eos dies pagani quasi sacrum ieiunium celebrabant;* Caesarius, *Serm.* 19.4 or 265 (*PL* 39.2240), with Klingshirn (1994) 234; or Conc. Narbonense a. 589 can. 15 (*CCSL* 148A.257) against the *execrabilis ritus de quinta feria, quod dicitur Iobis*, on which many Catholics do no work; and Harmening (1979) 155f.

25 Malal. in Roueché (1989) 72 on the Maiouma; Prudentius (d. 405), *Peristeph.* 10.160 on the Cybele *lavatio* in Rome, in Hepding (1903) 172f.; the Saturnalia in the 430s, Marinone (1967) 23, 36; Lupercalia with rites to Faunus, in Gelasius, *Adv. Andromachum* (*PL* 59.111f., 114), cf. Beugnot (1835) 2.274, Schultze (1887–92) 1.417, Pomarès (1959) 21, 140f. and passim, and Pasquato (1976) 199; the Megalensia, in Matthews (1975) 242, end of fourth century; the Neptunalia condemned in the Ps.-Aug., *Homil. de sacrilegiis* 3 of the eighth century, in Harmening (1979) 147; the winter solstice, Aug., *Serm.* 190.1 and 196.4.4 (*PL* 38.1007, 1021), *de solemnitate superstitiosa pagana*; the Cybele cult day

on March 24th, Aug., *Tract. in Joh* 7.1 (*PL* 35.1440), cf. Labriolle (1934) 447; Council of Tours a. 567 ca. 23 (*CCSL* 148A.191), on feasting and dancing as part of the family rites of February 18th–22nd, cf. Pontal (1989) 161 and Février (1977) 516ff., 521f.; Vulcanalia in Paulin. Nol., *Carm.* 32.138f., Caesarius, *Serm.* 192, and Pirminus, *Dicta.* 22 of the eighth century, in *RE Suppl.* 14 (1974) 957. Unidentified *dies festi* appear in Aug., *Ep.* 46 (*PL* 33.183) of a. 398, when sacrifices are offered to *simulacra* in the baths; the May kalends, in Gougaud (1914) 19, 21; the Spurcalia in February frowned on in the *Indiculus* 3 of a. 744 and the *sacra Mercurii vel Iovis,* ibid. 5 (*feriae,* §20), and the veneration to *simulacra quae per campos portant* (§28), in Dierkens (1984) 18ff., 22f.; the sacred vigil celebrating the summer solstice in southern Gaul, around June 24th, cf. Caesarius, *Serm.* 33.4 and Klingshirn (1994) 224f.; and the *dies idolorum* in Mart. Bracar., *De corr. rust.* 1, of ca. a. 573.

26 Examples of festival parade descriptions of 350–400 in Himerius ed. Colonna 194f., at Athens, in Trombley (1993–94) 1.19, who would find the custom past 410; Liban., *Or.* 8.538f. for Antioch and the area around; Heliodorus, *Aethiopica* 5.15, third/fourth century, Egypt, or more briefly but more surely of the date needed, Epiphanius, *Panarion* 4.31.22.9f.; Prudentius, *Peristeph.* 10.160ff.; Max. Tauron., *Serm.* 76; and Festugière (1961–64) 4, 1, *Enquête sur les moines d'Égypte* p. 54 = Greek text p. 56 §25. For baldachins sheltering and honoring images, as shown on third-century Syrian coins, see Collart and Coupel (1977) 86.

27 *CJ* 1.11.10, undated (Justinianic), that "some persons have been discovered given over to the error of the unholy and wicked pagans, performing acts that stir a loving God, φιλάνθρωπος, to just wrath, [who] offer sacrifice to insensate idols and celebrate festivals replete with every impiety, even those persons who have already been judged worthy of holy baptism," who henceforth shall be executed.

28 Aug., *Ep.* 91.8 (*PL* 33.316). Compare the shocked irritation of another bishop looking at another procession two generations earlier, Theodoret., *H. E.* 4.21 (*PG* 82.1184 = 4.24.2f., *GCS* 44.262), in Antioch, where "those enslaved to error celebrated their pagan mysteries . . . [and] Diasia [to Zeus], Dionysia, and festivals of Demeter were being conducted, not in secret, as in a devout realm, but right in the middle of the agora the bacchants paraded about."

29 Robert (1960) 120ff.

30 For the belief that the city is endangered by neglect of sacrifices, see the arguments of Christians themselves in the western capital rebuked by the pope in his letter to Andromachus, cited above n. 23 (§§3 and 29); toward the mid-sixth century, Symeon Stylites rebuking the pagans of Antioch "because of the wicked things they do, laying tables and libations and sacrifices to the demons in the name of the good fortune of the city, προφάσει τύχης τῆς πόλεως," in Ven (1962–70) 1.50 §57.

31 On scenes of what I call deluxe worship, see for a sampling Dölger (1964) 72, "blood sacrifices requiring a big altar and large expenditure . . . were reserved for major acts of official worship at temples," MacMullen (1981) 25–29, Quet (1981) 50, on Epaminondas and Dio Chrys., Schmitt-Pantel (1981) 85, 88, and Menander Rhet., *Epideiktikon* 1 p. 362, 2 p. 444, in Russell and Wilson (1981) 64, 220.

32 The best path through contradictory evidence is picked out by Bradbury (1994) pas-

sim, on Constantine's and Constantius' laws; but controversy goes on, cf. Lepelley (1994) 71, "the law of Constans of 341 prohibiting sacrifices," which is wrongly attributed to Constantius, "surely concerned only private rituals looked on as magic." Violations = sacrifices attested include those in Rome in the *Expositio totius mundi* 55.26f., in Montero (1991) 91; in Zeno's world of north Italy, in his I *Tract.* 5.8f. (*PL* 11.309ff.); in Publicola's world, where the butchers sell meat left over from sacrifice, in Aug., *Ep.* 46 (*PL* 33.182), a. 398; in Cappadocia around 375, Basil, *Ep. canon.* 217.81; at Touron in Syria, Trombley (1993–94) 2.277; at Chalcedon, tolerated by the bishop in 434/5, Callinicos, *Vita Hypatii* 33.6f. (*SC* 177.217); in the smaller Syrian towns in the mid-fifth century, honoring Tammuz = Adonis, Kawkabta, and the local Gadde = Tyche, in Klugkist (1974) 355, 358f., though most of the passages concern rooftop gatherings on private homes; at Baalbek in 555, Michael Syr., *Chron.* 9.31 = Chabot (1899–1910) 2.263; at Edessa to Zeus-Haddad in the last quarter of the sixth century, cf. John of Ephesus, *Hist. eccl., pars tertia* 3.28 ed. Brooks 114; at the isolated great Ammon temple in the Pentapolis in Justinian's reign, Procop., *Aed.* 6.2.15, and at Heliopolis still later, cf. John of Ephesus in Nau (1897) 490f.; at Harran, above, chap. 1 at n. 97; among the Franks, and so beyond my reach, in Greg. Magn., *Registr.* 8.4 (*MGH Epp.* 2.7 = *CCSL* 140.521) of a. 597; and elsewhere in the northwestern empire, below, note 37. For Libanius' clear sense of what the law said and didn't say, see his *Or.* 30, rightly stressed by Trombley (1993–94) 1.8. The antisacrifice laws include *CT* 16.10.2 a. 341, 4 a. 352, 6 a. 356, 7 a. 381, 10 a. 391, 11 a. 391, 12 a. 392, 17 a. 399, and 18 a. 399; *CJ* 1.11.7 a. 451, and 1.11.10 undated.

33 Ael. Arist., *Or.* 8.54, Sarapis *kline* invitations, Plut., and Ambrose in MacMullen (1985–86) 80; general background on eating at shrines, MacMullen (1981) 36–42 and notes, with instances of kitchens built on to temple enclosures, in *DE* s.v. "Culina" (e.g., *CIL* 9.2629 or 13.3650), and, on perceptions of the feasts, Milik (1972) 72 on the dining group "whom the goddess assembles," cf. the summons by Zeus of Panamara to μετέχειν εὐφροσύνης and τῶι κοινῶι τῆς φιλανθρωπίας, in Roussel (1927) 128, 135, and Hatzfeld (1927) 77; Caesarius, *Serm.* 47, in Manselli (1982) 76, on the pagan belief that the best way to honor the divine is to drink heavily; the pagan theology of religious feasting, Dio Chrysostom's and others' later, up through Julian, in Quet (1981) 45, 47, with Nock (1944) 150ff., 167, and his conclusion, "the gods formed a constant background and, we may say, a consecration of conviviality"(154); and condemnation of overindulgence by various Greek writers up through Dio Chrysostom in Schmitt-Pantel (1981) 93f.

34 Perdrizet (1914) 266f., 270f., and Deonna (1919) passim, hundreds of stamps from Ostia, Pompeii, and other western sites (e.g., for the *epulum Iovis*), as well as many eastern, up into the fourth century, many of the pagan with the wish "Health!" while many others are Christian, with cross, explained by literary sources, Pompeian frescoes, etc.; *RAC* s.v. "Brotstempel" (F. Eckstein and T. Klauser, 1954) 630f., correcting Deonna; for the spoons and strainers, see Johns and Potter (1983) 48, 71ff., dozens of articles of the late fourth century from Britain for Faunus cult, inscribed VIVAS or DEO FAUNI(sic), etc., with the names of individual worshipers added.

35 Constantine, *Or. ad sanctos* 11.7 (*PG* 20.1264A).

36 Nilsson (1945) 64.

37 Veyne (1976) 243f. finds, in the establishing of rites for a certain heroized young citizen, "everything that constituted a cult in Greece: a procession, games, banquet, and sacrifice. . . . A cult of the gods or of the dead? Religion or evergetism? For the Hellenistic spirit, these two ambiguities did not exist"; and similarly, "It is argued," says S. R. F. Price (1980) 41, "that sacrifices became merely an excuse for a good dinner . . . [but it is] a mistake to think that all banquets at this period were secular in tone. . . . [It is] a false problem. Modern scholars [of whom he cites several] wrongly tend to divide what was a single Greek semantic field into two and to distinguish between religious and secular aspects. The Greeks did not do this." And he goes on to find the evergetic emphasis "compatible with the idea that sacrifices formed a system in which the relationship with the god remained important."

38 *CT* 16.10.19.3 = *Sirm.* 12, trans. Pharr, capping *CT* 16.10.10 (391) and 11 (391) which forbade entrance into temples for any reason (though in a context of antisacrifice law).

39 Above, note 31, for eastern examples; for western, see Caesarius, *Serm.* 54.6, meat for sacrifice shared by Christians; II Conc. Aurel. a. 533 can. 20 (*CCSL* 148A.102); IV Conc. Aurel. a. 541 can. 15 (ibid. p. 136); Conc. Tur. a. 567 can. 23 (p. 191); Conc. Clippiacense a. 626/7 can. 16 (p. 294); Conc. sub Sonnatio episcopo Remensi habitum a. 627/30 can. 14 (*MGH Concilia* 1. 204f.); Greg. Turon., *Liber in gloria confess.* 2 (*MGH SRM* 1, 2.299), *mactantes animalia et per triduum epulantes,* in southern France; idem, *Vitae patrum* 6.2 (*PL* 71.1031A), near Cologne in Theuderic's time (511–534), "there was a temple there filled with various adornments, where the barbarians used to make their first offerings and gorge themselves with meat and wine until they vomited"; and Charlemagne's law against anyone who *ad honorem daemonum comederet (MGH Legum* 2,1.69 §21), in Harmening (1979) 57, with other eighth-century sources, 61f.

40 Some general background in MacMullen (1981) 41f.; on later periods, Grenier (1931–60) 4.912–16, the site with coins of Arcadius; of the first century, north of Dijon, a shrine with bones of hundreds of whole pigs, sheep, goats, oxen, deer, etc., in Deyts (1983) 39, 64–66, 154; bullock horns as offerings, left over from feasts and holocausts at water shrines, in Bourgeois (1991–92) 1.183f, 187; destruction of the grand shrine at Argentomagus "no doubt the work of the Christians" of the next town, ibid. 2.72; other water shrines in use to end of fourth century or later, ibid. 2.164, 183; a site forty miles west of Paris in use to the end of the fourth century, with bones of thousands of (mostly) pigs and sheep, in Méniel (1992) 27, 93, 98; or in the Cotswolds in southern Britain, the site with "a quarter-million animal bones," the shrine destroyed soon after 380 with deliberate "desecration . . . impact of Christianity," in Ellison (1980) 312f., 318.

41 Liban., *Or.* 30.20, Loeb trans. with reference also to 2.30, "in the past [pre-380] there were sacrifices in plenty: the temples used to be full of worshippers, there was good cheer, music, songs, garlands, and the treasure in every one was a means of assistance to those in need." Compare, earlier, the homeless seeking shelter in temples throughout the east, Tac., *Ann.* 3.60–63 and 4.14, the distributions to the poor at Lagina, Hatzfeld (1920) 74, 89, and at Panamara, Laumonier (1958) 267, and holy Damian feeding the poor in Ephesus, Philostr., *Vit. soph.* 605; also Basil, *Homil. dicta tempore famis*

8 (*PG* 31.325A), "Let us feel shame at the tales of loving-kindness among non-Christians. Among some of them, there is a law of the sort enjoining a single table and food in common," evidently uniting groups of worshipers and the self-invited poor at temples. I am sorry not to have had access to J. M. Strubbe's article, "Armenzorg . . . ," *Tijdschrift voor Geschiednis* 107 (1994) 163–83. For lodgings in temple precincts, see merely as examples Grenier (1931–60) 4.613, 897, dating up to Arcadius, or, at Karanis, Bowman (1990) 171f.; and a resident sacristan, in Robert (1948) 22. I assume that *CT* 16.10.28 a. 415, ordering priests to return from Carthage and all other African cities to their townships, was meant to drain religious services from the provincial capital; but the law is puzzling. For festivals as commercial fairs, see MacMullen (1981) 25ff.

42 E.g., temples' paintings at Luxor for the imperial cult, in Monneret de Villard (1953) 85ff., 105; at Dura, MacMullen (1981) 80; first- to second-century literary mentions of paintings in a variety of other shrines, ibid. 30 with notes.

43 MacMullen (1981) 18–21 on temple theatres; Levine (1988) 14 on lampooned versions of Shakespeare; and chaps. 21 and 23 of *Huckleberry Finn*.

44 On dancing, MacMullen (1981) 21–24, and above, n. 25, on the kalends.

45 Various passages antidance from Latin authors in MacMullen (1990) 146; Cic., *De off.* 1.42.151, distinguishing between *res honestae* and *saltatores*; *Cat.* II 23, *Pis.* 8.18, Catiline *illa saltatrix*, *Pro Plancio* 87 and *Post reditu in sen. 13*, *saltator* as a term of abuse, *Pro Murena* 6.13, *nemo fere saltat sobrius nisi forte insanit*; Nepos, *Epaminondas 1*, *saltare etiam in vitiis poni*; Aelius Arist. in a lost oration against certain kinds of degenerate style of hair, costume, and steps among even Spartans of his day, and again in *Or.* 29, see Mesk (1908) 60ff.; Philostr., *Vita Apollini* 4.21, the holy man rebuking the intrusion of luxurious costumes and sexy steps and postures into Orphic dancing; Dio Chrysos., *Or.* 7.119, rebuking dance as self-indulgence "except for sacred dances," and even these, too, if expressive of gods' sufferings; further, *Or.* 32.4; and quoted, Lucian, *De saltat.* 79 (Loeb trans.), also (§34) rebuking the rustics' style after excessive feasting.

46 Henzen (1874) 26, *tripodaverunt*, and passim; Hor., *Od.* 2.12.17f., in Diana festivals; Ovid, *Fasti* 3.537f.; Isiac dancing in Italy, Tibullus 1.7.43, Wetter (1922) 256f., Hepding (1903) 88, 144, 159, 172f. (with Prudentius' lines), and Malaise (1974) 58f., 252f.

47 Hand clapping with dance widespread in the east, cf. Dölger (1934) 254f. and Stander (1993) 76; Paus. 1.16.2ff. and 5.16.6f., Hera cult with women's dance choruses in Elis; 1.38.6, in Attica for Demeter; 3.10.7, in Sparta for Artemis, and 3.12.10, for Apollo; for Artemis near Sardis, Strabo 13.4.5; Dionysiac dances in Lucian, *De salt.* 22, Dionysios the Periegete, *Geographi graeci minores* 2.102f. lines 102f., in Nilsson (1988) 2.362, and in Pergamon, Conze and Schuchhardt (1899) 179f., along with choruses; May-festival dancing and singing ("heathen tales," narrative songs) in late fifth-century Edessa, Joshua the Stylite, *Chron.* 33, in Drijvers (1982) 39, with Epiphanius, *Panarion* 51.22 (*GCS* 31.285) describing the Kore Night festival in Alexandria, earlier, and mention by Ephraem [d. 373], in Lucius (1908) 437 n. 5; in Egypt in the first century, Juv. 15.47ff., and, for dancers hired and still others reflected in the hiring also of musicians for Egyptian festivals, cf. Vandoni (1964) 31, 35; also, past mid-fourth century, *Life of Apollon 25* in Festugière (1961–64) 56, οἱ ἱερεῖς βακχεύοντες μετὰ τοῦ

πλήθους; in Syria, in Ephraem, cf. Quasten (1983) 175; and in Africa, in Calama, Aug., *Ep.* 91. Sources for religious music in the northwest quadrant of the empire are nearly nonexistent, but see the pan pipes in use in Gallic cults, Deyts (1994) 11.

48 McKenna (1938) 130, of mid-seventh century; Caesarius, *Serm.* 193 (*CCL* 104.783), *tam demens . . . incompositis motibus et impudicis carminibus;* Conc. Romanum a. 743 can. 9 (*MGH Leg.* 3, 2.15f.), on January 1st, *per vicos et per plateas cantationes et choros ducere;* Greg. Tur., *Liber in gloria confess.* 76 (*MGH SRM* 1, 2.343f.), *pro salvatione agrorum ac vinearum suarum misero gentilitatis more . . . cantantes et saltantes* (the date of Simplicius around 400?); and Audeonius, *Vita Eligii* 2.19 (*PL* 87.553f.), *nefandae saltationes,* and §16 (*MGH SRM* 4.706), *ballationes* and *saltationes* on the Kalends.

49 See the preceding note, and Himerius (between 360 and 390) in Trombley (1993–94) 1.19; Epiphanius, *Panarion* cit. at n. 46, above, and 4.31.22.9–11, in Williams (1987–94) 2.51; at the Roman Lupercalia of a. 495, *cantilenae turpes,* Gelasius, *Adv. Andromachum* 19 (*PL* 59.114A); as work songs, Nägele (1905) 127f.; at rites for "Diana" near Trier, Greg. Turon., *Hist. Franc.* 8.15; Menander Rhet., *Epideiktikon* 2 p. 444, ἡμεῖς δὲ ὕμνοις ἱλασκόμεθα, trans. Russell and Wilson (1981) 220, with the same thought also in other writers, see that model work of scholarship now in its English dress, Quasten (1983) 1; in earlier centuries, in eastern settings, Nilsson (1945) 68, Fernández Marcos (1975) 35–39, and Quasten (1983) 88, 122, 130 (at feasts), 131; on singing over the dead, ibid. 74, 86, 153, 162f., and 176 quoting the thirteenth-century Bar Hebraeus. For more relevant texts pre-400, including those on temple walls, see MacMullen (1981) 16ff.

50 *Re* Minerva at loom, Pirmin of Reichenau (d. 753), *Dicta* 22, *mulieres in tela sua Minervam nominare . . . cultura diaboli,* cf. Barlow (1950) 198 and Harmening (1979) 277; Petropoulos (1989) 161ff.; Conc. in Trullo a. 691/2 can. 62 (Mansi 11.971), Dionysus called upon at the winepress.

51 Malal. 12 p. 288 (reign of Commodus); further on hymnodes, MacMullen (1981) 149 and Nilsson (1945) 67, on "oratorical displays in honor of the gods, and it may not be inappropriate to call these sermons."

52 Praise of Dio Chrys., *Or.* 12, from the best of modern critics, Kennedy (1972) 577; a little further background in MacMullen (1981) 31; and notice also *Or.* 17 with its weaving together of Euripides and other canonical authors in praise of the divine.

53 On various aspects of religious education available in temples, see Robert (1940) 513, MacMullen (1981) 10ff., and, especially relevant, the lectures in theology offered by Antoninus, cf. Eunap., *Vit. soph.* 470f., and by Egyptian philosophers in temples, Horst (1984) 16f.

54 Quoted, Dio Chrys., *Or* 11.19, Homer αἰνιττόμενος καὶ μεταφέρων; compare, of Plutarch, particularly the *De Iside et Osiride;* of Lucian, *Deorum conc.* 10f. defending even Egyptian animal deities as αἰνίγματα; Chaeremon doing likewise, in his Frgs. 2, 15d, and 22c, Horst (1984) 10f., 26f., 36f.; of Porphyry, particularly the *Antr. Nymph.;* further, the old standard, Zeller (1880) 3.36, concluding that allegorizing was "the only means to rescue the people's faith," and so thought the Stoics; Pohlenz (1948) 235; Grant (1952) 64–71, with various passages better selected than interpreted; Buffière (1956) 37, 69f., and passim (though his huge book emerges only incompletely from

his note cards); MacMullen (1981) 8ff., 29f., 64f., and 74–79, especially 78 on
Menander and αἰνίγματα; Meredith (1985) 423f., emphasizing the part played by
the first-century Cornutus; Most (1989) 2018f., 2020, with whose rejection of Zeller
I disagree; Lamberton (1992) 120ff., drawing Proclus into the picture; and Dawson
(1992) 25, 42, 47, 58ff.

55 Aug., *Enarr. in ps.* 96.11 (*PL* 37.1244), quoted, Augustine concluding that "the learned
in their own eyes do not worship idols, yet they worship demons." Cf. again, *Ep.*
102.3, acknowledging while trying to explain veneration for idols; also, below, chap. 4
n. 154; and a number of exactly similar imagined exchanges between the bishop and
his idolatrous neighbors, in Dolbeau (1993) 89, 101 at §8.

56 Augustine, below, at n. 62; Athanag., *Apol.* 26, οἱ ταῦτα ἐνεργοῦντες, says this second-century author, not denying the real efficacy of the statues but attributing it to
the action of demons (the Alexander in question is the Homeric hero, not the con-
queror, while Neryllinus is unknown); compare Lucian, *Deor. cons.* 12, and Paus. 7.11.9,
mentioning two other heroes receiving cult and healing actively through their statues,
cited by Weinreich (1909) 142f.

57 MacMullen (1976) 35f. with notes; above, nn. 3ff. and 9, on the imperial cult.

58 On hero cults across the centuries, see Nock (1944) 143–46, where the object of cult
is sometimes called θεos (p. 163), cf. also Ramsay (1897) 2.384, and in his first volume, pp. 72f., discussing *CIG* 3936, the "heroine" so declared by the town assembly
and senate; also Theodoret., *Graec. affect. curat.* 8 (*PG* 83.1016B); on Ammias, Robert
(1937) 130, tomb with the usual funerary altar, inscribed; and, on the memorial habit
of heroization, the third- or fourth-century Phrygian epitaph to a bishop in Ramsay
(1897) 521 with the later and preferable dating, or Guarducci (1978) 386; heroizing of
the young, best known, Cicero's daughter but also Antinous, with scores of others,
mainly the Latin/Roman, in Wrede (1981) 158, 319 (Greek) and passim; add Cadoux
(1984) 56f., on the possibility of hero cults in Gaul, but of a date perhaps too early
for my purposes; Fonquerle (1973) 8, 12, on the hero of Agde near Marseille; Antinous receiving prayers, Dörner (1952) 40; and heroizing of gymnasium youths, Cremer (1991) 1.57f., 62, 118. On Apollonius see principally Philostratus' biography,
noticing his ascetic diet (§1.8, 1.20), advice on right liturgy (§3.41, 4.40), mediation of
political disputes and stasis (§1.15f., 4.7f., 5.20, cf. *Epp. Apollonii* 11 and 76f.), sermonizing on general ethics (§4.2, 4.7, 4.21), and miraculous powers such as exorcism and
healing (§3.38f., 4.10, 4.20, 4.55, 8.13, 8.31), on account of which he is worshiped as
divine and a temple is built to him (§8.13, θεσπέσιον, 8.15, θεῖον, 8.31, ἀθάνατος,
and a temple); yet, he says, heroes are looked on more as "fathers," gods as "lords"
(§4.31, δεσπόται). On Thracian and Thessalian hero cults of his time, see Philostr.,
Heroicus, healing, 147.1 p. 17 and 148.1f. p. 17; 148.5 p. 17, temple and 151.3f. p. 20,
games; averts plague, 149.1f. p. 18; unidentified boons and miracles, passim; and the
Hector statue at Ilium πολλὰ ἐργάζεται χρηστά, p. 20. For the date of the Philostratus text, a. 215/9, see Eitrem (1929) 1 and Solmsen in *RE* s.v. "Philostratos" (1941)
154. For hymns and sermons in hero liturgy, see passages from Paus., Plut., etc., in
Pfister (1909–12) 2.498.

59 For Phidias' Zeus, burnt either under Theod. II (408–50) or in Constantinople in

475, see the Lucian scholia to the *Rhet. praecept.*, ed. H. Rabe (1906) 175f., and Cedrenus cited in Richter (1929) 219. Libanius, *Or.* 30.21 and 42 pleads the case for beauty in worship. The Phidias Athena was destroyed "probably in 485," Trombley (1993–94) 1.82, 310 (but I suspect the date should be a decade or more earlier).

60 Above, chap. 1 n. 48; *Martyrium S. Theodoti* 8, in Franchi de' Cavalieri (1901) 66; Lasaulx (1854) 32, citing Euseb., *Vita Const.* 3.54 (*PG* 20.1117Af.), where Constantine destroys bronze idols, and *De laude Const.* and Soz., *H. E.* 2.5, where he confiscates and melts down those of precious metals; and under Julian, the iconoclastic incident in Phrygia, Soz., *H. E.* 5.11 (*PG* 67.1248).

61 Rufin., *H. E.* 2.23 (*PL* 21.531); the presence of the soldier explained by Julian, *Ep.* 60.379a, the official in charge "brought in the army against the holy city," and the element of deliberate outrage against Sarapis cult emphasized by Soc., *H. E.* 5.16, καθυβρίσαι τὰ τῶν Ἑλλήνων μυστήρια, and Soz., *H. E.* 7.15 in similar words.

62 Aug., *Ep.* 50 (*PL* 33.191), declaring God to have acted through the mob, and on a Sunday, and *Serm.* 24.6f. (*CCSL* 41.331f.), of 399 or more likely 401, cf. discussions cited in MacMullen (1984) 162 n. 27 and Markus (1990) 116f. On Augustine's fondness for the treatment accorded the holy image, see his recommendation that, as to the true nature of such, "we may interrogate your [pagans'] god with an axe," in Dolbeau (1993) 99 §4, a sermon of ca. 403/4.

63 Above, chap. 1 n. 1; Aug., *Ep.* 232.3, in Lepelley (1994) 6, the images in one city actually all burnt and broken in 400 or 401; Conc. Afr. a. 401, Mansi 3.766 = C. Munier pp. 196 §58, *ut reliquias idolorum per omnem Africam iubeant* [*imperatores*] *penitus amputari*, and 205 §84, repeating the demand; and the response, *CT* 16.10.19.1 a. 408, that all images, *simulacra*, receiving cult shall be destroyed. Exceptions (aside from those in rural areas, on which see below, at nn. 124–27) include the image at Heliopolis in Macrobius' time, *Sat.*, 1.23.13, the Asclepius in Athens, to ca. 480, Frantz (1988) 70, the images seized from Philae by Narses, Procop., *Bell pers.* 1.19.37; images in Palestine cities up to a. 543 in Michael Syr., *Chron.* 9.28 = Chabot (1899–1910) 2.239; images destroyed at Antioch ca. a. 555 by Justinian's commander, cf. Ven (1962–70) 1.144, with further references to the pagans in the city, pp. 67, 130, 163 (§§78, 141, and 184 of the *Life of St. Symeon*, a. 551f.); the images (perhaps only from private houses?) in Constantinople in 562, Malal. 491.18f.; other Syrian household idols of the sixth century, in Ven (1962–70) 1.168; the Egyptian priest together with his idols burnt up by Christian villagers in the second half of the fifth century, cf. the *Paneg. on Macarius of Tkôou* in Amélineau (1888–95) 1.118; and "acts of idolatry" in early-seventh-century Egypt, with various scattered kinds of evidence for a persistent pagan population in this period in Amélineau (1887) 4–6, idem (1888–95) 1.44f., 158 (Besa, *Life of Shenute* 81, 83, at Panopolis and Blevit near Achmin of the mid-fifth century), Rémondon (1952) 71f., and Rochow (1978) 242. Bagnall (1993) ignores this late evidence and more indicated below in n. 97, along with such other items as Geraci (1971) 77, 132, 196 and passim for the third to fourth centuries at Thebes and fifth century at Philae, while he also minimizes (pp. 267–81 passim) other parts of the evidence, thus giving an unconvincing picture of the religious balance in the Nile valley. Further criticisms in Wipszycka (1988) 121f., 164f. Bowersock (1990) 37 asserts "the vigor of Syriac paganism

at the beginning of the sixth century," with undisturbed idolatry, on the basis of Jacob of Serûg's testimony, but in fact the source puts all the description in the past tense and sets it in time before the Crucifixion. See Martin (1875) 130–35, 138f., and Cramer (1980) 97f., who, however, rightly accepts (99 n. 17) "numerous [other] testimonies to the survival of pagan religion and practices into the sixth century."

64 Guarducci (1978) 400f.; on evidence of violent destruction of pagan edifices, see below, n. 124.

65 *CIL* 9.3375 a. 156 = Buecheler, *Carmina epigraphica* 1.118f., noticing the phrase from *Aen.* 9.157f.; a sampling of dedications of the same sort in MacMullen (1981) 31; Bakker (1994) 145 on a Silvanus portrayal "EX VISU" on the wall of an Ostian house; and one instance from hundreds of famous, canonical portrayals of a deity being replicated and fixed in the worshipers' minds far away in time and space, in Rossi (1992) 380, Phidias' Athena Hygia reappearing in a first- to fourth- century site near Brescia.

66 In Constantinople, evidence for Constantine's salvage work gathered by Mango (1963) 56f. and idem (1990) 58, declaring (I think mistakenly) that the emperor entertained pagan feelings toward the images, though they were indeed held sacred by some; on salvage in Italy, Lepelley (1992) 364ff., adducing inscriptions of the 370s forward from Africa and Italy (Verona etc.), and laws such as *CT* 16.10.15, 18, and 19 a. 399–407 and *Nov. Maj.* 4.1 a. 458; Trombley (1993–94) 1.82, on the survival of Phidias' Athena in Athens until perhaps the early 480s; further, Lepelley (1994) 6 and Saradi-Mendelovici (1990) 50.

67 *CT* 16.10.25, issued from the eastern capital and demanding action from city senates.

68 *CT* 16.10.19.2 declares, "the temples which are in cities or towns or outside the towns shall be vindicated to public use. Altars shall be destroyed in all places, and all temples situated on Our landholdings shall be transferred to suitable uses. The proprietors shall be compelled to destroy them." On the Athenian Asclepius temple violently demolished between 450 and 485, see Gregory (1986) 238; on Philae, cf. Nautin (1967) 25, comparing (6f.) a number of other uses of soldiers as wreckers; and add Geo. Alex., *Vita S. Joh. Chrysos.* 23, the bishop raises money to hire a gang of skilled and unskilled workmen for the destruction of shrines in Phoenicia; also Deichmann (1939) 108f., 110f., on the laboriously thorough demolition of temples to their very foundations at various sites in Syria, Palestine, and Egypt, regardless of expense—or sometimes responsive to cost limits. For the natural deterioration of temples, see e.g. Soc., *H. E.* 3.2, Soz., *H. E.* 2.5, Hier., *Ep.* 107.1 (*PL* 22.868) and *Adv. Iovin.* 2.38 (*PL* 23.352), or Zon. 13.12.30f.

69 Rufinus, *H. E.* 2.28, of course greatly exaggerating.

70 Quodvultdeus, *Liber de promiss.* 3.38.44 (*PL* 51.835A–C); Possidius, *Vita S. Augustini* 16 (*PL* 32.46); and *PLRE* 2.1192, the imperial procurator Ursus dated to ca. 421. "Aurelius" (the appearance of the name *mirum quoddam et incredibile*, Quodvultdeus says) was of course the most common of names in Antonine times. Bishop 392–429, he was a leader in persecution, cf. Joannou (1962a) 190, 295.

71 Devoted attendance at temples, e.g. *Didascalia Apost.* 13 (Syria, mid-third century?), cf. Philostr., *Heroicus* 148.5 p. 17, and the need for crowd control at the Apollo temple in Magnesia, where worshipers' names were taken in sequence for admission to the ora-

cle each in his turn, Robert (1948) 17ff., 22f.; further texts on daily prayers in Nilsson (1945) 64f. and Geraci (1971) 173 and 196, including PSI 236, third/fourth century; for lifelong loyalties, cf. the most familiar Aelius Aristides and Asclepius, or e.g. Philostr., *Heroicus.* 148.1f. p. 17, or Milik (1972) 183; tourism and pilgrimage in Grenier (1931–60) 4.632f., Geraci (1971) 77, 132 (at Philae, a. 452), and passim on Egypt alone, and more generally, MacMullen (1981) 29f., 73; for a sampling of the literary evidence on religious feelings, see Damascius, *Vita Isidori* 199 in Photius, *Bibliotheca* ed. R. Henry VI p. 42 §348, Hatzfeld (1927) 134, MacMullen (1981) 63f., MacMullen and Lane (1992) 79–82, with Christian insights offered into religious awe felt in idolatry in Aug., *Ep.* 102.3, and *CT* 16.10.12.2 a. 392. On pagan *horaria*, see e.g. Fernandez Marcos (1975) 39.

72 I find an odd reluctance to acknowledge the role, even the existence, of emotions in ancient paganism, e.g, in Dorcey (1992) 28 with n. 72 and 138, or S. Mitchell (1993) 12; but for a very broad statement on the role of feelings, see C. Geertz (1966), below, chap. 4 n. 13, and some illustrative texts in MacMullen (1984) 165.

73 POxy. 1380 line 152 (early second century) and other passages in Chapouthier (1932) 391, 393, 395 n. 2; add Philostr., *Vita Apollonii* 8.31, only the true disciple beholds the vision.

74 Junghaendel (1891) 862; Traunecker (1987) 222ff., ancient Egyptian illustrations, but also (228) of the Roman period. Compare the same basic idea of how superhuman power works in the description of the wonder-worker, a "Chaldaean," bringing back life to someone bitten by a snake, in Lucian, *Philops.* 11, "by fastening on to the foot a chip from the tombstone of a dead maiden," λίθον ἀπὸ τῆς στήλης, the maiden qualifying as that powerful thing in magic, a βιοθάνατος, someone cut off before his or her time.

75 Cure testimonials in general, in MacMullen (1981) 33f., adding, from Beugnot (1835) 1.369, Liban., *Ep.* 607, on examples in the Asclepius temple in his day, with *Or.* 1.143 and the Loeb ed. note ad loc. on his recourse to the Aegae temple for his own illnesses; in the west, the famous Sources-de-la-Seine shrine with its votive body parts and hundreds of wooden figures and figurines in a shrine used into the fourth century, in Grenier (1931–60) 4.639f., Romeuf (1986) 65ff., Deyts (1983) 35, 160f., and idem (1994) 13, with useful and convincing discussion of the question, whether votives showed hope or thanks, and showing heads of worshipers in pl. 13–15; Grenier (1931–60) 708, body-part effigies at an excavated third-century springside shrine; thousands of votive body parts at Royan (Puy-de-Dôme), in Chevallier (1992) 11; thousands at Chamalières, Romeuf (1986) 67f.; votive hands on Silvanus' altars at Glanum, Rolland (1958) 76 and Pl. 26; at Luxeuil among coins of Constantine, Bourgeois (1991–92) 1.137; at Senlis, among coins up to Valentinian's reign, Esperandieu (1907–28) 5.130f., 139f., and Grenier 4.815–18; at Mont-de-Sène and Alesia, Grenier 4.660 and 708; and the practice of anatomical votives noticed at Köln under Theodoric a. 511/534 by Greg. Turon., *Vitae patrum* 6.2 (*MGH SRM* 1.681 = *PL* 71.1031).

76 See POxy. 1382 (second century) on the miracle records in one Egyptian temple library, to which the editors compare the account of the collection of θεραπεῖαι

and ἀρεταί in the Canopus Serapeion, Strabo 17.1.17; further material in MacMullen (1981) 159.

77 On oracles and prophecy, sometimes through dreams, see MacMullen (1981) 153, 162, 174, through the third century. The long quotation is from Eusebius, *Theophania* 2.50, 52 (pp. 103*, 104* of the GCS ed.), where the author is speaking contemptuously, and contrasts the wise who "concern themselves rather with the relief of their spiritual pains."

78 Escape from drowning and travel dangers, *CIG* 2716 = LeBas-Wadd. 516, *CIG* 3669, *IG* 14.997 and 10, 2.67, *IGR* 1.107 = *IG* 14.1030; and many others. Cf. the miraculous preservation from drowning vouchsafed by Helios to Asclepiodotus around the turn of the sixth century, in Damascius, *Vita Isidori* 115 = Photius, *Bibliothèque* ed. R. Henry, 6 (1971) 31 §343.

79 Votive domestic animal figurines in Grenier (1931–60) 4.141f., Romeuf (1986) 68, and Deyts (1983) 66 with Pl. LXIX and LXXVI; specification of animals in prayers, MacMullen (1981) 169, eastern and western inscriptions.

80 Over two hundred known Asklepieia, cf. Kötting (1950) 13; local variants of the deity in *CIL* 6.2799 and *AE* 1975, 767; the argument for the marked primacy of health prayers in personal cult, in MacMullen (1981) 51.

81 On "right" powers of deities, e.g. where gardeners' or food-wholesalers' cult-clubs choose Demeter as their goddess, see Robert (1949) 202f., 204 n. 6; a *tabularius* dedicates a statuette to Minerva, *CIL* 2.4183; other examples in MacMullen (1981) 52; but Silvanus healing, above, n. 72 and Dorcey (1992) 26 n. 59; Mercury and Hercules heal, Thevenot (1968) 87ff., 99, 121, and Rolland (1958) 114; Mars a healer, Grenier (1931–60) 4.896; Minerva, too, in a north-Italian shrine, "monofunzionale . . . guaritrice," cf. Roda (1981) 248f., still with her devotees in the fifth/sixth century in baths at Lucus Feroniae (Etruria) as earlier at Bath and a north African site in association with Hygia and Aesculapius, cf. Fraschetti (1975) 318f., 327 and n. 33. For the eighty Gallic spring deities, cf. Bourgeois (1991–92) 1.59.

82 Kötting (1950) 316; Harnack (1924) 1.136.

83 On incubation, some evidence at random: in fourth-century eastern cities, Hier., *Comm. in Isaiam* 65 (*PL* 24.632Cf.), *incubare soliti erant . . . quod in fano Aesculapii usque hodie,* Cyrillus Hier., *Catechesis mystagogica* 1, *ad eos qui nuper illuminati sunt* 1.8 (*PG* 1072B), and Soz., *H. E.* 2.5 (the Asclepieion at Aegae); in Italy, see e.g. *CIL* 11.3296; in Gaul, *CIL* 13.2858, Grenier (1931–60) 4.458, Thevenot (1968) 113, MacKendrick (1971) 178, *AE* 1983, 711 (Metz, thanks to Silvanus and the Nymphs, *somnio monitus*), Bourgeois (1991–92) 242f., and Deyts (1994) 13, 125; in Egypt, Bernand (1969) 525 (third/fourth century) and 529f.; and more in MacMullen (1981) 60, 157–59, 175.

84 As examples of these offerings, notice *CIL* 8.22642, 6, from Mauretanian Caesarea, quoted (the ?sieves = strainers? for wine offerings); Zeno, *Liber* 1 *Tractatus* 15.6 (*PL* 11.563B = Ballerini 114f.), declaring the foolish pagans *lumen caecis* [= the gods] *inferre, thura non spirantibus concremare,* in northern Italy of the 350s; the ἔλαιον εἰς λυχναψίαν for the third-century emperor's birthday celebration in the Arsinoe temple, in Wilcken (1885) 432, 438, and Vandoni (1964) 48ff.; *Daremberg-Saglio* s.v. "Lucerna" (Toutain) 1336, with illustration of the deluxe offerings (Plin., *N. H.* 34.14, Paus.

1.26.7 and 7.22.2f., etc.); thousands of lamps in a Bas-Alpes site, Toutain (1907–20) 1, 3.343; thousands more, with statuettes and *unguentaria,* etc., at El-Kenissia, in Carton (1908) 28; Martin. Bracarensis, *De corr. rust.* 16, candles lit in offering to Mercury, a rite drawn from the Compitalia, cf. Meslin (1969) 520; Hier., *Comment. in Esaiam prophet.* 16.7 (*PL* 24.551Bf.), Tutela worship with candles; and general discussion in Lucius (1908) 39, MacMullen (1981) 42 with notes, and Nilsson (1960) passim, e.g. (p. 205) the lamps still lit in the Aphrodite temple in Augustine's time, *Civ. dei* 21.6, and idem (1961) 375f. Notice especially in a. 406 Hier., *Contra Vigilantium* 4 (*PL* 23.342f.), "It is almost pagan ritual we see brought into our churches under the pretense of honor, where a mass of candles is lit in broad daylight," and the characterization of torches in daylight as an act of worship among the *infideles,* in Conc. Aurel. II a. 452 can. 23, cf. Synod of Agde a. 506 can. 5, *candelae, Vita Eligii* 16 (*MGH SRM* 4.706), *luminaria,* and Conc. Tolet. XVI a. 693 can. 2 (*PL* 84.537), concerning the use of *faculae* by *idolorum cultores;* also "Joh. Chrysos.," *Sermo de pseudo-prophetis* 7 (*PG* 59.561), lamps hung by water shrines, and Dionysius quoted below, chap. 5 at n. 8; Macrob., *Sat.* 1.11.48, and Nilsson (1916–19) 63, showing that on the Saturnalia the candles are lit on Saturn's altars; and on Attis Days or, rather, nights (March 24th–25th), there is brilliant lighting, cf. Hepding (1903) 165 and Labriolle (1934) 447 on Aug., *Tract in Joh.* 7.1 (*PL* 35.1440), describing March 24th in north African cities. For mid-fifth-century Antioch usages, cf. Isaac of Antioch quoted in Klugkist (1974) 355. On incense as very common with prayer, see especially Nilsson (1945) 65, with Klauser (1964) 72, "incense offerings were the norm in the Empire," Fernandez Marcos (1975) 39, and fourth-century usage in *CT* 16.10.12.2 a. 392 and Aug., *Ep.* 46 (*PL* 13.183) and 47.3 (185) of a. 398; still in sixth-century Edessa offered to images in the theater during performances, cf. Jacob of Serûg in Cramer (1980) 104. For statuettes, just as examples, see Carton loc. cit., Ellison (1980) 312 (a British site, up to ca. 380), and Grenier (1931–60) 4.610, metal statuettes at the Sources de la Seine of the late third and fourth century. For offerings of coins, again merely illustrative, Mermet (1993) 105–13, 135, Pauli (1986) 850, and especially Kaminsky (1991) 173f., 180, 169ff., offerings-boxes at temples from all parts of the west and up into the third century. And for small gifts of edibles, Pauli loc. cit., and Deyts (1994) 10f.; other gifts (gold, silver, fine cloth) to "Aphrodite" of Aphaca in the time of Zosimus (1.38).

85 *CJ* 1.11.7.1 a. 451 directed the death penalty at incense and wine offerings, as well as *victima,* and people were informed on, physically punished, and stripped of property, Procop., *Hist. arcan* 11.31; but in the eastern provinces we have Zos. 1.38 reporting gifts of gold, silver, fine cloth, etc., to "Aphrodite" during her festival at Aphaca in the fifth century, and Trombley (1992–93) 2.155f. presents inscriptions of the 530s to 540s showing similar cult acts.

86 Wiseman (1970) 134–36; Garnett (1975) 173f., 186, and, on Eros stamps, 191 and 200; but notice (194f., 202) a proportion of the later ones with Christian symbols. Compare, at Ephesus in the fourth to sixth centuries, the pagans' lamps at the tomb of the Seven Sleepers, in Miltner (1937) 104f. 110f., 157f., 183, 223, and, with some correction of the chronology, Foss (1979) 11, 85. He (11) and Miltner (155, 233) also indicate a minority with crosses and OT figures.

87 On the first stripping of property and income from temples, see the reference to the legislation in *CT* 16.10.20.1 and the dating of it to 382 by His (1896) 37 and more recent studies in MacMullen (1984) 142 n. 3, the law perhaps explaining the reference to seized lands by Liban., *Or.* 30.11; further confiscation under Theodosius, Mac-Mullen loc. cit.; funds confiscated from all of Rome's temples in a. 394, Zos. 4.59; confiscation reasserted by *CT* 16.5.43 a. 407/8 from Rome and 16.10.19.1f. = *Sirm.* 12 a. 407/408; then, by *CJ* 1.11.8 a. 472. On earlier confiscation from temples, see Noethlichs (1986) 1154 and *CT* 5.13.3 and 10.1.8 a. 364, repossessing lands that had been taken from temples before Julian and by him given back; Constantius' confiscations in Italy and Syria, His loc. cit., Lasaulx (1854) 56 and 85, and Noethlichs (1986) 1156; Firmicus Maternus' summons to Constantius to "remove to your own uses and control all gifts to them" [the pagans], *De errore profan. relig.* 28.6; and Noethlichs 32 on Constantine's confiscations, adding Guida (1990) 49.

88 "Deluxe" worship, above, n. 31; and "upper parts" from my own 1981 book, pp. 130f., 136, "the most fragile" parts as opposed to "the more substantial" (Fr. tr. pp. 214f.), the words here quoted only because somehow they have been misread by Rousselle (1990) 44 and 266 n. 45. She (like most religious historians) sees the upper parts alone as the whole of paganism, and so supposes here a thesis "relevant du 'show-biz', la fin du financement fut la fin du culte. Pas de croyance. . . . " Besides such testimonies as the Fountain of the Lamps, I gather other material on "the more substantial part," below, from n. 97 on.

89 *CJ* 1.11.9.1 (post-472); 1.5.12 a. 527 and 1.5.17 a. 529 denying pagans the right to hold or inherit property; 1.5.12 revoked in 551 but reimposed in 572, cf. Köpstein (1978) 36.

90 Some useful titles on the subject in chap. 1 n. 70.

91 *CJ* 11.10.3 a. 427.

92 Bans on pagans as lawyers or imperial servants, cf. chap. 1 n. 70; bans on teaching by pagans, *CJ* 1.11.2 a. 527, 1.18.4; and, on the terror of 529, Theophanes, *Chron.* 1.276 Classen = de Boor, *Theophanis Chronographia* 1 (1883) 180, Malal. 18 p. 451 Dindorf, and Bury (1923) 367 and Constantelos (1964) 375.

93 Belief in control of the winds by a holy man, Eunap., *Vit. soph.* 463. Above, n. 57, on Apollonius; much on ascetic piety in the latter pages of Book 11 of Apul., *Met.*; the fourth-century Porph., *Vita Plotini* 7 (disciples) and 11 (able to detect a thief); and, in the first century, Chaeremon frg. 10 in Horst (1984) 16f., describing the Egyptian priests in their temples, ἐμφιλοσοφῆσαι τὰ ἱερά. It may be said of such ascetics that they constituted "a flagrant antithesis to the norms of civilized life in the Mediterranean," these being P. Brown's words applied exclusively to Christian ascetics but rightly extended to the pagan by Francis (1995) 193 n. 1. On the ascetic group, see POxy. 3069, quoted in P. J. Parson's translation, and reminiscent of many passages in Marcus Aurelius' *Meditations*.

94 Philostr., *Vita Apollonii* 3.38 and 4.20, and expulsion of the demon of plague, too, at 8.7; Plot., *Enn.* 2.9.14, on the (unidentifiable) "Gnostics," guilty of γοητεία, not claiming "like the philosphers" to work through a temperate and regulated life. He asks in scorn, do they suppose the demons of disease have physical needs by which they can be controlled? Ridiculous!—performances only for οἱ πολλοί, not for the

εὖ φρονοῦντες. For other pagan exorcists of the third and fourth centuries, see Mac-
Mullen (1981) 168 n. 3; and on the Syrian stylobates, Lucian, *De Syria* 28.

95 Among pagan professors prominent in Antioch, Iokasios, cf. Dagron (1978) 90f. and
PLRE 2.583 s.v. "Iacobus"; others condemned to death in the time of Isaac [d. ca.
460], cf. S. Brock's comments to Klugkist (1974) 368; in Alexandria, the trials in the
480s as sketched above, chap. 1 at n. 86; and, on the intellectual role of Athens in the
generation prior, Rémondon (1952) 63f., 66f., and Vian (1976) 1.xv.

96 On the (mostly neoplatonic) center for learning in Athens and its intellectual leaders, see Goodspeed (1908) 594, 597f., Frantz (1988) 85f., Chuvin (1990) 114, Trombley
(1993–94) 1.307f., and most fully Athanassiadi (1993), making good use of the text of
Damascius, *Vita Isidori* in Photius, ed. Henry. See *Vita* §179f. = Photius p. 40 §347,
concerning Julian and Athanasius; on the characterization of Christianity, Photius p.
48 §350 = *Vita Isidori* 238, taken to refer to Christians by Asmus (1911), Henry (note
ad loc.), and Athanassiadi (1993) 6. The words are a little more polite if no less
angry than those of John Chrysostom visiting the city as a distinguished orator and
in his oration to the to the city senate referring to Athena and Artemis as "those little whore women," cf. Geo. Alex., *Vita S. Joh. Chrysos.* 82.

97 Above, chap. 1 nn. 98f., on the afterlife of Greek learning in the Near East, with the
Agathias passage in Whitby (1991) 121.

98 Though *Daremberg-Saglio* s.v. "Lares" and Orr (1978) collect valuable material, there is
certainly room for a book about private and at-home religion in classical antiquity;
but my purposes perhaps don't require more than "gleanings," beginning with Mart.
Bracarensis, *De corr. rust.* 16, noting the practice *effundere in foco super truncum frugem et
vinum*, cf. the New Year's adorning of the hearth in Caesarius, *Serm.* 192. For earlier
Spanish evidence, cf. Orr (1978) 1588f., along with material from other northern
provinces, Pannonia, etc.

99 Lares and Penates, cf. Macrob., *Sat.* 1.24.22, the major domo, with the *cura vel adolendi
Penates vel struendi penum*, burns incense for the master to the household gods on the
Saturnalia; Prudentius, *Adv. Symm.* 1.208f. (post-384), to reach the statuette, the child
humeris positus nutricis, trivit et ipse / impressis labris, puerilia vota / fudit; SHA *Marcus Aur.*
18.2f. and 5f., statuettes of the emperor to be found in every *lararium*, recalling Sen.,
Ep. 64.9, with further passages in Fishwick (1992) 342–48; reporting on some five
hundred *lararia*, almost all in Pompeii and environs, Boyce (1937) 24, 58, 61, 64ff., 95f.,
98, and 100 (in Pompeian *lararia*, statuettes of Hercules, Jupiter, Juno, Minerva, Nep-
tune, Vulcan, Mercury, and Bacchus); Ostian evidence very well presented by Bakker
(1994), e.g. the fifty statuettes in one private shrine (147f.); briefly and generally,
Février (1977) 516f., Orr (1978) 1575 n. 128 on Marcus Aurelius and the emperor Tacitus' *lararia*, Orr (1988) 294, 297, Clarke (1991) 6ff., 9f. (including dedication to the
Lares of the first beard by males), and Fishwick (1992) 344, 348, adducing texts in
the poets like Horace and Tibullus and Petron., *Sat.* 60.8, with Trimalchio's twin silver statuettes brought in to start the meal; cf. ibid. 29.8, his *lararium;* and portable
altars, in Orr (1978) 1579. In Spain, notice the idols in Christians' homes, evidently
kept by their servants, Conc. Illiberit. can. 41, warning that *fideles prohibeant ne idola in
domibus suis habeant: si vero vim servorum . . .* , etc., though the passage reminds one of the

alleged idol kept by a priest in Italy, Greg. Magn., *Registr.* 10.2 (*MGH Epp.* 1, 1.238, a. 599); in Gaul, noted by Toutain (1907–20) 1, 3.404, "among the Gallo-Romans, piety toward native deities expressed itself not only by rites in cult centers; each house had no doubt its holy niche analogous to the lararia of Rome and Italy." Lar, Penates, or Genius worship banned by *CT* 16.10.12, the ban evidently ignored, cf. in Ostia, Bakker (1994) 33 and Hier., *Commentarii in Esaiam prophetam* 16.7 (*PL* 24.551Bf.), pagans *post fores domorum idola ponerent, quos domesticos appellant Lares, et tam publice quam privatim animarum suarum sanguinem funderent.* For cult signs in Greek homes, cf. an Asclepius icon mentioned by Philostr., *Vit. soph.* 2.4, a consul's house (Attalus, Severan cos. suff., *PIR*, 2d ed., s.v. "Claudius" no. 800) in Athens with the owner's statue of a goddess and votive inscription, Nilsson (1960) 206, and shrines discussed by Nilsson (1988) 2.187ff., little of the Roman period but a very wide range of loyalties to be seen, e.g. altars to Hestia but also to Zeus Soter, Hygieia, Tyche, etc.; and Nachtergael (1985) 225 on wall niches, not all for worship; for Sarapis busts, see Rufin., *H. E.* 2.29 (*PL* 21.557A); in other eastern settings, above, n. 63; in Egyptian houses, POxy. 1272 (a. 144) reporting the theft of a golden Bes statuette; much archeological evidence well treated in Nachtergael (1985) 228f. and passim, e.g. statuettes esp. of Harpocrates but also of Bes, Isis, etc., in, for instance, the Fayum in 350–450; also Lacau (1921–22) 194; at a late period, above, n. 63, also idols collected from pagan homes and burnt, in Zach., *Life of Severus,* Kugener (1903) 33; and household icons in Besa, *Life of Shenute* 125f., Amélineau (1888–95) 1.66f., sixth century; statues in north African gardens, cf. Aug., *Serm.* 62.18, and, in Gaul, Green (1993) 41 on Ausonius' statue of Liber Pantheus in his garden. On apotropaic figures by doors, see Caesarius, *Serm.* 193.2 (*CCL* 104.784); inscribed names on Greek house doors, esp. Hercules, in Merkelbach (1991) 41 and Trombley (1992–93) 2.258; Sarapis signs on doors in Alex., Rufinus loc. cit.; and "Sol lives here" in an Ostian house, with other similar testimonies, in Bakker (1994) 104, 110.

100 On birthday parties and cult acts, see esp. Argetsinger (1992) 181, with mention of annual cult on other family dates as well, 188; celebration of the *dies Kare cognationis* or Caristia discussed in Scullard (1981) 74ff., February 22nd, celebrated in the mid-fourth century in the west to judge from the Calendar of 354, up to Polemius Silvius in a. 448/9, cf. Février (1977) 519, and still in 567, cf. below, chap. 4 n. 153.

101 Legal contracts made secure by invoking a deity or deities, as in Giordano (1970) 218 of a. 39 (Jupiter and Numen Augusti); Basil, *Epp. class.* II 217 (*PG* 32.805); oaths with laborers at the turn of the fifth century, Aug., *Ep.* 46 (*PL* 33.182); Conc. Aurel. IV a. 541 can. 16; and Conc. Autessiodurense a. 578–585 can. 3.

102 Guarducci (1983) 115f.

103 Artemid., *Oneir.* 5.82 p. 271 Hercher, the passage drawn attention to by Nock (1944) 156, "receiving his friends [συμβιωταί] and being host at the meal at his grave," the source being "a good witness for popular beliefs at a fairly unsophisticated level."

104 A general practice in the world of Theodoret, *Graec. aff. curat.* 8 (*PG* 83.1020), where pagans still bring wine to the deceased in the evening, "against the laws," no doubt

referring to *CT* 16.10.19.3 of a. 408; in Asia Minor, funeral inscriptions with reliefs of the second to third centuries, in Dölger (1910–43) 5.468–75, and Trombley (1993–94) 2.107, adducing a Phrygian and a Galatian inscription; at Edessa, cf. Segal (1963) 204f., 214, third-century funeral feasts hosted by the deceased similar to Palmyrene funerary customs, cf. Milik (1972) 194, on the many *triclinia* at Palmyrene tombs where dead and living drank and dined together; Negev (1971) 110f. and 127, tombside tables according to Nabataean usages of the first century to Byzantine Mampsis and Petra, and (125ff., 129) pottery of many sorts, even indicating the usual number of diners, six to ten; and Barhebraeus (d. 1286) in his *Nomocanon*, cf. Quasten (1983) 176, on gatherings [but perhaps not feasts?] where there is singing and dancing to drums.

105 Lucian, *Charon* 22; Dyggve (1942) 226–28, with some Bulgarian as well as western material.

106 Dölger (1930) 95 or Snyder (1985) 111; Klauser (1956) 46 and fig. 6, showing a grave altar above the burial with the pipe leading down from it; and Klauser (1927) 13ff. on stone chairs for the dead at the tomb.

107 For the physical amenities described, see such inscriptions as *CIL* 2.266, a tomb *cum munitionibus tricleae* at Olisipo, 6.8860, *culina super tumulum*, 6.29958, *culina et puteum et iter at triclia*, both Roman, or 8.20780, a *mensa cum titulum refrigerationis* (Auzia in Mauretania Caes., a. 318); sarcophagi with pipes or similar arrangements, in Dyggve (1942) 226 (Ostia) and 231 (Aquincum), Wheeler (1929) 1–4, in Britain and Gaul, cf. for Gaul, P.-M. Duval (1952) 327f. and Conc. Arelatense III a. 452 can. 5; in Africa, Tert., *Apol.* 13 (*PL* 1.344B), and Trombley (1993–94) 1.68f. On the mood of *hilaritas*, see Testini (1958) 141.

108 Aug., *Ep.* 22, *foeditas flagitiosa et sacrilega*; Ambros., *De Helia et ieiunio* 17.62 (*CSEL* 32.449), against thinking like pagans *qui ebrietatem sacrificium putant*; and below, chap. 4.

109 See references accessible through MacMullen (1981) and, most recently, Pekary (1994) 101ff., stressing denial of belief in immortality.

110 Νεφοδιῶκται and *tempestarii*, in the east and in Gaul: Trombley (1985) 340f. and (1993–94) 1.318, resort to such persons banned in the fourth century, Ps.-Justin, *Quaestiones* (*PG* 6.1277Cf.) and Quinisextum can. 61, Joannou (1962) 196f.; Conc. in Trullo a. 691/2 can. 61; in the west, Plin., *N. H.* 17.267, on hail prevention through spells, which he doesn't believe in; Harmening (1979) 247f. on *immisores tempestatis et sim.*; Pirmin of Reichenau (d. 753), *Dicta* 22, *tempestarios nolite credere*; Agobard of Lyon (bishop 816–840), *Liber contra insulsam vulgi opinionem* 1 (*PL* 104.147), *in his regionibus pene omnes homines, nobiles et ignobiles, urbani et rustici, senes et iuvenes, putant grandines et tonitrua hominum libitu posse fieri*, and name the men able to do this *tempestarii*, while in truth only God has the power.

111 Holy men and women: Paus. 4.30.3, near Pharae in Messenia, men of a certain family able to heal; Dio Chrysos., *Or.* 1.54, a woman in the district near Olympia, with "the power given to her by the Mother of the Gods, and all the shepherds in the region and the farmers used her for the fertility and security of their crops and flocks"; Robert (1937) 132, the woman from a Phrygian region with "the gift of prophesy within the bounds" [of the region]; an elderly man in touch with an angel, serving a Bithynian village with his powers of prophecy, whom Hypatius (d.

446) locks up for life, till he is begged free by the elders, and soon dies, Callinicos, *Vita Hypatii* 43.9 (*SC* 177.259f.); another woman of superhuman powers in the 460s in Cilicia, Trombley (1993–94) 1.48; a woman seer and spell-maker near Emesa, Festugière and Ryden (1974) 152; and one of ca. a. 600 in central Galatia, Trombley (1985) 344; in the west, men of supernatural powers in Plin., *N. H.* 28.30.

112 Threads or ribbons = *vittae* on trees as prayers, Ovid, *Met.* 8.744, Stat., *Silv.* 4.4.92, Prudentius, *Contra Symm.* 2.1009f. (*PL* 60.261), Zeno, *Liber* I *Tract.* 15.6 (*PL* 11.563B), *allegare preces surdis* (= trees); and in the east, passages from Cyril and Chrysostom, in Nilsson (1955–61) 2.376, with the story of Roman times carried up further by Schiemenz (1986) 55; banned in *CT* 16.10.12.2 a. 392, from Constantinople. Destruction of sacred groves in Italy banned by Constantius, cf. His (1896) 37; by Benedict, Greg. Magn., *Dial.* 2.8.10 = Vogüé (1978–80) 2.168, and idem, *Registr.* 8.19 (*MGH Epp.* 2.21); in Corsica a. 597, ibid. 8.1 (2.1f.); in Africa, Conc. Carthag. a. 401 can. 84 = Joannou (1962a) 323, *luci vel arbores* to be destroyed, and Meer (1961) 39; in Spain ca. a. 573, Mart. Bracar., *De corr. rust.* 11, and Conc. Toletanum XII a. 681 can. 11 and XVI can. 2 (*PL* 84.537); in Gaul, sacred trees, in Toutain (1907–20) 1, 3.295ff., Drioux (1934) 174f. and Male (1950) 58; Sulp. Sev., *Vita S. Mart.* 13.1 (*PL* 20.167 = *CSEL* 1.122), the tree defended by a priest and a crowd; *Vita Eligii* 16 (*MGH SRM* 4.707); Conc. Arelatense II a. 452 can. 23; Caesarius, *Serm.* 1.11 (*CCSL* 103.8f.), 13.65f. (66f., 68), 14.70 (71), 53.1 (233), 54.229f. (238, 240), preaching vs. tree worship; Cyprian of Toulon, *Vita Caesarii* 55 (*MGH SRM* 3.479); *paganissimos ritus . . . lignicolas*; Conc. Turonense a. 567 can. 23. (Mansi 9.789), a practice of the *gentiles*; *Vita Amandi* 13 (*MGH SRM* 5.436f.), Amandus active to ca. a. 676; Conc. Nannetense a. 660 can. 20, ordering that trees *quas vulgus colet* (notice the tense) *et in tanta veneratione habet, ut nec ramum vel surculum inde audeat amputare, radicitus excidantur et comburantur*, in Wasserschleben (1840) 352; Greg. Magn., *Dial.* 2.8.11 and *Registr.* (*MGH Epp.* 2.7) a. 597; the eighth-century *Indiculus superstitionum et paganiarum* 6, in Markus (1990) 165, dating by Homann (1965) 209 or Karras (1986) 562 to the late eighth century; of the Germans, Tac., *Ger.* 9; in Armenia in John Chrysostom's time, in Geo. Alex., *Vita S. Joh. Chrysos.* 59 = Halkin (1977) 237 (if the source is reliable); tree cult at many points in the east, Trombley (1985) 334f.; in Lycia of the third and mid-sixth century, Anrich (1913–17) 2.224ff. and Robert (1955) 199; and in central Asia Minor, Joh. Ephes., *Lives of the Eastern Saints* 43 = Brooks (1924) 659.

113 Hilltop shrines, for example, *Vita S. Amantii* 12 (*MGH AA* 4, 2.56), at Rodez ca. mid-fifth century, Greg. Magn., *Dial.* 2.8.10f., Benedict destroys the Apollo idol on Monte Cassino; generally in Gaul, Male (1950) 32, 38f., and selected sites in Grenier (1931–60) 4.703, 707, 720, etc.; Nilsson (1955–61) 2.248, 376, Greece; for Syria, Theodoret, *Hist. relig.* 28.1, a hilltop temple to δαίμονες near Gabala in the author's day, and Cramer (1980) 98.

114 Sacred waters: Chevallier (1992) 5–27, a very full collection of references from all over the empire; in the east, Cyrillus Hier., *Catechesis mystagogica* 1, *ad eos qui nuper illuminati sunt* 1.8 (*PG* 1072B); Klugkist (1974) 355, 360, fifth-century Syria; Dölger (1932) 8, 14, sites of the first to fourth century (Oak of Mamre); in the west, Schultze (1887–92) 2.105, Hilary's time; of the late 580s, Greg. Turonensis, *Liber in gloria confess.* 2 (*MGH SRM* 1, 2.299); Pauli (1986) 851, Alpine areas into fifth century;

E. and S. Künzl (1992) 273–82, active site in the fourth century near Lake Bracciano; Male (1950) 56, Gaul, and a very full collection of evidence in Grenier
(1931–60) 4.608ff., 652f., 897, and passim, referring to Toutain (1907–20) and the
identification then of 760 cult sites, the most common for springs, of which Bourgeois (1991–92) 1.59 identifies some eighty in Gaul, of which the one active as
pagan to the latest date known to me (ca. a. 700) lies between Nancy and Stras-
bourg, cf. Demarolle (1992) 425, 432. See further most of the ecclesiastical evidence in n. 112, above, since bans and preaching, too, commonly linked *arbores* and
fontes. For the belief that some sacred waters would waste the flesh of perjurers
when applied (or similar practices = tests) of the first to fourth centuries in
many lands, see MacMullen (1981) 173 n. 33.

115 Theodoret, *Hist. relig.* 1.4, under Constantine; similarly the Apollo temple at Abydos
destroyed by an abbot's prayer, *Life of Moses*, in Amélineau (1888–95) 686f., and the
heathen idol shattered for the saint by lightning, *Vita S. Amantii* 18 (*MGH AA* 4, 2.56).

116 Cypresses at Plakoma, mid-sixth century, Anrich (1913–17) 2.224; ibid. 225 n. 2 for
more dendroclasm by John of Ephesus; Halkin (1977) 237 for still more in the
early fifth century; and, on destruction of sacred trees by monks at the same
period, see Callinicus, *Vita Hypatii* 30.1 (*SC* 177.201), near Chalcedon; Theodoret,
Hist. relig. 28.1–5 (*PG* 82.1489Af.), θαύματα at Gabala toward mid-fifth century;
Shenute's destruction of the temple at Panopolis, in Amélineau (1888–95) 1.xvii,
and the ideal or paradigm of monk behavior in such acts, seen ibid. xxvif. and
112–81 through Macarius and Besa and (506, 686–690) Moses; a slightly earlier
summing-up or tribute to the crucial role of monks in Syria against Ἑλληνίζειν, in
Soz., *H. E.* 6.34 (*PG* 67.1396C); and above, chap. 1 nn. 42, 47, 49, 54, and 57.

117 On the sheer size of the ecclesiastical hierarchy, including in the cities and *periodeu-
tai-chorespiscopi* in the fifth and later centuries, see Gain (1985) 35f., 94f., S. Mitchell
(1993) 71, and Wickham (1995) 6.

118 Joh. Chrysos., *In Acta apost. homil.* 18.4 (*PG* 60.146); pressure on rural districts
assumed by Rufinus, *H. E.* 2.28 (*PL* 21.536Cf.), *per vicos, per omnes rus, per eremum
quoque, . . . instantia unuiusquisque episcopi subrita* [*delubra*] in Egypt in the 390s.

119 Ownership of land by villages was a common pattern in the Near East, cf. e.g. the
two villages church-owned in Syria in 575, Tchalenko (1953–58) 1.177.

120 *CT* 16.10.13 a. 395 forbids entering a temple or sacrifices on fiscal estates and (§2)
governors' staff members who fail to enforce this shall be executed; also 16.10.19.2
= *Sirm.* 12 a. 408 assigns temples to secular uses; 16.10.16 a. 399 quoted in the Pharr
translation; and *CJ* 1.11.8 a. 472 follows through with landowners.

121 Const. Porph., *De admin. imperio* 50, lines 71ff., in Rochow (1978) 245, with other,
ninth-century, pagan localities in the Peloponnesus, p. 288; compare, only a few
miles from Antioch and in the last quarter of the sixth century, a wholly pagan village, *Vita S. Symeon.* 188ff. in Ven (1962–70) 1.166.; and Trombley (1985) 346ff.

122 Liban., *Or.* 30.9, a. 386 or 390; toasts, §18f.; gatherings of peasants at the residence
of the local magnates, §19; compare e.g. Sahin (1978) 775, 780f., a third-century
Bithynian gift by a landowner to the village to insure good harvests through an
annual feast to Zeus-of-Fertility-Festivals.

123 Joh. Ephes., *H. E.* in Nau (1897) 482, on the payment of a trimition = triens at
each baptism, fifty-five churches at fiscal expense (and forty-four paid for by converts) with special gifts from the emperor; seventy thousand converts, but, in his
Lives of the Eastern Saints 47 = Brooks (1924) 681, the figure is eighty thousand; further details ibid. 43 (pp. 658ff.) and *H. E.* 2.44 = Brooks (1936) 81. One or the
other of John's figures is accepted by Whitby (1991) 111f., Trombley (1985) 330f.,
and Bury (1923) 371. The last-named called the baptismal payment "a small sum,"
but its value appears in Jones (1964) 447 and Festugière (1961–64) 43 n. 58 and 116.
S. Mitchell (1993) 119 minimizes John's results, "not . . . a significant minority of
the rural population at large," representing, as he imagines, one hundred villages
over the four provinces. It seems to me more likely that John's boast rather indicated above two hundred thousand, since I cannot imagine him or his agents
bestowing a big sum of money each on anyone but males and heads of families
(the Syriac, describing the beneficiaries as plural males, is not decisive, but if
women and children were included in the gift, surely they would be specified). But
I think certainty is not within reach.

124 As a random sampling of iconclastic energy, comparable to much less eastern evidence (above, n. 66), see the evidence from the Danube lands in MacMullen (1981)
133, 205 n. 8; the remains indicated in southern Britain, Ellison (1980) 318, "soon
after 380"; in Gaul, Grenier (1931–60) 4.639, 705 (coins to 378), 916, "extrème
mutilation des statues réduites en menus morceaux et même des autels de dédicace
indiquerait . . . le zèle chrétien"; Male (1950) 37, 43 ("on s'étonne de recontrer, sans
cesse, des oeuvres mutilés"), and 45; Bulliot and Thiollier (1892) 240 and 44f.,
destruction of images and a shrine given to Mercury *ex stipibus vicani*, with coins to
375; more, in northern Italy at one rural site, Rossi (1992) 381, late fourth century.

125 Stancliffe (1979) 49; Pontal (1989) 292; Wood (1994) 191; and incidents of temple
destruction such as that by Saint Gall, Greg. Turon., *Vitae patrum* 6.2 (*PL* 71.1031).

126 Instances of conversions from preaching: Greg. Turon., *Liber in gloria confess.* 2 and 76
(*MGH SRM* 1, 2.299 and 344), preaching by a monk and a bishop of the later fifth
century; Greg. Magn., *Dial.* 2.19.1 = Vogüé (1978–80) 2.194; *Vita S. Eleutherii* 1.2 in
Vacandard (1899) 427; and *Vita S. Amantii* 15 (*MGH AA* 4, 2.56), preaching produces
only fury in the audience.

127 On the increasing number of rural churches, see Beck (1950) 72ff., 346, also Stancliffe (1979) 50 showing that within the Auxerre diocese "by the end of the fifth
century, most people would have had a church within 10 km of their homes," and
further, Caesarius, *Serm.* 13.68 and 53.224, 229 (*CCSL* 103.68 and 234), including the
rebuke (53.1 = *CCSL* 103.233) to members of his congregation who *paganorum fana
non solum destruere nolunt sed etiam quae destructa fuerant aedificare nec metuunt*; 54.5, calling
on landowners first to chide and warn the recalcitrant, then to shave them bald,
manacle, and (13.5) flog them; Max. Taur., *Serm.* 101 (*PL* 57.733) = 107.1f. and 23f. ed.
Mutzenbecher (*CCSL* 23.420f.); again, in *Serm.* 91.2 (Mutz. 369), 96f., 102, and 106.2
(Mutz. 417), with Dölger (1950) 306f. and Lizzi (1990) 168; Gaudentius, *Tract.* 13.28
(*CSEL* 68.122); around a. 430 in Ravenna, Peter Chrys., *Serm.* 155 (*PL* 52.611); and,
for the whole of Italy and in general terms, Cracco (1980) 362f., 367f.; in Sardinia a.

594, Greg. Magn., *Registr.* 4.23 (*MGH Epp.* 1, 1.257f.), to the *possessores*, advocating flogging and torture for slaves, incarceration if free men, with Tellenbach (1993) 7; and in Africa, Aug., *Ep.* 47.3 (*PL* 33.185) a. 398, 58.1 a. 401, and 62.11.17f. (*PL* 38.422f.), advocating action with moderation. By flogging etc., what were judged to be heresies or schisms were likewise expected to yield, e.g. *CT* 16.5.52.4 a. 412 directing masters to admonish their slaves and flog their *coloni*.

128 Conc. Illiberit. ca. a. 305 can. 40, aiming at sacrifices through *possessores*, and Conc. Bracar. a. 571 frg. 22 in Jonkers (1968) 50; Conc. Tolet. XII a. 681 can. 11, cf. McKenna (1938) 128f., miscalling the peasantry "slaves"; Conc. Arelat. II a. 443/452 can. 23, aiming at pagan acts and facilities through *domini aut ordinatores;* and Conc. Aurel. a. 549 in Vacandard 428. The Council of Soissons in 744 directed bishops to fine pagans, this, in Neustria, cf. Dierkens (1984) 16, but it is not clear how they were to do this.

129 The faithful are *pauci* and *idolatriae sacrilegium* overspreads the whole land, in the 580s, seen in McKenna (1938) 112.

130 *CT* 16.10.12.23 directed at estate owners too compliant to cult acts; legislation by Childebert (d. 558) in *MGH Leg.* 2, 1.2f., against idols on private property (rural, *per villas*), cf. Vacandard (1899) 424ff.; on Clovis, above, chap. 1 nn. 20, 67, and Geary (1988) 168, on his success with his nobles; Charlemagne's fine-laws, *MGH Leg.* 2, 1.69, §21, in Harmening (1979) 57, 62, and on his elevation to sainthood in 1165, Lecouteux (1982) 709; Brunigild's "Christian" subjects in fact not so at all, cf. Greg. Magn., *Registr.* 8.4 (*CCSL* 140.521) a. 597; and Egica in the *Lex Visigothorum*, Supplementa (*MGH Leg.* 1, 1.481f.) a. 693 to the Conc. Tolet. XVI, inviting the bishops to intercept for themselves whatever the *rustici* customarily contributed to forbidden cults.

131 On the recession of Christianity in Britain beginning with the fifth century, see Watts (1991) 223; in Spain, above, n. 129; in Provence, the *multitudo paganorum . . . rusticorum* in Greg. Turon., *Vitae patrum* 17.5 (*MGH SSR* 1.732 = *MGH SRM* 2d ed., 1, 2.282).

132 Above, n. 99; below, chap. 4 n. 139.

133 For the Romans, the god Terminus was the operative one; for the Greeks, see below, chap. 4 n. 121.

134 A large subject, with approach through such discussions as Weinreich (1991) 21, 33ff., Peterson (1926) 156f., Bonner (1950) passim, F. Eckstein and J. H. Waszink's in *RAC* (1950) s.v. "Amulett"; Plin., *N. H.* 28.29, quoted; and a hostile use of an amulet against Shenute, cf. Besa, *Life of Shenute* 83 = Amélineau (1888–95) 1.45f. = Campagnano and Orlandi (1984) 158; other practices in Plin., *N. H.*, 28.25, *fulgetras poppysmis adorare*, and §26, *sternumenta*.

135 MacMullen (1985/6) 68f. on *sortes Virgilianae* and children's play-chants.

136 Juv. 3.26, the coin mentioned not being the "third part" of an aureus, as the word meant in the time of Bishop John, above. For mid-fifth-century Merowingian burials, see Dhénin (1980) 201ff.

137 Regularly mentioned in western church councils, e.g. Conc. Aurel. a. 524 can. 33 or Conc. Bracar. a. 571/2 can. 20; Max. Taur., *Serm.* 30.2 or Caesarius, *Serm.* 52.3.

138 Above, n. 109, with recommendation of the use of private jails in various church documents, n. 127.

Chapter 3: Superstition

1 Max. Taur., *Serm.* 101 (*PL* 57.734), referring to "a *Dianiticus* or a *haruspex*"; Petrus
Chrysologus, *Homil. de Pythonibus* (*PG* 65.27), in Meslin (1970) 81; Mart. Bracar., *De
correct. rust.* 8, worship *in fontibus Nymphas, in silvis Dianas, quae omnia maligni daemones sunt;
Vita S. Eligii* 2.19 (*PL* 87.528B = *MGH SRM* 4.706); *Vita S. Eugendi, MGH SRM* 3.159,
near Ain, a sixth-century exorcism addresses a demon as *lunaticus et Dianaticus;* Messianus, *Vita Caesarii* 18 (*MGH SRM* 3.491), after the bishop's death a. 542, as recalled by
his priest, a local girl is possessed by *daemonium quod rustici Dianam appellant;* Greg.
Turon., *Hist. Franc.* 8.15, worship of a Diana image near Trier which is taken to be
Arduinna, by A. K. Michels, *RAC* s.v. "Diana" col. 970; and Regino of Prüm in
Wasserschleben (1840) viif., ix, 212, and 355 which concerns "certain wicked women
who have turned backwards after Satan, deluded by fancies and hallucinations, and
believe and claim they ride about on certain beasts with a numberless crowd of
women at night with the goddess of the heathens, Diana," traversing great spaces,
always obedient to her summons, etc.; and the believers in this are an *innumera multitudo,* simply *mulierculae* deceived by their dreams. The source Regino quotes is unidentifiable—possibly a chartulary, so ibid. 354n., J. B. Russell (1972) 76, and Ginzburg
(1989) 82.
2 On the medieval Diana cult, see J. B. Russell (1972) 49, 52 ("Diana's appearance in
Northern rites, a figment of the pedantic imagination"), 303 and passim, in contrast
to Margaret Murray's views of 1921 and a delayed succession to those, Ginzburg
(1961) 279, 282ff., idem (1966) xi n. 6, xii, 26, 46, 61f., 65, idem (1972) 608, 628, and
idem (1989) 66, 68, 82ff., arguing (p. 81) for "la stessa divinità romana, Diana,
sovrapposta a una o piu divinità celtiche," to be seen in the *Passio Kiliani* (though the
setting belongs east of the Rhine, cf. Wood [1994] 16), and with the determination
(Ginzburg [1989] 85) of "un sostrato celtico" at the root of various, and variously
modified, later manifestations. He goes on (pp. 187–205) to "conjetture eurasiatiche" reminiscent of Rhys Carpenter (1946). Ginzburg carries the story into the
early modern period, following on Verga (1899) 167ff., who, however, traces the
sources no further back than Regino (cf. also Bonomo [1971] 18) though willing to
imagine ties to the old Roman Diana as well.
3 For the assumption of a "folkloric" culture and its place in a sort of Ur-Welt (or, I
would call it, the Great Non Liquet), see LeGoff (1967) 782f., 785 n. 1, Manselli
(1975) 36, Musset (1976) 145f., Schmitt (1976) 945, 948f., Isambert (1982) 53, Gurevich
(1988) 4f., 21, 78, and Lauwers (1987) 227 and passim, perhaps the best discussion
I've seen of how scholars in various disciplines think about "magic," "superstition,"
and related terms; also Poly and Bournazel (1991) 452f., and Tellenbach (1993) 7, with
Boglioni (1974) 84 extending the term "folkloric" even to elements of Augustine's
world. "These speculations seem unprofitable today," says McManners (1982) 4,
regarding the possible existence or even reconstruction of a universal antecedent
"folk culture."
4 Plin., *N. H.* 28.135; 29.29f.; 28.10 (*sapientissimi cuiusque respuit fides, in universum vero omnibus
horis credit vita nec sentit,* trans. Loeb), 27, and 20 (*quae irridicula videri cogit animus*); 28.13,
confitendum sit de tota coniectatione; 28.29, "There are certain spells, *carmina,* to avert hail . . . ,

sed prodendo obstat ingens verecundia in tanta animorum varietate"; and a continuation, 28.112
—18, *pertaesum . . . vana atque intoleranda auribus*, etc. Views very similar to Pliny's may be
sensed in Roman Stoicism, so far as they regard the natural and supernatural, witness Seneca's friend bidding him "rid me of superstition," *Ad Lucilium* 121.4 (just like
Marcus Aurelius, at note 7, below); again, in the sense of estrangement from older
beliefs, though "our ancestors assigned a Genius or a Juno to every individual," ibid.
110.1; or in the sketch of the universe and everything in it moving according to the *lex
et naturae necessitas, Ad Helviam* 7f.; and *Ad Lucilium* 95.50 and 110.2 (like Pliny, below, n.
5, and below, chap. 4 n. 55), where he does not expect the gods to pay close attention
to little human affairs: they who are so grand are rightly *incuriosi singulorum*—with
the same thought in *De providentia* 1, the gods looking after the whole of humanity,
and only thereafter, *cura singulorum*. In his *Quaestiones naturales* Seneca unfolds most
clearly his point of view, showing himself widely read in Aristotle, Posidonius, and
other Greek predecessors, while also himself persistently empirical, e.g. at 2.28.2,
4B.4.2f., 6.1.11f., or 6.9.3, to pick passages at random; also in the passage quoted
below, chap. 4 n. 123. Add another observer similar to Pliny: Aul. Gell., *N. A.* 10.12.1,
quoting Pliny and expressing even sharper scepticism, adding more absurdities
(10.12.3), *aliud ultra humanam fidem*. Compare Lucian, *Philops.* passim, retailing all sorts
of miracle and magic and ghost stories against a background of completely disbe-
lieving commentary, which is the author's own.

5 Pliny's Stoicism is laid out quite programmatically at the start of his work, at 2.1ff.,
but even there (2.13) he characterizes the sun as *caeli rector, mundi animus, principale numen;*
he rejects (2.20) the belief *inridendum agere curam rerum humanarum illud quicquid est summum*, because it proposes a degree of condescension unworthy of a supreme being,
yet he acknowledges belief in the gods' responsiveness (28.13) and credits divine
benevolence with cures sent to men (25.17; 27.2; 37.60)—all this, notwithstanding
the different interpretation in Beagon (1992) 28f., 92.

6 Plut., *Moral.* 680Cf., where the speaker who defines the subject urges on everyone a
search for the true explanation of what is found in mere φήμη, for ὁ ζητῶν ἐν
ἑκάστωι τὸ εὔλογον ἀναιρεῖ τὸ θαυμάσιον . . . τουτ᾽ἔστι τὸ φιλοσοφεῖν. Note the
tone of confidence in thinking as opposed to tralatician authority (in contrast,
below, n. 15). The dramatic date (indicated in the person of Mestrius Florus) lies in
the third quarter of the first century. On Plutarch's theology, further, MacMullen
(1981) 74 and notes 1f. I have not found in Grant (1952) 64–73 a satisfactory, accurate treatment of Plutarch's and other second-century writers' religious views.

7 Plot., *Enn.* 2.9.14, on the group's ἐπαοιδαί, to believe which is beyond all serious
piety, τὸ σεμνόν; rejection of the δαιμόνια theory of disease, believed in only by οἱ
πολλοί but not by οἱ εὖ φρονοῦντες; disease to be rather addressed by the discipline
of οἱ φιλόσοφοι; and dismissal of the manner of thinking of gnostics as γελοῖον. For
a Roman elite view on cure by exorcism, see Marcus Aur., *Med.* 1.6, taught in his
youth "not to give credence to the statements of miracle-mongers and wizards about
incantations and the exorcism of demons," δαιμόνων ἀποπομπή (though, 1.17.20, he
does obey and profit from medical prescriptions in dreams), or Ulpian defining
physicians by excluding practitioners of incantations, prayers, and exorcism,

"although there are some people [i.e., of the respectable classes, but a minority] who affirm with commendation that these men have been of help to them" (*Dig.* 50.13.1.2f.).

8 Herodian 8.3.8, cf. Dio's fondness for reports of a giant female apparition, which he can swallow with difficulty (55.1.3f.), presents only as hearsay (79[78].25.5), or discounts (73.13.3); makes clear that a report is secondhand (39.61.1); but has a liking for tales of portents and the like, cf. Millar (1964) 77, 179. Of Apul., *Apol.*, a resumé conveniently in MacMullen (1966) 121ff.; and the Alexandrian opinion in Clement Alex., *Strom.* 4.80.

9 Ael. Arist., in the fourth of his *Sacred Tales* §39, trans. Behr (1968) 250: " . . . the following dream . . . I thought that I stood by the altar of Zeus . . . so I boldly sacrificed. As to what happened next, who is wont to have faith, let him have faith, and who is not, to him I say farewell! For the earthquakes came to an end." Compare Marcus Aurelius' army being saved from disaster by a great, a supernaturally severe, storm of rain, subsequently depicted on his Column, talked about in the day, and credited to the prayers or spells of various wonder-workers, cf. MacMullen (1966) 104, 319; earlier, Ps.-Plut., *Moral.* 775E, a god asserts his dignity by an earthquake; and Cic., *Harusp. respons.* 62, asserting that the divine may communicate with us through signs like earthquakes; but no one (i.e., of Cicero's circle) can believe some god will float down to earth and communicate his wishes to men in the way portrayed on the stage (Momigliano [1987] 273f. supplies some context).

10 Galen, *Subfiguratio empirica* 10 (K. Deichgräber, *Die gr. Empirikerschule*, 2d ed., 78f.), reporting on a man come from Thrace to Pergamon by advice of a dream, and there healed; *De libris propriis* 2 (I. Müller, *Galeni scripta minora* 2.99); these with a parallel in MacMullen (1981) 178; and compare Galen's emphatic willingness to trust dreams, omens, and portents reported by his patients, in treating them, whatever doubters may say, *Hippocratis de humoribus* 2.2 (16.222 Kühn).

11 Lucian, *Philops.* 8, where "Tychiades" of the dialogue is the author, ridiculing γοητεία and προσαρτώμενα and (§9) πυρετῶν αἱ ἀποπομπαί, where he requires a proof by reasoning, λόγος, "that the fever fears some holy name or gibberish," ῥῆσις βαρβαρική. He winds up, §10, with the quoted protestations of his piety. His friendship with Galen is shown by Strohmaier (1976) 119, 121, as also (p. 117) his being well known in his own day; further, MacCleod (1979) 327, on Lucian's conscious championing of tighter boundaries around belief, himself being in his own words "the humbug-hater, lie-hater, obfuscation-hater," and "Truth-Champion." A similar emphatic endorsement of cures through incubation sought from Sarapis "by the most distinguished men" in Strabo 17.1.17, of which there are in fact many known illustrations.

12 Aelian, frg. 89, in R. Hercher, *Aeliani opera* 2.231. He was also the author of a collection of wonder tales.

13 On contempt by the elite for the masses' views on religion, see illustrative texts assembled in MacMullen (1981) 8, 144, from Min. Felix, Clem. Alex., Eusebius, Lucian (cf. Francis [1995] 57 n. 9, 62, 125), Apul., Celsus as excerpted in Origen's rebuttal, Hierocles (cf. Cracco Ruggini [1981] 196 n. 89), Julian (frg. 7), and Hier.,

Ep. 75.3 (*PL* 22.687), contemptuous of the ridiculous beliefs spreading in Spain through the *imperiti et mulierculae . . . simplices . . . maximeque nobiles feminas* (an odd group for Jerome to criticize!); and further expressions of contempt for women and their religious opinions in Basil, Gregory of Nyssa, Joh. Chrysos., and other fourth-century writers, in Dickie (1995) 19 n. 32.

14 Plut., *Moral.* 822B, praises mass piety, and (1101Cf.) considers a mixture of piety and superstition among the ignorant masses better than unbelief; γοητεία, "magical fraud" or jugglery and divination should be rebuked or punished, 171Af.. For the broad background, cf. MacMullen (1966) 132–62.

15 The principle oracle was at Claros, but also at Didyma and elsewhere. See the sources indicated in MacMullen (1981) 13, 87, and esp. 147 n. 65, where L. Robert's work is the key; and, for the Chaldaean Oracles of the second century on which also Porphyry and then Proclus depended for much inspiration, see MacMullen (1966) 106f. In contrast, Cic., *De nat. deorum* 3.2.6, *a te philosopho rationem accipere debeo religionis, maioribus autem nostris etiam nulla ratione reddita credere*—so again, Cicero's generation sensed a different world among their ancestors.

16 Grodzinsky (1974) 50f., 55f., adding from much other material *Dig.* 48.19.30, on men of *leves animi* susceptible to "superstitious beliefs about the divine," *superstitio numinis.* For the edict vs. the Manichees, see *Mos. et Rom. leg. coll.* 15.3.1f., *FIRA*, 2d ed., (ed. Riccobono) 2.580f.

17 MacMullen (1990) 68, 120. Of Diocletian's associates (junior co-emperors like Galerius) or protegés or sons of associates, Licinius (307–324) is described as "a foe of letters, which in his boundless ignorance he declared a poison and public plague," *Epit. de Caes.* 41.8.

18 MacMullen (1988) 144.

19 Jones (1963) 28, 35 on the increase in government, "revolutionary change . . . formation of the new imperial nobility of service . . . This change was of crucial importance for the future of Christianity"—very closely (and wisely) followed by LeGoff (1967) 781ff.; further, MacMullen (1990) 118f., with some exceptions on the more educated side noted in MacMullen (1976) 234f. As to bishops, regarding the occasional illiterates, see Gain (1985) 61, 65f. and MacMullen (1990) 321; on bishops' class, most commonly curial (municipal senatorial), like Saint Patrick, with only two or three (imperial) senatorial like Ambrose, see Gilliard (1984) 154–57, 167f., 173f., noting some very poor, some definitely rich examples, and the higher-status antecedents of fifth-century bishops.

20 MacMullen (1990) 121–41 passim, esp. 126f., pointing out the confusions entailed in the "tier" terminology that Brown (1981) employs, cf. for example Brown p. 27, where he contradicts himself, or p. 29, more trouble; or see Wilson (1983) 324, saying of Brown's work that it "does not ultimately escape the two-tier model (popular and 'elite') of religion which it sets off by attacking." For the treatment of religious history in terms of "the educated" and "the peasant" in the early modern era, see, among a hundred illustrations, Lebreton (1923–24) 15, "savants" and "simples," or McManners (1982) 3f.; or "rural" and "the more intellectual" urban, in Frankfurter (1994) 27.

21 "Moving things"—I venture to repeat the phrase used in MacMullen (1981) 70, just
because it is the most specific I can think of to make plain what I mean at the heart
of "superstition." As to the irrelevance of "bookishness" as an index of difference,
I may instance any of the more finished productions of Greek astrology or Artemidorus' *Oneirocritica*, both of which, with gigantic exertion of disciplined intellect, nevertheless show a full acceptance of the "moving around" of tangibilia in the world
by divine forces; or again, the great powers of mind of Augustine in *Civ. dei* 22.8, or of
Gregory the Great in the midst of miracles, well brought out by Boglioni (1974) 71.

22 MacMullen (1966) 151–54.

23 *Asclepius* 1.12f., Nock and Festugière (1945) 311f., and Copenhaver (1992) 226, noting
the "anti-intellectualism" of the passage; the author is often cited by Lactantius as
correct and authoritative, albeit pagan (*Div. inst.* 2.16; 4.6; 4.9 [*PL* 6.335, 461f., 469];
also by Aug., *Civ. dei* 8.23, 24.26). For its quite standard paganism of a somewhat
intellectualized sort, see esp. §§16–18, 23f.

24 In both Greek and Latin, a shift in the meaning of the word "philosophy" can be
seen in the course of the Empire, cf. Stephanus s.v. Φιλοσοφία and Φιλόσοφος to
show the words meaning Christian asceticism and its devotees, from Clem. Alex.
through Joh. Chrysos.; G. W. H. Lampe, *Patristic Greek Lexicon* (1961) s.v. φιλοσοφέω,
φιλοσοφία, and φιλόσοφος; MacMullen (1966) 110f., 320; and Horst (1984) 57 n. 2,
instancing a text from Philo descriptive of the Therapeutai, φιλοσοφοῦσι τὴν
πατρίαν φιλοσοφίαν.

25 Geffcken (1907) 293: one should not investigate the natural universe (*Div. inst.* 2.8.64
and 69, cf. 3.3.4f.); for his "antiwissenschaftliche" views, ibid. 3.13.15, 3.15.6, 3.21.4,
6.4.23, etc., in Geffcken 294 n. 1; his denunciation of intellectual sophistication while
praising Apostolic simplicity, *Div. inst.* 5.2f. (*PL* 6.553A, 556B); and 3.8 (*PL* 6.369), the
passage quoted on the Nile and the lack of any *beatitudo* to be hoped for from the
rantings of *physici*, cf. Thomas Mann's *Der Zauberberg* (at 2.97 of the 1925 Berlin edition of the *Gesammelte Werke*).

26 Millennial panics and prophecies may be better attested in politically uncertain
times, and so suggest a rising credulity—so much for the positives that can be
asserted along these lines of explanation; but no more, I think. I am uncertain how
much ink to devote to clearing away the negatives. I may at least support what I say
about the reviving of the economy in the "Decline," cf. MacMullen (1988) 29–35,
and may instance my argument against the notion of a sort of empire-wide neurotic
reaction to the mid-third-century crisis, in MacMullen (1988) 1 and n. 1.

27 "Sfiducia nell'intelletto nel quarto secolo," *Rivista storica italiana* 84 (1972) 5–16, very
kindly translated for me by my friend Roberto Lopez from the original text of a lecture (of 1970) in English which, with its latter pages updated, became "Distrust of
the mind in the fourth century," MacMullen (1990)17–29; simultaneously, Momigliano
(1972), though professedly he focuses only on a narrow corner of the problem, that
is, on late Roman historiography. He notes (2f.) the earlier practice of Livy and
Livy's generation in isolating the miraculous as entertainment not history, "a paren-
thesis of amusement . . . outside the world of the educated," the separation of religion and superstition in the period "before Christianity complicated matters" (p. 4),

but then a real change with Eusebius which carries on among pagan authors also, Ammianus and Eunapius: "what we would normally call superstition, such as a readiness to believe in prodigies and magic practices, is quietly incorporated in religion" (p. 9). The cause of the change Momigliano doesn't explore, except to note in passing (p. 12) a revealing moment in the earlier-fifth century, in the bringing together of "the intellectuals and the beliefs of ordinary people," when the first persons able to build "a bridge" by which "the christian faith permeated the court in earnest" were certain women of the imperial family marked by their "devotion to the masses," who introduced "monks who came from peasant stock and whose command of Greek was dubious." The model of change here implicit is demographic, though of course a century and a half later than the actual, historic shift itself, as I see it. For the respectful use of Momigliano's essay, see Markus (1990) 13, "devastating critique," Cameron (1991) 36, or Brown (1981) 19, praising its "characteristic wisdom and firmness."

28 Tert., *De praescript. hereticorum* 7.9, with much more (§5–12) on the tedium and disgustingness of philosophy; quoted (§12), *nobis curiositate opus non est post Christum Iesum nec inquisitione post evangelium;* similar lines in *De testimonia animae* 1.6f., adduced with discussion by Fögen (1993) 297, parallel texts praising *simplicitas* from Irenaeus (299 n. 33, 302), Tertullian's attribution of *curiositas* to Satanic temptation (304, 311, on *De idol.* 9.1f., 7f., and Lact. passages), and 301, with the conclusion, "Der Verzicht auf die Wissbegierde bis hin zum Nichtwissen wird absolut und ohne Kompromissangebote eingefordert." For earlier discussion see also H. J. Carpenter (1963) 302ff., and Hällström (1984) 29, 32.

29 Arnob., *Adv. nat.* 2.10, "You have given credence to your wise men and those learned in every kind of study—those, forsooth, who know nothing and proclaim no one doctrine, who join battle over their views with their adversaries . . . and make all doubtful, and demonstrate from their disputes that nothing can be known."

30 Constantine's pronouncements gathered in MacMullen (1990) 128, where the emperor's similar dismissal of the niceties of jurisprudence (cf. *Paneg. vet.* 11[3].20.1), even of theological debate and the controversy over Arianism, is instanced: he waves aside all theological differences as "perfectly inconsequential and quite unworthy of such contentious debate . . . extremely minor and highly inconsequential."

31 In Bambeck (1983) 30, Ambrose, *De fide* 1.3.71f., raising the *stulta huius mundi* above the "wise," the *rusticus* over the *philosophus,* and, §§42f., damning the gymnasia and their *dialectica* and all those *qui copiose disputant* compared to simpler believers; other similar texts from this author, e.g. *De off.* 2.8 (*PL* 16.106), and references to modern discussions in Davidson (1995) 321, showing that Ambrose "seeks continually to depreciate philosophy" in a "consistently hostile spirit towards philosophy"; Bambeck (1983) 32, showing similar views in Chromatius, *Tract.* 16 *in Mt* 4.18f. (*CCSL* 9A.263), comparing *nobiles mundi aut divites, . . . sapientes saeculi,* and their *sapientia* with Christianity's *piscatores* and *idiotae* in a now-traditional Christian fashion; again, idem 4.4 (*PL* 20.339), on the *stultitia gentilium;* also Victricius, *De laude sanctorum* 11 (*PL* 20.453) of the early fifth century, inserting into his sermon, with no special reason, the demand, *non me hypothetici et categorici syllogismorum modi intricant, non inania philosophorum sophismata decipiunt; ipsa faciem*

suam veritas aperit, fides despuit argumenta. . . . My last quotation is from Philastr., *De haere-sibus* 102 (*PL* 12.1216A), of the 380s.

32 Aug., *Enchiridion* 9.3 (*PL* 40.235), *non rerum natura ita rimanda est, quemadmodum ab eis quos physicos Graeci vocant;* cf. 16.5 (239), *non nobis videatur ad felicitatem consequendam pertinere, si sciemus causas magnarum in mundo corporalium motionum . . . et cetera huiusmodi; Conf.* 10.35.54, out of his personal experience he laments, *inest animae . . . experiendi per carnem vana et curiosa cupiditas;* and *Ep.* 11.2 (*PL* 33.75), *illa namque quae de hoc mundo quaerentur nec satis ad beatam vitam obtinendam mihi videntur pertinere.* For such passages and comment, see Marrou (1937) 233f., 248f.; Boglioni (1974) 14f.; and Stancliffe (1983) 219, quoted.

33 Hällström (1984) 32, on Origen; and Origen protests, *Homil. in Ps.* 36.5.1 (*PG* 12.359), against "hating and opposing those who pursue the study of wisdom."

34 Soc., *H. E.* 2.9, Soz., *H. E.* 3.6, and other examples in MacMullen (1990) 316 n. 44, 319 n. 37.

35 Euseb., *Praep. ev.* 15.62.16, cf. Philostorgius, *H. E.* 12.10 (ed. Bidez-Winkelmann 147), on quakes, and the conclusion "that such happenings cannot come to pass through any of the aforesaid elements according to natural forces," only by God's wish. Further, a general statement on the change in the east, below, n. 39.

36 Basil, *Homil.* 1.9 (*PG* 29.24A), against πολυπραγμοσύνη; §10 col. 25A and §8 col. 20C, with other passages and discussion in Amand de Mendieta (1976) 29, 35, 40, 43; on Chrysostom, Bambeck (1983) 33, adding esp. *Homil. in Ep. 1 ad Cor.* 4.2ff. (*PG* 61.32ff.), ridiculing eloquence and Greek σοφία and δεινότης σοφισμάτων; and praising τοὺς ἀγροίκους and τοὺς ἰδιώτας. Compare, earlier, Didymus the Blind (ca. 313–398) in Theodoret, *H. E.* 4.29.1 (4.26, *PG* 82.1189C), praised because παιδείας οὐ γευσάμενος Ἑλλενικῆς τούς τε πολυσχιδεῖς τῶν Ἑλλήνων διήλεγξε πλάνους; likewise, Theodoret himself, *Graec. affect. curat.* 8.2ff. (*SC* 57 [1958]), glorying in the contrast between fancy Greek philosophy and its artificial expressions against the lowly simplicity of the apostles and disciples, however "untaught and uniniated into the refinements of language"; and the scene of Athens in the later fifth century where the studious young Severus, later bishop of Antioch, "was sitting one day reading the writings of Plato, and there appeared to him Leontius the martyr," saying, enough time wasted on "the abominations of the heathen, and mayest thou read the law of the Lord," cf. Goodspeed (1908) 594, 596f. on the date and circumstances. In Theodoret, notice the use of the word "philosophy" in the manner usual in these later times, to mean Christian asceticism, e.g. describing a monk's lodgings as φιλοσοφίας φροντιστήριον, *Hist. relig.* 4.2, 6.13, 8.2, 30.5, etc. (very far removed from the use in Aristophanes' *Clouds!*). Jerome may belong here, unless he should count in the Latin tradition: cf. in any case his own version of the topos *simplicitas = veritas, In Ps.* 81 (*PL* 26.1066B).

37 Festugière (1961–64) 1.77 and 3.118 n. 279, a long, rich note; similarly, Cracco Ruggini (1981) 196f. n. 89.

38 Athanas., *Vita Ant.* 72f., and even a visit from pagan intellectuals, §74; *Apophthegmata patrum, PG* 65.88f.; and Callinicos, *Vita Hypatii* 29.3, the σχολαστικοὶ τῆι τέχνηι τῆς παιδεύσεως αὐτῶν φιλοσοφῆσαι and are reproved by the saint's true-speaking.

39 Festugière (1961–64) 1.79ff.; σαλοί, "idiots for Christ," Egyptian and Syrian of the

mid-fourth to sixth century, in Grosdidier de Matons (1970) 282, 285ff., 297; Ryden (1981) 107ff., the first example of the σαλός in Egypt ca. 420; the gradual fading away of the phenomenon of σαλοί by the eleventh century, Morris (1995) 62; and the monk Evagrius quoted in MacMullen (1990) 125, "Blessed is he who has attained infinite ignorance." Speaking more generally, Gouillard (1976) 305f., points out how "philosophy in Byzantium became no more than a utilitarian discipline," focused on procedures of reasoning in Aristotelian fashion, and "wisdom was no more the truth gained through investigation, but truth granted through initiation, regulated for salvation and so taught that the orthodox pious, without special education, even illiterate, could claim the name of philosopher"—this, the Byzantine mentalité till some breakthroughs in the eleventh century and following.

40 Amm. 22.16.17, with comparable texts in MacMullen (1990) 318 n. 16; and Aeneas of Gaza, *Theophrastus* 23 (*PG* 85.876 = Colonna [1958] 3), on the low state of φιλοσοφία καὶ τὰ μουσεῖα, the date explained by Colonna pp. viif., and the author a pagan, cf. expressions in his *Ep.* 1, μὴ πρὸς Φιλίου Διός, or *Ep.* 2, μὰ τοὺς θεούς, Hercher (1873) 24f.

41 Grundmann (1958) 20ff.—though later rulers like Leo VI were educated, even literary figures.

42 Almost the only pagan sources to be drawn on are Eunapius and Damascius, the former (§463) reporting Constantine's belief that a certain philosopher could "chain the winds through his too-great σοφία," and another philosopher's introduction to superhuman wisdom through being taught by "either ἥρωες or δαίμονες" (§467) and thereby capable of far-sight (§470); still another philosopher's causing an image of Hecate to smile and laugh (§475), Porphyry's telling how he had cleansed a δαιμόνιον from a public building (§457), and Iamblichus (§459) evoking Erotes from sacred springs. Damascius retails an account of the combatants at the Catalaunian Fields, a. 451, who even in death continued standing and fighting for three days as εἴδωλα τῶν ψυχῶν, *Vita Isidori* 63 (Photius, *Bibl.* 339, ed. R. Henry 6.20). Notice (Photius §130, Henry 2.104) that Damascius was the author of four other works, on "Wonders," "Wonderful things about gods, δαίμονες," "Wonderful things about epiphanies after death," and "Wonders of nature." Momigliano (1972) 8ff. adduces texts from other pagan authors like Ammianus, the SHA, and Olympiodorus (and some from Eunapius, too), discovering in them (p. 11) no "distinction between religion and superstition" and (9) "no significant distinction between the beliefs of the upper classes and those of the lower classes." Saradi-Mendelovici (1990) 56 adds that there was no distinction to be drawn between the "intellectuals" and "the uneducated" in what they believed, whether pagan or Christian, and instances Libanius (*Or.* 19.5.29) and Chrysostom (*Homil* 15 and 21, *PG* 49.154, 214ff.) in agreement, that the civil outbreak of 387 in Antioch was caused by "evil demons," πονηροὶ δαίμονες.

43 For the background, see e.g. Origen, *C. Cels.* 1.31 and 8.31 (*PG* 11.717Df., 1564A), teaching that demons cause plagues, storms, famines etc.; Tertullian blaming them for diseases, even blights on trees, in *Dictionnaire de spiritualité* s.v. "Démon" p. 175; a good range of the more obvious second- and third-century texts and authors in E. Ferguson (1984) cap. 4; and in sources post-300, *RAC* s.v. "Geister" (1974/5) passim, esp. 779–81, and Graus (1989) 109 and (possession) 114. For the demonology taught in

baptismal ceremonies, see Kelly (1985) passim, e.g. 101f., 140ff., 166f. A clear direction is offered by Aug., *In ps.* 130.7 (*PL* 37.1708), *dolores autem in corporum plerumque immittuntur ab angelis Satanae;* cf. a representative eastern text showing prevailing ideas about man's infestation by demons, of date around 500, Philoxenus, *Homil.* 9.278–86, in Lemoine (1956) 259–64, and Greenfield (1988) 165f., on the ubiquity of demons in Byzantine thought. For a broad conclusion covering the fourth to the twelfth century, one might quote Schmitt (1986) 136 as representative of a consensus on medieval thought, often encountered and easily supported: "toute perturbation de l'ordre était rapporté au jeu des pouvoirs antagonistes qui étaient attribués à des intentionnalités, celles de personnages surnaturels (Dieu, démons, saints, etc.) ou de personnages humains (jeteurs de sorts, sorcières, etc.)." Painting of a cross on one's forehead is what distinguishes Christians according to Tert., *De corona* 3 (*PL* 2.80A); explained or assumed in Orig., *Selecta in Ezech.* 9 (*PG* 13.800), Cypr., *Test. adv. Iudaeos* 2.22, chap. title (*PL* 4.745), Julian, *Ep.* 79 (ed. Bidez, 2d ed., 1, 2.86), Hier., *In Ezech.* 9 (*PL* 25.88Bf.), Aug., *Serm.* 161.6, Cyril Alex., *C. Iulianum* 6 (*PG* 76.796D), and Lact., *Div. inst.* 4.26f. (*PL* 6.531)—these and other texts in Sulzberger (1925) 361, 365, 403, 432, 437.

44 On the attribution of hostile events to demons by Greg. Naz. et al., see the preceding note and Greenfield (1988) 52f., 67; on bishops' acceptance of hexing, 110f., Kelly (1985) 140f., and Dickie (1995) passim; notice, also, in the west, Augustine's matter-of-fact acceptance of hexing, the possession of a man's whole household of herds and flocks and slaves by *spiritus maligni, Civ. dei* 22.8.6 (*PL* 41.764); on the baptismal formula for exorcism, exactly resembling fourth-century magical spells, compare the text in Greenfield with *PGM* 4.3020–85 of ca. 300 in Betz (1986) 96f., exorcism by "Jesus, God of the Hebrews," followed by a long "arete" (possibly for use by Jews), or *PGM* 4.1227–64, using Jesus and the God of Abraham and "after driving out the demon, hang around him [= the healed] a phylactery" with a gibberish spell and a Chnoubis depiction, a lion-headed serpent, in Betz p. 62. On demons to be correctly seen as the cause of diseases and the church's consequent hostility toward and renunciation of medical science, see Severus of Antioch (patriarch 512–18, d. 538: *PO* 29.74f.), in *RAC* s.v. "Geister" 779, or again, in saints' biographies, the same hostility, with illustrative eastern texts collected in Magoulias (1964) 128–32.

45 Euseb., *H. E.* 8.7.2, 8.7.4f., 8.8.1, and Athanas., *Vita Ant.* 15 (*PG* 26.865), cf. also Soc., *H. E.* 4.23; *Vita Ant.* 59f., far-sight, §82, prediction with many witnesses, and §§14, 48, 71, exorcism; in later generations, among numberless similar examples, the holy man Emilis raises the dead to life, *Vitae patrum* 6.9 (*PL* 73.1002), as does Hormizd, Budge (1902) 37; for another wonder-worker, Bessarion, exorcizing in the presence of many witnesses, *Vitae patrum.* 3.121, 6.4, and 7.14 (*PL* 73.873, 1001, 1037), with *Bibliotheca Sanctorum* 3 (1963) 141 on the date and reliability of the source; Nikolaos (d. 564) near Myra in Lycia, raising the dead, restoring sight to the blind, or bringing fertility to the fields, §31 in Anrich (1913–17) 1.26f., §33 (1.28), §59 (1.46), and date of the saint, Anrich 2.214; with more resuscitations of the dead by the holy Hormizd in northern Mesopotamia, Budge (1902) 73, 82.

46 Patlagean (1968) 107ff., 113 n. 1 with exorcism scenes, and 123f. on imitation by the elite classes.

47 Soc., *H. E.* 6.6, 7.18; Paulin. Nolensis evidently reporting to Augustine the apparition of Saint Felix to save the town from Vandals, as reported *non incertis rumoribus sed testibus certis*, in Aug., *De cura pro mortuis* 16.19 (*PL* 40.606); Euseb., *H. E.* 3.8.5; John of Ephesus in Nau (1897) 458, a. 453, along with many other items of weather portents, pp. 457, 459, 462f., 473f., 476, 481f., etc.

48 Theodoret, *Hist. relig.* 1.1 (*PG* 82.1304D), on which see Adnès and Canivet (1967) 62f., the author writing in a. 444 crediting an event of 350 to a person already dead; for the dragon tale, *Hist. relig.* 3.7ff. (*PG* 82.1328C), an event of the 380s, with other miraculous destruction of dragons by Saint Symeon in Chaine (1948) 83 and Amélineau (1887) 135, drawing on bishop Moses' life of bishop Pisentios of Coptos of the early seventh century; on the supernatural defense of the eastern capital, accounts in Baynes (1949) 170, 174; in a western setting, below, n. 54, and the huge dragon seen in the air above Uzala, emptying the marketplace, whose crowds fly to the countervailing Saint Stephen, and so the dragon is destroyed, cf. the account by one of the clergy of Evodius, *De miraculis S. Stephani* 2.4 (*PL* 41.850).

49 Theodoret, *Graec. affect. curat.* 8 (*PG* 83.1012B = Canivet, *SC* 57.313), the population grateful to the martyrs, καὶ ἰατροὺς ὀναμάζουσι καὶ ὡς πολιούχος τιμῶσὶ καὶ φύλακας; cf. earlier, Asterius, *In ss. martyres* (*PG* 40.324A, προστάται); Evagrius, *H. E.* 4.35 (*PG* 86. 2768), the holy martyr guards Antioch from plague; Soc., *H. E.* 4.23 and other passages in Cracco Ruggini (1982) 65 n. 108. For western saints seen as patrons and defenders, see Guillot (1989) 210ff., 217f.

50 Theodoret, *Hist. relig.* 1.1 (*PG* 82.1297C–1300), bishop of Nisibis again; Eustratius, the priest of his subject, writing the *Vita Eutychii*, Eutychius being bishop of Constantinople (552–582), and the miracles at §§17 (Uranius, *PG* 86.2293D) and 45–60 (*PG* 86.2325C–28C, 2328D–44A), the biographer emphasizing that he had personally witnessed one miraculous cure (§51, col. 2332); further, Apollon bishop of Heracleopolis in Egypt under Justinian, curing a woman of an issue of blood when she touches his robe, etc., cf. Campagnano and Orlandi (1984) 185ff.

51 For festival honors, see, as examples of a practice universal by the early fifth century, Evagrius, *H. E.* 4.35 (*PG* 86.2768), and Theodoret, *Hist. relig.* 24.2 (*PG* 82.1457D), at Cyrrhus, and *Graec. affect. curat.*, (*PG* 83.1032Af. = *SC* 57.332); further examples in Lucius (1908) 550f.; and bishops as authors of eulogies such as the Cappadocian Fathers, cf. Delehaye (1912) 54; Joh. Chrysos., *Laudatio S. mart. Iuliani* (*PG* 50.669ff.), reminding his listeners that they can "take any deranged person, δαιμονῶντα, and mad, bring him here to that holy tomb where are the martyr's relics, and you will see the demon leap away and flee"; again, eulogizing, Moses, above; bishop Basil of Seleuceia in his *Vita Theclae*, *PG* 85.560Cff.; Cyril, *Oratiunculae tres in translatione reliq. SS. mart. Cyri et Joannis* (*PG* 77.1101–5); Theodoret (*Ep.* 4); and Sophronios in 610/20, cf. McGuckin (1993) 291.

52 Mango (1984) 48f., the date of the construction in the second quarter of the fifth century, the text of the ninth century.

53 Theodoret, *Hist. relig.* 17.10 (*PG* 82.1424Df.), regarding the processing of the remains of the bishop of Carrhae in 438 by Theodosius II, Pulcheria and Eudocia; idem, *H.*

E. 4.16 (*PG* 82.1161Af.), on Valens; and Evagrius, *H. E.* 4.36 (*PG* 86.2769), on the miracle of the furnace.

54 *De miraculis S. Stephani* 2.4.2 (*PL* 41.851), with 2.5.1 also for the title *patronus communis;* Ambros., *Ep.* 22.12, on the vision leading to the discovery of the relics of the two saints; Aug., *Civ. dei* 22.8 (*CCSL* 48.816–20), with other attestations of the use of such earth, in Meer (1961) 545, and (540) passages in other writings of Augustine relevant to miracles; and add *Civ. dei* 15.23.1 (*PL* 41.468), insisting on the credibility of witnesses to the reality and wicked works of demons, "Silvanuses" and "Faunuses," *quos vulgo incubos vocant,* visiting women with *quosdam daemones, quos Dusios Galli nuncupant,* and whom it would be reckless to deny.

55 Ibid. 820, thirty miles from Hippo (the miraculous replacing of a dislodged eye paralleled through a miracle of John, bishop of Caesarea, in Evagrius, *H. E.* 4.7 [*PG* 86.2716]); nearer the town of Hippo, the miracle of the ring, p. 821, and another healed fistula (822, recalling the fistula likewise healed a generation earlier by "the god" of the Neoplatonist Patricius, cf. Damascius, *Vita Isidori* 344, ed. Henry, Photius' *Bibl.* 6.35); blindness healed, gout (823) *per revelationem, quid adhiberet quando doleret* (i.e., a divine prescription through a dream), and the dead brought back to life, ibid., with a final set of miracles and the publicity they merit (826f.) to conclude. Meer (1961) 540 points to some scepticism in Augustine until past forty, when he was more detached from his books and "at last began to realize what the people themselves had known all along"; "the great mass of the people were not only credulous but absolutely athirst for miracles" (557); and "in his fully believing in miracles he is a typical child of his age" (553). For the special inventory of miracles, such a one as Augustine himself drew up, and the publicity attending on its frequent reading to festival crowds, see *De miraculis S. Stephani* 1.15 (*PL* 41.842) in Kötting (1950) 263f.

56 Sulpicius Sev., *Vita S. Martini* 11.4f., with more miracles at 5.4 (15f.), and innumerable cures, 6.1f. (16.1f.); 14.2 and *Dial.* 3.9.2, spectacular examples picked out by Stancliffe (1983) 222f.; but also Greg. Turon., *De virtutibus S. Martini* 1.11, etc., including the power of wax from candles at the shrine to protect fields from damaging weather, 1.34; restoring life, in a text of ca. 480, Constantius, *Vita Germani* 38 (*MGH SRM* 7.278), and healing miracles, 27 (p. 270), 29 (272); Messianus, *Vita Caesarii* 27 (*MGH SRM* 3.494); Nicetus, *CCSL* 117.421f., in Hillgarth (1969) 78, date ca. 560.

57 Victricius (ca. 380s), *De laude sanctorum* 11 (*PL* 20.453Af.), on the saints throughout the west as source of *medicina;* Faustus etc., in Beaujard (1991) 188.

58 Greg. Turon., *De gloria confess.* 35, the saint from within his tomb hurls off a bad man sitting on that tomb; *De gloria mart.* 33, regarding Saint Stephen as reported to Gregory by the bishop of Bordeaux; Augustine's belief that Saints Protasius and Gervasius will visibly punish foreswearing if disputants attempt it at their tombs, *Ep.* 78.3 (*PL* 33.269), as St. Martin in *his* tomb was known to punish oath-breakers, Greg. Turonensis, *Hist. Franc.* 7.29 (*MGH SRM* 1, 2.347); Demetrios' harsh punishment of someone who spoke against him, Lemerle (1979–82) 1.119f., and the saint's angry shouts from his tomb to protect his offerings, ibid. 99; cf. much similar pagan material in MacMullen (1981) 173 n. 33; for similar physical evidence of a saint's presence and operation, see e.g. Tolstoi (1920) 56, 58f., real oil and real blood left by an

epiphany in a Constantinopolitan shrine, or, among many examples, physical indications of an overnight miracle discovered on the suppliant sufferer in the morning, at the shrine of Saints Cosmas and Damian, Magoulias (1964) 140f.

59 Greg. Turon., *Vita patrum* 11.1 and 3, Caluppa in the Auvergne (526–76).

60 *De gloria mart.* 70; *De virtutibus S. Iuliani* 24f. (*MGH SRM* 1, 2.125); *De virtutibus S. Martini* 1.34, 2.2, and 3.10 (*MGH SRM* 1, 2.154, 160, and 185); and *De gloria mart.* 83, storms.

61 *De gloria mart.* 96 (*MGH SRM* 1, 2.103).

62 Greg. Turon., *Hist. Franc.* 2.23, 5.43 (*MGH SRM*, 2d ed., 1, 1, 1.68 and 249)—a favorite incident, cf. Athanas., *Ep. ad Serapionem de morte Arii* 3 (*PG* 25.688), Rufin., *H. E.* 1.13 (*PL* 21.485f.), Soc., *H. E.* 1.38 (*PG* 67.167), and Soz., *H. E.* 2.29 (*PG* 67.1020), and others later.

63 Severus Endelechius, *Carmen bucolicum* (*PL* 19.799f.); compare Paulin. Nolensis, *Carm.* 14.198f., where St. Felix cures sick stock; idem, *Carm.* 14.24f.,19.252ff., 18.98ff., and 26.318ff., exorcisms; and the tale of the sinner, *Carm.* 20.69–110.

64 Paulin. Mediolanensis, *Vita Ambrosii* 48, going on to mention how Ambrose' powers are operative not only in the church but in various provinces, too, up to the time of the writer.

65 Lucius (1908) 173 n. 2.

66 Greg. Magn., *Dial.* 1.10.5 (Vogüé [1978–80] 2.96); 1.10.8 (100); 1.10.17f. (108); by a *miraculum* cures a savage horse, too (1.10.9f.), and continues miracles from his tomb (1.10.19, p. 110); 2.27.3 (216) and 2.7, Benedict's cures and far-sight, and one of his priests walks on water (as does, for comparison, the holy Hormizd on the Tigris, in Budge [1902] 134); 3.10.2f., Sabinus of Placentia; 3.15, a bear is miraculously sent in answer to an ascetic's prayer to live with him and be company to him (compare the lion persuaded by the holy Zosimas in Palestine to serve as his ass and carry his loads to the very gates of Caesarea, δείκνυς τοῦ Θεοῦ τὴν δύναμιν, in Evagrius, *H. E.* 4.7 [*PG* 86.2717], or the bear made to serve as a beast of burden on a sixth-century road in Italy, *Miracula Martini abbatis Vertavensis* 1 [*MGH* SRM 3.568]); a restoration of life, Greg., Magn., *Dial.* 3.17.2f. (238); a holy abbot moves over in his grave to make room for a second burial, 3.23.4 (360); or *Hist. Franc.* 6.6, an ascetic "freezes" an unbeliever to discipline him.

67 Greg. Magn., *Registr.* 3.6 (*PL* 77.56Df.), in Boglioni (1974) 25f., with *Dial.* 2 praef. (Vogüé [1978–80] 2.126) on Benedict's fleeing from secular learning, *dispectis itaque litterarum studiis . . . scienter nescius et scienter indoctus;* 3.37.1 and 19f. (p. 424), a priest of Nursia, illiterate but all the more holy for that, in his *ignorantia* rising above *nostra indocta scientia;* and the passage quoted, *De trinitate* 3.2.6 (*CC* 50.132f.), in Boglioni (1974) 30.

68 Eugippius, *Vita S. Severini* 16.1–5, 18.1f., and 15.1–4, in Régerat (1991) 212, 220–24. The date of the mission lies in the 450s.

69 Muchembled (1978) 23, examining with another scholar, Mandrou, "a certain conception of human life, implying the omnipresence of the supernatural (God's or the Devil's) in all that happens," from which Europe escaped "to a conception plus raisonnée de l'existence." See the interpretation extended in idem (1978a) 220, that in the view of the rural population "nothing was natural and all events, good or bad,

were to be explained by the intervention of these [supernatural] forces"; or return to Gibbon insisting (1946, p. 369),"Since every friend of revelation is persuaded of the reality, and every reasonable man is convinced of the cessation, of miraculous powers" at some point before his present day, "there must have been *some period* in which they were either suddenly or gradually withdrawn from the Christian church." For something recent on the emergence of Enlightenment, with up-to-date bibliography, see for example Pott (1992) passim, e.g. 216–22 on the insistence by the Dutchman Balthasar Bekker (1634–98) that the Devil cannot influence the material world.

70 Bardy (1928) 128, "entrainement irraisonnée." For an instance of the consensus, see Grant (1952) 75, "the steady decline of rationality in the fourth century"; Sambursky (1962) 47, describing "the strange mental climate of the third century A.D. and the following centuries," and continuing, "It was a period in which obscurantist tendencies of all shades steadily increased their hold over the minds of religious sects, philosophical systems and practising scientists alike. Occult sciences flourished and magic and alchemy." Further, Graus (1965) 44, "Doch das Schlagwort, steretype vom kritiklosen Wunderglauben des Mittelalters ist leider, wie uns die Quellen eindeutig beweisen, zwar nicht falsch"; more recently (not to mention MacMullen [1966] chaps. 3f., e.g. 154, "twilight of irrationality"), see Uytfanghe (1981) 205, "Un des clichés les plus communément reçus pour caractériser la mentalité du Haut Moyen Age est 'l'invasion du miraculeux' . . . la régression mentale de cette époque . . . [mais] l'irrationalité n'est pas une innovation du haut Moyen Age . . . elle plonge ses racines très loin dans l'Antiquité tardive et même dans l'Antiquité classique."

71 For example, Cracco Ruggini (1982) 29, "sempre più rari si vanno facendo lo scetticismo razionalista di un Luciano, la cauta ricerca di spiegazioni 'scientifiche' alternative tipica degli Accademici e degli Epicurei" in the face of σημεῖα; or Hanson (1980) 959, detecting "a retreat from rationalism, a yearning for salvation, a flight from the disinterested search for truth, a tendency to rely on authority . . . , exaltation of revelation . . . there is no doubt that it was there in late antiquity."

72 Notes 4–6 and 10; MacMullen (1981) 144 nn. 33f. and 70ff. on the use of the term *superstition* in the second to fourth centuries.

73 See esp. Gibbon (1946) 902f.

74 On δεισιδαιμονία, much has been written, but good and recent is the discussion in Pott (1992) 36, also aligning the Latin word and idea (49), especially in Cicero, that it defies sense to fear rather than love and revere beings that are like parents; cf. Sen., *Ad Lucilium* 123.16, *superstitio error insanus est: amandos timet, quos colit, violat.* On cult acts inappropriate (= irrational) to such beings as the gods, ibid. 95.47, "Let us forbid lamps to be lighted on the sabbath, since the gods do not need light," cf. exactly the same thought (surely borrowed) in Lact., *Div. inst.* 6.2.5 (*PL* 6.639A), *num mentis suae compos putendus est* (. . . the person who does this). De Maistre is quoted in Meer (1961) 557, who goes on to conclude his discussion of Augustine's degree of "credulity" or "superstition" with the closing words to the chapter: "It was really not such a bad thing that historical criticism should have been kept back for a thousand years, if Christ was to continue to be preached and God's name to be magnified in all things."

75 Another controverted area, with a good entrance supplied by Prinz (1989) passim, citing e.g. Hincmar in the ninth century to show how different parts of his *Life of Remigius* is "volkstümlich" or for the *illuminati;* and notice (304) the difference between the degree of acceptance by Gregory of Tours and among those (evidently of any class) whom he rebukes as "unbelieving and envious," *Gloria confess.* 6 (*MGH SRM* 1, 2.752)—readers or listeners being evidently less accepting of miracles than the hagiographers, cf. the latter's "very numerous" assurances, not for mere form's sake, collected by Uytfanghe (1989) 183f. with n. 99. For the sense of distance between bishops and flock, see above, chap. 1 n. 15, and texts from Augustine, below, chap. 4 n. 37.

76 Agobard (see the *Enciclopedia cattolica* s.v.), *Liber contra insulsam vulgi opinionem de grandine et tonitruis* 1f., 4f., 7 (*PL* 104.147ff.), ending (§16 p. 158) with the complaint of the deluded, *nec rationabiliter pensabant....* Compare Plin., *N. H.* 2.104f., 131ff., meteorological phenomena have "fixed causes" which he examines; and Plut., *Moral.* 893Dff., collecting Greek philosophical explanations for thunder, all natural or empirical; 895Aff., on winds, droughts, storms; 896Cff., on earthquakes.

77 Cameron (1991) 42 devotes a considerable part of her book to the freeing of Christianity from nameless critics and from their detection in Christianity of "uncouthness" and "irrationality" (7), "popular culture" (36, 202), "naiveté" (39), "a general softening of the intellect" (147), and so forth.

78 For the term "superstition" where, as it seems to me, a definition of what is meant would be most useful, see for instance Meer (1961) 556 or Saradi-Mendelovici (1990) 57; for "folkloric," beyond n. 3, above, see Lauwers (1987) 230 with n. 5, on the body of scholarship assigning such a cultural category to paganism, or LeGoff (1967) 782f., where he evidently intends "folkloric" and "primitive" to indicate what preexisted Christianity and, indeed, preexisted the Roman empire among the "peasant masses." On "the masses" as defining beliefs in contrast to the elite, see for example Engemann (1975) 40f. discussing "Volksfrömmigkeit," Tellenbach (1993) 7 on beliefs "among the uncultured 'people,'" and other scholars in n. 80, below. Finally, for an example of how the apparently irrational or superstitious will be entirely rational within a person's basic assumptions, see Boglioni (1974) 71 on Gregory the Great: his "mentalité est, dans son orientation générale la plus profonde, suffisament 'surnaturaliste' pour pouvoir acceuillir le miraculeux comme chose obvie, avec une facilité psychologique et une disponibilité qui ne sont pas freinées par une précise exigence logico-rationnelle." Well said. The papal procession of 847 may be found in the *Liber pontificalis,* Duchesne (1955–57) 2.110, to which, add a striking parallel in the seventh-century challenge of Saint Marcianus to a dragon in a cave near Syracuse, *Acta Sanctorum, Iun.* II (1698) 788–95, especially 793, as in a third exorcizing of a basiliscus-haunted cave by the holy Paul near the Tigris, cf. John of Ephesus' *Lives* in Brooks (1924) 112.

79 A great deal of controversy centers in the word "survival"—needlessly, perhaps, if it is used to denote no more than parts of something otherwise largely perished. See Graus (1965) 166f.; Isambert (1982) 26, 35; for bibliography, Lauwers (1987) 228 n. 1; or Tellenbach (1993) 92f.

80 "Popular": Boglioni (1974) 11f., Engemann (1975) 40, Manselli (1975), Schmitt (1976), Isambert (1982) 72f.; Lauwers (1987) with bibliography at 229 nn. 1–4 and reference to *La piété populaire en France. Répertoire bibliographique;* Poly and Bournazel (1991) 452f., "vulgaire"; Cameron (1993) 36, 147.

81 For the apparent assumption that religion not Christian isn't religion at all, see, e.g. Van Engen (1986) 546, counting as "religious life" for "every European" only what went on within the church; or Cameron (1993) 222, "culture" which is not Christian is "secular"! Quoted is Schmitt (1976) 948f.

Chapter 4: Assimilation

1 Wetter (1922) 265f., quoted on "ritual dance" at the Saint Cyprian shrine and festival as noticed by Aug., *Serm.* 311.5 (*PL* 38.1415), and going on to instance the *Conc. Afr.* a. 401 can. 60 (Joannou [1962a] 297), on saints days *per nonnullas civitates, . . . saltationes sceleratissimae per vicos et plateas, ut matronalis honor et innumerabilium feminarum pudor devote venientium ad sacratissimum diem iniuriis lascivientibus appetatur, ut etiam ipsius sanctae religionis pene fugiatur accessus;* cf. Aug., *Serm.* 311.5 (*PL* 38.1415), dancing in Carthage on Cyprian's anniversary rebuked, and again, 326.1 (*PL* 38.1449), at Hippo on the martyr's birth-day, and *En. in Ps.* 32(33).5 (*PL* 36.279), dance and song to the cithara at martyrs' tombs (just as in Antioch, Joh. Chrys., *Homil. de Lazaro* 1.1 [*PG* 48.963]); *Homil.* 265 attributed to Augustine (*PL* 39.2239), likewise rebuking *saltationes ante ipsas basilicas sanctorum . . . paganorum observatione.* For dance apparently universal, or close to it, in non-Christian worship, see cap. 2 nn. 44–47.

2 The call for dancing for the Saint Polyeuctos festival in a saint's-day sermon (so, by a bishop), in Aubé (1882) 9f., 38, and 79, is best dated a. 363/375, at one of the saint's several shrines (known in Constantinople and elsewhere), the text at p. 79, τί τοίνυν ἡμεῖς ἀντάξιον δῶρον, . . . ποῖα δὲ χαριστήρια; . . . χορεύσωμεν αὐτῶι; also in Gougaud (1914) 10, Quasten (1983) 175, and Pasquato (1976) 233f. and 259; in Antioch, Joh. Chrysos., *Ad pop. Ant. homil.* 19.1 (*PG* 49.188) on the city dancing.

3 Joh. Chrysos., *In illud, vidi Dominum homil.* 1.2 (*PG* 56.99) in Pasquato (1976) 149, compared with *In Ep. ad Coloss. homil.* 12.5 (*PG* 62.387), reproaching dance, or *De Lazaro* 1.1 (*PG* 48.963) congratulating those who on New Year's day did not indulge in σκιρτήματα (which, nevertheless, continued, cf. Conc. Trullanum a. 691/2 can. 62). Notice the similar strictures against less restrained steps and styles, by pagans, above, chap. 2 n. 45. Sacred dance likely derived from Greek cult practices—so, Wetter (1922) 273.

4 On Glycerius, Greg. Naz., *Epp.* 246–48 ("Basil" *Epp.* 169–71), Ramsay (1893) 451–60, correctly identifying the letters and suggesting links with the cult of Zeus Ouranios at Venasa; further on Glycerius, Gain (1985) 256 n. 128, Trombley (1993–94) 2.120ff., and ibid. 1.29 for Gregory's rebukes; generally in the east, Conc. Laodicense a. 341–83 (the date, Hefele and Leclercq [1907–52] I, 2.995), can. 53; for Basil's rebukes, see *In ebriosos homil.* 14.1 (*PG* 31.445C), against those "who form up their dance groups in the martyria before the city," shamelessly "waving their long locks, trailing their tunics, playfully stepping, with lascivious glances and rolling laughter," and so forth; in

Edessa in Ephraem's time (d. 373), *De poenitent. et iudicio* in Lucius (1908) 437 n. 5, noting the need for the bishop's plea μὴ πρόθυμα στεφανώμεθα, μὴ χοροὺς συστησώμεθα, μὴ αὐλαῖς καὶ κιθάραις τὴν ἀκοὴν ἐκθηλύνωμεν; mentioned with approval in the mid-fifth century *Miracles of Saint Thecla* no. 36, Dagron (1978) 356; and Evagrius, *H. E.* 1.14 (*PG* 86.2461A), τῶν ἀγροίκων περὶ τόν κίονα χορευόντων; at Gaza, festival-time dancing not disapproved, in Litsas (1982) 435; and eastern bishops opposed to clapping that they saw around them, references offered and minimized by Stander (1993) 76, 79. In the early sixth century, Jacob of Serugh, *Homil.* 3, spoke against a fondness for dancing, sounding as if it were an active indulgence, not merely witnessed on the stage, Moss (1935) 105; similarly condemnatory, the Conc. Trullanum can. 62, see Joannou (1962) 198f. (Gougaud [1914] 20 in error, I think, in taking the dancing to be in the churches); also opposed to dancing at month's commencement, can. 65, p. 203.

5 Messalians, cf. Epiphan., *Haer.* 80.8f., in Wetter (1922) 268, and in Egypt, Meletian dancing with hand clapping, Theodoret., *Haeret. fab. compend.* 4.7 (*PG* 83.425f.), in Gougaud (1914) 9 and Dölger (1934) 245. For the pagan origins, see above, chap. 2 n. 47.

6 Victricius (bishop of Rouen a. 380–ca. 408, perhaps at the Saint Gelasius church), *De laude sanctorum* 3 and 5, quoted, *psallite . . . , tramites . . . pede pulsate* (*PL* 20.445, 447), *pede pulsare* being ordinary Latin for "dance," as *laetitia* was a common term for the festival, cf. Gougaud (1914) 9 or Meer (1961) 519. Caesarius notes for disapproval at martyrs' feast days the singing and dancing, both, *Serm.* 13.4 and 55, 2 in Klingshirn (1994) 198.

7 *Saltare spiritaliter,* in Ambros., *De poenitentia* 2.6.42 (*PL* 16.508), and quoting Cicero, *Pro Murena* (above, chap. 2 n. 45), without getting the joke; reproving of dance at weddings, though he singles out *extrema saltatio,* the more decent being permissible? Cf. Aug., *Serm.* 311.7 (*PL* 38.1415), let there be dancing only metaphorically and of the spirit.

8 Dance as worship in Judaism: Gougaud (1914) 5, 8f., Wetter (1922) 264, and Unnik (1964) 1, 3.

9 Sex was seen lurking in celebratory and social customs, cf. MacMullen (1990) 142, 144, 146; ridicule of dance which is clumsy leaping, e.g. Caesarius, *Serm.* 16.3, or Conc. Trullanum can. 65, or too wild, Joh. Chrys., *In illud, vidi Dominum* 1.2 (*PG* 56.99).

10 The character of sacred dance was recognized in both eastern and western sources, see above, chap. 2 nn. 56f., or Aug., *Homil.* 265 (*PL* 39.2239), or Joh. Chrysos., *Homil. in Ep. ad Coloss.* 12.5 (*PG* 62.387), Ephraem (cited n. 2, above), the canons of the patriarch John III (ninth century) against women's graveside dancing, especially accompanied by priests, cf. Quasten (1983) 114 n. 155, or Barhebraeus (d. 1286) in his *Nomocanon* regarding women's dancing at graveside rites "in pagan fashion," cf. Quasten (1983) 176. For Caesarius' strictures, see *Serm.* 1.11 (*CCSL* 103.9), 13.65 (p. 67), and 19.85 (p. 89), Gougaud (1922) 18, 21, and Klingshirn (1994) 198; more widely, the Councils of Orleans (a. 533) to Chalons (a. 639–654), in Gougaud (1922) 10f. and Homann (1965) 174, and so up to Pirmin (d. 753), *Dicta* 22, in Harmening (1979) 277, *nullus Christianus neque ad ecclesiam neque . . . in trivios . . . ballationes . . . saltationes . . . facere.*

11 I have made no exploration of the folklore or anthropological literature, but notice sacral dance in Egypt today (more accurately, in the Monophysite church of Ethiopia), in MacMullen (1985/6) 76; in western Europe, Gougaud (1914) 8 (Flemish and Spanish churches of the eighteenth century), 11–14, 238 (Barjols, described), 240, 242f.; in the 1950s a Pentecostal dance around a tree by the young women of an Argonne village, Isambert (1982) 60f.; cf. dances and games in cemeteries in the late Middle Ages, Muchembled (1978a) 241.

12 For the denial, see for example Markus (1990) 1ff., quoted at the outset on "religion" as distinct from "culture" and, 4f. and 8, adducing in support that one out of A. D. Nock's two mutually contradictory definitions of conversion offered in 1933, whereby "conversion" is a form of attachment excluding all others (for the other definition, see MacMullen [1985/86] 74); similarly, James (1982) 95f., also quoted; similarly Musset (1976) 145, discovering in Merovingian France "a setting characterized as much by folkloric superstitions as by a real pagan *credo*"—there being, of course, no such thing, ever, as that latter. For a more recent example, see Gurevich (1988) passim, e.g. 90 or all of chap. 3, distinguishing all but idols, temples, and the named gods of Roman-empire times as "pagan" in quotation marks, otherwise, "practices," "rituals," "superstitions," "magic" in general, never "religion."

13 For the interpretations that seem to me the better, among historians, see Schmitt, quoted at the end of the preceding chapter; among anthropologists, C. Geertz (1966) 14f., regarding religion as a construct to relieve anxiety induced by the incomprehensible, the construct consisting (p. 4) of "a system of symbols" which include (5) "cultural acts . . . social events" induced and accompanied (9) by "moods" and "motivations" such as shame, reverence, worshipfulness [=awe], solemnity, or playfulness. In the same spirit, under the term "worship" and "religion," I included every thought or act directed to a superhuman being, cf. (1981) 20–28, 40, and passim, and (1984) 8, citing to disagree with the view "that all forms of religion have one common structure," a structure only of theology and moral system, and "that religion means doctrine"; also (1985/6) 75f., emphasizing the word "*structure*" like Schmitt, speaking of dance as worship, and instancing parallels from anthropological studies (notes 20, 31, 36, C. Geertz), while unaware of Schmitt's remarks (until 1995).

14 On ascetics, see below, at nn. 111ff.

15 Chap. 2 nn. 49f.

16 Wild lamentation at eastern funerals, Pasquato (1976) 341 n. 71, quoting texts from John Chrysostom, and Quasten (1983) 87, 163; as is better known, the women hired to keen at ancient Roman funerals; keening in the early medieval period, forbidden in the *Indiculus superstitionum et paganiarum* 2, cf. Homann (1965) 26; and wedding songs in Augustine's world, Zellinger (1933) 83, as in Chysostom's, Quasten (1983) 131.

17 Strictures against indecent songs, evidently at parties, in the third- to fourth-century Syrian *Apostolic Constitutions*, cf. Quasten (1983) 122, 173 (and a text from Basil, *Ep.* 207.3, *PG* 32.764); also Joh. Chrysos., *Exposit. in Ps.* 41.1ff. (*PG* 55.156f.) and *In Mt homil.* 7.6 (*PG* 57.79), Pasquato (1976) 270–75 and Zellinger (1933) 83. Kalends-singing, above, chap, 2 nn. 13f.; New-Month singing forbidden in the early eighth-century collection of earlier bans by Pirmin of Reichenau, the *Dicta* 22, in Harmening (1979)

277, 335, *Luna quando obscuratur, nolite clamores emittere. Nullus carminum diabolicum credire.* Propagandistic and processional singing in eastern churches from at least the mid-fourth century, MacMullen (1990) 272 with n. 49, p. 392. Singing apparently in ordinary church services, Zellinger, loc. cit. and Meer (1961) 327f.; or flutes, see Greg. Naz., *Ep.* 193, in Dölger (1934) 255; cithara, above, n. 1.

18 In Cappadocia, Basil, *Or.* 8 (*PG* 35.805), Pasquato (1976) 228, and Quasten (1983) 173; at Nola, Paulinus (*Carm.* 23.111f., cf. 27.561), ibid. 174; in the west, besides Augustine's remarks in the notes above, the Conc. Turonense a. 567 can. 18, Autessiodurum a. 573/603 can. 9 (*MGH Conc. Meroving.* 1. 180), Toletanum III a. 589 can. 23 (Mansi IX 999), and Cabillon. a. 639/54 can. 19, 22, 28, in Gougaud (1914) 10f.; ibid. 16, on Caesarius' strictures, blaming *rustici* and *rusticae;* and ibid. 18, on the legislation of barbarian kings; and Quasten (175) on the opposition of Eligius (d. 659). In Egypt, see Shenute's blast at the wicked at the very church doors who play their pipes and horns, Pasquato (1976) 347 n. 123.

19 Chap. 1 n. 10, and 2 at nn. 100–108.

20 *CIL* 13.633, wife apparently Christian setting up a stone to a ?pagan husband, with "D. M.," in J. Ferguson (1970) 240f.; Charles-Picard (1965) 116, Mactar; other examples in MacMullen (1984) 116 with n. 14, 153 n. 21, and in the excellent and comprehensive work of Giuntella (1985) 42 with n. 75, and 45f., examples of the fifth century; Mazzoleni (1985) 4f., likewise with Italian Christian texts with "D.M.S.," up to a. 557; fifth-century(?) threats against disturbers of the dead on a stone from near Athens, recalling pagan formulae and invoking against even the clergy "the All-Powerful God" plus "the Celestial Powers and those of the Air and Earth and Beneath," cf. Feissel (1980) 459, 470. For the customs of burial goods, lack of orientation, and cremation shared indistinguishably in France among pagans and Christians post-400 to Carolingian times, cf. Dierkens (1985) 144; Graus (1965) 177f. and James (1982) 97 on grave-goods in Merowingian lands and times; the earlier Christian burials indistinguishable from the pagan in Rome and throughout the empire, cf. Périn (1987) 11; and, in Watts (1991) 38–98, a most careful attempt to identify the differentia of Christian burials in Britain, yet with some inevitable circularity in argument and uncertain conclusions. For the Charon obol in Christian tombs, see generally Rush (1941) 95, Spain, Dölger (1910–43) 5.85 (Spain, Sicily), and the *Lexikon für Theologie und Kirche* 2 (1958) 303, "manchenorts"; in fifth-century France, Dhénin (1980) 202f.; in fourth-century Britain and elsewhere in the west "still widespread" at the end of the seventh century, Watts (1991) 192; in Palestine, apparently Christian, Negev (1971) 119; and coins in the hands or at the feet of the deceased in the nineteenth century, *DACL* 12 (1936) s.v. "Obole" and Pekary (1994) 96, Pius IX's burial in St. Peter's.

21 E.g., above, chap. 3 nn. 58, 66, on saints physically present and active in their tombs; Conc. Iliberr. can. 34 and Aug., *Ep.* 22.6 (*PL* 33.92) and *Enchiridion* 110 (*PL* 40.283), that *oblationes* rejoice the *spiritus dormientium*—all three references in Lucius (1908) 37f.; and fourth-century inscriptions from Syracuse and elsewhere, with the prayer, "In this tomb may the holy spirit rejoice," cf. Testini (1958) 148f. For the general Christian view of the presence of the dead in their tombs, cf. Klauser (1928) 606f. and Snyder (1985) 46 (against one contrary assertion, though many others could be cited) and 145.

22 Stone chairs of the third to fourth centuries for the dead, cf. Klauser (1927) 98f. (Rome), 118f. (Naples), and 121f. (Africa), comparing above, chap. 2 n. 106; Giuntella (1985) 59, on a Sardinian example; a fifth-century custom, cf. Synesius (*PG* 66.1234), ibid. 16f. and Février (1977a) 37; inscriptions on nearby walls, πίε ζῆσης or *care refrigera*, in Klauser (1928) 605; the inscription with the invitation, *refrigera cum spirita[!] sancta*, *ICUR* 17, in Snyder (1985) 126, or "Dear one, enjoy the party," *care refrigera*, or variations, in Klauser (1927) 135f.; the text, *Ianuaria bene refrigera et roga pro nos*, in the Callixtus catacomb on the Via Appia to the south of Rome, cf. Février (1978) 259, the text with a relief of a pitcher, goblet, and lamp. The pagan custom and model, above, chap. 2, n. 106.

23 For the pagan graveside banquets and the physical amenities for them, see chap. 2, nn. 103–6; third-century Christian amenities in Bonn, Snyder (1985) 88; in Tipasa (Mauretania Caesariensis), Albertini and Leschi (1932) 79, 81; the best known Tipasa funerary mosaic and *triclinium* effectively brought to notice by Février (1977a) 29 and Marrou (1979), cf. also Giuntella (1985) 58, with parallels from Tarraco, 29; the well-known Roman catacomb frescoes in Ferrua (1970) 24, 34, 38ff., and 81f. (giving them a Constantinian date), in Dölger (1910–43) 5.492–500, and in Février (1977a) 29–36 or idem (1978) 241, 250, 256. Note in the *Apostolic Constitutions* 8.44.1, the injunction, ἐν δὲ ταῖς μνείαις αὐτῶν μετὰ εὐταξίας ἑστιᾶσθε, the document, though of the later fourth century, preserving mostly third century materials, cf. Klauser (1928) 601 and Quasten (1950–60) 2.184; Marrou (1979) 262 presents the mosaic with depiction of fish for the meal; for fish bones and other animal remains, and pipes for wine, in early Spanish burials, Giuntella (1985) 29, 31; and third-century Roman burials equipped with benches and receptacles for drink, in Février (1978) 218.

24 Celebration of the altar, *mensa*, food and drink and memorializing of the deceased in *CIL* 8.20277 = *Inscriptiones Christianae Latinae veteres* 1570, Diehl, placed in a context of Christian practices by Février (1977a) 36; but pagan according to Brown (1981) 24 and "pre-Christian" for Trombley (1993–94) 1.69 n. 290—who, however, points to many other undoubtedly Christian parallels. For the reuse of pagan sarcophagi by Christians, see Février (1978) 325.

25 Ibid. 268, 272, 306f. (distinguishing between history and apologetic), and 320ff. (retaining the word "cult"). Février's discussion seems to me especially careful and authoritative.

26 In Africa, Giuntella (1985) 37f., 42; Spain, cf. McKenna (1938) 36 and 105, Martin of Braga's publication in 572 of church bans on *prandia* (as below, Council of Arles); also Giuntella (1985) 36; in the Vatican in 397, Paulin. Nol., *Ep.* 13 (61.213), *congregatos per accubitus ordinari, et profluis omnes saturari cibis*, cf. Grossi-Gondi (1915) 230; elsewhere in Rome, Dölger (1930) 84f., 90, Testini (1958) 142f., Février (1978) 218, 226, 241, and Giuntella (1985) 29 and 31 (Isola Sacra); in Naples (catacomb of Saint Gennaro), Klauser (1927) 118ff. and Giuntella (1985) 52; Nola, a sarcophagus of a. 541 equipped as a *mensa*, Korol (1992) 96; Milan in the fourth/fifth century, food and wine amphorae in cemetery, Cuscito (1993) 98ff.; Syracuse, Testini (1958) 148; Salona, in Marrou (1949) 197 or Snyder (1985) 90f.; Sardinia, in Giuntella (1985) passim, including (78f.) the rich collection of lamps associated with the cult; Conc. Arelat. III can. 5, *non liceat Christianis prandia ad defunctorum sepulchra deferre et sacrificare de re mortuorum;*

Conc. Turinense a. 567 can. 22 regulating what the church intended as a substitute for the Caristia, that is, the festival of the *cathedra domni Petri*, cf. Février (1977) 521; later church reprobation of the practices, Dierkens (1985) 144, and in the *Indiculus superstitionum* 1, cf. Homann (1965) 22, noting the primacy here of the ban *De sacrilegio ad sepulchra mortuorum* "because this practice and the forms it took constituted the most common and widespread insignia of pagan usages"; and the practices in mid-eighth century Germany, reported by Boniface, *Ep.* 56 (*MGH Epp. select.* ed. Tangl, p. 100), *sacrificia mortuorum*, with the pope's comments, *Ep.* 80 (p. 174), on such sacrifices. In the east, notice the Syrian Saint Michael shrine near Apamea with adjoining burials, that is, sarcophagi with holes in their side, reminiscent of the Timgad one, says Canivet (1980) 95, 98; for Egyptian tomb amenities for eating, Giuntella (1985) 49; and for the miniature stone sarcophagi, see Dyggve (1942) 245 n. 31, from Bulgaria and elsewhere. On the calendar of family graveside memorializing, see Meer (1961) 526 (February etc.).

27 Description of graveside banquets for ordinary deceased, in Aug., *Ep.* 22(23).3, 6 (*PL* 33.91f.); *Serm.* 62.7, 10; *De moribus eccl. cath.* 1.34.75 (*PL* 32.1342), *novi multos esse sepulcrorum et picturarum adoratores; novi multos esse qui luxuriossissime super mortuos bibant et epulas cadaveribus exhibentes . . . et voracitates ebrietatesque suas deputent religioni;* other passages by Augustine in Zellinger (1933) 77 n. 63, and Meer (1961) 503, on the usual days for graveside memorial attendance; Zeno, *Serm.* 1.16.15 (*PL* 11.366), reprobating heavy eating and drinking seen at banquets for the dead, in Klauser (1927) 133 n. 134; further, in the west, at Noyon, on the traditional family day of February made over into the Feast of the Apostle Peter, music and dancing toward the mid-sixth century, cf. Quasten (1983) 175; and in the east, a range of texts gathered by Maraval (1985) 218, including the testimony of Gregory Nazianzenus, to which Dölger (1910–43) 5.495f. adds the Jamnia incident.

28 Dölger (1930a) 320; Dyggve (1942) 234, 238 fig. 12, and 245 n. 29, proof of "an unbroken tradition from Antiquity to the present day," to which compare Dölger (1910–43) 2.571 and 3 fig. 46, on practices in modern Serbia and Greece, where the family spreads the food and the patriarch pours the wine into the tomb; and Nilsson (1945) 63, quoted on the Psychosabbaton. Cf. Février (1977) 522, instancing a fifteenth-century north Italian will with provisions for feasting on the Feast of Saint Peter in February—that would be on the 22d, the Caristia—as an indication that "les repas funéraires ne seraient pas un reste antique."

29 Euseb., *H. E.* 4.15.44, ἐν ἀγαλλιάσει καὶ χάραι . . . ἐπιτελεῖν τὴν τοῦ μαρτυρίου ἡμέραν γενέθλιον, "in gladness and joy" = *Passio S. Polycarpi* 18.3; on the practices at the eastern capital, Const., *Or. ad sanctos* 12 (*PG* 20.1272B), ὕμνοι δὴ μετὰ ταῦτα [the martyr's death] καὶ ψαλτήρια καὶ εὐφημίαι, along with lights and συμπόσια; next, high spirits at the celebrations recalled by Greg. Nyss., *Vita Greg. Thaumat.* (*PG* 46.95), in Lucius (1908) 100, and *Ep.* 1.24, in Maraval (1985) 218, to which one might add *Vita S. Macrinae* (*PG* 46.992), in Quasten (1983) 162, for its evident adapting of a martyr's vigil to a funeral; Julian, *Adv. Galilaios* 339Ef.; Greg. Naz.'s epigrams, in Nilsson (1945) 63; Joh. Chrys., *In Homil. in mart.* (*PG* 50.663) on the παννυχίδες and *Iulianum mart.* 4 (ibid. 673), describing delightful picnic scenes, although in both pas-

sages warning against too much wine; and Basil and Asterius in Lucius (1908) 436f. and Vryonis (1981) 211.

30 Cypr., *Ep.* 12.2 and 39.3 (*CSEL* 3, 1.503 and 583 = *PL* 4.331 and 337), *oblationes et ob commemorationes eorum* [= the martyrs], or *sacrificia . . . offerimus, quotiens martyrum passiones et dies anniversariae commemorationes celebramus,* in Lucius (1908) 98 n. 1; cf. the celebratory procession accompanying the body to its grave "with candles and torches," in *Acta proconsularia S. Cypriani* 5; Aug., *Sermo* 310.2, where, surely, because graveside memorials were normally on birthdays, the bishop feels called on to explain that Cyprian's is not known, the name of the site for the memorial being given as the *Mensa Cypriani* here and in *Sermo* 49 and 131 (*PL* 8.320, 729); and Y. M. Duval (1982) 1.34–39, on the text of about a. 400 at Dougga (which I recall inspecting with my friend E. Tengström); and the Timgad tomb, Marrou (1949) 193f. and 196, supposing (201) that the chapel may be Donatist, though his chief argument for this, reasoning from what Augustine does *not* say, at *Contra Faust.* 20.21 (*PL* 42.385), seems to me of no force; the whole question left up in the air by Meer (1961) 482; supposed to be a martyr's burial, less likely, of a bishop, Giuntella (1985) 56.

31 "I have made the party," *refrigerium feci,* or "I offered the gift of a party to them," *votum is* [= *iis*] *promisit refrigerium,* in Grossi-Gondi (1915) 221f.; and notice the description of "the banquet, an act of devotion dedicated to the Apostles in the hope that they might be of help to the dedicant's salvation," as C. Pietri (1989) 72 puts it in discussing *refrigerium* graffiti; the tomb cover pierced, *DACL* s.v. "Paul (Saint)" 2665, in S. Paulo fuori le Mura; the memorial in Saint Peter's, in Gerkan (1964) 59ff. and Guarducci (1989) 25 and (1967) 46; for Saint Sebastiano, see Klauser (1928) 601ff. and (1956) 23f., Tolotti (1982) 171ff., 176 Fig. 7, and Snyder (1985) 98–104, 141–45, comparing the *triclia* arrangements under Saint Gennaro, cf. Giuntella (1985) 52.

32 For sacred art on the walls of pagan temples, see chap. 2 n. 42; for versified glorifications of the object of cult in pagan shrines, see chap. 2 n. 53; for the dedication of his beard, Paulin. Nolensis, *Carm.* 21.377, in the tradition not only of the old Italian *depositio barbae* but of many eastern communities, cf. above, chap. 2 n. 99, MacMullen (1984) 153 n. 23, and, for the east in general, MacMullen (1981) 160 n. 1 and idem (1985/86) 78 with nn. 26ff.; testimonials, *Carm.* 21.369, *admiranda operum documenta sacrorum pro foribus,* compared with chap. 2 n. 74, above.

33 Slab — as Dyggve (1942) 245 n. 35 notices; frescoes intended to catch the rustic mind, *Carm.* 27.580ff.; inscriptions, *Ep.* 32; unguent poured on and recovered from the tomb, *Carm.* 18.38ff. (*PL* 61.491B) and wine as well, 27.566f.; wine also drunk, 27.561; offerings, 18.29ff., cf. above, chap. 2 n. 84, with much comparative material on donations to churches and martyria; for a western example, in fourth-century Britain, Painter (1977) 21f., or in the east, Kötting (1950) 156 or Maraval (1985) 231; illumination both day and night, *Carm.* 14.100ff., 18.35ff.; incense, 26.38f.; banquets paid for by local patrons, *Carm.* 18.44f., and above, chap. 2. n. 83; the roast meats seen as offerings, *hostia,* 21.105f., cf. 20.312ff., 389ff., animals offered, *qui mos esse videtur persolvenda . . . sua vota . . . martyribus,* and 20.72, a petitioner with a *pingue pecus voti iugulat, de more voventum* (notice that it is in the customary way, i.e., pagan); compare in the east, at Beirut in 513, "the rustics made offerings to the Christian God in the same manner

as to their former divinities," that is, sacrificing a cock, as Severus of Antioch explains in his *Laudatio S. Leontii* 12, in Trombley (1993–94) 2.50; the meats shared with poor, Paulinus Nolensis, *Carm.* 18.45ff. (495Bf.), cf. above, chap. 2 n. 41, and supplied by the rich, above, chap. 2 nn. 29, 32; singing, *Carm.* 14.109, 23.111ff.; all-night vigil, *laetitia*, 14.49ff., 27.556f.; and a general narrative of the vigil, 30. 286ff., 511–635.

34 Augustine acquainted with Nola, *Ep.* 78.3 (*PL* 33.269), referring to Saint Felix's *notissima sanctitas*; on his mother's routine of visiting around at various martyr shrines, below, n. 35.

35 Toasts, Aug., *Serm.* 225.4, 154.9, "for the ordinary man . . . the culminating point of the feast," Meer (1961) 171; drinking, ibid. 516, 520, the most often quoted passage being the description of the loud joyful scenes and music in the Saint Cyprian church, *Serm.* 311.5 (*PL* 38.1415), cf. 326.1 (1449), in Gougaud (1914) 10, Pasquato (1976) 348, etc.; cf. also *En. in ps.* 32.5 (*PL* 36.279), *Ep.* 22.4 (*PL* 33.91), and *Contra Faust.* 20.21 (*PL* 42.385); above, n. 30, feasting and drinking at Timgad and Dougga; also Ps.-Cyprian, *De duplici martyrio* 25 (*PL* 4.975C), post-Diocletianic, as G. Hartel points out, *CSEL* 3, 3.lxiv, but otherwise undatable, where Christians egg each other on into drunkenness; Aug., *Conf.* 6.2.2 (*PL* 32.719), also often cited, where it was Monica's *consuetudo* to bring cakes, bread, and wine to many different martyr tombs in Africa, *ut solebat*, and similarly in Milan; dancing and singing, above, nn. 1, 6, and 18, including the France of Caesarius, with dancing, too, deplored in the Conc. Toletanum III a. 589, cf. above, nn. 1 and 18—deplored as by non-Christian moralists, above, chap. 2 n. 35; and Chrysologus, *Serm.* 129 (*PL* 52.555B), indicating big feasts in his see, in Lucius (1908) 435 n. 1.

36 Church-feasting "almost daily," Aug., *Serm.* 273.8; the *basilica Tricliarum* in Carthage, *En. in ps.* 32.2.29 (*PL* 36.300), cf. *PL* 38.364 note c; feasting in French cathedrals of Caesarius' day at festivals of all sorts, in Klingshirn (1994) 197; *convivia* in churches, Conc. Carth. a. 419 (Hippo, 393) can. 30, forbidden to bishops and clergy, in Quasten (1983) 176; church festival feasts with dancing, Conc. Romanum a. 826, ibid.

37 Paulinus' tone, caught by Meer (1961) 512ff.; Ambrose, in Aug., *Ep.* 22(23).3 (*PL* 33.91) and Ambros., *De Helia* 62; Sidon. Apoll., *Epp.* 5.17.3ff.; Aug., *Ep.* 29.8f., on the feast of Saint Leontius, a former bishop, trans. based on Quasten (1983) 172, a. 395, a passage in which Augustine decries the *imperita multitudo*, cf. *De moribus eccl. cath.* 1.34.75 (*PL* 32.1342), the *turbae imperitorum*.

38 *Contra Faust.* 20.21 (*PL* 42.384); cf. above, chap. 2 n. 34 on the pagan perception of wine-drinking and feasting as an offering; Augustine's opinion on the gifts of food and wine to the martyrs' tombs, *Conf.* 6.2.2 (*PL* 32.719), *illa quasi parentalia superstitioni gentilium . . . simillima.*

39 Above, nn. 22, 27, 30, 31, 37; from the outset, in Cyprian's phrases quoted above, n. 30; Faustus' protests against offerings to saints, Aug., *Contra Faust.* 20.4; further texts and contexts in Lucius (1908) 390f., with a wrong reference which may be to Gregory of Tours, *Liber de gloria mart.* 96 (*MGH SRM* 1, 2.103), Sergius martyr *multa signa in populis facit, curans infirmitates sanansque languores fideliter deprecantium; unde agitur, ut ex hoc ingentia basilicae vel promittantur vota vel munera deferantur;* idem, *Liber de virtutibus S. Iuliani* 31 (*MGH SRM*, 1st ed., p. 577 = *SRM*, 2d ed., 1, 1.127), describing the miraculous good behavior

of the votive animals stabled in the church before being slaughtered; Conc. German-
icum a. 742 can. 5, *hostias immolatitias, quas stulti homines iuxta ecclesias ritu pagano faciunt . . .
sub nomine sanctorum martyrum vel confessorum*, and the *Indiculus superstitionum* 9 (later
eighth century), *de sacrificio, quod fit alicui sanctorum*, both with context in Homann
(1965) 67f. and Dierkens (1984) 19f.; in the east, Theodoret, *Grace. affect. curat.* 8.62f.
(*PG* 83.1032Bf.), explaining that offerings, even very modest ones from the poor, are
invited and welcome to the tombs of the saints; and below, chap. 5 n. 11.

40 Hier., *Contra Vigilantium* 4 (*PL* 23.342, 346), a. 406, conceding the use of candles in
honor to the relics of martyrs; denounced as a rite of idolatry, by Athanas., *Ep. ad
orthodox.* 4 (*PG* 25.229C), when the Arians light candles to their "idols" (meaning
depictions of martyrs?); on daytime lighting, examples above at nn. 30 and especially
33 (at Nola), noticed as prescribed in western liturgy from the fifth century, cf.
DACL s.v. "Chandelier" col. 212, on the *Statuta eccl. antiqua* and Isidore; and below,
chap. 5 n. 11.

41 On dance, etc., above, nn. 3f.; on wine permitted *ad laetitiam*, but not in excess, cf. the
Didascalia et constitutiones apostolorum 8.44.3 (ed. F. X. Funk p. 554f.); on the luxury or
heaviness of feasting, music, etc., Shenute, in Lucius (1908) 437, Pasquato (1976) 347
n. 123, or Quasten (1983) 175, along with fairs, decried by Asterius, *Homil.* 3 (*PG*
40.193Df.) at Amasea around the turn of the fifth century and, with displays of
foods for sale in the churches, banned by the Conc. Trull. can. 17; more again from
Shenute, in Egypt and (Lefort [1954] 228) at Ephesus; similar features noted in
Egypt in the *Miracula S. Colluthi*, in Maraval (1985) 218; Greg. Nyss., *De vita Macrinae*,
PG 46.992; ibid., on Severus of Antioch, *Homil.* 27 (*PO* 36.573) describing Antioch in
the first half of the sixth century; eastern Asia, *Certamen S. Blasii* 12 (*PG* 116.829),
remarking on celebrations μέχρι καὶ νῦν . . . μετὰ λαμπάδων καὶ ὕμνων καὶ
εὐωχίας πολλῆς; further details in Lucius (1908) 435 n. 5, Pasquato (1981) 228f., 233,
or Maraval (1985) 216. For the quotation, see Eusebius Alex., *Serm.* 8 (*PG* 86.357Bf.),
comparing above, chap. 2 nn. 31, 33; ibid. n. 41, on exactly similar fairs at pagan shrines.

42 On invited encomiasts, I instance Greg. Nyss. on Saint Theodore, celebrated at
Euchaita (a hundred miles south of Sinope), cf. *PG* 46.736ff., Delehaye (1923) 131,
and *Lexikon für Theologie und Kirche* 10.39; in western settings, see above, chap. 2 n. 51; on
Thecla's, cf. Vryonis (1981) 201; other details in Dagron (1978) 350, her sacred birds
and the pilgrims' offerings to them; 356, the πανήγυρις famous and thronged and its
delightful amenities and joyful doings described; and 378, the culminating banquet.
Compare pagan sermons or encomia as prominent features of religious festivals,
above, chap. 2 nn. 31, 51f.

43 Above, at nn. 23ff.; cf. Dom Cabrol quoted in Isambert (1982) 43, "le culte des idoles
fleurit de plus belle sous couleur de culte des saints, de culte des martyrs"; and to the
same effect, Delehaye (1912) 160, in a work first published in the year before Cabrol's
observation. For a more recent assertion of the identity in accommodations for the
nonsanctified and the sanctified dead, from the Roman evidence, see Février (1978)
268, 272f.; from the Tipasa evidence, ibid. 224, concluding, "there is no difference
architecturally between the late third to early fourth century cult of the dead, and
cult of martyrs"; and Pani Ermini (1989) 840 n. 10, in agreement. On the identity of

pagan and Christian cult of the dead, see e.g. Grossi-Gondi (1915) 227, Dyggve (1942) 246, or Giuntella (1985) 52, agreeing with Jastrzebowska on the "prima testimonianza monumentale del refrigerio in onore dei martiri, la continuazione di un tradizione funeraria precristiana," in Rome; or more generally, Snyder (1985) 65 and, on the derivation of martyr cult from pagan cult of the dead/heroes, Pasquato (1981) 212, 341.

44 Above, chap. 1 nn. 10, 12; MacMullen (1984) 153 n. 22; Conc. Laodicense a. 381 or late fourth century, can. 39, in Joannou (1962a) 146; of about the same date, in Syria, the direction in the *Constitutiones apost.* 8.44, ed. Funk 1.555, *in mortuorum vera memoriis, cum moderatione ac Dei metu epulamini;* Basil, *Ep. canonica* 81, on Christians joining pagan banquets; similarly, Joannou (1962a) 190, Conc. Carth. a. 419 can. 60 (the decree of a. 401), Caesarius, *Serm.* 54.6, or Conc. Turon. a. 567 can. 23 (Mansi 9.789). Notice also the likelihood of interfaith mingling in upper-class Athens in the late fifth century, Frantz (1988) 57, as in Beirut, Alexandria, Aphrodisias, and other eastern cities, the centers of action as described in chap. 1, above, with further touches in Rémondon (1952) 63f. Two sources of the earlier fourth century which give a specially clear sense of the realities of intermingling are the *Acta purgationis Felicis,* conveniently in MacMullen and Lane (1992) 242ff., and the Theophanes archive, cf. Wipszycka (1988) 143.

45 Dolbeau (1991) 53, 77; above, chap. 1, from nn. 65 on, passim.

46 The pagan Jacob, imperial physician, cf. Whitby (1991) 120; Christian consultation of pagan healers, in e.g. Caesarius, *Serm.* 184 (*CCL* 104.750), *solet fieri* (notice, it is a common thing); see further, below, n. 125. Basil, *Ep. canonica* 83, would bar Christian resort to pagan diviners; pagan and Christian are seen quite comfortably together at sanctuaries of ambiguous holiness, e.g. Epiphanius, *Panarion* 30.4ff., trans. MacMullen and Lane (1992) 2ff., and a large number of Holy-land and other eastern examples in Maraval (1985) 53, 144; and pagans apply to Christian holy places or holy men, *Vita S. Symeon. iun.* 184, Ven (1962–70) 1.163, or many examples above, chap. 1 nn. 22 and 24. Quoted are Hassall and Tomlin (1982) 404, where, despite the word *gentilis* in the text (certainly not what a pagan called himself), the authors hesitate to call the writer of the *defixio* a Christian.

47 *Passio S. Polycarpi* 18.3, celebration of Polycarp's anniversary; Grossi-Gondi (1915) 228; Lucius (1908) 233 n. 3.

48 Cf. *Lexikon für Theologie und Kirche* 5.105, and, most clearly, Cypr., *Ep.* 10(6).4 (*PL* 4.262A), 12(25).1(265B), etc., on *libelli* of forgiveness of sin; and, on relics, below, nn. 93ff..

49 Above, chap. 2 at nn. 56f.; below, at n. 91; Lucius was the principle proponent of a "heroic" origin for saints, which has found some acceptance, e.g. in Pfister (1909–12) 2.498 or Pasquato (1976) 344, but more often, rejection, of which C. Pietri (1991) 17 represents the most dismissive: "L'expérience des enquêtes antérieures démontrent qu'il n'est pas utile de s'attarder à la quête d'antécédents païens"; but cf. also Brown (1976) 9, denying the phenomenon outside of the Christian sphere: "Unlike paganism and much of Judaism, the Christian communities were prepared to invest individual human beings with supernatural powers or with the ability to exercise power

on behalf of the supernatural." For a wiser view, by no means a novelty, cf. Fréret (1751) 278, writing actually in 1743: "Une histoire détaillée de la destruction de l'idolatrie, et des recherches sur les nouveaux cultes introduits dans le paganisme, répandroient un grand jour sur nos antiquités ecclésiastiques."

50 Lucius (1908) 186, finding still in mid-fourth century "an astonishingly small number of martyrs' tombs" around Rome, compared (108f.) with Africa by Augustine's time seen by Augustine as crammed with saints, while (144, the passage in italics) "the era of the most intense growth of martyr cult and its definitive naturalizing within all circles of Christian society" in the twenty-five years leading up to Julian was also the period of an increase in converts by two, three, or four times. On the speed of the change, see e.g. Brown (1981) 75, "geyserlike force," Maraval (1985) 63, "like mushrooms," or Markus (1990) 150, "dramatic rise"; and the particularly visible ubiquity of the martyr shrines in Africa, Meer (1961) 478.

51 Lucius (1908) 453.

52 For Egypt, see Lefort (1954) 225f., the quotation from Shenute; *CT* 9.17.7; Fontaine (1967–69) 2.709; Conc. Carth. a. 419 can. 83, Joannou (1962a) 323, going on to specify dreams and *inanes quasi revelationes;* Conc. Romanum II a. 745 can. 3 (*MGH Legum 2*, 1: *Concilia,* p. 39), Aldebert a man of France.

53 Lucius (1908) 144f., the surge in conversions constituting thus the period when the church was "most under the influence of the ideas and tendencies born of the old religion." For the surge as sensibly placed in time, see confirmation for some regions of the west in Galvao-Sobrinho (1995) figs. 1 and 6 (Rome and Belgica), pp. 463, 465, the peaks in the graphs coming ten to twenty years after conversion, as the author says (461); a decade or so earlier at three African sites (fig. 3 p. 464), still later at other western points.

54 Apollonius' saying, above, chap. 2 n. 58; the same thought long familiar in various forms in the Platonic stream and equally in the Stoic, e.g. (as Seneca puts it, *Ep. ad Lucil.* 110.2), "whether the gods have enough time on their hands to care for the concerns of private individuals," or again, idem, *De providentia* 1 or *De beneficiis* 4.3f., or Pliny, *N. H.* 2.20, *inridendum agere curam rerum illud quicquid est summum;* Aug., *En. in ps.* 34.1.7 (*PL* 36.326), *In Ioann. ev. tract.* 34.3f. (*PL* 35.1652f.), and *En. in ps.* 26.2.19 (*PL* 36.209), all three quoted; *Civ. dei* 6.1, there are persons who turn to the heathen deities for concerns of this life, cf. 6.10; also *En. in ps.* 40.3 (*PL* 35.456) and 62.7 (*PL* 35.752), those in need of anything lowly like bread, water, wine, food, money, a draught animal, *a Deo petere debet, non a daemoniis et idolis et nescio quibus potestatibus; Retractationes* 2.43; Zellinger (1933) 10, Meer (1961) 56f., and Klugkist (1974) 353. For a modern parallel, Calvin contesting Erasmus' view that it would be wrong to ask God for something as common as food, cf. Graham (1971) 66.

55 Lucius (1908) 160 n. 3, quoting Basil, *In ps.* 45.1 (*PG* 29.417Cf.), to which Aug., *In Ioann. ev. tract.* 7.7 (*PL* 35.1441) is very closely similar; cf. also below, at nn. 149ff.

56 Paulin. Nolensis, *Carm.* 18.198ff., 19.200ff.; Callinicus, *Vita S. Hypatii* 22.21, of the 420s or 430s; *Miracle* 36 of Thecla, Dagron (1978) 386f.; Theodoret., *Hist. relig.* (*PG* 82.1489Af.), the holy man heals not only mules but camels; *Vita S. Symeon. iun.* 148, in Ven (1962–70) 1.135; *Vita S. Theodori* 98f., of roughly a. 600; other eastern examples in

Maraval (1985) 149; Sulp. Sev., *Dial.* 2.9 (*PL* 20.207 = *CSEL* 1.190f.), cf. *Vita S. Leobini* 10 (*MGH AA* 4, 2.29ff.), the holy man sought out for healing, or exorcism of a horse by the bishop of Todi, in Greg. Magn., *Dial.* 1.10.9f.; on Saint Foy, Bouillet (1897) 209, cf. 21 and 23 for other animal cures; compare above, chap. 2 n. 79. For the cure of a farmer's rooster, see Constantius, *Vita Germani* 11 (*MGH SRM* 7.258f.).

57 Saints' favors or miracles more often regarding health than anything else, clearly implied in Paulin. Nolensis, *Carm.* 26.384ff., and in Greg. Magnus, *Homil. Ev.* 2.32.6 (*PL* 76.1237C); cf. Kötting (1950) on Felix and Stephen as well; true of miracles at Saint Martin's tomb as with other saints of France, L. Pietri (1983) 562ff., with the summary, that Saint Martin "was viewed almost exclusively as a healer" until the twelfth century (K. Mitchell [1987] 78, quoting Leclercq); true of Saint Fides (Foy), Bouillet (1897) passim; centrality of healing in saints' cult generally in the west, cf. Wilson (1983) 18 and Schmitt (1976) 141 n. 12, in the early Middle Ages as still in the eleventh to twelfth centuries; true of Thecla, cf. Dagron (1978) 103; true of Saint Nikolaos, cf. Anrich (1913–17) 226, of Saint Symeon the Younger in Ven (1962) 1.73 (healing central to over 95 percent of over 150 miracles); true of Demetrios' cures, "numberless as the sands" and the chief part of the catalog, Lemerle (1979–82) 53, 75; and of eastern saints in general, cf. Browning (1981) 121 or Maraval (1985) 149. Similarly, the primacy of health in the business of the gods, above, chap. 2 n. 80.

58 POxy. 1150 (sixth century), to which the editors compare questions of identical form and purpose submitted, in somewhat earlier pagan times, to temples (POxy. 1148, first century). On προστάτης, see above, chap. 1 n. 59.

59 Theodoret., *Graec. affect. curat.* 9 (*PG* 83. 1032A–C), ending, ταῦτα δὲ κηρύττει τῶν κειμένων τὴν δύναμιν; further eastern witnesses in Maraval (1985) 232; western, below, n. 108. On the pagan usage, see above, chap. 2 n. 75.

60 Not by but through the saints, so runs the continual reminder by the bishops, e.g. Augustine in Lucius (1908) 451–53 or Meer (1961) 488, or on a wider choice of texts, Uytfanghe (1989) 171 n. 53, quoting Aug., *Sermo Lambot* 26.2 (*PL Suppl.* 2.831), *vos ergo fratres, admoneo hortor atque obsecro . . . non enim eos* [= *martyres*] *tamquam deos colimus, sed eos propter deum colimus;* idem loc. cit., Latin hagiographers show the same care; or eastern bishops like Asterius in Lucius loc. cit. or Maraval (1985) 145, 158.

61 In Nineham (1993) 86, Joh. Damasc., *De imaginibus or.* 3.33 (*PG* 94.1352Bf.), only God is ἅγιος but he shares his φύσις with his elect who are thus ἀληθῶς θεῖοι and προσκυνητοί. John was no revolutionary. Cf. good pages on hagiolatry in Lucius (1908) 451f.

62 Cf. a range of passages easily extended, where only the saint appears as actor, e.g. Paulin. Mediolanensis, *Vita Ambros.* 14.3, or 48 (demons tortured *ab illo*, i.e. the saint), Paulin. Nolensis, *Carm.* 14.24f. or 28.60ff., 148f.; Sulp. Sev., *Vita Mart.* 5.2 (13.9) or 6.3 (19.2) on Martin's *virtutes* which, at ibid. 14.2 and *Dial.* 3.9.2, Stancliffe (1983) 222 takes to be angels at Martin's command; as also in those many contexts where a saint is called *patronus*, e.g. *De miraculis S. Stephani* 1.1 (*PL* 41.834) and above, chap. 1 n. 60, or generally throughout the accounts of the Thecla miracles, as Dagron (1978) 96 points out, and as is especially to be seen at the end of the *Thaumata* (364f.) where, in summary, it is said "she has favor and power to help those who should be helped," "she knows how to reward and to punish the sacrilegious and those who venture any

impiety, with Christ her model." On the quoted inscription, see Vikan (1984) 70, the younger Saint Symeon being addressed; on the oracle lots, Papaconstantinou (1994) 282ff.

63 Vigilantius and Fortunatus, above; cf. also Euseb., *H. E.* 8.6.7. This was, for the church, a very ancient point of difficulty, hence ancient discussions, e.g. Mansi 2.265ff., or more modern, e.g. Uytfanghe (1989) 173, exploring the ambiguity a little; Lucius (1908) 451f., distinguishing what the theologians wanted, but "distinctions of this sort could make little sense for the great majority" of Christians; Croon in *RAC* 13 (1986) 1224f., s.v. "Heilgötter," declaring that, whatever the church authorities wished, "yet in practice and especially in Volksfrömmigkeit, it was certainly something different." The Augustine quotation is from *De moribus eccl. cath.* 1.34.75 (*PL* 32.1342), on which see Maraval (1985) 146, "Ces précisions [such as προσκύνησις and λατρεία in Greek, *adorare, colere* in Latin] des théologiens n'empêcheront pas que le terme adorer soit bientôt directement appliqué aux reliques bibliques, aux reliques des saints et même aux images"—as indeed the Augustine passage illustrates.

64 Cyril. Alex., *Oratiunculae tres* 2 and 3 (*PG* 77.1102Bf. and 1105A); they two can drive out demons, 3 (1105A); and they become the first of the ἀνάργυροι, "Gratis" healers of a long tradition, cf. Kötting (1950) 204; further on the pair, Sophronios, *Laudes in S. Cyrum et Ioannem* (*PG* 87.3409) and Fernandez Marcos (1975) 48f.

65 Greg. Magn., *Registr.* 11.56 (*MGH Epp.* 2.331), a. 601, with advice on changing the slaughtered oxen into *religiosa convivia*.

66 Martyria challenge or displace pagan shrines: in the east, the first attested being the translation of the relics of Saint Babylas from inside Antioch to a martyrium in suburban Daphne, home of famous pagan festivals and Apollo cult, by prince Gallus, cf. Mango (1990) 52, supposing "the motive may have been to counteract the strongly pagan character of Daphne"; another translation, of relics of Saint Timothy, in Paulin. Nolensis, *Carm.* 19.317ff., a. 357; broad claims in Theodoret., *Graec. affect. curat.* 8.69 (*PG* 46.1033B), of the 420s; Thecla displaces Sarpedonius at Seleuceia, cf. Vryonis (1981) 200 and Maraval (1985) 133; at Philippi, a church of Saint Paul built directly atop a shrine for hero worship, cf. Gregory (1986) 237; a Saint Therapon shrine replaces a famous Asclepieion at Mytilene, Lane Fox (1986) 676; many examples in Maraval (1985) 53f.; in Syria, no demonstrable instances of a martyrion on top of a pagan temple until the fifth century, cf. Pasquato (1976) 311; in the west, Greg. Turonensis, *Liber in gloria confess.* 2 (*MGH SRM* 1, 2.299), of ca. a. 588, relics of Saint Hilary housed by a lake in southern France, to displace the cult offered to the lake, named Helarius, where remains of the pagan shrine have been excavated, cf. Grenier (1931–60) 4.518 n. 5 seeing in the local bishop's arrangement "a pious subterfuge"; a church for Saint Michael, archangel of peaks, on a hilltop in place of a Mercury-shrine, cf. Male (1950) 32; further illustrative sites, ibid. 707f.; further texts in Graus (1965) 185; and tree-cult shrines turned into martyria, in Bulliot and Thiollier (1892) 360; and many instances dependent on circumstantial evidence, e.g. Roblin (1976) 235–42.

67 Above, chap. 1 n. 23.

68 Deubner (1907) 43ff. and 58, "the Dioscuri were clothed by the church in Christian

costume; only the names Cosmas and Damian were new in the forms of the saints";
also Kötting (1950) 218f. and Croon in *RAC* 13 (1986) 1225, s.v. "Heilgötter."

69 Wittmann (1967) 22; cf. the sixth/seventh century PAmst. 1.22, "Holy Cosmas and
Damian, command your servant So-and-So to bathe" in healing water, Papaconstantinou (1994) 283f.

70 Rohland (1977) 98 and 101 and Trombley (1993–94) 1.159 n. 270, quoted

71 Rohland (1977) 101, Perge, etc.; Canivet (1980) 103, on εὐκτήρια to Michael by Leo and
Zeno; Soz., *H. E.* 2.3 (*PG* 67.940Cf.), recounting not only his own healing but that of
other contemporaries, through nocturnal visions and prescriptions, one beneficiary
being a pagan converted by his cure; Rohland 95f. and Mango (1984) 54, on Colossae
= Chonae and pagans; finally, Nau (1908) 548, §2f. on the Laodicean pagan etc.

72 Conc. Laodicense can. 35, against invoking angels and assembling in their honor, the
date uncertain, often cited as of the 360s, e.g. in Rouche (1989) 536, also more loosely
as of the later fourth century, see above, n. 4 or Joannou (1962a) 145 or Canivet
(1980) 99. For angel cult in other moments, see second- and third-century texts
assembled by Sheppard (1980–81) 77ff., 88, 94, 98, drawing out their connections
with pagan and Jewish cults; further, S. Mitchell (1993) 46; third- to fifth-century
inscriptions from Thera addressing angels, in Grégoire (1922) 56f., 58ff.; the fifth-
century Bithynian seer deriving his predictions from consultation with angels, above,
chap. 2 n. 111; a Church of the Angels supported by a great official of the 530s, cf.
Trombley (1993–94) 2.115 n. 214; fifth- and sixth-century invocations of angels' aid at
Aphrodisias, in Roueché (1989) 156; the angels worshiped at Corinth, above, chap. 2
n. 86; sixth-century invocation of a local Lydian pagan deity and Raphael etc. to
ward off hail from fields, Trombley (1993–94) 2.132f.; and in the west, Aug., *En. in ps.*
85.12 (*PL* 37.1090), acknowledging the perception of Christians that *angelos colimus,*
angelos habemus deos, with depictions in church art at Ravenna, Mango (1984) 42, and
invocation to angels, with mystic signs, to protect vineyards in fifth- and sixth-century Sicily, Jordan (1984) 297ff.; also archangelic aid invoked on a gold plate by the
empress Maria, buried beneath Saint Peter's, cf. Rouche (1989) 536.

73 Invoked by Didymus Alex., *De trinitate* 2.92a (*PG* 39.859Af.), therefore respected in
Egypt of the later fourth century; Rohland (1977) 76 describing Michael's frequent
attestation as a healer in third- to fifth-century magical papyri, in company with
other Powers, but also (81ff.) in fourth- to seventh-century Coptic Christian legends,
the Christian angel being a clear follow-through of the pagan; special prominence of
Michael in the *Life of Nikolaos*, cf. Anrich (1913–17) 2.255; a chapel dedicated to him by
a deacon he had healed, Mango (1984) 48f.; requested in a Thera inscription to aid
the suppliant and his children, Grégoire (1922) 57; depicted in sixth-century Syrian
church art, ibid. 42f.; but also a pervasive presence in magic, ibid. 54, and stigmatized
by the Conc. Romanum a. 492 (Mansi 8.151), in Rouche (1989) 536.

74 Sincere belief the key to receiving a miraculous cure, seen in Rohland (1977) 97, also
in Cosmas-and-Damian cult, in *Miracle* no. 1 lines 24ff. (Rupprechts p. 2, ἀδύνατον
ἔλεγον εἶναι τῶν δωρεῶν τοῦ θεοῦ ἄνευ πίστεως μετασχεῖν), in Deubner (1907)
98f., or again, in Bede, *H. E.* 3.13; similarly and familiarly in Mk 5.34, 9.23, 10.52, and
other texts; and in paganism, above, chap. 2 n. 73. For water cures, cf. Nau (1908)

548f. §2f. and 550; Mango (1984) 47f., 53f.; Kötting (1950) 209; Maraval (1985) 229; at the Cyrus and John shrine of Menuthis, ibid. and Fernandez Marcos (1975) 44; at Thecla's shrine, Vryonis (1981) 201; and fish in pagan cults, Dölger (1910–43) 5 passim and MacMullen (1981) 35f.

75 Ibid. 35, with Picard (1922) 58f., 61; POxy. 1382 col. ii line 1, healing water borne off to Pharos; MacMullen (1981) 147, pagan sacred birds; Dagron (1978) 352, 354, Thecla's birds; and Greg. Turonensis, *Liber de virtut. S. Iuliani* 25 (*MGH SRM* 1, 2.125).

76 Instances of healing advice delivered in a dream by Michael, in Soz. loc. cit. and Rohland (1977) 95f. Notice that Michael's aid is sought in the magical papyri through dream-revelations, ibid. 77f., e.g. *PGM* 2.44 and 149, even consulted from one's own bedroom at home, p. 80 (*PGM* 1.29); and he appears in Coptic legends also advising through dreams at Michael churches, pp. 82f., 96.

77 Incubation rewarded by Thecla in eleven different miracles, Dagron (1978) 103, noting the wording; also 336, *Miracle* 17, 340 no. 18, etc.; an ὀπτασία to one "sleeping in the usual place in the baptistery" of a Cosmas-and-Damian church, Deubner (1907) 117f.; Cyrus-and-John epiphanies, Cyril, *Oratiunculae* 3 (*PG* 77.1105A), the eulogist saying that Christian suppliants at the shrine, unlike the pagan of yore, don't have to pay for their dreams vouchsafed to an intermediary, cf. Deubner (1907) 104ff. and 112f., the two saints appealed to by a woman with an illness, and they respond φανέντες αὐτῆι ἐν ὀπτασίαις κατὰ τὸ σύνηθες αὐτοῖς; an epiphany to Justinian, Procop., *Aed.* 1.6.5f.; also Fernandez Marcos (1975) 34 noting the terminological echoes in the Christian wonder-accounts from those of the Epidauran Asclepieion; at Ephesus, a prediction offered to Theodosius in a dream, in Momigliano (1972) 14; in Egypt earlier (the 360s), Lefort (1954) 225f.; in Palestine in the 420s, at the tomb of the saint, Cyril Scythopolitanus, *Vita S. Euthymii* 10.20f., in Festugiére (1961–64) 3, 1.74; in Pontus toward a. 550, in Eustratius, *Vita Eutychii* 17 (*PG* 86.2293D–2296A), at Saint Uranius' tomb; in Constantinople, in an account of the seventh century, with a study of parallels in wording between this cult and the pagan, e.g. at Epidaurus, by Tolstoi (1920) 53–59 passim; incubation at the Saint Demetrios shrine in Thessaloniki, including mass incubations in time of plague, Lemerle (1979–82) 1.65, 79, 97 n. 1; 2.32ff., the bulk of the miracles in the collection assembled in the second half of the sixth century by one bishop, written up by another by ca. 620, and (73) vouched for by the second from personal observation or first-hand report; and a miscellany in Maraval (1985) 225 n. 102; incubation and special buildings for it at Pachomian Egyptian sites alleged by McCoull (1991) 125f. but not apparent to me in her cited studies by Grossman (1985) 75f. and idem and Jaritz (1980) art. cit. Above, chap. 2 n. 83 on pagan incubation in the east.

78 On the date of the Athenian Asclepius shrine's destruction, see above, chap. 2 n. 63 (ca. a. 480) and Gregory (1986) 238, setting it post-450, etc. (quoted). He goes on to draw the church's ties to Saint Andrew, known as a patron of healing in early Christian Greece.

79 *De miraculis S. Stephani* (*PL* 41.840), in Kötting (1950) 264; Aug., *Civ. dei* 22.8.14 (*PL* 41.767), the mode of healing prescribed to the suppliant *per revelationem*. On pagan antecedents in Gaul, see above, chap. 2 n. 83.

80 Greg. Magn., *Dial.* 3.38, Ferentinum, with many later attestations at this site and numerous others in Naples of the eighth to tenth centuries, in Mallardo (1949) 465, with mention of long stays and explanation by priests, 497f., cf. eastern examples to the same effect in Maraval (1985) 225; in France, Constantius, *Vita Germani* 45 (*MGH SRM* 7.282); Greg. Turonensis, *Vita patrum* 2.2 and 3.1; idem, *Hist. Franc.* 8.16; "accounts of healing miracles that take place after a period of incubation at the tomb of a saint are, in Gregory of Tours, very frequent," says Flint (1991) 270, who certainly knows this author, though she supplies no references for her statement. Brown (1976) 18 insists, "There is nothing in Gregory [of Tours]. . . . The right to dream in the presence of the holy is denied. There is no incubation in Gaul." The denial is repeated, idem (1981) 174, "with all that this implies"; and similarly, Delehaye (1961) 155, minimizing the practice of incubation in churches. For incubation further into the Middle Ages, cf. the routine of healing in the tenth-century resort to Saint Fides (Foy), in Bouilliet (1897) 9, 36f., 137f., especially 48 (reporting a *multitudo decumbentium* on an apparently ordinary night), and beyond the boundaries of this study up into eleventh-century France, even Norway, cf. Gessler (1946) 664–67.

81 Beck (1950) 346 finds about a quarter of bishops sanctified from about 150 of the sixth century in a section of France. I have seen no comparable study of the proportions in other times and regions, but Lucius (1908) 565–67 collects a good number of examples.

82 Above, nn. 32, 60, 62; *De miraculis S. Stephani* 2.4.2 (*PL* 41.851).

83 Greg. Nyss., *De S. Theodoro*, PG 46.737D– 740A; and Gendle (1981) 183f., instancing (with several wrong references) Asterios (*PG* 40.336A, not improved by F. Halkin in *Subsidia Hagiographica* 41 [1965]), Basil (*PG* 31.489), Gregory Nazianzenus (*PG* 37.737f.), and John Chrysostom (*PG* 50.516).

84 Severus Ant., *Homil.* 72, in Brière (1991) 83; Eustratius, *Vita Eutychii* 53 (*PG* 86.2233D–36B), the grateful patient ἔστησεν τὴν εἰκόνα τοῦ ἁγίου ἀνδρός; Venantius Fortunatus, bishop of Poitiers, *Carm.* 10.6.92ff., in L. Pietri (1983) 828, 830f., or Van Dam (1993) 130, speaking also of many murals dating from the later fifth century.

85 Nautin (1967) 6, the temple taken over by Narses in 535/537 in the episcopacy of Theodore (525–c. 577!); p. 18, the votive inscription of the painting; and p. 27, the painting itself with others now lost.

86 Chap. 2 n. 42.

87 Bouillet (1892) xf., 50, 53f., and idem (1897) viif., the statue basically assembled in the ninth century, promptly working miracles, ornaments etc. added in the tenth and still later, and the write-up of miracles from the tenth century into early eleventh; on the practice of stauettes as reliquaries, J. and M.-C. Hubert (1982) 236f., 239f. (Late Empire date for the face); Taralon (1978) 16 (fourth- to fifth-century date), 19 (reconstitution of elements ca. 880 and ca. 1000), and 21 n. 47, comparing the gold head of Avenches which he supposes is Marcus Aurelius; but, better, the emperor Julian, cf. Balty (1980) 58ff., rightly comparing (p. 63) the Conques Majesté de Ste. Foy; and Remensnyder (1990) 352, 357, 364 n. 82, on the proposed dating of the image in its present form, including an unsupported view (M.-M. Gauthier's) that no part is later than the ninth century.

88 Bouillet (1897) 40, *Liber* 1.11, Bernardus broaching his fears *de qua imagine, quamvis super-*
sticiosa res esse videatur . . . , and 47, *Liber* 1.13 (quoted), contrasting the *sapientes* and *rustici;*
Taralon (1978) 20; and Remensnyder (1990) 358ff., underlining the final acceptance
by Bernard of a simpler piety. For a ninth-century attack on images of the saints,
supported by citations from Augustine, Bede, and many others, cf. Claudius Tauri-
nensis (d. 827), *Liber de imaginibus sanctorum, PL* 104.199f.; in all of the churches in
Torino, again, idem, *Apologeticum, PL* 105.460.

89 Bouillet (1897) 40 (*Vita S. Fide* 1.11, the image paraded *ut mos est*) and 100 (2.4), the
processions "with laity and clergy, cymbals and horns," and frequent; cf. also J. and
M.-C. Hubert (1982) 260f.; Homann (1965) 132 on the western pagan antecedents of
processions and subsequent church bans on them, fifth to tenth centuries (though he
seems to me too certain about the *Indiculus* text he begins with); MacMullen (1981)
28f., on hundreds of known localities with annual, or more frequent, pagan processing of idols, of which a famous one in Athens was still to be seen in the late fourth
century, Trombley (1993–94) 1.18, another in Rome still later, Macrob., *Sat.* 1.23.13, a
third ca. 360 in Egypt, in the *Life of Apollon* §24, Festugière (1961–64) 4, 1.54, a fourth
also Egyptian reported from the 370s by Epiphanius, *Panarion* 4.31.22.9f., in Williams
(1987–94) 2.51, a fifth from the late fourth century in northern Italy, Max. Taur.,
Serm. 76, and a sixth still later in France reported by Greg. Turon., *Gloria confess.* 76
(*MGH SRM* 1,2.343); compare Greg. Naz., *Or.* 44 (*PG* 36.620C), the martyrs
αἰθριάζουσι . . . πομπευουσι borne upon λαμπροῖς βήμασι.

90 See Huskinson (1974) 68, partially endorsing T. Klauser's derivation of Christian art
from the unregulated laity, and providing a good discussion (69–72) of Jesus as
Orpheus; Breckenridge (1978) 365 quoting to endorse Kitzinger (1954) 86, that Christian art began unnoticed by the ecclesiastical authorities; idem 365f., collecting references to scores of portrayals of Jesus on sarcophagi and others, too, in frescoes;
Gendle (1981) 182 on Jesus as a young bearded male, to which J. Ferguson (1970) 238
or Lane Fox (1986) 676 would add the Dorset (Hinton Saint Mary) mosaic of perhaps the 330s. For the church position, cf. Conc. Illiberr. can. 37 (Mansi 2.253, *ne pic-*
turae in ecclesia fiant, Mansi commenting, *ne quod colitur et adoratur in parietibus depingatur*).

91 Drawing on Mt 9.20ff., Mk 5.25, or Lk 8.43, Euseb., *H. E.* 7.18, at Paneas = Caesarea
Phillipi in Phoenicia; cf. Philostorg., *H. E.* 7.3 (ed. J. Bidez, *GCS* 21 [1913] 78), repeating the story of the curative plant and emphasizing that there was no "worship" of
the image resulting.

92 *Liber pont.* 34 (*MGH Gesta Pont. Roman.* 1.52), in Smith (1970) 149f., 158ff. The *fastigium*
(as it was called) recalls the emperor's ideas of glorification of his own image among
the Apostles, or on a porphyry column in the eastern capital, above, chap. 2 n. 2.

93 Soc., *H. E.* 1.9 (*PG* 67.84C), the emperor's letter to the church of Alexandria.

94 *Liber pont.* 46 (*MGH Gest. Pont. Roman.* 1.98), Jesus' *imaginem auream* to Xystus (a.
432–440) from Valentinian II; depictions of sacred figures at Ravenna, in Kötzsche
(1992) 110f., with fourth- and fifth-century sarcophagi also; at Naples in S. Gennaro,
cf. Pariset (1968) 13–16, datable to the last third of the fourth century; Jesus, Peter,
Paul, and Mary on church walls of Augustine's day and region, the references gathered by H. Chadwick (1996) 80f.; Greg. Turonensis, *De gloria mart.* 21f. (*MGH SRM*

1,2.51), contemporary examples; in various eastern localities, ibid. 96ff. or Chabot (1899–1910) 2.159, at a Syrian (Amida) church, a painting of Jesus in the sixth century. On cult images in private hands, see Aug., *De haeresibus* 7 (*PL* 42.27) in Zellinger (1933) 81, Nikephorus, *Vita S. Andreae Sali* 130 (*PG* 111.777C), and the Council of Hiereia a. 787 (Mansi 13.328B) outlawing proskynesis to icons in the home. On the controversy, see e.g. in the sixth century Hypatius Ephesinus, in Kitzinger (1954) 94f. or Markus (1978) 152f., in the east, and in the west, in the early eighth century, Claudius Taurin., *Liber de imag. sanct.* (*PL* 104.199ff.) and *Apol.* (*PL* 105.460).

95 Markus (1978) 152f., Gregory's letters, *Ep.* 9.208 and 11.10 (*MGH Epp.* 2.195f., 269f.), reacting to the report of *quidam imaginum adoratores* in Marseilles churches, where the *imagines* shouldn't be smashed, but accepted as teaching devices.

96 Picard (1922) 62.

97 For example (from much material): Aug., *Civ. dei* 22.8.10 (*PL* 41.766), the instrument being flowers held by a bishop who in turn holds relics of Saint Stephen (comparing the means of a beneficent miracle wrought by Isis through flowers "for me," the petitioner, Apul., *Met.* 11.13); plants from saints' tombs, Greg. Turonensis, *Liber de gloria mart.* 70; *Vita patrum* 6.7; and the incident drawn from the *Miracula S. Demetrii* by Magoulias (1967) 256f.

98 Above, chap. 2 n. 74; Nautin (1967) 33, cf. the continuation of the practice also in modern France reported by Bulliot and Thiollier (1892) 298f. and Traunecker (1987) 230; ibid. 228f., fifth-century Egypt (Coptic); Dagron (1978) 340, Thecla's *Miracle* no. 18; in Syria, given to suppliants by Saint Symeon the Younger, Ven (1962–70) 1.145, 212; in Palestine and Pontus of the early sixth century, cf. Brière (1919) 87; dust from Hormizd's cross works miracles, seventh century or later, cf. Budge (1902) 73, 82; Aug., *De civ. dei* 22.8.6 (*PL* 41.764) and *Ep.* 52.2 (*PL* 33.194), earth from Jesus' grave is put to good use or bad (the Donatists "adore" it); Greg. Turonensis, *Liber de virtut. S. Iuliani* 24 and 46a (*MGH SRM* 1, 2.125 and 132), the latter incident where Greg. prescribes dust from the tomb and it works, and dust from Martin's tomb applied to the ailing by Gregory personally with successful results, *De virtut. S. Mart.* 4.37 (*MGH SRM* 1, 2.209), cf. Traunecker (1987) 232f.; Greg. Magn., *Dial.* 3.17.2ff. (Vogüé [1978–80] 2.338), dust from altar base brings a dead man to life; in connection with St. Martin cult, L. Pietri (1983) 578; and other examples in Lucius (1908) 180 n. 3. For the continuation of the use of dust, see western examples of the thirteenth century on in Traunecker (1987) 230, 233.

99 Acts 19.12, σουδάρια ἢ σιμικίνθια, cf. Kotansky (1995) 244 n. 4, and the *Acta proconsularia S. Cypr.* 4, *linteamina et manualia*; Prudentius, *Peristeph.* 5.41ff. (*CSEL* 61.346) of ca. 400, *plerique vestem lineam stillente tingunt sanguine*, at Saint Vincent's execution; and Cyril of Jerusalem quoting Acts 9.12 to argue that, if garments, then even more the bodily remains of martyrs can work miracles of healing, *Catechesis* 18.16 (*PG* 33.1037A); and so into the first half of sixth-century France, cf. Meyer (1904) 17, 60; Greg. Turon., *In gloria mart.* 27 (*MGH SRM* 1,2.54); then in Greg. Magn., *Registr.* 5.57 (*MGH Epp.* 1,1.364), magical properties in recent popes' burial dalmatics; and in Bede, *H. E.* 1.18 and 3.10. Merkelbach and Totti (1991) 155, on the well-known special powers of βιαιοθάνατοι when invoked, point to a most useful text, the *Passio S. Pionii* 13.6, con-

veniently in Musurillo (1972) 152, who sets the date around the turn of the fourth century, p. xxix (the place was Smyrna, cf. Euseb., *H. E.* 4.15.47, who knew the account): "by the name of what executed person, βιοθανοῦς ἀνθρώπου, have so many demons been exorcized, and are still and will be exorcized?" Next, perhaps, the statement in a. 363 by Greg. Naz., *Or.* 4 (*Contra Iulianum* 1).69 (*PG* 35.589C), that "demons are driven out and the sick made well, some by visions, some by foretelling . . . by mere drops of blood" of the martyrs; and then, the routine of the miraculous supplying of blood from St. Euphemia's relics, sought at her tomb by bishops and laity alike, to work more miracles, Evagrius, *H. E.* 2.3 (*PG* 86.2493Bf.). Further, that human or animal blood was used as a convenient essence in magic spells, cf. Betz (1986) 38, 168, and 93 (*PGM* 1.2876 and 2887, οὐσία . . . παρθένου ἀώρου and βιαίου αἷμα, relics and blood of someone who died young or cut off). Frankfurter (1994) 30f. uses a third-century Coptic text to suggest an antecedent to Christian martyr-blood veneration, but I think his argument exceeds his evidence

100 Lucius (1908) 99 n. 4, on Euseb., *Mart. Pal.* 12; Sulp. Sev., *Vita S. Martini* 18.3; Aug., *Civ. dei* 22.8.12 and 16 (*PL* 41.766f.), a piece of clothing touched to holy relics carries their healing to a sufferer; cf. *Vita S. Leobini* 20 (*MGH AA* 4, 2.66f.); later, Gerontius, *Vita S. Melaniae* 61, Melania wears a saint's belt and applies it in healing; *Vita Apollinaris* 5 (*MGH SRM* 3.199), where the instrument of healing is a cloak and the saint is bishop of Valence (ca. 453–520); also Graf (1994) 128, clothing used in hexing; and splinters from a stake on which a martyr's head had been impaled used by bishop Acca, toward the mid-seventh century, to work a healing miracle (on the model of the Rood), Bede, *H. E.* 3.13.

101 A saint gives his toenail to work wonders, Brooks (1924) 69, cf. *PGM* 1.3f., fingernails and hairs; Graf (1994) 162, nails of the victim used in hexing; Aug., *Civ. dei* 22.8.8 (*PL* 41.765), a holy priest's tears drive out a demon; body parts or fluids commonly believed to represent the whole person in working magic, as in Lucian, *Dialogue of Courtesans* 4.288.

102 Above, n. 66, the translation in the 350s; *Liber pont.* ed. Duchesne 1.212, of Pope Damasus (d. 384), "this man sought out and found many saints' bodies," cf. his dreams in Delehaye (1912) 89 n. 3, 90; his example immediately followed by Ambrose's dream a. 386 revealing the resting place of Gervasius and Protasius, in response to the earlier shouted demands of his congregation for something to match the martyr-relics found at Rome, *Ep.* 1.22.1 (*PL* 19.1019), cf. Aug., *Civ. dei* 22.8.2 (*PL* 41.761), *per somnium*, etc., and Augustine's significant choice of words in regard to the discovery of Gervasius' and Protasius' remains in Milan, *nuper, sicut solent apparere sanctorum corpora martyrum, revelatione dei, Serm.* 318.1 (*PL* 38.1438). A *somnium* to a nun authenticated the relics of Saint Stephen in Africa, *De miraculis S. Stephani* 1.1 (*PL* 41.834); another to a local devout of Syria in 515, or rather, οὐ καθ᾽ὕπνον ἀλλὰ φανερῶς, in Trombley (1993–94) 1.104; still another to the bishop of Langres authenticates a martyr tomb discovered by the people, in Greg. Turonensis, *Liber in gloria mart.* 50 (*MGH SRM* 1, 2.72). Revealing is the phrase in Eugippius' *Vita S. Severini* 22.1, Régerat (1991) 236f., "for a church being built outside the walls of Batava, . . . a martyr's remains were being sought" (mid-fifth century); or

again, praise of a bishop in the 720s for energetic collection of relics and building of martyria for them, Bede, *H. E.* 5.20. In the east, cf. an example in Zebennus' dreams (the bishop of Eleutheropolis in the 390s) which revealed the relics of Habakkuk and Micah, cf. Soz., *H. E.* 7.29 (*PG* 67.1505C). Maraval (1985) 41–44 collects many references to relics discovery authenticated (46f.) by miracles; the material is very extensive.

103 Beaujard (1991) 187, quoted, speaking of the west, and adding, "It was he [the bishop] who presided over the cult offered to him" [the martyr].

104 Joh. Chrysos., *De S. Babyla* 1 (*PG* 50.529).

105 Soc., *H. E.* 7.14 (*PG* 67.765Bf.), on the origin of Saint Thaumasius.

106 "Battle-logic": cf. Pasquato (1976) 311, "lottare," and Maraval (1985) 51 describing Christians engaged "dans la lutte contre le paganisme," which dictated the location of many eastern church sites. On Hilarius, see above, n. 66; on Christians and water shrines, chap. 2 n. 114; and continual condemnation of Christians for water-deity worship or, at least, for the sacrilegious acts of such cults, e.g. in Caesarius, *Sermo* 53.224, 54.229f.

107 Lucius (1908) 1f. began his study with a brief survey of the subject of temples remade into churches, and Deichmann (1939) 107ff. and idem, *RAC* 2 (1954) s.v. "Christianisierung II (der Monumente)," cols. 1230ff., supplied an update. As a random sample of archeological data from the second half of this century, see for Egypt, Rees (1950) 93 and (though not archeological) Thelamon (1981) 264, a martyrion for John the Baptist in the ruins of the Alexandrian Serapeion; in Asia Minor, Trombley (1993–94) 1.82 (Aphrodisias) and 2.23 (a Klaros inscription of 457/474); and N. Thierry (1977) 102 n. 20 (Comana); in fourth- to fifth-century Britain, examples gathered in Watts (1991) 106ff, 138; in France, Male (1950) 32f., 37f., 40f., 56, 58f., Grenier (1931–60) 4.707f., and Roblin (1976) 236ff. Much more might be listed.

108 Above, nn. 58 (Theodoret), 74 (pagan origins and instances), and 32 (Nola). The grateful display of representations of healed body parts was condemned (as I understand the reference to *sculptilia*) by the Conc. Autessiodurense a. 573/603 can. 3, but went on nevertheless.

109 Gibbon (1946) 902f., ending his chapter, "The religion of Constantine achieved, in less than a century, the final conquest of the Roman empire; but the victors themselves were insensibly subdued by the arts of the vanquished rivals." For Paulinus' attitude toward the peasantry, cf. e.g. *Carm.* 27.581f., on the frescoes at the shrine, *pictura . . . sancta / Si forte attonitas haec per spectacula mentes / Agrestum caperet fucata coloribus umbra.*

110 On clerical, usually episcopal, warranty of miracles, see above, chap. 3 nn. 47, 50, 55, 58, and passim; above, n. 77 (Demetrios' miracles recounted by bishops); miracles by Eutychius (Constantinopolitan patriarch 552–565) vouched for personally by his priest and biographer, Eustratius, *Vita* 51 (*PG* 86.2332); or similarly, Messian in his *Vita Caesarii* 19 (*MGH SRM* 3491); Aug., *Serm.* 286.5(4)(*PL* 38.1299), on the punishments expected of Saints Gervasius and Protasius; and above, chap. 3 n. 58.

111 Aside from examples of bishops and ascetics performing miraculous cures, above,

chap. 1 n. 22 and chap. 3 n. 50, notice, further, Theodoret., *H. E.* 4.16 (*PG* 82.1161f.);
Paneg. on Makarius of Tkôou in Amélineau (1888–95) 1.158, miracles from the grave; *Life
of Apollo* bishop of Heracleopolis, §16, in Campagnano and Orlandi (1984) 210f.;
Victor Vitensis, *Hist. persecut. Afr. prov.* 2.47f. (*CSEL* 7.42f.), Eugenius bishop of
Carthage (d. 505); *Vita Melaniae iun.* 34 (*SC* 90.190f.); Sulp. Sev., *Vita S. Mart.* 6.1f.
(16.1f.); Constantius, *Vita Germani* 45 (*MGH SRM* 7.282), miracles from the tomb,
beyond the healing the bishop did in his lifetime; Eugippius, *Vita S. Severini* 16.1ff.,
46.1ff., in Régerat (1991) 222f., 294 (in 488 in Naples, p. 11); Messian, *Vita Caesarii* 19
(*MGH SRM* 3.491); *Vita Lupi* 6, 8, 9a, etc. (ibid. 7.299f.); *Vita S. Gaugerici* 5, 10 (ibid.
3.653, 656), the bishop of Carignan (d. 623/9) cures leprosy and blindness; Venantius Fortunatus, *Vita S. Leobini* 10, 17, 20f. (garment), and 24, heals; and 8f. and 19,
checks conflagrations (*MGH AA* 4, 2.76, 79f.); idem, *Vita S. Amantii* 41ff. (ibid.
59–64); *Vita S. Consortiae, Acta Sanctorum Iunii* 4 (1707) 253, exorcizes, restores sight
and heals, in Provence of the late sixth century; *Vita Audoini* 9 (*MGH SRM* 5.59) of
the seventh century; and *Vita Iuliani* 10 (ibid. 3.379) of the ninth/tenth.

112 Above, chap. 2 at nn. 58ff.; Acts 14.11, 28.6; and Xen. Ephes. 1.7.

113 Above, chap. 2 at nn. 58 and 93; Heussi (1936) 286, 292ff., whose discussion of the
origins of Christian asceticism, and its relations to Hellenistic movements and traditions in the hundred years leading up to Antony, seems to me still the most bal-
anced and careful. O'Neill (1989) seems to me to stretch his evidence in the search
for pre-Antonian monasticism, rather to be counted as ascetic ideals occasionally
preached and followed; but for early Egyptian monks beyond Antony, see ibid. 274,
276.

114 Above, chap. 1 at nn. 47 and 54.

115 *Life of Nikolaos of Sion* 54ff. (55, quoted), in Anrich (1913–17) 1.42f., with 2.244f. (date,
540s); Robert (1955) 199, commenting on the description, "One might suppose one
was reading a description of the ancient post-sacrifice banquets, under the guise,
always repeated with minor variations, ἀπελθόντες ἐν τῶι εὐκτήριου τοῦ ἁγίου."
Compare Concilia Afr. a. 397 can. 42 (*Register ecclesiae Carthaginiensis*, ed. C. Munier,
1974), *ut in ecclesiis convivia minime celebrentur*, with the added directive that "no bishops
or clergy" should banquet in churches, "so far as the prohibition can be enforced"
(a despairing note), cf. above, n. 36 and Lucius (1908) 434.

116 E.g. *Vita S. Symeon. iun.* 95f., Ven (1962–70) 1.73f.; Rees (1950) 91; MacMullen (1984)
152.

117 Greg. Nyss., *Vita Greg. Thaumat.*, *PG* 46.932B–C, trans. in MacMullen and Lane
(1992) 212f.; Georgios' *Life of Theodore of Sykeon* 141, ed. Festugière (1970); Eugippius,
Vita S. Severini 15.1ff., in Régerat (1991) 220ff.; and Greg. Magn., *Dial.* 3.10.2f., Vogüé
(1978) 2.290.

118 Against fire: Sulp. Sev., *Vita S. Mart.* 14.2; *Vita S. Leobini* 8f. and 19 (*MGH AA* 4, 2.25,
28, 64f.), scenes toward the mid-sixth century.

119 Eugippius, *Vita S. Sevrini* 12.1f., 18.1f., Régerat (1991) 212, 223f.; Aphraates, in Lucius
(1908) 527.

120 Lucius (1908) 527 with many examples of monks controlling weather and natural
phenomena; further, on pagan holy men and women insuring good harvests, above,

chap. 2 n. 111; on miraculous weather control, above, chap. 1 n. 24; add, Festugière (1970) 1.ixf. and 2.47ff., *Vita S. Theodori* 51; ibid. 52 or Brooks (1923) 14 on the blessed Habib, the saint controls hail by prayer; ibid. 118 (from John of Ephesus, *Vitae patrum* 6.118), the skull of Paul the Anchorite is carried around the countryside and averts plague, hail, or locusts; further, Callinicus, *Vita Hypatii* 46.3f.; Cyril Scyth., *Vita S. Euthymii* 25.39, Festugière (1961–64) 3, 1.93, drought relieved by rain, e.g. by the prayers of Quintianus, Greg. Turonensis, *Vitae patrum* 4.4; Thalaleios defeats storms believed to be demons, Theodoret., *Hist. relig.* 18.1, the historian vouching for the report; the bishop, later saint, Germanus stills the storm roused by *inimica vis daemonum*, cf. Constantius, *Vita Germani* 13 (*MGH SRM* 7.260); hailstorms averted by Julian, Stancliffe (1979) 58; idem (1983) 221, quoting Sulp. Sev., *Dial.* 3.7.3, on Martin's control against hailstorms both in his life and afterwards; Gregory of Tours uses holy relics against storms, *Liber de gloria mart.* 83, in Graus (1965) 44 n. 138; in mid-sixth century, Symeon the Younger's prayers gain good weather, in Ven (1962–70) 1.153, *Vita* §171; similarly, Nikolaos, *Vita* 59, in Anrich (1913–17) 1.46; and so forth.

121 Georgios' *Life of Theodore of Sykeon* 52 in Festugière (1970) 1.45, which Trombley (1985) 340 very well explains in terms of Nilsson (1955–61) 1.113f., Nilsson in turn citing Lucian, *Philopseudes* 12 and other data concerning magic circles; earlier, Messian, *Vita Caesarii* 27 (*MGH SRM* 3.494); later, texts like the Sicilian ones in n. 72, above.

122 Trombley (1993–94) 2.133.

123 *Quaest. nat.* 4B.5.2; for Pliny's view and the context for Seneca's attitude, cf. above, chap. 3 n. 5.

124 On hail spells of Pliny's times, above, chap. 3 n. 4; in Mauretania Caesariensis, *CIL* 8.9180; around Hippo, the Christian farmer resorts to the sortilege for help against hail, Aug., *En. in ps.* 70.17 (*PL* 36.887); and Gatier (1986) 143f. and *Lexikon für Theologie und Kirche* s.v. "Elias," noting the pagan tradition that shaped the prophet, in the popular mind, into this rural rain and lightning god.

125 Iambl., *Vita Pythag.* 92, 135; Ps.-Justin, *Quaest. et resp. ad orthodoxos* of the fourth century, *PG* 6.1277Cf., banning resort to νεφοδιῶκται, cf. Trombley (1993–94) 1.318; Conc. Trullanum a. 691 can. 61, Joannou (1962) 197; repeated directives against *immisores tempestatis* etc. in western penitentials, cf. Harmening (1979) 247f.; Agobard bishop of Lyon a. 816–40, *Liber contra insulsam vulgi opinionem* 1 and 13 (*PL* 104.147, 155), speaking out of personal observation and of the common belief in *tempestarii*. On the prevalence of alternatives, I agree with Treadgold (1994) 154, speaking of the eastern provinces but still more truly of the western: "It seems improbable that as much as 5% of the population of the Later Roman Empire ever saw a holy man."

126 On haruspices, astrology, laws, etc. in the the fourth century, see Montero (1991) 91, 123–43 or Fögen (1993) 258ff., 283; on *haruspicina* thereafter, in Cyril of Jerusalem and into Justinian's reign, and up to the Conc. Tolet. can. 29, *de clericis magos aut aruspicos consulentibus*, see Montero (1991) 162; Salvian, *De gub. dei* 6.12 (*MGH AA* 1, 1.69), consuls consult augurs, *adhuc gentilium sacrilegiorum more, . . . paene omnia fiunt . . .* etc., quoted; and on astrology, Hendrikx (1954) 329ff.

127 On oracle-seeking at Egyptian shrines of St. Philoxenus or Kollouthos in the sixth

century and later, by the traditional device of double questions, Yes or No, cf. Papaconstantinou (1995) 281ff.; on prophetic powers, for example, of pagan wonder-workers, cf. above, chap. 2 n. 111; of Nestorios, above, n. 111; of Severinus, in Eugippius, *Vita S. Severini* 39.1, Régerat (1991) 272, or of Zosimas, near Tyre in the sixth century, Evagrius, *H. E.* 4.7 (*PG* 86.2713); of Symeon Stylites, ibid. 5.21 (*PG* 86.2836C); of Symeon Stylites the Younger, *Vita S. Symeon. iun.* 7, 78, in Ven (1962–70) 1.50, 67; of Symeon the Mad, in Syria of the sixth century, Festugière and Ryden (1974) 132; around a. 600, Eleusios, *Vita S. Theodori* 120; and other eastern examples in Patlagean (1968) 116 n. 2.

128 Conc. Ankyranum a. 314 can. 24 (Mansi 2.522) and Basil, *Ep. canonica* 217.83 in Gain (1985) 242 n. 63; in mid-fifth century Antioch, see Klugkist (1974) 361; Conc. Trull. a. 692 can. 61, against consultation with μάντεις; in the west, condemnation of *sortilegi et aruspices* in Aug., *In Joh. evang. tract.* 6.17 (*PL* 35.1433), and Dolbeau (1993) 102 §10, for help with a minor ailment or major decision, and other passages in Zellinger (1933) 40f. n. 34; Cyprian of Toulon, *Vita Caesarii* 55 (*MGH SRM* 3.479); church commands against *sortilegi* and *caragii* or *caraii* reflected in *Vita Eligii* 2.15 (*PL* 87.529A = *MGH SRM* 4.707), various mentions from Gregory of Tours and Charlemagne's Capitulary a. 789 cap. 20, in Flint (1991) 60f. and 217, Conc. Autessiodurense a. 578 can. 4 (Hefele and Leclercq [1907–52] 4.410), Toletanum IV a. 633 can. 29 (ibid. 453, aiming at clergy who consult diviners), Greg. III's *Canons* 16, and Conc. Rom. a. 721 can. 12 (Mansi 12.292, 264), and Pirmin, *Scarapsus* (*PL* 89.1041), the latter three texts in Flint (1991) 62 and 91, who (69) emphasizes the impression conveyed of a society permeated by magical practices.

129 Reliance on sneezing (above, chap. 2 n. 134), omens, bird flight, presages and "observances" attacked by Basil, *Comment. in Isaiam* 2.77 (*PG* 30.2483), Cyril Hierosolymitanus, *Catechesis mystagogica* 1, *ad eos qui nuper illuminati sunt* 1.8 (*PG* 33.1073), Joh. Chrysos., 1 *Catechesis* 39, Wenger (1970) 128, and John of Damascus, *De haeres.*, *PG* 94.757, in Rochow (1978a) 483f.; observation of *sternutationes*, bird song, etc., condemned by Caesarius, *Serm.* 54.1, and other passages in Harmening (1979) 82 and Klingshirn (1994) 219, and *Vita Eligii* 2.15 (*PL* 87.528A = *MGH SRM* 4.705); Conc. Clippiacense a. 626/7 can. 16 (*MGH Conc.* 1.199) condemning augury by Christians, and repeated a few years later (ibid. 204f.); a bishop's use of the flame on the altar as a prognostic, Evagrius, *H. E.* 5.21 (*PG* 86.2836Bf.); chants by children at play in Ael. Arist., *Or.* 50.10 of a. 153, cf. MacMullen (1985/6) 69, and Thelamon (1981) 335 n. 17 comparing the special grace of children in Paulin. Mediolan., *Vita Ambros.* 48 (*PL* 14.43D).

130 MacMullen loc. cit., on Augustine's use; and add various Augustine texts from Brox (1974) 177; but Augustine also expresses slight misgivings, *Ep.* 55.20.37 (*PL* 33.222). For recent discussions of the literariness of the garden scene (not relevant to the actual Christian use and perception of sortition), see the references in a book review by G. J. P. O'Daly, *JRS* 85 (1995) 345. Klingshirn (1994) 220 shows the usage continuing up into the seventh century; but it is condemned by councils at Vannes a. 461/91 can. 16 (Mansi 7.955: aimed at *clerici*), Agde a. 506 can. 21 (*sortes sanctorum*) and 42, Conc. Aurel. I a. 511 can. 30 (Hefele and Leclercq [1907–52] 4.92), Autess.

a. 578 can. 4 (ibid. 410), and Leptines a. 743; by the *Poenitentiale Egberti* 8.1, in Clemen (1928) 40, of the 720s, threatening both clergy and laity who resort to to *auguria vel sortes sanctorum;* further, Greg. Turonensis, *Hist. Franc.* 4.10(16), 5.8(14) (*MGH SRM* 1.149, 210, the bishop uses the *sortes biblicae* himself, as does a king), and Sulp. Sev., *Vita S. Mart.* 9.5ff. (for the election of a bishop), in Kisch (1970) 360f. and Poulin (1979) 131; *Vita S. Consortiae,* in *Acta Sanctorum Iunii* 4 (1707) 251, *ponatur Evangelium super altare;* and Nineham (1993) 125.

131 Poulin (1979) 131f., looking at sixth- to ninth-century manuscripts with marginalia; eastern equivalents in Harris (1901) 46, 56 (western), 70 (tenth century); Klingshirn (1994) 220, on clerical use and condemnation, both, of several sorts of lot devices; the "Astrampsachos" book of oracular responses given a Christian revision, cf. Lane Fox (1986) 677; and questions submitted with prayer to St. Philoxenus' God, of a form similar to those given in at pagan temples in Egypt, cf. Rees (1950) 87.

132 As Adnès and Canivet (1967) 178 put it, describing an instance of suspected hexing, "Like everyone of his time, and Christians in particular, when it has to do with magic, Theodoret [bishop of Cyrrhus near Antioch, 427–449] sees demoniac intervention in such practices"; and notice the conclusion from the finds of amulets and stamps at one small Isaurian town mostly datable to the decades pre-650, "magic amongst the ordinary people of Anemurium . . . was as commonplace a function of daily living as any other activity represented amongst the small finds," cf. J. Russell (1982) 543; also, much additional good material in Engemann (1975) passim.

133 Exorcisms, above, chap. 3 n. 43; *Miracula SS. Cyri et Iohann.* no. 55, in Magoulias (1967) 236.

134 Above, chap. 2 n. 134; Plin., *N. H.* Bk. 30, passim, especially 30.51, cf. e.g. 30.140, various kinds of tied-on packages of odd things; but he is plainly sceptical of phylacteries, at 28.29.

135 On amulets and phylacteries, see Bonner (1950) 50 and 218ff., on the first, and on the second, Betz (1986) 38, 63f., 88, 96, 134, etc.; against *phylacteria* and *ligaturae,* reminders by Basil, *Homil. in ps.* 45.2 (*PG* 29.417); also by Chrysostom and Jerome (*In Mt* 4.23.6 [*PL* 26.168Af.], against *superstitiosae mulierculae*), in Rapp (1981) 35; by Ps.-Athanas., *Syntagma doctrinae ad monachos* 2 (*PG* 28.837) and Athanasius in *PG* 26.1319, cf. *RAC* 1.407f.; also Theodoret, *Graec. affect. curat.* 8.62ff.; Cyril Hierosolymitanus, *Catechesis* 18.8 (*PG* 33.1072Bf.), against περιάμματα and spells on plates; Isaac of Antioch's sermonizing against invocation of the archangel Raphael on amulets, Klugkist (1974) 362f.; and Caesarius, *Serm.* 1.11, 19.86, 50.1 and 215f. (clergy-supplied), 218f., and 221; 54.229; and Eligius (ca. 588–659) preaching a model sermon, *Vita Eligii* (*PL* 87.528C = *MGH SRM* 4.706), condemning Christians who use *ligamina, etiamsi a clericis fiant,* though containing a scriptural text; Kubinska (1974) 153, on a spell invoking the specially favored four archangels, attributed to Gregory I, the angels' names being common on εὐλογία stamps, concerning which, cf. J. Russell (1995) 41; and Rouche (1989) 596, on Conc. Laodicense a. 363 can. 35f. (Mansi 2.569), against invocation of angels and phylacteries, the latter sometimes made by clergy, and Conc. Rom. a. 492 (Mansi 8.151), likewise against *phylacteria omnia quae angelorum*

. . . *nominibus conscripta sunt*; likewise Council of Agde a. 506, in Harmening (1979) 236, with many other Spanish and Gallic bans up to Pirmin in the eighth century, 237, 242ff., 277, 335. For the phylactery of a. 603 from Gregory I, *Registr.* 14.12 (*MGH Epp.* 2.431), see Dölger (1932a) 110; ibid. 90 on the pope's phylactery. For a model, earlier, see Constantius, *Vita Germani* 15 (*MGH SRM* 7.262), blindness healed by application of cross relics carried by the bishop in a *capsula* around his neck.

136   For the quoted passage from the *Vita S. Eugendi* (abbot, d. 510), see *MGH SRM* 3.158; the complaint by Boniface (672/5–754) about "women in pagan fashion with phylacteries and ligatures fastened about their arms and legs and publicly offering them to others for sale," in his *Ep.* 50 (*MGH Epp.* 3, 1.301); apotropaic properties of the fish symbol in Dölger (1910–43) 5.39 (twentieth-century Italy and Sicily), 44, 50f., 325; and more on Christian amulets = medallions in Schultze (1887–92) 309; Naldini (1981) 180ff., discussing spells of Ps. 90 or Paternoster or some other text with a cross, some fourth- to sixth-century examples from Egypt; Vikan (1984) 74–86 on hundreds of surviving "medico-amuletic armbands," etc.; or Jordan (1991) 61f., a representative jumble of Christian and non-Christian elements from Beirut. For clearly pagan models, see e.g. Betz (1986) 134f., comparing exorcistic texts in Kelly (1985) 164 or 177, or Greenfield (1988) 145; for a Christian spell against fever, Aug., *Tract. in Ioann evang.* 7.12 (*PL* 35.1443), or another, with much pagan material, Daniel and Maltomini (1990–92) 1.35ff., 55ff. Compare the Christian Marcellus Empiricus of Bordeaux, *De medicamentis* 8.57, 59, 170f., and 192f., 10.55f., and 15.89, 105f., 108, in Niederman (1968) 128, 156, etc., with *RE* s.v. "Marcellus 58" col. 1498; Daniel and Maltomini (1990–92) 64ff., a purely Christian spell with parts of the Credo, recalling its use exorcistically in Justin's day. For western Christian amulets, see for example Monceaux (1909) 62ff. or Meer (1961) 58, 528.

137   The concluding sentence of Vikan (1984).

138   Spell-casters most often Christian, as seems most likely (and clear in Conc. Aspasi episcopi Elusani a. 551 can. 3, *CCSL* 148A.163f.); Aug., *Tract. in Iohann. evang.* 7.7 (*PL* 35.1441—notice, quotidie *invenio ista*, says Augustine), *Serm.* 87.8.7 (*PL* 38.1300f.), *En. in ps.* 34.6 (*PL* 36.326), Dolbeau (1993) 102 §10, and with special vividness in one of the Lambot sermons, Dölger (1950a) 57; Flint (1991) 60ff., 245ff., and 68, finding in the abundance of attestations proof of "a whole alternative world of intercession"; and above, n. 128. As to the rituals to accompany the culling of medicinal plants, the whole story is compressed into Plin., *N. H.* 33.137, describing the uses etc. of a certain simple (but no mention of magic in picking it), Marcellus Emp., *Med.* 31.33 (p. 333 Helmreich, with a three-phrase word-set prescribed in picking), and McNeill and Gamer (1979) 330f., where Burchard of Worms (early eleventh century) condemns non-Christian spells but prescribes correct Christian: singing of Credo and Paternoster. Delatte (1938) passim provides, not these texts, but their whole context; cf. 94, church condemnation from sixth century on, but (50f.) thirteenth-century specification of Saint John's Day, summer solstice, for picking, with proper prayer, use of the local church for preliminaries and address to pagan deities (71f.) plus (100) other names from the New Testament, even prayers recited

by the priest or the process prayed over (110f., medieval Italian; 154, Anglo-Saxon text and sixth-century *Dynamidia*), accompanied by kneeling, bowing East, or propitiatory offerings (82, 114f., 126).

139 Crosses on doorposts, noticed by Julian the Apostate, cf. Cyril Alex., *C. Iulianum* 6 (*PG* 76.796D), in Sulzberger (1925) 432; Betz (1986) 17, regarding doorpost spells written in mud in Egypt; Engemann (1975) 42f. on Syrian doorway crosses, chrisms, etc., noting the identity of rite between ἰησοῦς Χριστὸς ἐνθάδε κατοικεῖ and the pagan word-set, *Heracles hic habitat;* on which, see also Dölger (1964) 21–25 and Merkelbach (1991) 41f.; Thelamon (1981) 268, 270, and 272 on the ankh (with Rufin., *H. E.* 11.29 and Trombley [1993–94] 1.141); doorpost kisses, both pagan and Christian, in Lucius (1908) 387 n. 3; Nautin (1967) 14f., 24, and 18, noting the Christian translation of the pagan doorway word-set, "Good may the outcome be!" Also, Peterson (1926) 157 on Syrian and Egyptian apotropaic acclamations. In the west, Theodoret, *Hist. relig.* 26.11 (*PG* 82.1473A); Conc. Bracar. a. 571/2 can. 20 (Mansi 9.858), in Jonkers (1968) 51, repeated by Martin of Braga, *Capitula coll.* 72 = Barlow (1950) 141, *inanem signorum fallaciam pro domo facere* (*signa* are apotropaic marks?).

140 Endelechius, *PL* 19.797f.; the friend of Paulinus of Nola, Severus Rhetor, *Carm. bucolicum* 105ff. (*PL* 18.800); and *RAC* 1 (1950) s.v. "Amulett" 409, the Lausanne amulet of lead with "Abrasax."

141 Above, chap. 2 n. 34.

142 Apotropaic properties of psalms, often in the lives of Egyptian monks, and in Basil, *Homil. in ps.* 1 (*PG* 29.212D); also in John Moschus, *Pratum spirituale* 152 (*PL* 74.196f.), an anecdote of ca. a. 600; compare the pagan tradition of sacral music in Quasten (1983) 30; ibid. 16, 29f. n. 117, on Christian apotropaic bells hung on children's necks and wrists, some surviving, and mention in Joh. Chrysos., *Homil.* 12 *in ep. 1 ad Corinth.* 7 (*PG* 61.105f.); also *Daremberg-Saglio* s.v. "Tintinnabulum" 342 and Hübner (1894) 188, second-century bell = *ILS* 8622.

143 Above, chap. 2 nn. 84, 86; Nilsson (1960) 212 on lamps in cult, quoting Eitrem, "The Christian church showed itself here too a true heir of the ancient ritual"; and Kitzinger (1954) 97 on "the use of lights before images" of saints by ca. a. 600.

144 Above, n. 13. Among anthropologists, Goode (1949) 172f., 176f., and idem (1951) 50f. reflected on the distinction, and is still sometimes cited, e.g. by Aune (1980) 1512, who ends (1516) with the inclusion of magic within religion; more recently among anthropologists, H. Geertz (1975) 72ff. An early historian to take the modern view was Schmitt (1976) 945, saying, "It goes without saying that religion cannot be distinguished from magic"; in agreement, Engemann (1975) 41ff., Vikan (1984) 86, Beltz (1992) 167, or Sünskes Thompson (1994) 109f. and 112 n. 23, citing an early (1957) dismissal by O. Pettersson of magic-vs.-religion as no more than "an artificial problem"; and excellent discussion in Fögen (1993) 189, 191–201. For an illustration of the errors that can enter where magic and religion are wrongly separated, see Graf (1994) 241f.

145 An incident of ca. a. 420 in Cyril of Scythopolis, *Vita Euthymii* 10, in Trombley (1993–94) 2.169, who terms it a "conversion" in quotation marks—and so, not a "real" one? Exactly my question in discussing an exactly similar case from

Theodoret, MacMullen (1984) 3. See further George Alex., *Vita S. Joh. Chrysos.* 59, in Halkin (1977) 238, ἐπίστευσαν πάντες ὁμοθυμαδὸν πρὸς κύριον καὶ ἐβαπτίσθησαν πολὺ πλῆθος ἀναρίθμητον, everything done in an instant; and Greg. Turonensis, *De passione et virtut. S. Iuliani* 5f.

146 MacMullen (1984) 3 with nn. 5–8; or as illustration, Aug., *De fide et operibus* 9 (*PL* 40.202), accepting the sequence, *prius, baptizetur; deinde doceatur quid ad bonam vitam moresque pertineat* (and the longer the subsequent instruction, of course, the better).

147 John Ephes., *Lives of the Eastern Saints*, on Symeon the Mountaineer, in Brooks (1923) 229, 232ff.

148 Klugkist (1974) 355, 365f., and passim on "the nominal Christians."

149 Among the "spuria" of John Chrysostom, because of the indications of tinkering with the text: *Sermo de pseudoprophetis* 7 (*PG* 59.561). Cf. Joh. Chrysos., *Laudat. S. mart. Iuliani* 3 (*PG* 50.672f.), deploring "some of those persons gathered here today" before his eyes "who will tomorrow, leaving us, be off to [the Apollo park at] Daphne." Compare Severus of Antioch's lament over the withered little crowds at church, while such large crowds attended theaters, wild beast shows, and races, *Homil.* 76, in Brière (1919) 135; similarly, Augustine's regret that so many women of his congregation were absent to attend the Cybele festival, H. Chadwick (1996) 71.

150 *CJ* 1.11.10; Rochow (1978) 238; above, chap. 1 at nn. 74, 89f., 93ff.; and a similar crypto-pagan among the clergy in Italy a. 599, Greg. Magn., *Registr. epp.* 10.2 (*MGH Epp.* 2.238).

151 Aug., *En in ps.* 26.2.19 (*PL* 36.209).

152 Aug., *Serm.* 196.4.4 (*PL* 38.1021); cf. Caesarius, *Serm.* 33.4, warning his people "not to dare to bathe in springs, lakes, or rivers during the night before or on the morning of the feast of Saint John, for this unfortunate custom carries over from the devotion of the pagans." I am not clear whether both passages refer to June 24th or December 25th, cf. *Lexikon für Theologie und Kirche* s.v. "Johannes" col. 1087.

153 On Christians at pagan celebrations, see Basil, above, n. 44, *Epp. class II* 217 (*PG* 32.805), and *Ep.* 188; at Cybele celebrations in Hippo, above, n. 149; specifically the Kalends, Conc. Bracarense can. 24 (Mansi 9.858), in Jonkers (1968) 52, and a great deal of further material above, chap. 2 n. 13; in unspecified rites, Conc. Valentinum a. 374 can. 3 (Hefele 1, 2.982), Zeno, *Tract.* 21 *de ps.* 100.2 (*PL* 11.460B), Caesarius, *Serm.* 53.1, 54.6 (*CCSL* 103.233—cross-signing meat), and Salvian, *De gub. dei* 8.2f. (*PL* 53.154f.), specifying the sin especially among the *ditissimi ac potentissimi* of Africa, this in the 440s; and Conc. Aurelianense a. 533 can. 20 (*MGH Conc.* 1.64). The Council of Tours a. 567 can. 23 specified the festival of Saint Peter's Throne as the occasion of Christians joining in pagan rites, cf. above, nn. 28ff., on February 22nd.

154 Stancliffe (1983) 213 takes note, with some good discussion, of Aug., *En. in ps.* 78 *Serm.* 2.14 (*PL* 37.1140). The quotation, of the teens of the fifth century, continues with Augustine's remark, *Tenens matrem, offendisti patrem.* Compare above, chap. 2 n. 55, and Aug., *Serm.* 62.7ff. (*PL* 38.417ff.), rebuking Christians who join the sacrificial feasts in temples, to which the errant reply (§10 p. 419), "He [the object of the feast] is no god but the Genius of Carthage," not like Mars or Mercury. For a similar protest by a Christian against what he saw as an unfair rebuke, see Jacob of

Serugh, *Homil.* 5, in Moss (1935) 108f., regarding attendance at miming of gods' stories; or the protest "openly and officially" by Christian magistrates in Rome, that
the Lupercalia rites must be kept up to secure good fortune during the year, cf.
Gelasius, *Adv. Andromachum* 3, in Pomarès (1959) 164.

155 Aug., *De moribus eccl. cath.* 34.75 (*PL* 32.1342), *professores nominis christiani*; other Augustine passages with similar ones from other bishops and a good number of instances
of calculating conversion in MacMullen (1984) 144f. nn. 24–26, 28; Liban., *Or.*
30.28f., on coerced insincere pretense of Christianity; Procop., *Anecdota* 11.32, on
converts in their public acts who risked death in secret sacrifices. On Kourion, I
recall my friend with affection: Mitford (1971) 354ff. Trombley (1993–94) 1.178f.
apparently misreads Mitford's words, attributing the "hint" of pagan feeling (not
"supposition") to the benefactor not to the town (i.e., the curia), and taking the
"House" of the benefactor to be a residence, not a public complex of halls. How
much belief in the old gods must be supposed in the minds of the composers of
the inscriptions, or similar users of traditional motifs and personifications, is
impossible to say—no doubt less and less as time went on, and, by the later sixth
century, none at all, cf. Liebeschuetz (1995) 202 and n. 56.

156 On Nonnus, Vian (1976) xv; the penetrating essay by Livrea (1989) 20ff. and nn. 5f.
and 28ff., gathering writers like Dracontius into his net of discussion; also Wipszycka (1988) 144f., with *RE* s.v. "Kyros (11)" as later bishop of Kotyaeion, cols. 188f.;
Bregman (1982) 179f. and passim; and some references on Claudian, Palladas, et al.,
in MacMullen (1984) 154.

157 On Ausonius, see above, chap. 2 n. 99, and Green (1993) 40ff.; on the persistent col-
oring of later Greek (Byzantine) Christian literature by the past, see e.g. Gregory
(1986) 230f.; of Latin literature, the older broad surveys have been outdated by nar-
rower ones, e.g. on Paulinus, Erdt (1976) 288ff.; but some bibliography in Pack
(1989) 188f. n. 9.

158 N. Thierry (1977) 111, Il. 16.675 on a Christian Cappadocian tombstone of ca. a.
400; Vergil on many tombstones, Sanders (1983) 256f. or Pailler (1986) 152f., 156–64;
J. J. Thierry (1963) 28, 37, on Hier., *Ep.* 22.30; and compare a slightly similar
reproach to secular reading, above, chap. 3 n. 36.

159 On the various attempts to displace Homer, Vergil, and the rest, the principle text
is Soz., *H. E.* 5.18, on such figures as Apollinarios (*PG* 33.1313ff.); on controlling education, above, chap. 2 n. 92, 96, Pack (1989), Schwenk (1992), and Irmscher (1992);
and on church bans on pagan literature, see the *Statuta eccl. antiqua* 5 (*CCSL* 148.167),
Conc. Carth. IV can. 16 (Mansi 3.952), and Isidore of Seville, *Sententiae* 3.13.1 (*PL*
83.685A).

160 On Christian adoption and adaptation of various common symbols, see Biamonte
(1992) on the wreath = corona; Ferguson (1970) 238 on birds, fruits, etc., in S.
Costanza (Rome); Cremer (1991) 2.42ff. on the grapevine; Février (1983) 31ff. on
rural leisure scenes; Celtic apotropaic forms on reliquaries, in Elbern (1989) 957,
962; and Dölger (1964) 67ff. and Chapeaurouge (1984) 14ff. on *orantes* and shepherd
figures. On Coptic rider saints, see Parlasca (1982) 19, 26; on Endymion, see especially Crossan (1992), also Lawrence (1961) 324f., Allenbach (1971), Engemann

(1973) 70f., and Snyder (1985) 43–49, with good introduction to many other motifs of the third century, and a still broader survey in Chapeaurouge 18–68.

161 Pasquato (1976) 293 on thrones; on baldachins, above, chap. 2 n. 26 and Smith (1974) 379–82 and 380 n. 4; on imperial ceremonial symbols and perquisites, Mac-Mullen (1981) 81f.

162 MacMullen (1986) 5f. with nn. 21ff.

163 Ibid. 8, with older literature; add Charles-Picard (1965) 112, 115ff., and 121–25 with useful parallels in other arts and settings; and more recently, Shelton (1981) 27.

164 The logic behind the thought that no one who might be called "Christian" would ever do anything "pagan," or if he did, saw in it no pagan content, is often to be found: e.g., long ago, in Loisy of 1902, quoted in Isambert (1982) 44, "If we suppose that one can demonstrate the pagan origin of some part of Christian ritual, that ritual ceased to be pagan when it was accepted and interpreted by the Church"; or more recently, to explain away "pagan survivals," in Markus (1990) 110 and elsewhere: no Christian saw these survivals as pagan. The logic is the same as Burkhardt's in reverse, when he denies the supposed conversion of Constantine, because the emperor thereafter nevertheless broke certain commandments!

165 A definition might be reached through n. 13, above. I find an awareness of the need to define "religious" hardly registering on all the pages I have read for this book: by exception, but strictly in passing, "autenticamente religioso" (Cracco Ruggini [1982] 10). A reader might certainly expect better in Markus (1990), who from the outset of his interesting and serious discussion concerns himself with the distinction between "culture" and "religion"; but it doesn't appear. It is much easier to find scholars defining what is Christian!—bypassing entirely the preliminary, "religious": "true Christianity" (Festugière quoted in MacMullen [1984] 8), "authentic Christianity" (Brown [1981] 290), or "genuine" (Markus [1990] 8), as opposed to "nominal" Christianity (Henig [1986] 164), echoing Augustine, *Serm.* 17.6 (*PL* 38.127), *ethnicus gentilis est qui . . .* , or the bishops assembled at Tours in 567, Conc. Tur. can. 23, *non potest integer Christianus dici qui. . . .*

166 Cf. John Chrysostom's rebuke to those who saw a service as a παίγνιον, *PG* 51.174, with similar passages in Natali (1985) 464ff. Occasional pagans attended church services, above, chap. 1 n. 11; and Christians very frequently attended pagan services, above, chap. 4 n. 153.

167 I take the liberty of quoting what I confessed once before, MacMullen (1986) 5; cf. similar difficulties confessed, MacMullen (1984) 124 n. 13.

Chapter 5: Summary

1 Trombley (1985) 346ff.; above, chap. 1 at n. 96 and chap. 2 at n. 23

2 Above, chap. 1 n. 65 and passim, chap. 4 n. 155, on insincere conversions; and R. A. Markus in McManners (1993) 71, the whole century post-313, "The Age of Hypocrisy," Christianity being in that period "a passport to office, power, and wealth" (to say nothing of humbler but no less important rewards for humbler persons).

3 Above, fig. 1 and Kitzinger (1963) 110, "I feel fairly safe . . . in asserting that in all Byzantine painting and sculpture there is not a single laughing figure. When one considers the popularity of such figures in Hellenistic art. . . . "

4 That not very important officer, the "Curator of Martyrs," *custos martyrum* in the Roman church of the 530s (*Liber pont.* 33, *MGH Gesta pont. Rom.* 1.51), was not created on any pagan model, whatever martyr cult itself may have owed to beliefs and models outside of Christianity.

5 Above, chap. 4 n. 154.

6 Chap. 2 n. 40, chap. 4 n. 38.

7 Harmening (1979) 271, conciliar condemnation of 1582; Nilsson (1916–19) 90, still in ninteenth and twentieth century Albania and Bulgaria; and note in the late twelfth century Theodore Balsamon saying (*Canones, PG* 137.728Bf.) that the rites of the opening of January are still celebrated (he means around Constantinople?) "up to the present among some of the rural population," including the clergy.

8 Dionysius Bar-Salibi, bishop of Amida, whom I quote from the Latin of G. S. Assemani, *Bibliotheca orientalis Clementino-Vaticanae* 2 (Rome 1721) 164; and compare such other festivals as that of the Natale Petri of February, particularly in Février (1977) 515, who protests against apologetic arguments to insulate the choice of date from any pagan antecedents or competition.

9 Above, chap. 2 n. 24. Bakker (1994) 166 on the Robigalia-Laetania, and the Conc. Turonense 11 can. 18, making clear the strategy behind the church's innovation: "because festivals are held daily between Natale Domini and Epiphany, so they (Christians) will feast and, moreover, for three days, they (the bishops) determined that, to bring an end to the pagan custom," they should celebrate Letaniae on the January Kalends. For the pagan division of the day into hours of worship at its temples, see above, chap. 2 n. 71, though the relation between this model and the canonical hours (or between the latter and possible Jewish models) can't be traced.

10 Above, chap. 4 nn. 78, 107.

11 On gifts to divine benefactors, see above, chap. 4 nn. 33, 35, 38f., and random illustrations of the practice, which gigantically enriched the martyrs' chapels, in *Carm.* 18.29ff. (*PL* 61.491Bf.) of Paulinus of Nola, or in Ross (1964) 101f., donative bronze hands of the sixth and seventh centuries in the pagan tradition; a number of fourth-century chi-rho inscribed votive plaques from Water Newton, one with the Anicilla text, quoted, in Toynbee (1978) 144, compared (129–43) with pagan predecessors offered to Epona, Jupiter Dolichenus, etc., in Galatia, Dacia, Gallia, Germania, etc. of the second and third centuries; in Festugière (1961–64) 3, 2.116, a text describing an annual endowment in the age-old form of gift; and above, chap. 2 n. 86, Christian gifts along with pagan, at pagan shrines. Saint Demetrios' saying I quote from Lemerle (1979–82) 1.99 §65, from the bishop Eusebius to John of Thessaloniki, the story coming out of the second half of the sixth century.

12 Above, chap. 2 n. 75; Jonkers (1968) 52, conciliar condemnation at Rouen a. 1445 up to Bordeaux a. 1583 (and later?); and a striking photo of 1967 in a Greek church, the walls covered with exactly the same little metal representations of body parts healed that are so abundantly attested in antiquity, Kriss-Rettenbeck (1972) 66 Tafel 15.

13 Above, chap. 4 n. 127, for an example of predictive practices continued; on oath-tak-
ing, above, chap. 2 n. 101, the pagan practice, and its continuation among Christians,
e.g. MacMullen (1981) 133, Basil, *Epp. class.* II 217 (*PG* 32.805), Aug., *Ep.* 46 (*PL* 33.182),
iuramentum per daemones, and swearing on the depictions of sacred animals' heads,
banned in Conc. Aurel IV a. 541 can. 15f. or by other pagan means, Conc. Clippiacense a. 626/7 can. 3, in Pontal (1989) 104, 293. For divinity punishing perjurers from
the tomb, cf. above, chap. 3 n. 58.

14 On the question of divine concern for the minutiae of life, above, chap. 4 at n. 55; in
the basic teachings, emphasis on salvation, cf. chap. 1 nn. 30f.; the emphatic contrast
drawn by Eusebius in the passages above, chap. 4 n. 77; or Aug., *De cat. rud.* 5(9),
16(24), and 17(26), teaching the importance of focus on *requies post hanc vitam* as
opposed to *vitae praesentis aliquod commodum* or *humana* or *temporalia commoda*.

15 Above, chap. 2 n. 99 and chap. 4 n. 139; Leo I (pope, 440–461), *Sermo* 27 (*PL*
54.218f.), in Dölger (1925) 3; and idem (1964) 11 (Macedonia in 1905).

16 For bishops perceiving pagan rites as religious/sacrilegious, see, from abundant evidence, above, chap. 2 nn. 15, 33, 48, and 108, and chap. 4 nn. 10 and 38; chap. 4 n. 14;
also chap. 2 n. 37, Price seeing the important truth regarding the matter of religious
structure.

17 *CT* 16.10.12.2 a. 392, cf. above, chap. 2 at n. 112; fillets most recently photographed by
my friend F. G. Maier, whom I thank; and cf. also the report from many other modern lands, including Cyprus, today, in Schiemenz (1986) 55, or Turkey today, in J.
Russell (1995) 35.

18 On Italy, Ramage (1985) 64.

19 Schmidt (1876) 273, 278ff., where the dragon legends clustered around the statue are
also presented; Hamilton (1906/7) 350, on Saint Demetrios and Greek fertility cult;
and Nilsson (1988) 352. Cf. the appearance of Demeter on the route to Eleusis in
1940, according to reliable witnesses, in Picard (1940) 102, 106.

20 Thevenot (1968) 191ff., with description of the offerings made to her; cf. Bulliot and
Thiollier (1892) 298f., a statue of a female, "a water fairy squeezing out water from
her hair with her fingers. People used to come and still come to this shrine every
Thursday to ask healing for their sick children and for infertility. To win this result,
the women scratched a little dust from the bas-reliefs and mixed it in a glass of
water from the spring, which they drank. . . . They gave to the spirit the name of
Saint Freluchot, found again at several springs in Brittany." For the preservation of
sacred fish in an eastern shrine of the twentieth century in Syria, see Mango (1984)
54. For the scratching of dust from holy images or structures, cf. above, chap. 2 n. 74
and chap. 4 n. 98, the practice persisting in nineteenth- and even twentieth-century
Europe and Egypt, cf. Junghaendel (1891) 862, Nautin (1967) 33, and Traunecker
(1987) 230, 233.

21 On Bock, see Delatte (1938) 155, with discussion of adaptation of pagan procedures
by the church; for sacrifices and feasts in nineteenth-century Armenia, Maraval
(1985) 219; and elsewhere, above, chap. 4 n. 28.

22 Above, chap. 4 n. 20 ("Charon's obol").

23 See chap. 4 n. 11.

Bibliography

◆ ◆ ◆

(*ANRW* = *Aufstieg und Niedergang der römischen Welt*, ed. H. Temporini et al. [Berlin]; other abbreviations to be found in *The Princeton Encyclopedia of Classical Sites*, ed. R. Stillwell, Princeton 1976, or *The Oxford Dictionary of Byzantium*, ed. A. Kazhdan, New York 1991)

Adnès and Canivet (1967)—Adnès, A., and P. Canivet, "Guérisons miraculeuses et exorcismes dans l'*Histoire philothée* de Théodoret de Cyr," *Rev. de l'hist. des religions* 171 (1967) 53–82, 149–79.

Albertini and Leschi (1932)—Albertini, A., and L. Leschi, "Le cimetière de Sainte-Salsa à Tipasa de Maurétanie," *CRAI* 1932, 77–88.

Allenbach (1971)—Allenbach, J., "La figure de Jonas dans les textes préconstantiniennes, ou l'histoire de l'exégèse au secours de l'iconographie," *La bible et les pères. Colloque . . . 1969*, Paris 1971, 97–112.

Amand de Mendieta (1976)—Amand de Mendieta, E., "The official attitude of Basil of Caesarea as a Christian bishop towards Greek philosophy and science," *Papers Read at the Fourteenth Summer Meeting and the Fifteenth Winter Meeting of the Ecclesiastical History Society: The Orthodox Churches and the West*, Oxford 1976, 25–49.

Amélineau (1887)—Amélineau, E., *Etude sur le christianisme en Egypte au septième siècle*, Paris 1887.

Amélineau (1888–95)—Amélineau, E., *Monuments pour servir à l'histoire de l'Egypte chrétienne aux IV* et V* siècles*, 4 vols., Paris 1888–95.

Angelini Bertinelli (1990)—Angelini Bertinelli, G., "Frammenti epigrafici inediti di *fasti* femminili, da Luna," *Epigraphica* 52 (1990) 41–60.

Anrich (1913–17)—Anrich, G., *Hagios Nikolaos. Der heilige Nikolaos in der griechische Kirche*, 2 vols., Leipzig 1913–17.

Arbesmann (1979)—Arbesmann, R., "The 'cervuli' and 'anniculae' in Caesarius of Arles," *Traditio* 35 (1979) 89–119.

Argetsinger (1992)—Argetsinger, K., "Birthday rituals: friends and patrons in Roman poetry and cult," *Class. Antiquity* 11 (1992) 175–93.

Athanassiadi (1993)—Athanassiadi, P., "Persecution and response in Late paganism," *JHS* 113 (1993) 1–29.

Aubé (1882)—Aubé, B., *Polyeucte dans l'histoire. Etude sur le martyre Polyeucte,* Paris 1882.

Aune (1980)—Aune, D. E., "Magic in early Christianity," *ANRW* 2, 23 (Berlin 1980), 1507–57.

Bagnall (1993)—Bagnall, R. S., *Egypt in Late Antiquity,* Princeton 1993.

Bakker (1994)—Bakker, J. T., *Living and Working with the Gods. Studies of Evidence for Private Religion and Its Material Environment in the City of Ostia (100–500 AD),* Amsterdam, 1994.

Balty (1980)—Balty, J. C., "Le prétendu Marc-Aurèle d'Avenches," *Eikones: Studien zum griechischen und römischen Bildnis H. Jucker . . . gewidmet,* Bern 1980, 57–63.

Bambeck (1983)—Bambeck, M., "Fischer und Bauern gegen Philosophen und sonstige Grosskopfeten—ein christlicher 'Topos' in Antike und Mittelalter," *Mittellateinisches Jb* 18 (1983) 29–50.

Bardy (1928)—Bardy, G., "Origène et la magie," *Recherches de science réligieuse* 18 (1928) 128–42.

Barlow (1950)—Barlow, C. W., *Martini episcopi Bracarensis opera omnia,* New Haven 1950.

Barnes (1995)—Barnes, T. D., "Statistics and the conversion of the Roman aristocracy," *JRS* 85 (1995) 135–47.

Bartelinck (1994)—Bartelinck, G. J. M., *Athanase, "Vie d'Antoine,"* Paris 1994.

Baynes (1949)—Baynes, N. H., "The supernatural defenders of Constantinople," *Analecta Bollandiana* 67 (1949) 165–77.

Beagon (1992)—Beagon, M., *Roman Nature: The Thought of Pliny the Elder,* Oxford 1992.

Beaujard (1991)—Beaujard, B., "Cités, évèques et martyrs en Gaule à la fin de l'époque romaine," *Les fonctions des saints dans le monde occidental (IIIᵉ-XIIIᵉ) siècle. Actes du colloque . . . 1988,* Rome 1991, 175–91.

Beck (1950)—Beck, H. G. J., *The Pastoral Care of Souls in South-East France during the Sixth Century,* Rome 1950 (*Analecta Gregoriana* 51).

Behr (1968)—Behr, C. A., *Aelius Aristides and the Sacred Tales,* Amsterdam 1968.

Beltz (1992)—Beltz, W., "Zum Berliner Zaubertext P. 20 892," *Byzantinische Forschungen* 18 (1992) 167–70.

Bernand (1969)—Bernand, E., *Inscriptions métriques de l'Egypte gréco-romaine. Recherches sur la poésie épigrammatique des Grecs en Egypte,* Paris 1969.

Bernardi (1968)—Bernardi, J., *La prédication des pères cappadociens. Le prédicateur et son auditoire,* Paris 1968.

Betz (1986)—Betz, H. D., *The Greek Magical Papyri in Translation including the Demotic Spells,* Chicago 1986.

Beugnot (1835)—Beugnot, A. A., *Histoire de la destruction du paganisme en Occident,* 2 vols., Paris 1835.

Biamonte (1992)—Biamonte, G., "Dal segno pagano al simbolo cristiano," *Studi e materiali di storia delle religioni* 16 (1992) 93–123.

Bidez (1972)—Bidez, J., *Philostorgius Kirchengeschichte met den Leben des Lucian von Antiochien und den Fragmenten eines ariansichen Historiographen*, 2d ed., Berlin 1972.

Boglioni (1974)—Boglioni, P., "Miracle et nature chez Grégoire le Grand," *Cahiers d'études médiévals*, 1: *Epopées, légendes, miracles*, Montreal 1974, 11–102.

Bolognesi Recchi Franceschini (1995)—Bolognesi Recchi Franceschini, E., "Winter in the Great Palace: the persistence of pagan festivals in Christian Byzantium," *Byzantinische Forschungen* 21 (1995) 117–33.

Bonamente (1988)—Bonamente, G., "Apoteosi e imperatori cristiani," *I Cristiani e l'Impero nel IV secolo. Colloquio sul cristianesimo nel mondo antico*, ed. G. Bonamente and A. Nestori, Macerato 1988, 107–42.

Bonner (1950)—Bonner, C., *Studies in Magical Amulets, Chiefly Greco-Egyptian*, Ann Arbor 1950.

Bonomo (1971)—Bonomo, G., *Caccia alle streghe. La credenza nelle streghe dal sec. XIII al XIX con particolare riferimento all'Italia*, Palermo 1971.

Bouillet (1892)—Bouillet, A., *L'église et le trésor de Conques (Aveyron). Notice descriptive*, Mâçon 1892.

Bouillet (1897)—Bouillet, A., *"Liber miraculorum Sancte Fidis" publié d'après le manuscrit de la Bibliothèque de Schlestadt*, Paris 1897.

Bourgeois (1991–92)—Bourgeois, C., *Divona*, 1: *Divinités et ex-voto du culte gallo-romain de l'eau*, and 2: *Monuments et sactuaires du culte gallo-romain de l'eau*, Paris 1991–92.

Bowersock (1972)—Bowersock, G. W., "Greek intellectuals and the imperial cult in the second century," *Le culte des souverains dans l'empire romain*, ed. W. den Boer (*Entretiens sur l'antiquité classique* 19, Fondation Hardt), Geneva 1972, 177–212.

Bowersock (1990)—Bowersock, G. W., *Hellenism in Late Antiquity*, Ann Arbor 1990.

Bowman (1990)—Bowman, A. K., *Egypt after the Pharaohs*, Oxford 1990.

Boyce (1937)—Boyce, G. K., "A corpus of the lararia of Pompeii," *MAAR* 14 (1937) 5–112.

Bradbury (1994)—Bradbury, S., "Constantine and the problem of anti-pagan legislation in the fourth century," *AJP* 89 (1994) 120–39.

Breckenridge (1978)—Breckenridge, J. D., "The reception of art into the early church," *Atti del IX congresso int. di archeologia cristiana . . . 1975*, Rome 1978, 1.363–69 (*Studi di antichità cristiana* 32).

Bregman (1982)—Bregman, J., *Synesius of Cyrene, Philosopher-Bishop*, Berkeley 1982.

Brière (1919)—Brière, M., *Les homiliae cathédrales de Sévère d'Antioche. Traduction syriaque de Jacques d'Edesse. Homélies LXX à LXXVI* (*Patrologia orientalis* 12), Paris 1919, 3–161.

Brière (1943)—Brière, M., *Les homiliae cathédrales de Sévère d'Antioche* (*Patrologia orientalis* 25), Paris 1943.

Brock (1983)—Brock, S., "A Syriac collection of prophecies of the pagan philosophers," *Orientalia Lovanensia Periodica* 14 (1983) 203–46.

Brooks (1923)—Brooks, E. W., *John of Ephesus, Lives of the Eastern Saints* (*Patrologia orientalis* 17), Paris 1923.

Brooks (1924)—Brooks, E. W., *John of Ephesus, Lives of the Eastern Saints* (*Patrologia orientalis* 18), Paris 1924.

Brooks (1936)—Brooks, E. W., *Iohannis Ephesini Historiae Ecclesiasticae pars tertius*, Louvain 1936 (*Corpus Scriptorum Christianorum Orientalium, Scriptores Syri* 3).

Brown (1971)—Brown, P., "The rise and function of the holy man in late antiquity," *JRS* 61 (1971) 80–101.

Brown (1976)—Brown, P., "Eastern and western christendom in late antiquity: A parting of the ways," *The Orthodox Churches and the West*, ed. D. Baker, Oxford 1976, 1–24.

Brown (1981)—Brown, P., *The Cult of the Saints: Its Rise and Function in Latin Christianity*, Chicago 1981.

Brown (1983)—Brown, P., "The saint as exemplar in Late Antiquity," *Representations* 1.2 (1983) 1–25.

Browning (1981)—Browning, R., "The 'low-level' saint's life in the early Byzantine world," *The Byzantine Saint*, ed. S. Hackel, London 1981, 117–27.

Brox (1974)—Brox, N., "Magie und Aberglaube an den Anfängen des Christentums," *Trierer theologische Zeitschr.* 83 (1974) 157–80.

Budge (1902)—Budge, E. A. W., ed. and trans., *The Histories of Rabban Hormizd the Persian and Rabban Bar-'Idta 2, 1: English Translations*, London 1902.

Budge (1932)—Budge, E. A. W., *The Chronography of Gregory Abû'l Faraj the Son of Aaron, the Hebrew Physician, Commonly Known as Bar Hebraeus*, 2 vols., London 1932.

Buffière (1956)—Buffière, F., *Les mythes d'Homère et la pensée grecque*, Paris 1956.

Bulliot and Thiollier (1892)—Bulliot, J.-G., and F. Thiollier, *La mission et le culte de Saint Martin d'après les légendes et les monuments populaires dans le pays éduen. Etude sur le paganisme rural*, Autun 1892.

Bury (1923)—Bury, J. B., *History of the Later Roman Empire from the Death of Theodosius I to the Death of Justinian (A.D. 395 to A.D. 565)*, 2 vols., London 1923.

Cadoux (1984)—Cadoux, J.-L., "L'ossuaire gaulois de Ribemont-sur-Ancre (Somme). Premières observations, premières questions," *Gallia* 42 (1984) 53–78.

Cameron (1991)—Cameron, A., *Christianity and the Rhetoric of Empire. The Development of Christian Discourse*, Berkeley 1991.

Campagnano and Orlandi (1984)—Campagnano, A., and T. Orlandi, *Vite di monaci copti*, Rome 1984.

Canivet (1980)—Canivet, P., "Le *Michaelion* de Huarte (Ve s.)," *Byzantion* 50 (1980) 85–117.

Canivet (1989)—Canivet, P., "Le christianisme en Syrie des origines à l'avènement de l'Islam," *Archéologie et histoire de la Syrie* 2, ed. J.-M. Dentzer and W. Orthmann, Saarbrücken 1989, 117–48.

H. J. Carpenter (1963)—Carpenter, H. J., "Popular Christianity and the theologians," *JTS* 14 (1963) 294–310.

R. Carpenter (1946)—Carpenter, R., *Folk Tale, Fiction, and Saga in the Homeric Epics*, Berkeley 1946.

Carr (1898)—Carr, S. J., *Thomae Edesseni tractatus de nativitate domini nostri Jesu. Textum syriacum*, Rome 1898.

Carton (1908)—Carton, L., "Le sanctuaire de Tanit à El-Kénissia," *Mémoires de l'Acad. des Inscriptions et Belles-Lettres* 12, 1 (1908) 1–60.

Chabot (1899–1910)—Chabot, J.-B., *Chronique de Michel le Syrien, patriarche jacobite d'Antioche*, 4 vols., Paris 1899–1910.

H. Chadwick (1958)—Chadwick, H., "Ossius of Cordova and the presidency of the Council of Antioch," *JTS* 9 (1958) 292–304.

H. Chadwick (1981)—Chadwick, H., "Pachomios and the idea of sanctity," *The Byzantine Saint*, ed. S. Hackel, London 1981, 11–25.

H. Chadwick (1996)—Chadwick, H., "New sermons of St Augustine," *JTS* 47 (1996) 69–91.

N. K. Chadwick (1955)—Chadwick, N. K., *Poetry and Letters in Early Christian Gaul*, London 1955.

Chaine (1948)—Chaine, M., *La vie et les miracles de Saint Syméon Stylite l'Ancien*, Cairo 1948 (*Bibliothèque d'Etudes Coptes* 3).

Chapeaurouge (1984)—Chapeaurouge, D. de, *Einführung in die Geschichte der christlichen Symbole*, Darmstadt 1984.

Chapoutier (1932)—Chapouthier, F., "De la bonne foi dans la dévotion antique," *REG* 45 (1932) 391–96.

Charles-Picard (1965)—Charles-Picard, G., *La Carthage de saint Augustin*, Paris 1965.

Chevallier (1992)—Chevallier, R., "Introduction au colloque," *Les eaux thermales et les cultes des eaux en Gaule et dans les provinces voisines. Actes du colloque . . . 1990*, ed. R. Chevallier (*Caesarodunum* 26), Tours 1992, 5–27.

Chuvin (1990)—Chuvin, P., *A Chronicle of the Last Pagans*, trans. B. A. Archer, Cambridge 1990.

Clarke (1991)—Clarke, J. R., *The Houses of Roman Italy 100 B.C.–A.D. 250. Ritual, Space, and Decoration*, Berkeley 1991.

Clemen (1928)—Clemen, C., ed., *Fontes historiae religionis Germanicae*, Berlin 1928.

Collart and Coupel (1977)—Collart, P., and P. Coupel, *Le petit autel de Baalbek*, Paris 1977.

Colonna (1958)—Colonna, M. E., *Teofrasto [Enea di Gaza]*, Naples 1958.

Constantelos (1964)—Constantelos, D. J., "Paganism and the state in the age of Justinian," *Catholic Historical Rev.* 50 (1964) 372–80.

Conze and Schuchhardt (1899)—Conze, A., and C. Schuchhardt, "Die Arbeiten zu Pergamon 1886–1898," *Ath. Mitt.* 24 (1899) 97–240.

Copenhaver (1992)—Copenhaver, B. P., *Hermetica. The Greek "Corpus Hermeticum" and the Latin "Asclepius,"* Cambridge 1992.

Cormack (1985)—Cormack, R., *Writing in Gold: Byzantine Society and Its Icons*, London 1985.

Cracco (1980)—Cracco, G., "Chiesa e cristianità rurale nell'Italia di Gregorio Magno," *Medioevo rurale. Sulle tracce della civiltà contadina*, ed. V. Fumagalli and G. Rossetti, Bologna 1980, 361–79.

Cracco Ruggini (1981)—Cracco Ruggini, L., "Il miracolo nella cultura del tardo impero: concetto e funzione," *Hagiographie, cultures et sociétés IVᵉ–XIIᵉ siècles. Actes du colloque . . . 1979*, Paris 1981, 161–202.

Cracco Ruggini (1982)—Cracco Ruggini, L., "Imperatori romani e uomini divini (I–VI secolo d.C.)," *Governanti e intellettuali, popolo di Roma e popolo di Dio (I–VI secolo)*, Turin 1982, 9–91.

Cramer (1980)—Cramer, W., "Irrtum und Lüge. Zum Urteil des Jacob von Sarug über Reste paganer Religion und Kultur," *Jb für Antike und Christentum* 23 (1980) 96–107.

Crawford (1920)—Crawford, J. R., "De Bruma et Brumalibus festis," *Byzantinische Zeitschrift.* 23 (1920) 365–96.

Cremer (1991)—Cremer, M., *Hellenistisch-römischen Grabstelen im nordwestlichen Kleinasien, 1: Mysien* and 2: *Bithynien,* Bonn 1991.

Crossan (1992)—Crossan, J. D., "Bias in interpreting earliest Christianity," *Numen* 39 (1992) 233–35.

Cumont (1920)—Cumont, F., "La célébration du 'Natalis Invicti' en Orient," *Rev. de l'hist. des religions* 82 (1920) 85–87.

Cumont (1929)—Cumont, F., *Les religions orientales dans le paganisme romain,* 4th ed., Paris 1929.

Cuscito (1993)—Cuscito, G., "L'area cemeteriale di S. Lorenzo maggiore per il *Corpus* delle iscrizioni paleocristiane di Milano," *Epigraphica* 55 (1993) 75–102.

Dagron (1978)—Dagron, G., *Vie et miracles de sainte Thècle. Texte grec, traduction et commentaire,* Brussels 1978.

Daly (1971)—Daly, L. J., "Themistius' plea for religious toleration," *GRBS* 12 (1971) 65–79.

Daniel and Maltomini (1990–92)—Daniel, R. W., and F. Maltomini, *Supplementum Magicum,* 2 vols., Opladen 1990–92.

Dattrino (1987)—Dattrino, L., "La conversione al cristianesimo secondo la *Historia ecclesiastica* di Rufino," *Augustinianum* 27 (1987) 247–80.

Davidson (1995)—Davidson, I. J., "Ambrose's *De officiis* and the intellectual climate of the late fourth century," *Vigiliae Christ.* 49 (1995) 313–33.

Dawson (1992)—Dawson, D., *Allegorical Readers and Cultural Revision in Ancient Alexandria,* Berkeley 1992.

Deichmann (1939)—Deichmann, F. W., "Frühchristlichen Kirchen in antiken Heiligtümern," *JDAI* 54 (1939) 105–36.

Dekkers (1980)—Dekkers, E., "Les limites sociales et linguistique de la pastorale liturgique de saint Jean Chrysostome," *Augustinianum* 20 (1980) 119–29.

Delage (1971)—Delage, M.-J., *Césare d'Arles,* Paris 1971 (*Sources Chrétiennes* 175).

Delatte (1938)—Delatte, A., *Herbarius. Recherches sur le cérémonial usité chez les anciens pour la cueillette des simples et des plantes magiques,* 2d ed., Liège 1938.

Delehaye (1912)—Delehaye, H., *Les origines du culte des martyrs,* Brussels 1912.

Delehaye (1923)—Delehaye, H., "Euchaïta et la légende de S. Théodore," *Anatolian Studies Presented to Sir William Mitchell Ramsay,* ed. W. H. Buckler and W. M. Calder, Manchester 1923, 129–34.

Delehaye (1961)—*The Legends of the Saints. An Introduction to Hagiography,* trans. V. M. Crawford [of the French of 1905], London 1961.

Demarolle (1992)—Demarolle, J.-M., "D'Hygie à Sainte Valdrée: Autour des vertus d'une source de la cité des Leuques," *Les eaux thermales et les cultes des eaux en Gaule et dans les provinces voisines. Actes du colloque . . . 1990,* ed. R. Chevallier (*Caesarodunum* 26), Tours 1992, 425–37.

Deonna (1919)—Deonna, W., "Notes d'archéologie suisse," *Anzeiger für Schweizerische Altertumskunde,* 2d series 21 (1919) 85–96.

Deubner (1907)—Deubner, L., *Kosmas und Damian. Texte und Einleitung.,* Leipzig 1907.

Devauges (1973)—Devauges, J. B., "Le fanum de Crain (Yonne). Fouille de sauvetage," *Rev. arch. de l'Est et du Centre-Est* 24 (1973) 169–213.

Deyts (1983)—Deyts, S., *Les bois sculptés des Sources de la Seine*, Paris 1983.

Deyts (1994)—Deyts, S., *Un peuple de pèlerins. Offrandes de pierre et de bronze des Sources de la Seine*, Dijon 1994.

Dhénin (1980)—Dhénin, M., "Monnaies des Vᵉ-VIᵉ siècles des nécropoles de Vron (Somme) et de Hordain (Nord)," *Mélanges de numismatique, d'archéologie et d'histoire offerts à Jean Lafaurie*, Paris 1980, 201–7.

Dickie (1995)—Dickie, M. W., "The Fathers of the church and the evil eye," *Byzantine Magic*, ed. H. Maguire, Washington, D.C., 1995, 9–34.

Diehl (1901)—Diehl, C., *Justinien et la civilisation byzantine au VIᵉ siècle*, Paris 1901.

Dierkens (1984)—Dierkens, A., "Superstitions, christianisme et paganisme à la fin de l'époque mérovingienne," *Magie, sorcellerie, parapsychologie*, ed. H. Hasquin, Brussels 1984, 9–26.

Dierkens (1985)—Dierkens, A., "Les survivances du paganisme (en Neustrie mérovingienne)," *La Neustrie. Les pays au Nord de la Loire, de Dagobert à Charles le Chauve (VIIᵉ-IXᵉ siècles)*, ed. P. Périn and L.-C. Feffer, Rouen 1985, 142–45.

Dihle (1992)—Dihle, A., "La fête chrétienne," *Rev. des études augustiniennes* 38 (1992) 323–35.

Dodds (1965)—Dodds, E. R., *Pagan and Christian in an Age of Anxiety. Some Aspects of Religious Experience from Marcus Aurelius to Constantine*, Cambridge 1965.

Dölger (1910–43)—Dölger, F. J., *ΙΧΘΥΣ*, 5 vols., Münster 1910–43.

Dölger (1925)—Dölger, F. J., *Sol Salutis. Gebet und Gesang im christlichen Altertum*, 2d ed., Münster in Westfal. 1925.

Dölger (1930)—Dölger, F. J., "Darstellungen einer Totenspende mit Fisch auf einer christlichen Grabverschlussplatt aus der Katakombe Pietro e Marcellino in Rom," *Antike und Christentum. Kultur- und Religionsgeschichtliche Studien* 2, Münster in Westfalen 1930, 81–99.

Dölger (1930a)—Dölger, F. J., "Wein als Totenspende bei Armeniern und Griechen in Anatolien," *Antike und Christentum. Kultur- und Religionsgeschichtliche Studien* 2, Münster in Westfalen 1930, 320.

Dölger (1930b)—Dölger, F., "Echo aus Antike und Christentum 20: Wein als Totenspende bei Armeniern und Griechen in Anatolien," *Antike und Christentum. Kultur- und Religionsgeschichtliche Studien* 2, Münster in Westfalen 1930, 320.

Dölger (1932)—Dölger, F. J., "Die Münze im Taufbecken und die Münzen-Funde in Heilquellen der Antike," *Antike und Christentum. Kultur- und Religionsgeschichtliche Studien* 3, Münster in Westfalen 1932, 1–24.

Dölger (1932a)—Dölger, F. J. "Das Anhängekreuzchen dr hl. Makrina und ihr Ring mit der Kreuzpartikel . . . ," *Antike und Christentum. Kultur- und Religionsgeschichtliche Studien* 3, Münster in Westfalen 1932, 81–116.

Dölger (1934)—Dölger, F. J., "Klingeln, Tanz und Händelklatschen im Gottesdienst der christlichen Melitianer in Agypten," *Antike und Christentum* 4, Münster in Westfalen 1934, 245–65.

Dölger (1950)—Dölger, F. J., "Christliche Grundbesitzer und heidnische Landarbeiter,"

Antike und Christentum. Kultur- und Religionsgeschichtliche Studien 6, Münster in Westfalen 1950, 297–320.

Dölger (1950a)—Dölger, F. J., "Das Ei im Heilzauber nach einer Predigt des hl. Augustins," *Antike und Christentum. Kultur- und Religionsgeschichtliche Studien* 6, Münster in Westfalen 1950, 57–60.

Dölger (1964)—Dölger, F. J., "Beiträge zur Geschichte der Kreuzzeichens VII," *Jb für Antike und Christentum* 7 (1964) 5–38.

Dörner (1952)—Dörner, F. K., *Bericht über eine Reise in Bithynien . . . 1948* (*Denkschr. der Oesterr. Akad. der Wiss., Phil.-Kl.* 75), Vienna 1952.

Dolbeau (1991)—Dolbeau, F., "Nouveaux sermons de saint Augustin pour la conversion des païens et des donatistes," *Rev. des études augustiniennes* 37 (1991) 37–77.

Dolbeau (1993)—Dolbeau, F., "Nouveaux sermons de saint Augustin pour la conversion des païens et des donatistes (V)," *Rev. des études augustiniennes* 39 (1993) 57–108.

Dorcey (1992)—Dorcey, P. F., *The Cult of Silvanus: A Study in Roman Folk Religion*, Leiden 1992.

Drijvers (1982)—Drijvers, H. J. W., "The persistence of pagan cults and practices in Christian Syria," *East of Byzantium: Syria and Armenia in the Formative Period*, ed. N. Garsoian et al., Washington, D.C., 1982, 35–43.

Drioux (1934)—Drioux, G., *Cultes indigènes des Lingons. Essai sur les traditions religieuses d'une cité gallo-romaine avant le tromphe du Christianisme*, Paris 1934.

Duchesne (1955–57)—Duchesne, L., *Le Liber pontificalis. Texte, introduction et commentaire*, 2d ed., 3 vols., Paris 1955–57.

P.-M. Duval (1952)—Duval, P.-M., *La vie quotidienne en Gaule pendant la paix romaine*, Paris 1952.

Y. M. Duval (1982)—Duval, Y. M., *Loca sanctorum Africae. Le culte des martyrs en Afrique du IVᵉ au Vᵉ siècle*, 2 vols., Rome 1982.

Dyggve (1942)—Dyggve, E., "A sarcophagus lid with a tricliniarch," *From the Collections of the Ny Carlsberg Glyptothek* 3 (1942) 225–46.

Eitrem (1929)—Eitrem, S., "Zu Philostrats Heroikos," *Symbolae Osloenses* 8 (1929) 1–56.

Elbern (1989)—Elbern, V. H., "Heilige, Dämonen und Magie an Reliquiaren des frühen Mittelalters," *Settimane di studio del centro italiano di studi sull'alto medioevo* 36 (1989) 951–80.

Ellison (1980)—Ellison, A., "Natives, Romans and Christians on West Hill, Uley: An interim report on the excavations of a ritual complex of the first millennium A.D.," *Temples, Churches and Religion: Recent Research in Roman Britain with a Gazetteer of Romano-Celtic Temples in Continental Europe*, ed. W. Rodwell, Oxford 1980, 305–28.

Engemann (1973)—Engemann, J., *Untersuchungen zur Sepulkralsymbolik der späteren römischen Kaiserzeit*, Münster 1973.

Engemann (1975)—Engemann, J., "Zur Verbreitung magischer Übelabwehr in der nichtchristlichen und christlichen Spätantike," *JbAC* 18 (1975) 22–48.

Erdt (1976)—Erdt, W., *Christentum und heidnisch-antike Bildung bei Paulin von Nola*, Meisenheim 1976.

Espérandieu (1907–28)—Espérandieu, E., *Receuil générale des bas-reliefs, statues et bustes de la Gaule romaine*, 10 vols., Paris 1901–28.

Feissel (1977)—Feissel, D., "Notes d'épigraphie chrétienne, II," *BCH* 101 (1977) 209–28.

Feissel (1980)—Feissel, D., "Notes d'épigraphie chrétienne (IV)," *BCH* 104 (1980) 459–75.

E. Ferguson (1984)—Ferguson, E., *Demonology of the Early Christian World*, New York 1984.

J. Ferguson (1970)—Ferguson, J., *The Religions of the Roman Empire*, London 1970.

Fernández Marcos (1975)—Fernández Marcos, N., *Los Thaumata de Sofronio: Contribucion al estudio de la incubatio cristiana*, Madrid 1975.

Ferrua (1970)—Ferrua, A., "Una nuova regione della catacomba dei SS. Marcellino e Pietro," *Riv. di arch. crist.* 46 (1970) 7–83.

Festugière (1961–64)—Festugière, A.-J., *Les moines d'Orient*, 4 vols., Paris 1961–64.

Festugière (1970)—Festugière, A.-J., *Vie de Théodore de Sykéôn*, 2 vols., Brussels 1970.

Festugière and Ryden (1974)—Festugière, A.-J., and L. Ryden, *Léontios de Néapolis, Vie de Syméon le Fou et Vie de Chypre*, Paris 1974.

Février (1977)—Février, P.-A., "Natale Petri de Cathedra," *CRAI* 1977, 514–31.

Février (1977a)—Février, P.-A., "A propos du repas funéraire: culte et sociabilité," *Cah. arch.* 26 (1977) 29–45.

Février (1978)—Février, P.-A., "Le culte des morts dans les communautés chrétiennes durant le IIIᵉ siècle," *Atti del IX congresso internazionale di archeologia cristiana . . . 1975*, Rome 1978, 1 pp. 211–74.

Février (1983)—Février, P.-A., "Une approche de la conversion des élites au IVᵉ siècle: le décor de la mort," *Miscellanea historiae ecclesiasticae VI. Congrès de Varsovie . . . 1978, I: Les transformations dans la société chrétienne au IVᵉ siècle*, Brussels 1983, 22–46.

Fishwick (1987–92)—Fishwick, D., *The Imperial Cult in the Latin West*, 2 vols., Leiden 1987–92.

Fishwick (1991)—Fishwick, D., "Ovid and divus Augustus," *CP* 86 (1991) 36–41.

Fishwick (1992)—Fishwick, D., "Prayer and the living emperor," *The Two Worlds of the Poet. New Perspectives on Vergil*, ed. R. M. Wilhelm and H. Jones, Detroit 1992, 343–55.

Flint (1991)—Flint, V. I. J., *The Rise of Magic in Early Medieval Europe*, Princeton 1991.

Fögen (1993)—Fögen, M. T., *Die Enteignung der Wahrsager. Studien zum kaiserlichen Wissensmonopol in der Spätantike*, Frankfurt on Main 1993.

Fonquerle (1973)—Fonquerle, D., "Sur les traces d'Agathé-Tyché," *Archéologia* 61 (1973) 8–12.

Fontaine (1967–69)—Fontaine, J., *Sulpice Sévère, "Vie de saint Martin,"* 3 vols., Paris 1967–69.

Foss (1979)—Foss, C., *Ephesus after Antiquity: A Late Antique, Byzantine and Turkish City*, Cambridge 1979.

Fowden (1978)—Fowden, G., "Bishops and temples in the eastern Roman empire, A.D. 320–435," *JTS* 29 (1978) 53–78.

Franchi de' Cavalieri (1901)—Franchi de' Cavalieri, P., *Studi e Testi 6: I martirii di S. Teodoto e di S. Ariadne con un appendice sul testo originale del martirio di S. Eleuterio*, Rome 1901.

Francis (1995)—Francis, J. A., *Subversive Virtue. Asceticism and Authority in the Second-Century Pagan World*, University Park 1995.

Frankfurter (1994)—Frankfurter, D., "The cult of the martyrs in Egypt before Constantine: The evidence of the Coptic "Apocalypse of Elijah," *Vigiliae Christ.* 48 (1994) 25–47.

Frantz (1988)—Frantz, A., *The Athenian Agora. Results of Excavations Conducted by the American School of Classical Studies at Athens* XXIV: *Late Antiquity:* A.D. 267–700, Princeton 1988.

Fraschetti (1975)—Fraschetti, A., "A proposito di un graffito tardoantico da Lucus Feroniae," *Archeologia class.* 27 (1975) 317–30.

Frend (1984)—Frend, W. H. C., *The Rise of Christianity*, Philadelphia 1984.

Fréret (1751)—Fréret, M., "Observations sur les fêtes religieuses de l'année Persane, et en particulier sur celles de Mithra, tant chez les Persanes que chez les Romains," *Mémoires de littérature . . . de l'Académie royale des Inscriptions et Belles-Lettres* 16 (1751) 267–85.

Gain (1985)—*L'église de Capadoce au IVᵉ siècle d'après la correspondance de Basile de Césarée (330–379)*, Rome 1985.

Gajeri (1992)—Gajeri, E., *Ipazia: Un mito letterario*, Rome 1992.

Galvao-Sobrinho (1995)—Galvao-Sobrinho, C. R., "Funerary epigraphy and the spread of Christianity in the West," *Athenaeum* 83 (1995) 431–66.

Gandolfo (1989)—Gandolfo, F., "Luoghi dei santi e luoghi dei demoni: Il riuso dei templi nel medioevo," *Santi e demoni nell'alto medioevo occidentale (secoli V–XI)*, Spoleto 1989, 883–916.

Garnett (1975)—Garnett, K. S., "Late Corinthian lamps from the Fountain of the Lamps," *Hesperia* 44 (1975) 173–206.

Garnsey (1984)—Garnsey, P., "Religious toleration in classical antiquity," *Persecution and Toleration*, ed. W. J. Sheils, Padstow 1984, 1–27.

Gascou (1967)—Gascou, J., "Le rescrit d'Hispellum," *MEFR* 79 (1967) 609–59.

Gatier (1986)—Gatier, P.-L., ed., *Inscriptions de la Jordanie*, 2: *Région centrale (IGLS)*, Paris 1986

Geary (1988)—Geary, P. J., *Before France and Germany. The Creation and Transformation of the Merovingian World*, New York 1988.

C. Geertz (1966)—Geertz, C., "Religion as a cultural system," *Anthropological Approaches to the Study of Religion*, ed. M. Banton, London 1966, 1–46.

H. Geertz (1975)—Geertz, H., "An anthropology of religion and magic," *Jnl of Interdisciplinary Hist.* 6 (1975) 71–89.

Geffcken (1907)—Geffcken, J., *Zwei griechische Apologeten*, Leipzig 1907.

Gendle (1981)—Gendle, N., "The role of the Byzantine saint in the development of the icon cult," *The Byzantine Saint*, ed. S. Hackel, London 1981, 181–86.

Geraci (1971)—Geraci, G., "Ricerche sul proskynema," *Aegyptus* 51 (1971) 3–211.

Gerkan (1964)—Gerkan, A. von, "Weitere Uberlegungen zum Petrusgrab. Zu den neuen Veröffentlichungen von A. Prandi und M. Guarducci," *Jb. für Antike und Christentum* 7 (1964) 58–66.

Gessler (1946)—Gessler, J., "Notes sur l'incubation et ses survivances," *Le Muséon* 59 (1946) 661–70.

Gibbon (1946)—Gibbon, E., *The History of the Decline and Fall of the Roman Empire*, ed. J. B. Bury, 3 vols., New York 1946.

Gilliard (1984)—Gilliard, F. D., "Senatorial bishops in the fourth century," *HThR* 77 (1984) 153–75.

Ginzburg (1961)—Ginzburg, C., "Stregoneria e pietà popolare. Note a proposito di un processo modenese del 1519," *Annali della Scuola normale superiore di Pisa. Lettere, storia e filosofia,* 2d series 30 (1961) 269–87.

Ginzburg (1966)—Ginzburg, C., *I benandanti. Stregoneria e culti agrari tra Cinquecento e Seicento,* Turin 1966.

Ginzburg (1972)—Ginzburg, C., "Folklore, magia, religione," *Storia d'Italia* 1, Turin 1972, 601–76.

Ginzburg (1989)—Ginzburg, C., *Storia notturna. Una decifrazione del sabba,* Turin 1989.

Giordano (1970)—Giordano, C., "Nuove tavolette cerate pompeiane," *Rend. Accad. Arch. Lett. e Belle Arti di Napoli,* 2d series 45 (1970) 211–28.

Giuntella (1985)—Giuntella, A. M., *Mensae e rite funerari in Sardegna: la testimonianza de Cornus,* Tarentum 1985 (Mediterraneo tardoantico e medioevale. Scavi e ricerche 1).

Goode (1949)—Goode, W. J., "Magic and religion: a continuum," *Ethnos* 14 (1949) 172–82.

Goode (1951)—Goode, W. J., *Religion among the Primitives,* Glencoe 1951.

Goodspeed (1908)—Goodspeed, E. J., *The Conflict of Severus, Patriarch of Antioch (Patrologia Orientalis* 4), Paris 1908, 591–18.

Gougaud (1914)—Gougaud, L., "La danse dans l'église," *Rev. de l'hist. eccl.* 15 (1914) 5–22, 229–45.

Gouillard (1976)—Gouillard, J., "La religion des philosophes," *Travaux et mémoires* 6 (1976) 305–24.

Graf (1994)—Graf, F., *La magie dans l'antiquité gréco-romaine. Idéologie et pratique,* Paris 1994.

Graham (1971)—Graham, W. F., *The Constructive Revolutionary John Calvin. His Socio-Economic Impact,* Richmond 1971.

Grant (1952)—Grant, R. M., *Miracle and Natural Law in Graeco-Roman and Early Christian Thought,* Amsterdam 1952.

Graus (1965)—Graus, F., *Herrscher und Heiliger im Reich der Merowinger: Studien zur Hagiographie der Merowingerzeit,* Prague 1965.

Graus (1989)—Graus, F., "Hagiographie und Demonenglauben—zu ihren Funktionen in der Merowingerzeit," *Santi e demoni nell'alto medioevo occidentale (secoli V–XI),* Spoleto 1989, 93–120.

Green (1993)—Green, R. P. H., "The Christianity of Ausonius," *Studia patristica* 28 (1993) 40–48.

Greenfield (1988)—Greenfield, R. P. H., *Traditions of Beliefs in Late Byzantine Demonology,* Amsterdam 1988.

Grégoire (1922)—Grégoire, H., *Recueil des inscriptions grecques-chrétiennes d'Asie Mineure,* Paris 1922.

Gregory (1986)—Gregory, T. E., "The survival of paganism in Christian Greece: A critical essay," *AJP* 107 (1986) 229–42.

Grenier (1931–60)—Grenier, A., *Manuel d'archéologie gallo-romaine,* 4 vols., Paris 1931–60.

Grodzinski (1974)—Grodzinski, D., "Superstitio," *REA* 76 (1974) 36–60.

Grosdidier de Matons (1970)—Grosdidier de Matons, J., "Les thèmes d'édification dans la Vie d'André Salos," *Travaux et mémoires* 4 (1970) 277–328.

Grossi-Gondi (1915)—Grossi-Gondi, F., "Il 'Refrigerium' celebrato in onore dei SS.

Apostoli Pietro e Paolo nel sec. IV ad Catacumbas," *Römische Quartalschr.* 29 (1915) 221–39.

Grossman (1985)—Grossman, P., "Archäologische Funde aus dem Raum von Abu Mina," *Acts of the Second Int. Congr. of Coptic Study* . . . *1980*, Rome 1985, 75–82.

Grossman and Jaritz (1980)—Grossman, P. and H. Jaritz, "Abu Mina. Neunter vorlaüfiger Bericht," *Mitt. des deutschen arch. Inst, Kairo* 36 (1980) 203–27.

Grundmann (1958)—Grundmann, H., "Litteratus-illiteratus. Der Wandel einer Bildungsnorm vom Altertum zum Mittelalter," *Archiv für Kulturgeschichte* 40 (1958) 1–65.

Guarducci (1967)—Guarducci, M., *Le reliquie di Pietro sotto la Confessione della Basilica vaticana: Una messa a punto,* Rome 1967.

Guarducci (1978)—Guarducci, M., *Epigraphia graeca 4: Epigrafi sacre pagane e cristiane,* Rome 1978.

Guarducci (1983)—Guarducci, M., "Aspetti religiosi pagani nella necropoli sotto la Basilica Vaticana," *Studi e materiali di storia delle religioni* 7 (1983) 103–22.

Guarducci (1989)—Guarducci, M., *La tomba di San Pietro. Una straordinaria vicenda,* Milan 1989.

Guida (1990)—Guida, A., *Un anonimo panegirico per l'imperatore Giuliano (Anon. Paneg.Iul .Imp.) Introduzione, testo critico, commento,* Florence 1990.

Guidi (1929)—Guidi, I., *Les homiliae cathedrales de Sévère d'Antioche (Homélies XCIX à CIII),* Paris 1929 (*Patrologia orientalis* 22, Paris 1930).

Guillot (1989)—Guillot, O., "Les saints des peuples et des nations dans l'Occident des VIᵉ–Xᵉ s.," *Santi e demoni nell'alto medioevo occidentale (secoli V–XI),* Spoleto 1989, 204–51.

Gurevich (1988)—Gurevich, A., *Medieval Popular Culture: Problems of Belief and Perception,* trans. J. M. Bak and P. A. Hollingsworth, Cambridge 1988.

Gutas (1988)—Gutas, D., "Plato's *Symposium* in the Arabic tradition," *Oriens* 31 (1988) 36–60.

Gutas (1994)—Gutas, D., "Pre-Plotinian philosophy in Arabic," *ANRW* 2, 36, Berlin 1994, 4941–73.

Hadot (1972)—Hadot, P., "La fin du paganisme," *Histoire des religions,* 2, Paris 1970, 81–113.

Haehling (1978)—Haehling, R. von, *Die Religionszugehörigkeit der hohen Amtsträger des Römischen Reiches seit Constantins I. Alleinherrschaft bis zum Ende der Theodosianischen Dynastie (324–450 bzw. 455 n. Chr.),* Bonn 1978.

Haehling (1980)—Haehling, R. von, "Damascius und die heidnische Opposition im 5. Jahrhundert nach Christus. Betrachtungen zu einem Katalog heidnischer Widersacher in der Vita Isidori," *JbAC* 23 (1980) 82–95.

Halkin (1977)—Halkin, F., *Douze récits byzantins sur Saint Jean Chrysostome,* Brussels 1977.

Hällström (1984)—Hällström, G. af, *Fides simpliciorum according to Origen of Alexandria,* Ekenäs 1984.

Hamilton (1906/7)—Hamilton, M., "The pagan elements in the names of saints," *BSA* 13 (1906/7) 348–56.

Hanson (1980)—Hanson, R. P. C., "The Christian attitude to pagan religions up to the time of Constantine the Great," *ANRW* 2, 23, Berlin 1980, 910–73.

Harl (1990)—Harl, K. W., "Sacrifice and pagan belief in fifth- and sixth-century Byzantium," *Past and Present* 128 (1990) 7–27.

Harmening (1979)—Harmening, D., *Superstitio. Ueberlieferungs- und theoriegeschichtliche Untersuchungen zur kirklich-theologische Aberglaubensliteratur des Mittelalters*, Berlin 1979.

Harnack (1924)—Harnack, A., *Die Mission und Ausbreitung des Christentums in der ersten drei Jahrhunderten*, 4th ed., 2 vols., Leipzig 1924.

Harris (1901)—Harris, J. R., *The Annotators of the Codex Bezae (with some Notes on Sortes Sanctorum)*, London 1901.

Hassall and Tomlin (1982)—Hassall, M. W. C., and R. S. O. Tomlin, "Roman Britain in 1981: II, Inscriptions," *Britannia* 13 (1982) 396–422.

Hatzfeld (1920)—Hatzfeld, J., "Inscriptions de Lagina en Carie," *BCH* 44 (1920) 70–100.

Hatzfeld (1927)—Hatzfeld, J., "Inscriptions de Panamara," *BCH* 51 (1927) 57–122.

Hefele and Leclercq (1907–52)—Hefele, C. J., and H. Leclercq, *Histoire des conciles d'après les documents originaux*, 11 vols., Paris 1907–52.

Hendrikx (1954)—Hendrikx, E., "Astrologie, Waarzeggerij en Parapsychologie bij Augustinus," *Augustiniana* 4 (1954) 325–52.

Henig (1986)—Henig, M., "*Ita intellexit numine inductus tuo:* Some personal interpretations of deity in Roman religion," *Pagan Gods and Shrines of the Roman Empire*, ed. M. Henig and A. King, Oxford 1986, 159–69.

Henzen (1874)—Henzen, G., *Acta fratrum arvalium quae supersunt*, Berlin 1874.

Hepding (1903)—Hepding, H., *Attis, seine Mythen und sein Kult*, Giessen 1903.

Hercher (1873)—Hercher, R., *Epistolographi graeci*, Paris 1873.

Hermann (1959)—Hermann, A., "Der Nil und die Christen," *Jb. für Antike u. Christentum* 2 (1959) 30–69.

Herzog (1939)—Herzog, R., "Der Kampf um den Kult von Menuthis," *Pisciculi. Studien zur Religion und Kultur des Altertums F. J. Dölger . . . dargeboten*, Münster 1939, 117–24.

Heussi (1936)—Heussi, K., *Der Ursprung des Mönchtums*, Tübingen 1936.

Hillgarth (1969)—Hillgarth, J. N., *The Conversion of Western Europe 350–750*, Englewood Cliffs 1969.

His (1896)—His, R., *Die Domänen der römischen Kaiserzeit*, Leipzig 1896.

Homann (1965)—Homann, H., *Der Indiculus superstitionum et paganiarum und verwandte Denkmäler*, Diss. Göttingen 1965.

Horst (1984)—Horst, P. W. van der, *Chaeremon, Egyptian Priest and Stoic Philosopher*, Brussels 1984.

J. and M.-C. Hubert (1982)—Hubert, J. and M.-C., "Piété chrétienne ou paganisme? Les statues reliquaires de l'Europe carolingienne," *Cristianizzazione ed organizzazione ecclesiastica delle campagne nell'alto medioevo. Espansione e resistenze . . . 1980*, Spoleto 1982, 235–68 (Settimane di studio del Centro italiano di studi sull'alto medioevo 28).

Hübner (1894)—Hübner, E., "Eine römische Glocke aus Tarraco," *Arch. Anzeiger* 9 (1894) 187–88.

Huskinson (1974)—Huskinson, J., "Some pagan mythological figures and their significance in early Christian art," *PBSR* 47 (1974) 68–97.

Irmscher (1981)—Irmscher, J., "Paganismus im justinianischen Reich," *Klio* 63 (1981) 683–88.

Irmscher (1992)—Irmscher, J., "Inhalte und Institutionen der Bioldung in der Spätantike," *Spätantike und Christentum. Beiträge zur Religions- und Geistesgeschichte der griechisch-römischen Kultur und Zivilisation der Kaiserzeit,* ed. C. Colpe et al., Berlin 1992, 159–72.

Isambert (1982)—Isambert, F.-A., *Le sens du sacré. Fête et religion populaire,* Paris 1982.

James (1982)—James, E., *The Origins of France: From Clovis to the Capetians, 500–1000,* London 1982.

Joannou (1962)—Joannou, P.-P., *Discipline générale antique (IIe–IXe s.),* Rome 1962 (Pontificia Commissione . . . Fonti, Fascicolo IX).

Joannou (1962a)—Joannou, P.-P., *Discipline générale antique (IVe–IXe s.)* I, 2: *Les canons des synodes particuliers,* Rome 1962 (Pontificia Commissione . . . , Fonti, Fascicolo IX).

Joannou (1972)—Joannou, P.-P., *La législation impériale et la christianisation de l'empire romain (311–476),* Rome 1972 (*Orientalia Christiana analecta* 192).

Johns and Potter (1983)—Johns, C., and T. Potter, *The Thetford Treasure. Roman Jewellery and Silver,* London 1983.

Jones (1963)—Jones, A. H. M., "The social background of the struggle between paganism and Christianity," *The Conflict Between Paganism and Christianity in the Fourth Century,* ed. A. Momigliano, Oxford 1963, 17–37.

Jones (1964)—Jones, A. H. M., *The Later Roman Empire. A Social, Economic and Administrative Survey,* 2 vols., Norman 1964.

Jonkers (1968)—Jonkers, E. J., "Die Konzile und einige Formen alten Volksglaubens im fünften und sechsten Jahrhundert." *Vigiliae Christ.* 22 (1968) 49–53.

Jordan (1984)—Jordan, D. R., "Two Christian prayers from southeastern Sicily," *GRBS* 25 (1984) 297–302.

Jordan (1991)—Jordan, D. R., "A new reading of a phylactery from Beirut," *ZPE* 88 (1991) 61–69.

Junghaendel (1891)—Junghaendel, M., "Rillen an aegyptischen Tempeln," *Zeitschr. für Ethnologie* 23 (1891) 861–63.

Kaminsky (1991)—Kaminsky, G., "Thesauros. Untersuchungen zum antiken Opferstock," *JDAI* 106 (1991) 63–181.

Karras (1986)—Karras, R. M., "Pagan survivals and syncretism in the conversion of Saxony," *Cath. Hist. Rev.* 72 (1986) 553–72.

Kearsley (1986)—Kearsley, R. A., "Asiarchs, *archiereis* and the *archiereiai* of Asia," *GRBS* 27 (1986) 183–92.

Kelly (1985)—Kelly, H. A., *The Devil at Baptism. Ritual, Theology, and Drama,* Ithaca 1985.

Kennedy (1972)—Kennedy, G., *The Art of Rhetoric in the Roman World, 300 B.C.–A.D. 300,* Princeton 1972.

Kisch (1970)—Kisch, Y. de, "Les *sortes Vergilianae* dans l'*Histoire Auguste,*" *Mél. Rome* 82 (1970) 321–62.

Kitzinger (1954)—Kitzinger, E., "The cult of images in the age before iconoclasm," *DOP* 8 (1954) 83–150.

Kitzinger (1963)—Kitzinger, E., "The Hellenistic heritage in Byzantine art," *DOP* 17 (1963) 96–115.

Klauser (1925)—Klauser, F. J., *Sol Salutis,* 2d ed., Münster 1925.

Klauser (1927)—Klauser, T., *Die Cathedra im Totenkult der heidnischen und christlichen Antike*, Münster in Westfalen 1927.

Klauser (1928)—Klauser, T., "Das altchristliche Totenmahl nach dem heutigen Stande der Forschung," *Theologie und Glaube* 20 (1928) 599–608.

Klauser (1956)—Klauser, T., *Die römische Petrustradition im Lichte der neuen Ausgrabungen unter der Petruskirche*, Cologne 1956.

Klauser (1964)—Klauser, T., "Studien zur Entstehungsgeschichte der christlichen Kunst VII," *Jb für Antike und Christentum* 7 (1964) 67–76.

Klein (1991)—Klein, R., "Die Bestellung von Sklaven zu Priestern—ein rechtliches und soziales Problem in Spätantike und Frühmittelalter," *Klio* 73 (1991) 601–5.

Klein (1993)—Klein, R., "Spätantike Tempelzerstörungen im Widerspruch christlicher Urteil," *Papers Presented at the Eleventh International Conference in Patristic Studies . . . 1991* (Studia Patristica 24, 1993) 135–42.

Klingshirn (1994)—Klingshirn, W. E., *Caesarius of Arles. The Making of a Christian Community in Late Antique Gaul*, Cambridge 1994.

Klugkist (1974)—Klugkist, A., "Pagane Bräuche in den Homilien des Isaak von Antiocheia gegen die Wahrsager," *Symposium Syriacum 1972* (*Orientalia Christiana analecta* 197), Rome 1974, 353–69.

Köpstein (1978)—Köpstein, H., "Zu den Agrarverhältnissen," *Byzanz im 7. Jahrhundert. Untersuchungen zur Herausbildung des Feudalsimus*, Berlin 1978, 1–72.

Kötting (1950)—Kötting, B., *Peregrinatio religiosa: Wahlfahrten in der Antike und das Pilgerwesen in der alten Kirche*, Münster 1950.

Kötzsche (1992)—Kötzsche, L., "Das herrscherliche Christusbild," *Spätantike und Christentum. Beiträge zur Religions- und Geistesgeschichte der griechisch-römischen Kultur und Zivilisation der Kaiserzeit*, ed. C. Colpe et al., Berlin 1992, 99–123.

Korol (1992)—Korol, D., "Neues zur Geschichte der verherten Gräber und des zentralen Bezirks des Pilgerheiligtums in Cimitile/Nola," *Jb. für Antike u. Christentum* 35 (1992) 83–118.

Kotansky (1995)—Kotansky, R., "Greek exorcistic amulets," *Ancient Magic and Ritual Power*, eds. M. Meyer and P. Mirecki, Leiden 1995, 243–77.

Kreider (1995)—Kreider, A., *Worship and Evangelism in Pre-Christendom*, Cambridge 1995.

Kriss-Rettenbeck (1972)—Kriss-Rettenbeck, L., *Ex voto. Zeichen, Bild und Abbild im christlichen Votivbrauchtum*, Zurich 1972.

Kubinska (1974)—Kubinska, J., *Faras IV: Inscriptions grecques chrétiennes*, Warsaw 1974.

E. and S. Künzl (1992)—Künzl, E. and S., "Aquae Apollinares / Vicarello," *Les eaux thermales et les cultes des eaux en Gaule et dans les provinces voisines. Actes du colloque . . . 1990*, ed. R. Chevallier (*Caesarodunum* 26), Tours 1992, 273–96.

Kugener (1903)—Kugener, M.-A., *Sévère patriarche d'Antioche 512–518. Textes Syriaques, 1: Vie de Sévère par Zacharie le Scholastique*, Paris 1903 (*Patrologia orientalis* 2, 1, Paris 1907, 2–115).

Kugener (1904)—Kugener, M.-A., *Sévère patriarche d'Antioche 512–518. Textes syriaques, 2: Vie de Sévère par Jean*, Paris 1904 (*Patrologia orientalis* 2, 1, Paris 1907, 199–400).

Labriolle (1934)—Labriolle, P. de, *La réaction païenne. Etude sur la polémique antichrétienne du Ier au VIe siècle*, 2d ed., Paris 1934.

Lacau (1921–22)—Lacau, P., "Les 'statues guérisseuses' dans l'ancienne Egypte," *Monuments et Mémoires, Fondation Piot (Acad. Inscr. et Belles-Lettres)* 25 (1921–22) 189–209.

Lackner (1968)—Lackner, W., "Zu einem bislang unbekannten Bericht über die Translation der Ignatios-Reliquien nach Antiochien," *Vigiliae Christ.* 22 (1968) 287–94.

Lamberton (1992)—Lamberton, R., "The Neoplatonists and the spiritualization of Homer," *Homer's Ancient Readers. The Hermeneutics of Greek Epic's Earliest Exegetes*, ed. idem and J. J. Keaney, Princeton 1992, 115–33.

Lane Fox (1986)—Lane Fox, R., *Pagans and Christians*, London 1986.

Lasaulx (1854)—Lasaulx, E. von, *Der Untergang des Hellenismus und die Einziehung seiner Tempelgüter durch die christlichen Kaiser*, Munich 1854.

Laumonier (1958)—Laumonier, A., *Les cultes indigènes en Carie*, Paris 1958.

Lauwers (1987)—Lauwers, M., " 'Religion populaire,' culture folklorique, mentalités. Notes pour une anthropologie culturelle du moyen-âge," *Rev. d'hist. ecclés.* 82 (1987) 221–58.

Lavagne (1992)—Lavagne, H., "Le problème des 'Nymphées' en Gaule," *Les eaux thermales et les cultes des eaux en Gaule et dans les provinces voisines. Actes du colloque . . . 1990*, ed. R. Chevallier (*Caesarodunum* 24), Tours 1992, 217–25.

Lawrence (1961)—Lawrence, M., "Three pagan themes in Christian art," *De opuscula XL. Essays in Honor of E. Panofsky*, ed. M. Meiss, New York 1961, 323–34.

Lebreton (1923–24)—Lebreton, J. "Le désaccord de la foi populaire et de la théologie savante dans l'Eglise chrétienne du IIIe siècle," *Rev. d'hist. ecclesiastique* 19 (1923) 481–506; 20 (1924) 5–37.

Lecouteux (1982)—Lecouteux, C., "Paganisme, christianisme et merveilleux," *Annales* 37 (1982) 700–716.

Leeb (1992)—Leeb, R., *Konstantin und Christus: Die Verchristlichung der imperialen Repräsentation unter Konstantin und seines Groben als Spiegel seiner Kirchenpolitik und seines Selbverständnisses als christlicher Kaiser*, Berlin 1992.

Lefort (1954)—Lefort, L. T., "La chasse aux reliques des martyrs en Egypte au IVe siècle," *La nouvelle Clio* 6 (1954) 225–30.

LeGoff (1967)—LeGoff, J., "Culture cléricale et traditions folkloriques dans la civilisation mérovingienne," *Annales* 1967, 780–91 [= "Clerical culture and folklore traditions in Merovingian civilization," *Time, Work, and Culture in the Middle Ages*, trans. A. Goldhammer, Chicago 1980, 153–58, 324–28].

Lemerle (1979–82)—Lemerle, P., *Les plus anciens receuils des miracles de St. Démétrius et la pénétration des Slaves dans les Balkans*, 2 vols., Paris 1979–82.

Lemoine (1956)—Lemoine, E., *Philoxène de Mabboug, Homélies. Introduction, traduction et notes* (*Sources chrétiennes* 44), Paris 1956.

Lepelley (1979)—Lepelley, C., *Les cités de l'Afrique romaine au Bas Empire*, Paris 1979.

Lepelley (1992)—Lepelley, C., "Permanences de la cité classique et archaïsmes municipaux en Italie au Bas Empire," *Institutions, société et vie politique dans l'empire romain au IVe siècle ap. J.-C. Actes . . . 1989*, ed. M. Christol et al., Rome 1992, 353–71.

Lepelley (1994)—Lepelley, C., "Le musée de statues divines. La volonté de sauvegarder le patrimoine artistique païen à l'époque théodosienne," *Cahiers archéologiques* 42 (1994) 5–15.

Levine (1988)—Levine, L. W., *Highbrow / Lowbrow*, Cambridge 1988.

Liebeschuetz (1979)—Liebeschuetz, W., "Problems arising from the conversion of Syria," *The Church in Town and Countryside. Papers Read at the Seventeenth Summer Meeting and the Eighteenth Winter Meeting of the Ecclesiastical Hist. Soc.*, ed. D. Baker, Oxford 1979, 17–24.

Liebeschuetz (1995)—Liebeschuetz, W., "Pagan mythology in the Christian empire," *International Jnl of the Classical Tradition* 2 (1995) 193–208.

Lieu (1992)—Lieu, S. N. C., *Manichaeism in the Later Roman Empire and Medieval China. A Historical Survey*, 2d ed., Tübingen 1992.

Litsas (1982)—Litsas, F. K., "Choricius of Gaza and his description of festivals at Gaza," *Jahrbuch der Oesterr. Byzantinistik* 32 (1982) 427–37 (*XVI. Internationaler Byzantinistenkongress . . . 1981, Akten* II, 3, Vienna 1982).

Livrea (1989)—Livrea, E., ed., *Nonno di Panopoli, Parafrasi del Vangelo di S. Giovanni, Canto XVIII*, Naples 1989.

Lizzi (1990)—Lizzi, R., "Ambrose's contemporaries and the Christianization of northern Italy," *JRS* 80 (1990) 156–73.

Longosz (1993)—Longosz, S., "L'antico mimo anticristiano," *Papers Presented at the Eleventh International Conf. in Patristic Studies . . . 1991, Studia patristica* 24 (1993) 164–68.

Lucius (1908)—Lucius, E., *Les origines du culte des saints dans l'Eglise chrétienne*, trans. (from the German of 1904) E. Jeanmaire, Paris 1908.

MacCleod (1979)—MacCleod, M. D., "Lucian's activities as a μισαλάζων," *Philologus* 123 (1979) 326–28.

MacCoull (1991)—MacCoull, L. S. B., "Duke University MS. C25: Dreams, visions, and incubation in Coptic Egypt," *Orientalia Lovanensia Periodica* 22 (1991) 123–28.

MacKendrick (1971)—MacKendrick, P., *Roman France*, London 1971.

MacMullen (1966)—MacMullen, R., *Enemies of the Roman Order. Treason, Unrest, and Alienation in the Empire*, Cambridge 1966.

MacMullen (1974)—MacMullen, R., *Roman Social Relations*, New Haven 1974.

MacMullen (1976)—MacMullen, R., *Roman Government's Response to Crisis A.D. 235–337*, New Haven 1976.

MacMullen (1980)—MacMullen, R., "Response," *Protocol of the Thirty-fifth Colloquy: The Role of the Christian Bishop in Ancient Society . . . 1979* (Center for Hermeneutical Studies), Berkeley 1980, 25–29.

MacMullen (1981)—MacMullen, R., *Paganism in the Roman Empire*, New Haven 1981.

MacMullen (1984)—MacMullen, R., *Christianizing the Roman Empire (A.D. 100–400)*, New Haven 1984.

MacMullen (1985/6)—MacMullen, R., "Conversion: A historian's view," *The Second Century* 5 (1985/6) 67–81.

MacMullen (1986)—MacMullen, R., "The meaning of A.D. 312: The difficulty of converting the empire," *The 17th International Byzantine Congress, Major Papers*, New Rochelle 1986, 1–15.

MacMullen (1988)—MacMullen, R., *Corruption and the Decline of Rome*, New Haven 1988.

MacMullen (1989)—MacMullen, R., "The preacher's audience (A.D. 350–400)," *JTS* 40 (1989) 503–11.

MacMullen (1990)—MacMullen, R., *Changes in the Roman Empire. Essays in the Ordinary*, Princeton 1990.

MacMullen and Lane (1992)—MacMullen, R., and E. N. Lane, *Paganism and Christianity 100–425 C. E.*, Minneapolis 1992.

Magoulias (1964)—Magoulias, H. J., "The lives of saints as sources of data for the history of Byzantine medicine in the sixth and seventh centuries," *Byzantinische Zeitschrift* 57 (1964) 127–50.

Magoulias (1967)—Magoulias, H. J., "The lives of Byzantine saints as sources of data for the history of magic in the sixth and seventh centuries A.D.: Sorcery, relics and icons," *Byzantion* 37 (1967) 228–69.

Malaise (1974)—Malaise, M., *Inventaire préliminaire des documents égyptiens découverts en Italie*, Leiden 1974.

Male (1950)—Male, E., *La fin du paganisme en Gaule et les plus anciennes basiliques chrétiennes*, Paris 1950.

Mallardo (1949)—Mallardo, D., "L'incubazione nella cristianità medievale napoletana," *Analecta Bollandiana* 67 (1949) 465–98.

Mango (1963)—Mango, C., "Antique statuary and the Byzantine beholder," *DOP* 17 (1963) 55–75.

Mango (1984)—Mango, C., "St. Michael and Attis," *Deltion tes Christianikes Archaiologikes Etaireias* 12 (1984) 39–62.

Mango (1990)—Mango, C., "Constantine's mausoleum and the translation of relics," *BZ* 83 (1990) 51–62.

Manselli (1975)—Manselli, R., *La religion populaire au Moyen Age. Problèmes de méthode et d'histoire*, Montreal 1975.

Manselli (1982)—Manselli, R., "Resistenza dei culti antichi nella pratica religiosa dei laici nelle campagne," *Cristianizzazione ed organizzazione ecclesiastica delle campagne nell'alto medioevo. Espansione e resistenze . . . 1980 (Settimane di Studio del Centro italiano di studi sull'alto medioevo 28)*, Spoleto 1982, 57–108.

Maraval (1985)—Maraval, P., *Lieux saints et pèlerinages d'Orient. Histoire et géographie des origines à la conquête arabe*, Paris 1985.

Marinone (1967)—Marinone, N., *I Saturnali di Macrobio Teodosio*, Turin 1967.

Markus (1978)—Markus, R. A., "The cult of icons in sixth-century Gaul," *Jnl Theol. Studies* 29 (1978) 151–57.

Markus (1990)—Markus, R. A., *The End of Ancient Christianity*, Cambridge 1990.

Marrou (1937)—Marrou, H.-I., *Saint Augustin et la fin de la culture antique*, Paris 1937.

Marrou (1949)—Marrou, H.-I., "Survivances païennes dans les rites funéraires des donatistes," *Hommages à J. Bidez et à F. Cumont*, Brussels 1949, 2.193–203.

Marrou (1979)—Marrou, H.-I., "Une inscription chrétienne de Tipase et le réfrigerium," *Ant. afr.* 14 (1979) 261–69.

Martin (1875)—Martin, Abbé, "Discours de Jacques de Saroug sur la chute des idoles," *Zeitschr. der deutschen morgenländischen Gesellschaft* 29 (1875) 107–47.

Matthews (1975)—Matthews, J., *Western Aristocracies and Imperial Court, A.D. 364–425*, Oxford 1975.

Mazzoleni (1985)—Mazzoleni, D., ed., *Regio VII: Centumcellae* (*Inscriptiones christianae Italiae* 2), Bari 1985.

McGuckin (1993)—McGuckin, J. A., "The influence of Isis cult on St. Cyril of Alexandria's Christology," *Papers Presented at the Eleventh International Conf. in Patristic Studies . . . 1991, Studia patristica* 24 (1993), 291–99.

McKenna (1938)—McKenna, S., *Paganism and Pagan Survivals in Spain up to the Fall of the Visigothic Kingdom,* Washington 1938.

McLynn (1992)—McLynn, N., "Christian controversy and violence in the fourth century," *Kodai. Jnl. for Ancient Hist.* 3 (1992) 15–44.

McManners (1982)—McManners, J., *"Popular Religion" in 17th and 18th Century France. A New Theme in French Historiography,* London 1982.

McManners (1993)—McManners, J., ed., *The Oxford History of Christianity,* Oxford 1993.

McNeill and Gamer (1979)—McNeill, J. H., and H. M. Gamer, *Medieval Handbooks of Penance: A Translation of the Principal libri poenitentiales and Selections from Related Documents,* New York 1979.

Meer (1961)—Meer, F. van der, *Augustine the Bishop. The Life and Works of a Father of the Church,* trans. B. Battershaw and G. R. Lamb, London and New York 1961.

Méniel (1992)—Méniel, P., *Les sacrifices d'animaux chez les Gaulois,* Paris 1992.

Meredith (1985)—Meredith, A., "Allegory in Porphyry and Gregory of Nyssa," *Papers Presented to the Seventh International Conference on Patristic Studies . . . 1975, Studia Patristica* 16 (1985) 423–27.

Merkelbach (1991)—Merkelbach, R., "Weg mit dir, Herakles, in die Feuershölle," *ZPE* 86 (1991) 41–43.

Merkelbach and Totti (1991)—Merkelbach, R., and M. Totti, ed., *Abrasax. Ausgewählte Papyri religiösen und magischen Inhalts,* 2: *Gebete (Fortsetzung),* Opladen 1991.

Mermet (1993)—Mermet, C., "Le sanctuaire gallo-romain de Châteauneuf (Savoie)," *Gallia* 50 (1993) 95–138.

Mesk (1908)—Mesk, J., "Des Aelius Aristides Rede gegen die Tänzer," *Wiener Studien* 30 (1908) 59–74.

Meslin (1969)—Meslin, M., "Persistances païennes en Gaule vers la fin du VIe siècle," *Hommages à M. Renard,* Brussels 1969, 2.512–24.

Meslin (1970)—Meslin, M., *La fête des kalendes de janvier dans l'empire romain. Etude d'un rituel de Nouvel An,* Brussels 1970.

Meyer (1904)—Meyer, W., "Die Legende des h. Albanus des Protomartyr Angliae in Texten vor Beda," *Abhandlungen der Königlichen Gesellschaft der Wiss. zu Göttingen,* 2d series *Phil.-hist. Kl.* 8 (1904) 3–82.

Milik (1972)—Milik, J. T., *Recherches d'épigraphie proche-orientale* 1: *Dédicaces faites par des dieux,* Paris 1972.

Millar (1964)—Millar, F., *A Study in Cassius Dio,* Oxford 1964.

Miltner (1937)—Miltner, F., *Das Cömeterium der Sieben Schläfer* (*Forschungen in Ephesos* 4, 2), Vienna 1937.

Miltner (1958)—Miltner, F., *Ephesos, Stadt der Artemis und des Johannes,* Vienna 1958.

K. Mitchell (1987)—Mitchell, K., "Saints and public Christianity in the *Historiae* of

Gregory of Tours," *Religion, Culture, and Society in the Early Middle Ages. Studies in Honor of R. E. Sullivan*, ed. T. F. X. Noble and T. J. Contreni, Kalamazoo 1987, 77–94.

S. Mitchell (1993)—Mitchell, S., *Anatolia. Land, Men, and Gods in Asia Minor*, II: *The Rise of the Church*, Oxford 1993.

Mitford (1971)—Mitford, T. B., *The Inscriptions of Kourion*, Philadelphia 1971.

Momigliano (1972)—Momigliano, A., "Popular religious beliefs and the late Roman historians," *Popular Belief and Practice*, ed. G. J. Cuming and D. Baker, Cambridge 1972, 1–18 [= *Quinto contributo alla storia degli studi classici e del mondo antico*, Rome 1975, 73–92].

Momigliano (1987)—Momigliano, A., "The theological efforts of the Roman upper classes in the first century B.C.," *Ottavo contributo alla storia degli studi classici e del mondo antico*, Rome 1987, 261–77.

Monaci Castagno (1987)—Monaci Castagno, A., *Origene predicatore e il suo pubblico*, Milan 1987.

Monceaux (1909)—Monceaux, P., "Cachets-amulettes du cercle de Tébessa," *Bull. arch. du Comité des travaux hist.* 1909, 62–67.

Monneret de Villard (1953)—Monneret de Villard, U., "The temple of the imperial cult at Luxor," *Archaeologia* 95 (1953) 85–105.

Montero (1991)—Montero, S., *Politica y adivinación en el Bajo Imperio Romano: Emperadores y haruspices (193 D.C.–408 D.C.)*, Brussels 1991.

Morris (1995)—Morris, R., *Monks and Laymen in Byzantium, 843–1118*, Cambridge 1995.

Moss (1935)—Moss, C., "Jacob of Sarugh's homilies on the spectacles of the theatre," *Muséon* 48 (1935) 87–112.

Most (1989)—Most, G. W., "Cornutus and Stoic allegories: A preliminary report," *ANRW* II 36, 3, Berlin 1989, 2014–65.

Muchembled (1978)—Muchembled, R., "Satan ou les hommes? La chasse aux sorciers et ses causes," *Prophètes et sorciers dans les Bas-Pays, XVIe–XVIIIe siècle*, ed. M.-S. Dupont-Bouchat et al., Paris 1978, 13–39.

Muchembled (1978a)—Muchembled, R., "Sorcières du Cambrésis. L'acculturation du monde rural aux XVIe et XVIIe siècles," *Prophètes et sorciers dans les Bas-Pays, XVIe–XVIIIe siècle*, ed. M.-S. Dupont-Bouchat et al., Paris 1978, 155–261.

Munier (1960)—Munier, C., *Les Statuta ecclesiae antiqua. Edition, études critiques*, Paris 1960.

Musset (1976)—Musset, L., "De saint Victrice à saint Ouen: La christianisation de la province de Rouen d'après l'hagiographie," *Revue d'histoire de l'église de France* 62 (1976) 141–52.

Musurillo (1972)—Musurillo, H., *The Acts of the Christian Martyrs. Introduction Texts and Translations*, Oxford 1972.

Nachtergael (1985)—Nachtergael, G., "Les terres cuites 'du Fayoum' dans les maisons de l'Egypte romaine," *Chron. d'Egypte* 60 (1985) 223–39.

Nägele (1905)—Nägele, A., "Über Arbeitslieder bei Johannes Chrysostomus," *Berichte über die Verhandlung der Kaiserlich Sächsische Gesellschaft der Wissenschaften, Phil.-hist. Kl.* 57 (1905) 101–42.

Naldini (1981)—Naldini, M., "Testimonianze cristiane negli amuleti greco-egizi," *Augustinianum* 21 (1981) 179–88.

Natali (1985)—Natali, A., "Tradition ludique et sociabilité dans la pratique religieuse à

Antioche d'après Jean Chrysostome," *Studia patristica* 16, II (1985) 463–70 (*Papers Presented to th 7th Int. Conf. on Patristic Studies* . . . *1975*, Part II).

Nau (1897)—Nau, F., "Analyse de la seconde partie inédite de l'Histoire ecclésiastique de Jean d'Asie," *Revue de l'Orient chrétien* 2 (1897) 455–93.

Nau (1908)—Nau, F., "Le miracle de S. Michel à Colosses (récit de Saint Archippos)," *Patrologia orientalis* 4, Paris 1908, 542–62.

Nautin (1967)—Nautin, P., "La conversion du temple de Philae en église chrétienne," *Cah. arch.* 17 (1967) 1–43.

Nautin (1977)—Nautin, P., *Origène. Sa vie et son oeuvre*, Paris 1977.

Negev (1971)—Negev, A., "The Nabataean necropolis of Mampsis (Kurnub)," *Israel Exploration Jnl* 21 (1971) 110–29.

Nicholls (1993)—Nicholls, W., *Antisemitism. A History of Hate*, Northvale 1993.

Niederman (1968)—Niederman, M., *Marcellus, Über Heilmittel*, 2d ed., Berlin 1968.

Nilsson (1916–19)—Nilsson, M. P., "Studien zur Vorgeschichte des Weinnachtsfestes," *Archiv für Religionswissenschaft* 19 (1916–19) 50–150.

Nilsson (1945)—Nilsson, M. P., "Pagan divine service in late paganism," *HThR* 38 (1945) 63–69.

Nilsson (1955–61)—Nilsson, M. P., *Geschichte der griechischen Religion*, 2d ed., Munich 1955–61.

Nilsson (1960)—Nilsson, M. P., "Lampen und Kerzen im antiken Kult," *Opuscula selecta* 3, Lund 1960, 189–214 [originally, *Acta Instituti Romani Regni Sueciae* 15, 1950, 96–111].

Nilsson (1988)—Nilsson, M. P., *Geschichte der griechischen Religion, 2: Die hellenistische und römische Zeit*, 4th ed., Munich 1988.

Nineham (1993)—Nineham, D., *Christianity Medieval and Modern. A Study in Religious Change*, London 1993.

Nock (1944)—Nock, A. D., "The cult of heroes," *HThR* 37 (1944) 141–74.

Nock and Festugière (1945)—Nock, A. D., and A.-J. Festugière, *Corpus Hermeticum* 2. *Traités XIII–XVIII Asclepius*, Paris 1945.

Noethlichs (1986)—Noethlichs, K. L., "Heidenverfolgung," *Reallexikon für Antike und Christentum* 13 (1986) 1149–90.

Nürnberg (1988)—Nürnberg, R., "'Non decet neque necessarium est, ut mulieres doceant.' Ueberlegungen zum altkirchlichen Lehrverbot für Frauen," *JbAC* 31 (1988) 57–73.

O'Neill (1989)—O'Neill, J. C., "The origins of monasticism," *The Making of Orthodoxy. Essays in Honour of H. Chadwick*, ed. R. Williams, Cambridge 1989, 270–87.

Orr (1978)—Orr, D. G., "Roman domestic religion: The evidence of the household shrines," *ANRW* 2, 16, Berlin 1978, 1557–91.

Orr (1988)—Orr, D. G., "Learning from *lararia*: Notes on the household shrines of Pompeii," *Studia Pompeiana et classica in Honor of W. F. Jashemski*, ed. R. I. Curtis, New Rochelle 1988, 293–99.

Pack (1989)—Pack, E., "Sozialgeschichtliche Aspekte des Fehlens einer 'christlichen' Schule in der romischen Kaiserzeit," *Religion und Gesellschaft in der römischen Kaiserzeit. Kolloquium zu Ehren F. Vittinghoff*, ed. W. Eck, Cologne-Vienna 1989, 185–263.

Pailler (1986)—Pailler, J.-M., "L'énigme Nymfius," *Gallia* 44 (1986) 151–65.

Painter (1977)—Painter, K. S., *The Water Newton Early Christian Silver*, London 1977.

Pani Ermini (1989)—Pani Ermini, L., "Santuario e città fra tarda antichità e altomedioevo," *Santi e demoni nell'alto medioevo occidentale (secoli V–XI)*, Spoleto 1989, 837–77.

Papaconstantinou (1994)—Papaconstantinou, A., "Oracls chrétiens dans l'Egypte byzantine: Le témoignage des papyrus," *ZPE* 104 (1994) 281–86.

Pariset (1968)—Pariset, P., "Un monumento della pittura paleocristiana a Napoli. L'affresco di S. Gennaro extra moenia," *Cah. arch.* 18 (1968) 13–20.

Parlasca (1982)—Parlasca, K., "Pseudokoptische 'Reiterheilige,'" *Studien zur spätantiken und frühchristlichen Kunst und Kultur des Orients*, ed. G. Koch, Wiesbaden 1982, 1.19–30.

Pasquato (1976)—Pasquato, O., *Gli spectacoli in S. Giovanni crisostomo. Paganesimo ad Antiochia e Constantinopoli nel IV secolo*, Rome 1976.

Pasquato (1981)—Pasquato, O., "Religiosità popolare e culto ai martiri, in particolare a Costantinopoli nei secc. IV–V, tra paganesimo, eresia e ortodossia," *Augustinianum* 21 (1981) 207–42.

Patlagean (1968)—Patlagean, E., "Ancienne hagiographie byzantine et histoire sociale," *Annales* 23 (1968) 106–26.

Pauli (1986)—Pauli, L., "Einheimische Götter und Opferbräuche im Alpenrraum," *ANRW* 2,18, Berlin 1986, 816–71.

Pekary (1994)—Pekary, T., "Mors perpetua est. Zum Jenseitsglauben in Rom," *Laverna. Beiträge zur Wirtschafts- und Sozialgeschichte der alten Welt* 5 (1994) 87–103.

Perdrizet (1914)—Perdrizet, P., "ΥΓΙΑ ΖΩΗ ΧΑΡΑ," *REG* 27 (1914) 266–80.

Périn (1987)—Périn, P., "Des nécropoles romaines tardives aux nécropoles du Haut-Moyen Age. Remarques sur la topographie funéraire en Gaule mérovingienne et à sa périphérie," *Cah. arch.* 35 (1987) 9–30.

Peterson (1926)—Peterson, E., Εἷσ θεός. *Epigraphische, formengeschichtliche, und religionsgeschichtliche Untersuchungen*, Göttingen 1926.

Petropoulos (1989)—Petropoulos, J. C. B., "The Church Fathers as social informant: St. John Chrysostom on folk-songs," *Papers Presented to the Tenth International Conference on Patristic Studies . . . 1987, Studia Patristica* 22 (1989) 159–64.

Pfister (1909–12)—Pfister, F., *Der Reliquienkult im Altertum*, 2 vols., Giessen 1909–12.

Picard (1922)—Picard, C., *Ephèse et Claros*, Paris 1922.

Picard (1940)—Picard, C., "Déméter, puissance oraculaire," *Rev. de l'hist. religieuse* 122 (1940) 102–24.

C. Pietri (1989)—Pietri, C., "Saints et démons: L'héritage de l'hagiographie antique," *Santi e demoni nell'alto medioevo occidentale (secoli V–XI)*, Spoleto 1989, 15–90.

C. Pietri (1991)—Pietri, C., "L'évolution des saints aux premiers siècles chrétiens: Du témoin à l'intercesseur," *Les fonctions des saints dans le monde occidental IIIᵉ–XIIIᵉ siècle). Actes du colloque . . . 1988*, Rome 1991, 15–36.

L. Pietri (1983)—Pietri, L., *La ville de Tours du IVᵉ au VIᵉ siècle: Naissance d'une cité chrétienne*, Rome 1983.

Piganiol (1972)—Piganiol, A., *L'empire chrétien (325–395)*, 2d ed., Paris 1972.

Plaine (1883)—Plaine, F., "Vita S. Brioci episcopi et confessoris ab anonymo suppari conscripta," *Analecta Bollandiana* 2 (1883) 161–90.

Poethke (1981)—Poethke, G., "Der Papyrus-Kodex BGU 1024–1027 aus Hermupolis Magna," *Proceedings of the Sixteenth Int. Congress of Papyrology . . . 1980*, Ann Arbor 1981, 457–62.

Pohlenz (1948)—Pohlenz, M., *Die Stoa. Geschichte einer geistigen Bewegung*, Göttingen 1948.

Poly and Bournazel (1991)—Poly, J. P., and E. Bournazel, *La mutation féodale, Xᵉ–XIIᵉ siècles*, 2d ed., Paris 1991.

Pomarès (1959)—Pomarès, G., *Gélase Iᵉʳ, Lettre contre les Lupercales et dix-huit messes du sacramentaire léonien. Introduction, texte critique, traduction et notes*, Paris 1959 (*Sources chrétiennes* 65).

Pontal (1989)—Pontal, O., *Histoire des conciles mérovingiens*, Mayenne 1989.

Pott (1992)—Pott, M., *Aufklärung und Aberglaube. Die deutsche Frühaufklärung im Spiegel ihrer Aberglaubenskritik*, Tübingen 1992.

Poulin (1979)—Poulin, J.-C., "Entre magie et religion," *La culture populaire au Moyen Age. Etudes présentées au quatrième colloque de l'Institut d'études médiévales de l'Université de Montréal . . . 1977*, Montreal 1979, 121–43.

Praet (1992–93)—Praet, D., "Explaining the Christianizing of the Roman Empire: Older theories and recent developments," *Sacris erudiri* 33 (1992–93) 5–119.

R. M. Price (1993)—Price, R. M., "Pluralism and religious tolerance in the empire of the fourth century," *Papers Presented at the Eleventh Conference in Patristic Studies . . . 1991, Studia patristica* 24 (1993) 184–88.

S. R. F. Price (1980)—Price, S. R. F., "Between man and god: Sacrifice in the Roman imperial cult," *JRS* 70 (1980) 28–43.

Prinz (1989)—Prinz, F., "Der Heilige und seine Lebenswelt. Überlegungen zum gesellschafts- und kulturgeschichtlichen Aussagewert von Viten und Wundererzählungen," *Santi e demoni nell'alto medioevo occidentale (secoli V–XI)*, Spoleto 1989, 286–311.

Quasten (1950–60)—Quasten, J., *Patrology*, 3 vols., Utrecht 1950–60.

Quasten (1983)—Quasten, J., *Music and Worship in Pagan and Christian Antiquity*, trans. B. Ramsey, Washington 1983.

Quet (1981)—Quet, M.-H., "Remarques sur la place de la fête dans le discours de moralistes grecs et dans l'éloge des cités et des évergètes aux premiers siècles de l'empire," *La fête, pratique et discours d'Alexandrie hellénistique à la mission de Besançon*, Paris 1981, 41–84.

Ramage (1985)—Ramage, C. T., *Ramage in South Italy. The Nooks and By-Ways of Italy*, ed. E. Clay, Chicago 1985.

Ramsay (1893)—Ramsay, W. M., *The Church in the Roman Empire before A.D. 170*, 2d ed., London 1893.

Ramsay (1897)—Ramsay, W. M., *Cities and Bishoprics of Phrygia I, 2: West and West-Central Phrygia*, Oxford 1897.

Rapp (1991)—Rapp, C., "Libri e lettori cristiani nell'Oriente greco del IV secolo," *Bisanzio fuori di Bisanzio*, ed. G. Cavallo, Palermo 1991, 19–36.

Rees (1950)—Rees, B. R., "Popular religion in Graeco-Roman Egypt, II: The transition to Christianity," *JEA* 36 (1950) 86–100.

Régerat (1991)—Régerat, P., *Vie de Saint Séverin*, Paris 1991.

Remensnyder (1990)—Remensnyder, A. G., "Un problème de cultures ou de culture?:

La statue-reliquaire et les *joca* de sainte Foy de Conques," *Cahiers de civilisation médiévale* 33 (1990) 351–79.

Rémondon (1952)—Rémondon, R., "L'Egypte et la suprème résistance au christianisme," *Bull. Inst. Fr. d'arch. orientale* 51 (1952) 63–78.

Richter (1929)—Richter, G. M. A., *The Sculpture and Sculptors of the Greeks*, New Haven 1929.

Robert (1937)—Robert, L., *Etudes anatoliennes. Recherches sur les inscriptions grecques de l'Asie Mineure*, Paris 1937.

Robert (1940)—Robert, L., "'Ἀμφιθαλής," *Athenian Studies Presented to W. S. Ferguson*, Cambridge 1940, 509–19.

Robert (1948)—Robert, L., "Sur l'oracle d'Apollon Koropaios," *Hellenica. Receuil d'épigraphie, de numismatique et d'antiquités grecques* 5 (1948) 16–28.

Robert (1949)—Robert, L. "Inscription honorifique de Tarse," *Hellenica. Receuil d'épigraphie, de numismatique et d'antiquités grecques* 7, Paris 1949, 197–205.

Robert (1955)—Robert, L. "Villes et monnaies de Lycie," *Hellenica. Receuil d'épigraphie, de numismatique et d'antiquités grecques* 10, Paris 1955, 188–222.

Robert (1960)—Robert, L., *Hellenica. Receuil d'épigraphie, de numismatique et d'antiquités grecques* 11–12, Paris 1960.

Roblin (1976)—Roblin, M., "Fontaines sacrées et nécropoles antiques, deux sites fréquents d'églises paroissales rurales dans les sept anciens diocèses de l'Oise," *Rev. de l'hist. de l'Eglise de France* 62 (1976) 235–51.

Rochow (1978)—Rochow, I., "Zu einigen oppositionellen religiösen Strömungen," *Byzanz im 7. Jahrhundert. Untersuchungen zur Herausbildung des Feudalismus*, Berlin 1978, 225–88.

Rochow (1978a)—Rochow, I., "Zu 'heidnischen' Brauchen bei der Bevölkerung des Byzantinischen Reiches im 7. Jahrhundert, vor allem auf Grund der Bestimmungen des Trullanum," *Klio* 60 (1978) 483–98.

Rochow (1994)—Rochow, I., *Kaiser Konstantin V (741–775), Materialen zu seiner Leben und Nachleben*, Frankfurt 1994.

Roda (1981)—Roda, S., "Religiosità popolare nell'Italia nord-occidentale attraverso le epigrafi cristiane nei secoli IV–VI," *Augustinianum* 21 (1981) 243–57.

Rodgers (1986)—Rodgers, B. S., "Divine insinuation in the *Panegyrici Latini*," *Historia* 35 (1986) 69–99.

Rohland (1977)—Rohland, J. P., *Der Erzengel Michael, Arzt und Feldherr. Zwei Aspekte des vor- und frühbyzantinischen Michaelskultes*, Leiden 1977.

Rolland (1958)—Rolland, H., *Fouilles de Glanum 1947–1956*, Paris 1958.

Romeuf (1986)—Romeuf, A.-M., "Ex-voto en bois de Chamalières (Puy-de-Dôme) et des Sources de la Seine. Essai de comparaison," *Gallia* 44 (1986) 63–89.

Ross (1964)—Ross, M. C., "Byzantine bronze hands holding crosses," *Archaeology* 17 (1964) 101–3.

Rossi (1992)—Rossi, F., "Breno (BS): Il Santuario di Minerva," *Les eaux thermales et les cultes des eaux en Gaule et dans les provinces voisines. Actes du colloque . . . 1990*, ed. R. Chevallier (*Caesarodunum* 26), Tours 1992, 379–84.

Rouche (1989)—Rouche, M., "Le combat des saints anges et des démons: La victoire de saint Michel," *Santi e demoni nell'alto medioevo occidentale (secoli V–XI)*, Spoleto 1989, 532–60.

Roueché (1989)—Roueché, C., *Aphrodisias in Late Antiquity. The Late Roman and Byzantine Inscriptions*, London 1989.

Roussel (1927)—Roussel, P. "Les mystères de Panamara," *BCH* 51 (1927) 123–37.

Rousselle (1983)—Rousselle, A., "Paulin de Nole et Sulpice Sévère, hagiographes, et la culture populaire," *Les saints et les stars. Le texte hagiographique dans la culture populaire*, ed. J.-C. Schmitt, Paris 1983, 27–40.

Rousselle (1990)—Rousselle, A., *Croire et guérir. La foi en Gaule dans l'Antiquité tardive*, Paris 1990.

Rupprecht (1935)—Rupprecht, E., *Cosmae et Damiani sanctorum medicorum vitam et miracula*, Berlin 1935.

Rush (1941)—Rush, A. C., *Death and Burial in Christian Antiquity*, Washington, D.C., 1941.

J. B. Russell (1972)—Russell, J. B., *Witchcraft in the Middle Ages*, Ithaca 1972.

J. Russell (1982)—Russell, J., "The evil eye in early Byzantine society. Archeological evidence from Anemurium in Isauria," *Jahrb. der oesterr. Byzantinistik* 32 (1982) 539–48.

J. Russell (1995)—Russell, J., "The archeological context of magic in the early Byzantine period," *Byzantine Magic*, ed. H. Maguire, Washington 1995, 35–50.

Russell and Wilson (1981)—Russell, D. A., and N. G. Wilson, *Menander Rhetor*, Oxford 1981.

Ryden (1981)—Ryden, L., "The holy fool," *The Byzantine Saint*, ed. S. Hackel, London 1981, 106–13.

Sahin (1978)—Sahin, S., "Zeus Bennios," *Studien zur Religion und Kultur Kleinasiens. Festschrift für Friedrich Karl Dörner*, Leiden 1978, 2.771–90.

Salzman (1992)—Salzman, M. R., "How the West was won: The Christianization of the Roman aristocracy in the years after Constantine," *Studies in Latin Literature and Roman History* 6, ed. C. Deroux, Brussels 1992, 451–79.

Sambursky (1962)—Sambursky, S., *The Physical World of Late Antiquity*, New York 1962.

Sanders (1983)—Sanders, G., "La mort chrétienne au IVᵉ siècle d'après l'épigraphie funéraire de Rome. Nouveauté, continuité, mutation," *Miscellanea historiae ecclesiasticae VI. Congrès . . . 1978, I: Les transformations dans la société chrétienne au IVᵉ siècle*, Brussels 1983, 251–66.

Saradi-Mendelovici (1990)—Saradi-Mendelovici, H., "Christian attitudes toward pagan monuments in late antiquity and their legacy in later Byzantine centuries," *DOP* 44 (1990) 47–61.

Sartre (1985)—Sartre, M., *Bostra. Des origines à l'Islam*, Paris 1985.

Schiemenz (1986)—Schiemenz, G. P., "Fische und Löwen in Kappadokien—ein Beitrag zur Geisteswelt der anatolischen Christen," *Studien zur frühchristlichen Kunst*, ed. G. Koch, 3, Wiesbaden 1986, 55–105.

Schmidt (1876)—Schmidt, B., "Demeter in Eleusis und Herr François Lenormant," *RhM* 31 (1876) 273–82.

Schmitt (1976)—Schmitt, J.-C., " 'Religion populaire' et culture folklorique," *Annales* 32 (1976) 941–53.

Schmitt-Pantel (1981)—Schmitt-Pantel, P., "Le festin de la fête de la cité grecque hellénistique," *La fête, pratique et discours d'Alexandrie hellénistique à la mission de Besançon*, Paris 1981, 85–99.

Schultze (1887–92)—Schultze, V., *Geschichte des Untergangs des griechisch-römischen Heidentums*, 2 vols., Jena 1887–92.

Schwenk (1992)—Schwenk, B., "Hellenistische Paideia und christliche Erziehung," *Spätantike und Christentum. Beiträge zur Religions- und Geistesgeschichte der griechisch-römischen Kultur und Zivilisation der Kaiserzeit*, ed. C. Colpe et al., Berlin 1992, 141–58.

Scullard (1981)—Scullard, H. H., *Festivals and Ceremonies of the Roman Republic*, London 1981.

Segal (1963)—Segal, J. B., *Edessa and Harran. An Inaugural Lecture . . . 1962*, London 1963.

Segal (1963a)—Segal, J. B., "The Sabian mysteries. The planet cult of ancient Harran," *Vanished Civilizations. Forgotten Peoples of the Ancient World*, ed. E. Bacon, London 1963, 201–20.

Seiber (1977)—Seiber, J., *The Urban Saint in Early Byzantine Social History*, Cambridge 1977.

Shboul (1979)—Shboul, A. M. H., *Al-Mas'udi & His World. A Muslim Humanist and His Interest in Non-Muslims*, London 1979.

Shelton (1981)—Shelton, K. J., *The Esquiline Treasure*, London 1981.

Sheppard (1980–81)—Sheppard, A. R., "Pagan cults of angels in Roman Asia Minor," *Talanta* 12 / 13 (1980–81) 77–101.

Sivan (1993)—Sivan, H., "On hymns and holiness in Late Antiquity," *Jahrbuch für Antike und Christentum* 36 (1993) 81–93.

Smith (1970)—Smith, M. T., "The Lateran *fastigium* a gift of Constantine the Great," *RAC* 46 (1970) 149–75.

Smith (1974)—Smith, M. T., "The development of the altar canopy in Rome," *Riv. di arch. christ.* 50 (1974) 379–414.

Snyder (1985)—Snyder, G. F., *Ante Pacem. Archaeological Evidence of Church Life before Constantine*, Macon 1985.

Stancliffe (1979)—Stancliffe, C. E., "From town to country: the Christianisation of the Touraine, 370–600," *The Church in Town and Countryside*, ed. D. Baker, Oxford 1979, 43–59.

Stancliffe (1983)—Stancliffe, C. E., *St. Martin and His Hagiographer. History and Miracle in Sulpicius Severus*, Oxford 1983.

Stander (1993)—Stander, H. F., "The clapping of hands in the early church," *Papers Presented at the Eleventh International Conference in Patristic Studies . . . 1991, Studia patristica* 26 (1993) 75–80.

Stark (1996)—Stark, R., *The Rise of Christianity. A Sociologist Reconsiders History*, Princeton 1996.

Stein (1949)—Stein, E., *Histoire du Bas-Empire*, 2: *De la disparition de l'empire d'Occident à la mort de Justinien*, ed. J.-R. Palanque, Paris 1949.

Stevens (1995)—Stevens, S. T., "A late-Roman urban population cemetery of Vandalic date at Carthage," *Jnl. Rom. Arch.* 8 (1995) 263–70.

Strohmaier (1976)—Strohmaier, G., "Ubersehenes zur Biographie Lukians," *Philologus* 120 (1976) 117–22.

Sünskes Thompson (1994)—Sünskes Thompson, J., "'Der Tod und das Mädchen': Zur Magie im römischen Reich," *Laverna* 5 (1994) 104–33.

Sulzberger (1925)—Sulzberger, M., "La symbole de la croix et les monogrammes de Jésus chez les premiers Chrétiens," *Byzantion* 2 (1925) 337–448.

Taralon (1978)—Taralon, J., "La majesté d'or de sainte Foy au trésor de Conques," *La revue de l'art* 40–41 (1978) 9–22.

Tchalenko (1953–58)—Tchalenko, G., *Villages antiques de la Syrie du Nord. Le massif du Bélus à l'époque romaine*, 3 vols., Paris 1953–58.

Teitler (1985)—Teitler, H. C., *Notarii and Exceptores. An Inquiry into Role and Significance of Shorthand Writers in the Imperial and Ecclesiastical Bureaucracy of the Roman Empire (from the Early Principate to c. 450 A.D.)*, Amsterdam 1985.

Tellenbach (1993)—Tellenbach, G., *The Church in Western Europe from the Tenth to the Early Twelfth Century*, trans. T. Reuter, Cambridge 1993 [Ger. ed. 1988].

Testini (1958)—Testini, P., *Archeologia cristiana. Nozioni generali dalle origini all fine del sec. VI*, Rome 1958.

Thébert (1983)—Thébert, Y., "L'évolution urbaine dans les provinces orientales de l'Afrique romaine tardive," *Opus* 2 (1983) 99–130.

Thébert (1988)—Thébert, Y., "A propos du 'triomphe du christianisme,'" *Dialogues d'hist. ancienne* 14 (1988) 277–345.

Thelamon (1981)—Thelamon, F., *Païens et chrétiens au IVᵉ siècle. L'apport de l'Histoire ecclésias-tique' de Rufin d'Aquilée*, Paris 1981.

Thevenot (1968)—Thevenot, E., *Divinités et sanctuaires de la Gaule*, Paris 1968.

J. J. Thierry (1963)—Thierry, J. J., "The date of the dream of Jerome," *Vigiliae Christ.* 17 (1963) 28–40.

N. Thierry (1977)—Thierry, N., "Un problème de continuité ou de rupture. Le Cap-padoce entre Rome, Byzance et les Arabes," *CRAI* 1977, 98–144.

Thompson (1982)—Thompson, E. A., *Romans and Barbarians*, Madison 1982.

Thurman (1968)—Thurman, W. S., "How Justinian I sought to handle the problem of religious dissent," *Greek Orthodox Theol. Rev.* 13 (1968) 15–40.

Tolotti (1982)—Tolotti, F., "Le basiliche cimiteriali con deambulatorio de suburbio romano: Questione ancora aperta," *Röm. Mitt.* 89 (1982) 153–211.

Tolstoi (1920)—Tolstoi, J., "Un poncif arétalogique dans les Miracles d'Asklèpios et d'Artémios," *Byzantion* 3 (1920) 53–63.

Toutain (1907–20)—Toutain, J., *Les cultes païens dans l'empire romain*, 3 vols., Paris 1907–20.

Toynbee (1978)—J. [M. C.] Toynbee, "A Londinium votive leaf or feather and its fellows," *Collectanea Londiniensia: Studies . . . R. Merrifield*, ed. J. Bird et al., London 1978, 128–47.

Traunecker (1987)—Traunecker, C., "Une pratique de magie populaire dans les tem-ples de Karnak," *La magia in Egitto ai tempi dei Faraoni . . . Atti, convegno int. di studi, Milano . . . 1985*, ed. A. Roccati and A. Silotti, Verona 1987, 221–42.

Treadgold (1994)—Treadgold, W. T., "Taking sources on their own terms and on ours: Peter Brown's Late Antiquity," *Antiquité tardive* 2 (1994) 153–59.

Trombley (1985)—Trombley, F. R., "Paganism in the Greek world at the end of antiq-uity. The case of rural Anatolia and Greece," *HThR* 78 (1985) 327–52.

Trombley (1993–94)—Trombley, F. R., *Hellenic Religion and Christianization c. 370–529*, 2 vols., Leiden 1993–94.

Trombley (1994)—Trombley, F. R., "Religious transition in sixth century Syria," *Byzantinische Forschungen* 20 (1994) 153—95.

Turcan (1972)—Turcan, R., "Les religions orientales dans l'empire romain," *Histoire des religions* 2 (Paris 1972) 33—80.

Unnik (1964)—Unnik, W. C. van, "A note on the dance of Jesus in the 'Acts of John,'" *Vigiliae Christ.* 18 (1964) 1—5.

Uytfanghe (1981)—Uytfanghe, M. van, "La controverse biblique et patristique autour du miracle, et ses répercussion sur l'hagiographie dans l'Antiquité tardive et le haut Moyen Age latin," *Hagiographie cultures et sociétés IVe–XIIe siècles. Actes du Colloque . . . 1979*, Paris 1981, 205—31.

Uytfanghe (1989)—Uytfanghe, M. van, "Le culte des saints et l'hagiographie face à l'écriture: Les avatars d'une relation ambiguë," *Santi e demoni nell'alto medioevo occidentale (secoli V–XI)*, Spoleto 1989, 155—202.

Vacandard (1899)—Vacandard, E., "L'idolâtrie en Gaule au VIe et au VIIe siècles," *Rev. des questions historiques* 65 (1899) 424—54.

Van Dam (1993)—Van Dam, R., *Saints and Their Miracles in Late Antique Gaul*, Princeton 1993.

Vandoni (1964)—Vandoni, M., ed., *Feste pubbliche e private nei documenti greci*, Milan 1964.

Van Engen (1986)—Van Engen, J., "The Christian Middle Ages as an historiographical problem," *American Hist. Rev.* 91 (1986) 519—52.

Ven (1962—70)—Ven, van den, P., *La vie ancienne de S. Syméon Stylite le Jeune (521—592)*, 2 vols., Brussels 1962—70.

Verga (1899)—Verga, E., "Intorno a due inediti documenti di stregheria milanese del secolo XIV," *Rend. del R. Ist. Lombardo di scienze e lettere*, 2d ed., 32 (1899) 165—88.

Veyne (1976)—Veyne, P., *Le pain et le cirque. Sociologie historique d'un pluralisme politique*, Paris 1976.

Vian (1976)—Vian, F., *Nonnos de Panopolis, "Les Dionysiaques"* I, Paris 1976.

Vikan (1984)—Vikan, G., "Art, medicine, and magic in early Byzantium," *Dumb. Oaks Papers* 38 (1984) 65—86.

Vogel (1952)—Vogel, C., *La discipline pénitentielle en Gaule des origines à la fin du VIIe siècle*, Paris 1952.

Vogliano (1933)—Vogliano, A., "La grande iscrizione bacchica del Metropolitan Museum," *AJA* 37 (1933) 215—31.

Vogt (1931)—Vogt, A., "Etudes sur le théâtre byzantin, II," *Byzantion* 6 (1931) 623—40.

Vogüé (1978—80)—Vogüé, A. de, *Grégoire le Grand, Dialogues*, 3 vols., Paris 1978—80.

Vryonis (1981)—Vryonis, S., "The panegyris of the Byzantine saint," *The Byzantine Saint*, ed. S. Hackel, London 1981, 196—226.

Wasserschleben (1840)—Wasserschleben, F. G. A., ed., *Reginonis abbatis Prumiensis libri duo de synodalibus causis et disciplinis ecclesiasticis*, Leipzig 1840.

Watts (1991)—Watts, D., *Christians and Pagans in Roman Britain*, London 1991.

Weinreich (1919)—Weinreich, O., *Neue Urkunden zur Sarapis-Religion*, Tübingen 1919.

Wenger (1970)—Wenger, A., *Jean Chrysostome, Huits catéchèses baptismales inédites*, Paris 1970 (Sources Chrétiennes 50 bis).

Werner (1976)—Werner, K. F., "Le role de l'aristocratie dans la christianisation du Nord-Est de la Gaule," *Rev. d'hist. de l'Eglise de France* 62 (1976) 45–73.

Wetter (1922)—Wetter, G. P., "La danse rituelle dans l'Eglise ancienne," *Rev. de l'hist. et litt. religieuses*, ser. 2, 8 (1922) 254–75.

Wheeler (1929)—Wheeler, R. E. M., "A Roman pipe-burial from Caerleon, Monmouthshire," *Antiquaries Jnl* 9 (1929) 1–7.

Whitby (1991)—Whitby, M., "John of Ephesus and the pagans: Pagan survivals in the sixth century," *Paganism in the Later Roman Empire and in Byzantium*, ed. M. Salamon, Cracow 1991, 111–31.

Wickham (1995)—Wickham, L. R., "Aspects of clerical life in the early Byzantine church in two scenes: Mopsuestia and Apamea," *Jnl Eccl. Hist.* 46 (1995) 3–18.

Wilcken (1885)—Wilcken, U., "Arsinoitische Tempelrechnungen aus dem J. 215 n. Chr.," *Hermes* 20 (1885) 430–76.

Williams (1987–94)—Williams, F., trans., *The Panarion of Epiphanius of Salamis*, 2 vols., Leiden 1987, 1994.

Wilson (1983)—Wilson, S., ed., *Saints and Their Cults. Studies in Religious Sociology, Folklore and History*, Cambridge 1983.

Wipszycka (1988)—Wipszycka, E., "La christianisation de l'Egypte aux IVᵉ–VIᵉ siècles. Aspects sociaux et ethniques," *Aegyptus* 68 (1988) 117–65.

Wiseman (1970)—Wiseman, J., "The Fountain of the Lamps," *Archaeology* 23 (1970) 130–37.

Wissowa (1912)—Wissowa, G., *Religion und Kultus der Römer*, 2d ed., Munich 1912.

Wittmann (1967)—A. Wittmann, *Kosmas und Damian: Kultausbreitung und Volksdevotion*, Berlin 1967.

Wood (1994)—Wood, I., *The Merovingian Kingdoms 450–751*, London 1994.

Wrede (1981)—Wrede, H., *Consecratio in Formam Deorum. Vergöttlichte Privatpersonen in der römischen Kaiserzeit*, Mainz 1981.

Zeller (1880)—Zeller, E., *Philosophie der Griechen in ihrer geschichtlichen Entwicklung*, 3d ed., 4 vols., Leipzig 1880.

Zellinger (1933)—Zellinger, J., *Augustin und die Volksfrömmigkeit. Blicke in den frühchristlichen Alltag*, Munich 1933.

Zoega (1810)—Zoega, G. *Catalogus codicum Copticorum manuscriptorum qui in Museo Borgiano Velitris adservantur*, Rome 1810 (Leipzig repr. 1903).

Index